TAIM BILONG MASTA

To Roger Lee

With best wishes

from Max Bulley

TAIM BILONG MASTA

The Australian Involvement with Papua New Guinea

HANK NELSON

Based on the ABC Radio series produced by Tim Bowden

Published by the Australian Broadcasting Commission
145–153 Elizabeth Street, Sydney, NSW
Postal Address: GPO Box 487, Sydney 2001

Printed in Australia at Griffin Press Limited
© Australian Broadcasting Commission 1982

National Library of Australia card number
and ISBN 0 642 97566 3

Typesetting at Griffin Press Limited
Text type 10 on 12 point Bembo Roman

Designed by Leigh Nankervis

Edited by Helen Findlay and Nina Riemer
Index Compiled by Suzanne Ridley

Contents

Introduction		7
1	Never a Colony	11
2	The Good Time Before	23
3	God's Shadow on Earth	33
4	The Loneliness and the Glory	43
5	On Patrol	51
6	Sailo!	57
7	The Boat Came Every Six Weeks	67
8	Masta—Me Like Work	75
9	The Violent Land	83
10	Moneymakers and Misfits	91
11	Wife and Missus	99
12	Growing Up	107
13	Into the Highlands	115
14	The Promised Land	123
15	First Contact	133
16	Gold!	141
17	The Good News	149
18	The Mission Rush	157
19	You Had to be Firm	165
20	Across the Barriers	175
21	Courts and Calaboose	185
22	War	193
23	A Reason for Being There	201
24	Going Finish	209
Acknowledgments		220
Index		221

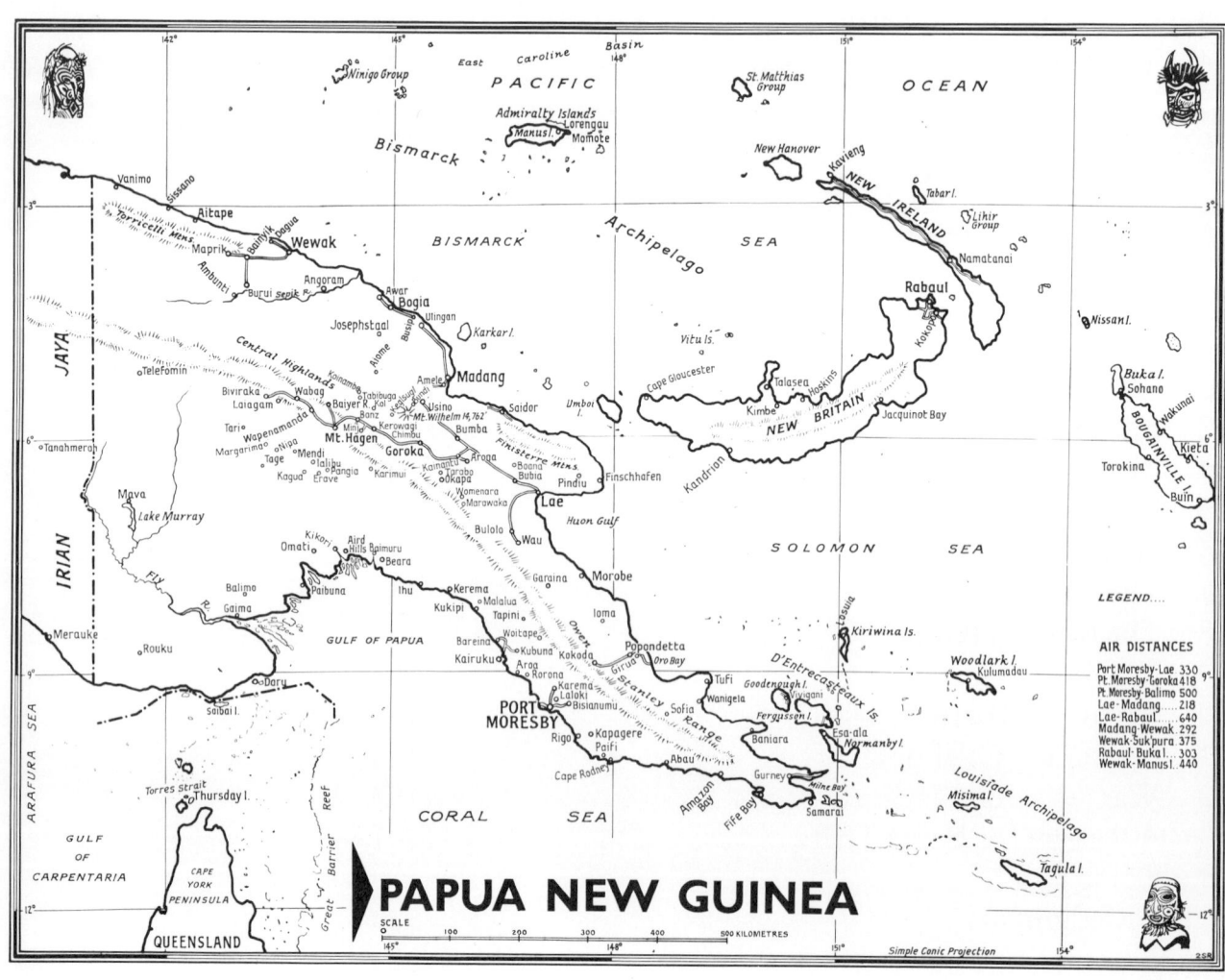

PAPUA NEW GUINEA

LEGEND....

AIR DISTANCES
Port Moresby-Lae 330
Pt.Moresby-Goroka 418
Pt.Moresby-Balimo 500
Lae-Madang.....218
Lae-Rabaul.....640
Madang-Wewak..292
Wewak-Suk'pura 375
Rabaul-Buka I...303
Wewak-Manus I...440

SCALE
100 200 300 400 500 KILOMETRES

Simple Conic Projection

Introduction

The aim of the radio series *Taim Bilong Masta* was to persuade many different Australians to talk about themselves in Papua New Guinea. We wanted them to say why they went, what they did, and what they took away. Most interviews were recorded in 1980, five years after Independence. They cover an apparent telescoping of massive change. People speak of their sense of privilege at being the first foreigners to walk into the homelands of thousands of people, the bringing of the first health services and building the first airstrips, the breaking of the old *masta-boi* relationships, and of deciding whether or not they would become citizens of the nation of Papua New Guinea. Received as spirits of the dead ancestors, they stayed as *mastas*, and must now be citizens or aliens under the political direction of communities that they helped introduce to the outside world. Informants were also invited to go beyond a personal level and make broad comments on Australian policies and performance in bringing three million people to independence. Australians at home have rarely been excited by the achievements and failures of their fellow countrymen in Papua New Guinea although those actions may be the most significant that Australians have undertaken beyond their own

shores. Only the dramatic details of a missionary eaten, a fabulous gold strike, a lost valley, a man bites crocodile and war have attracted the attention of the Australian public.

The *Taim Bilong Masta* radio series had its real beginning in 1979 when Tim Bowden and Daniel Connell pooled their ideas and energy. Bowden had previously demonstrated an interest in Australians on the margin by making the radio features *The Top End, It's Different Up There*, a weaving of song and anecdote to create a picture of life in the Northern Territory, and *The West Coasters* in which he enabled Tasmanian timber cutters and miners to talk sensitively, even lyrically, about their lives. Early in 1979 he proposed a major project on Australians in Papua New Guinea. Unknown to Bowden, Connell, on secondment to the National Broadcasting Commission of Papua New Guinea and alert to the rich material available, had already collected some thirty hours of reminiscences. Now back in Australia and transferred to television, Connell was looking for an opportunity to extend and exploit his material. He offered his tapes and such time as he could spare from his other commitments to *Taim Bilong Masta*. After some exploratory talks Bowden asked me to provide

Tim Bowden with 300 hours of
taped source material

research and comment. At that stage
Bowden probably had many misgivings
about asking me to do anything. One early
conversation with Connell took place at
my house on Saturday afternoon of
September 8, 1979. It was Grand Final day
in the Victorian Football League, and I
could devote only parts of quarter and
half time to events north of the Murray.
Perhaps it was the football which also kept
me blissfully unaware of the magnitude of
the project.

Through many conversations and draft
programs the scope of the series was
gradually defined. Armed with a fifty-
page document headed 'For the perusal of
interviewers with hangovers who fear
that inspiration will not strike with the
turning on of the recorder' Bowden
began the bulk of the recording. Connell
again began collecting material, and other
ABC or freelance interviewers were employed from time to time. Eventually
over 300 hours of conversation were
recorded. Interviews with such central
figures as Michael Leahy, Father William
Ross, the Reverend Ben Butcher and (as
he was then) Sergeant John Guise were
taken from the ABC archives and added
to the mass of reels that covered a wall of
Bowden's office. The collection, classifica-
tion and preservation of some 350 interviews would alone have justified the
expense of the project.

The first program was recorded in
September 1980 and the last in November 1981. Working part-time as a research
assistant Susan Crivelli heard all the tapes,
wrote a commentary and made an index.
Connell selected material according to
agreed themes. Although he was rejecting
much, Connell was gathering up to ten
hours of tape. Bowden then began cutting
thirty-six minutes from Connell's massive
assemblage. At various times we talked
(with me on the telephone) as we struggled to find a coherent structure and
adjusted our plans in accordance with the
strengths of the material. With the
dialogue down to about forty minutes and
the shape of the program fixed, Bowden
posted a copy to me on cassette. When I
had checked three or four programs for
accuracy Bowden came to Canberra
where we recorded my comments.
Bowden returned to Sydney to do the
fine editing and add effects and continuity.

The makers of any radio series such as
Taim Bilong Masta owe a debt to Michael
Mason's *Plain Tales from the Raj* first
broadcast by the BBC in 1974. Indeed
immediately *Plain Tales* was broadcast in
Australia listeners wrote suggesting that
the ABC attempt a comparable series. But
while we hoped to make *Taim Bilong
Masta* as evocative of time, place and
values, we also aimed to do something
different. We interviewed more people
covering a greater range of ages and occu-
pations; and to exploit the breadth of
accents and experience Bowden cut more
quickly from one speaker to another. We
were more prepared to examine central
political issues and less willing to accept
speakers on their own terms. While we
did not wish to be guilty of a final colonial
arrogance and present the people of Papua
New Guinea with their own history, we
wanted them to give something of their
experiences in relation to Australians and
to assess and counterpoint.

Problems of selection were constant.
There was always a temptation to tape
more informants, some of whom we
knew had had extraordinary experiences
or had held key positions. In selecting
themes we regretted omitting several

potentially rich subjects, particularly the testimony of two overlapping groups, school teachers and women in paid employment. These and other programs may still be made from material already collected. As the programs were put together many sharp, sensitive comments and humorous stories were discarded because other speakers made the same points equally well and more concisely. In compiling the book I have further reduced the program transcripts by about a half. As a result many two hour interviews, valuable by any other count, appear only in fragments.

At their best the radio programs were good history, good entertainment, and art. Their value as history lies in the way they have opened subjects not yet dealt with in published accounts and in the presentation of so much first-hand testimony. They are basic sources in the history of Australians in Papua New Guinea. The high craft, the imposition of a structure, and the whole having something worthwhile to say carries them beyond the level of clever compilation. The skills and the hundreds of hours applied cutting and splicing tape on the Tandberg recorder were largely Bowden's.

Early I feared a situation in which the members of a particular group would consistently praise themselves. In practice the harshest and most perceptive comments were made from within groups. It was not a case of a speaker excluding himself while he condemned his fellows; the sharpest critics passed judgment on themselves. In general the interviews confirm the value of oral evidence for the historian, demonstrate the articulateness of ordinary people talking about their own lives, and show that nearly all will go to considerable effort to contribute.

In transferring the spoken word to print I have omitted repetitions and changed the structure of some sentences. I have, of course, kept as close to the sense and style of the transcript as possible.

The presentation of Pidgin always raises problems for writers on Papua New Guinea. Pidgin has become a language in its own right, but if it is printed with its own orthography it is unintelligible to the ordinary reader. To avoid frequent translations in brackets I have sometimes presented Pidgin as though it were broken English although I concede that this may be unjust to both speaker and language.

Through the last one hundred years parts of the islands of New Guinea have suffered frequent changes of name. The north-east became German New Guinea in 1884 and came under Australian military rule in 1914. This area was transformed to an Australian Mandated Territory in 1921, and to a Trust Territory in 1945. Called British New Guinea in 1884, the south-east became the Territory of Papua in 1906. From 1945 the combined Territories were officially Papua-New Guinea, then Papua and New Guinea. At times my use of the terms 'Papua New Guinea' and 'Papua New Guinean' has been anachronistic. Both came into use in 1971 and were confirmed at Independence in 1975.

Towards the end of making the programs, deadlines had so disturbed our sense of time that dates seemed to be rushing erratically towards us. Bowden was spending seven days a week, cutting and splicing, ankle-deep in the confetti of stumbling lips. His wife, Ros, remarked that she felt like a single parent sharing a house with a grumpy lodger. At the same time my wife commented on the difficulty of having a satisfactory relationship with a typewriter. We thank those who tolerated us while we were dominated by intolerant material and dates.

1 Never a Colony

I wouldn't say that any Australians thought we had a colony. That was not in any way the thinking. The first time I heard 'colony' mentioned was about 1965; and it gave me a distinct shock.

Dame Rachel Cleland, wife of Administrator

Australians have always been uncertain about that great island to their north. They know it as close but alien; they have ruled half of it, but never possessed it; they are periodically fascinated by it, then they ignore it for years; they put it on their maps of the region but can never match its colours with those of their flat, arid, stable homeland; and they see its peoples in fleeting contradictory images as bow and arrow warriors, mission converts, 'kanaka' labourers, fuzzy wuzzy angels and visiting grey-suited politicians.

Australians first demonstrated their interest—and their uncertainty—in the 1880s. The separate Australian colonies wanted New Guinea to be part of the British Empire and have a special link with themselves. After failing to persuade the British Government to act, the Queensland Premier, Thomas McIlwraith, sent Henry Chester north from Thursday Island in a 'little tub of a cutter' to annex all of the east of New Guinea to Queensland. The British Government considered such memorable advice as the Empire 'already had black subjects enough' and that Queensland regarded its own Aboriginals as 'vermin to be cleared off the face of the earth': it repudiated the annexation. The British were not willing to allow colonies to gather colonies.

The other Australian colonies had generally supported the Queensland move of 1883. They feared that another European power would seize the island if the British did not act. Already the Dutch claimed the west of the island as an extension of their empire in the East Indies. The French were in New Caledonia. The German traders were moving west and south from their other points of interest in the island Pacific. And some Australians even thought they saw the Italians poised to take the burden of colonial rule. What worried the Australians was that if some non-British power seized the east, and if there were war in Europe, then there was every chance that they would have an enemy at their door. The oceans and the British navy would no longer be their great barriers against the world.

Australians also had a shrewd concern about their pockets—as well as their security. Most knew little about the north. They came by boats that favoured the southern routes and they settled in the temperate zones. Apart from the miners who risked their health on the northern fields, the pearlers and traders who were drifting through the islands and reefs of Torres Strait and into Melanesia, and a few missionaries, hardly any Australians ventured across the Coral Sea. But those

Officers' Mess Rabaul, previously the German Rabaul Club (left) Dame Rachel Cleland (below)

Across Hanuabada to Port Moresby and Paga, 1942

southern Australians were determined that if there was money to be made in New Guinea then they ought to have first choice. It was an area to be reserved for their exploitation. And if anybody wanted to get highminded about it, then Australians, they asserted, were going to bring more practical benefits to the local inhabitants than the woolly-minded armchair do-gooders of the English humanitarian movement.

In 1884 the British agreed to annex eastern New Guinea. At the same time the Germans raised their flag in what they now called the Bismarck Archipelago and claimed all of the north-east. Here was one of those classic scrambles for territory of nineteenth-century colonialism. At meetings in Europe the colonial prize was divided: the Germans took the north-east and the British the south-east. The line of compromise ran down the centre of much of the mainland, through territory never seen by any foreigners. Most of the people were not to know for decades how their national allegiance had been decided in 1884. The Australians were most indignant. They derided the British for tardiness and blamed them for losing half the island. They felt that they had been robbed of half what was rightly theirs.

Control in British New Guinea was shared. The British supplied most of the senior officers and the Australian colonies reluctantly gave much of the money. Decision-making was divided—or confused. It was a British colony with the line of command diverted through the eastern Australian capitals of Brisbane, Sydney and Melbourne before it finally reached

the heart of the Empire in London. This, it was assumed, was a temporary measure until the Australian colonies federated and then the new government would take responsibility for the remnants of empire on the Australian fringe. And in fact one of the first decisions of the new Australian government then meeting in Melbourne was to make British New Guinea the Australian Territory of Papua. It was now to be staffed, financed and directed by Australians.

The decision to call south-eastern New Guinea a Territory was important. It was an unusual word to choose. No other land had then been designated an Australian Territory. What did the word mean? Did it carry the same meaning as it did for Americans, that it was an area on its way to becoming a State? Some of the Australians thought just that. In some distant future Papua would be an Australian State. But a lot of Australians disagreed. They regarded Papua as overseas, in a way that Tasmania was not overseas. For them Tasmania was clearly part of Australia, and Papua was not. That ambiguity in the Australian perception of the area to their north remained until the 1960s. It affected the motives of those who went there. Some thought that they were Australian pioneers, extending the Australian frontier. Others thought that they were to be civilisers in a foreign land; they were going to one of the outposts of that great and vast British Empire. They might make it British, but not necessarily Australian. That word Territory also helped some Australians avoid the idea that they were in a colony. Colonies were something

Papuan Administration Legislative Council Meeting c1906

possessed by the old European powers: they were parts of empires and alien to the egalitarian, pioneering, settler or humanitarian traditions in which the Australians wished to see themselves.

It is easy to say why most Australians went to Papua New Guinea: they went as soldiers to war. Over 1000 went with the expeditionary force and the garrison in the First World War and nearly half a million followed in the Second. But other than that mass of men and few women who left in uniform, Australians went north for a variety of reasons. Most combined the romantic and the pragmatic:

Papua was always a country that I wanted to visit. As a young fellow I'd read Jack Hides and ever so many books on Papua New Guinea.

Ron Galloway,
government officer

I was interested in doing anything really because it was the Depression. I thought it was an exciting thing to do, and as I had been brought up in the navy, in Jervis Bay, I still had a strong desire to work for my country in some way.

Ian Downs,
government officer

They were brought up on Kipling, the *Boy's Own Paper*, and the whole attitude of the supremacy of the white race and their duty to enlighten the savages. Whether they actually said it or not, they accepted the complete right of Europeans to sweep through the world and scoop up anything they happened to think would make some money for them. I don't say that everybody had that notion, but most had it in their background: they were so imbued with it that it never occurred to them to question it.

Penelope Hope,
planter's daughter

I lived in Ballarat in Victoria, and there was nothing very exciting about living in Ballarat. Distant places attracted me: it was the spirit of adventure. And there was the fact that I was getting married and I looked upon the security of a government job. Another thing that attracted me very strongly was the three months' holiday every twenty-one months.

Vince Bloink,
government printer

Well, I always wanted to get away. I didn't want to be an office-type. I

Papuan Courier January 1935

PERSONALIA

Mr. & Mrs. Osborne Grimshaw left Port by the "Montoro" last week, Mr. Mr. Grimshaw being on leave prior to retirement from the Public Service after over 20 years' service in the Magisterial Department. We understand Mr. and Mrs. Grimshaw will spend some months in Australia after which they intend settling down in England.

Capt. A. S. Fitch, managing director of Steamships Trading Co. Ltd., returned to Port on the "Macdhui" after a short business trip to Melbourne.

Another passenger who returned by the "Macdhui" was Mr. E. B. Bignold, Crown Law Officer, who has been South on long leave. Mrs. Bignold is not returning for another month or so, after the hot weather.

Mr. A. L. Clarke, manager of Tiveri Gold Dredging Co. Ltd., returned from South last week and left by 'plane on Sunday last for Bulldog 'drome, via Wau.

Macdhui berthed at Samarai

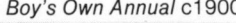

Boy's Own Annual c1900

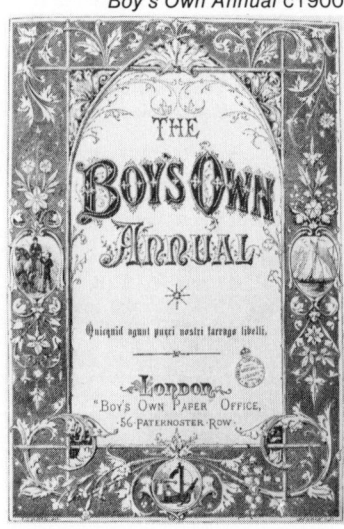

humanity. Perhaps all people put a noble gloss on the most ordinary of actions, but the idealism is so strong in the words that they now choose that it almost certainly influenced their behaviour in the past. A surprising number remember the books of their childhood; or like Dudley McCarthy the magic of a particular story in the *Boy's Own Annual*. Papua New Guinea was Australia's one frontier where any boy could imagine playing out the deeds that won an empire. And they went with another aim: they wanted to do well. Whether they were planters, public servants, prospectors or schooner captains, they wanted success. Even the missionaries could not completely escape the human frailty of wanting to come home to applause and honour.

> *We are not colonials. The Germans were colonials. The British were colonials . . . Am I going to be called a bloody colonial in this country?*
> **Bertie Heath,
> pioneer pilot**

Whatever their motives, they all soon had one experience in common: the trip. The schooners that took erratic passage from Thursday Island, Cooktown and Cairns soon gave way to the regular government-subsidised Burns Philp steamers: the *Marsina*, *Matunga*, *Montoro*, *Macdhui* and *Bulolo*. The old coalburners reeking with the smell of copra were replaced by the more spacious oil-fired liners. The boats, captains and crews are remembered with affection. Mrs Andrée Millar, horticulturalist:

> You came up and down on the boats, and you knew everybody on board. There weren't that many people in the country in those days, and if there was a group coming from some other part of the country that you hadn't met, you soon got to know them on the ship. And the crews—they were BP's boats—the crews were marvellous. They looked after the kids and they looked after you: it really was ten days of heaven. No one really cared two hoots if there was a strike and you got

would have liked to have gone out on the land, but the old man just couldn't afford it. There were nine of us kids, and he just couldn't put me there.

> **Bob Cole,
> government officer**

It was largely a sense of adventure and I was a real right royalist. Building the British Empire meant a lot to me then. And I've never been ashamed of that, of course.

> **Ian Skinner,
> government officer**

I came from New South Wales and I had a spot of trouble socially speaking, in Sydney, mainly at Government House at the Queen's Birthday levee. Being socially unacceptable, I decided to come to the islands and I've been here ever since.

> **Harry Lawson,
> Territorian**

As people reflected on why they went to Papua New Guinea, they kept returning to several reasons. Among the forces that pushed them out of Australia were the Depression, failure to get their first choice, boredom—and social embarrassment. Papua New Guinea seemed to offer the opposites: adventure, opportunity, the exotic and a chance to serve. Whether they left Australia in the 1920s or the 1960s many spoke of a duty to something beyond self: an empire, a nation, Christ, or

held up in Brisbane. And even in stormy weather it was still beautiful. You talked with people that you mightn't see again unless you were lucky enough to come on the same ship with them in two years' time. It was a wonderful way to travel.

They travelled often. Many had jobs with regular leave, pregnant women sometimes 'went south' for the birth and returned with the baby, and older children went to boarding schools. Government officers of the 1930s New Guinea service accumulated leave at the rate of one day for every week served and the most durable or optimistic among them looked forward to an additional six months' furlough at the end of eighteen years. Miners took a 'spell' and planters a holiday when their funds allowed or their health determined. It was that meeting on the boats that helped give the Territory whites their sense of community. 'There would be a sports committee elected,' Professor Ian Hogbin, anthropologist, remembers. 'It ran the various deck games and competitions, and there would be a fancy dress ball and so on. People drank of course. And certainly there was a captain's table. If a prominent planter didn't get put at the captain's table there would be awful ructions.'

> *We belonged then to the British Empire and we were very proud of that fact. I suppose I regarded Port Moresby as an outpost of Empire. I do remember when we came up in the old* Katoomba *and I saw Paga Hill at the entrance to Port Moresby harbour. It looked like the old British lion crouched; and I was very impressed.*
> **Geoff Elworthy,**
> **planter**

On the eve of the Second World War Carpenters established a regular flight from Sydney to Rabaul, and after the war most Australians crossed the Coral Sea by air. Denys Faithful, government officer:

We went from Sydney to Brisbane to Port Moresby in a DC4. At that time it was a twelve-hour flight. We left at six at night and we got in at six in the morning.

The early exhausting flights shortened with each generation of aircraft. By the eve of independence travellers could take one meal in Moresby and the next in Sydney or Manila. (But the custom of airlines ensured that they ate and drank through more than a thousand air miles.)

Old Territorians quickly recall their first meeting with their second home:

The first impression was the great crashing of sound as we landed on the marsden matting runway. The second was the tremendous heat when they opened the door of the aircraft and the third was being called *masta* by all the people who were taking the bags out of the aeroplane and into the cars.

Denys Faithful

As another new-arrival said, stepping onto the runway at Jacksons Airport in Moresby was like dropping into a warm malted milk.

There was a wave of the new. Amirah Inglis, historian:

Everything was very strange, and I heard strange noises. The tropics has got that sort of rotten smell. And everything seemed to be growing. I felt that things were going to grow all over me.

But Port Moresby in the dry season could be a disappointment for those expecting the lush, wet tropics. It was just 'a makeshift colonial-style of town with a lot of temporary buildings'. Port Moresby's poverty of nature and industry was repugnant to many old New Guinea hands. Norman Sandford, planter:

It looked like a primitive Townsville. The buildings were very ordinary, most of them lacked paint, and I was very disappointed with the place. You must remember that I am an old dyed-in-the-wool New Guinean, not a Papuan, and we of course looked down on the Papuans. Those people walked around with their braces showing and that sort of thing.

Dame Rachel Cleland flew to Port Moresby to join her husband, Donald,

The New Guinea Handbook 1937

Sir Donald Cleland
Port Moresby

who had been appointed Assistant Administrator in September 1951. Warned that she was arriving in the dry season, she was prepared for the change from the brilliant turquoise of the reefs to the brown of the hills, but not to the degree of aridity: 'it was like central Australia in a drought'. The plane bumped to a halt and she looked at

> a painted white galvanised iron shed, and that was Moresby airport. My husband was standing beside it, also in white. There were a few other people waiting to pick up other passengers. It was all very informal. The pilots pulled the luggage out of the plane, and everybody helped. We got into an old Buick with a very smart police driver who gave me a beaming smile, held out his hand and shook mine warmly. Well that impressed me very much indeed; it was a spontaneous reaction. He had given me a warm welcome on his own account. He had offered his hand: I hadn't offered him mine. I thought, 'What friendly people.'

Sir William MacGregor served ten years as head of the administration of British New Guinea. A tough, energetic Scot from a poor crofter-farmer background, MacGregor was an ideal man to be the pioneering Lieutenant-Governor. If there was a river that could be navigat-

ed by a small boat, he took a government party to its headwaters. He was a man to cut trails and climb mountains. In the ten years that he held office from 1888 to 1898 he made the government known to most of the coastal and accessible peoples. It is true that he and his officers shot people. Confronted by warriors with their bowstrings taut and spears poised, MacGregor would shoot. He thought it was to the government's long-term disadvantage if it withdrew in the face of violence. But at the same time, he was a shrewd protector of Papuans. He was careful to protect their lands from white speculators and he made sure that the villagers were not bashed or abused by traffickers in guns or booze. And he passed legislation to safeguard those who volunteered to work for the white men.

When in 1906 the control of British New Guinea passed to the Commonwealth of Australia some commentators thought that the special protective policies of the British would be lost and that the Papuans would be in for a tough time. Again they said that the Papuans would suffer the same deprivation and neglect as the Aboriginals of neighbouring Queensland. In fact that did not happen. The Australians were as keen for Papuans to possess their own lands and be free from obvious exploitation by labour overseers as the British had been. The new Australian administration from 1906 to the Second World War was to be dominated by one man, Sir Hubert Murray.

Murray went to Papua in 1904 as the colony's Chief Judicial Officer. A brilliant scholar and sportsman, he stood six feet three inches tall. Born in Australia, he had returned from Oxford with First Class Honours and the British amateur heavyweight boxing title. He was forty-three when he arrived in Papua: he had done little in Australia to exploit his great natural gifts.

> *When I think of Judge Murray I see somebody in a blue shirt and khaki trousers on a horse riding round the countryside.*
> **Mrs Eric Ure,**
> **missionary's wife**

Murray had arrived at an opportune time. The Australian government set up a Royal Commission to help it decide its policies in British New Guinea. The three commissioners came ashore at the sleepy, hot little galvanised iron town of Port Moresby. They took evidence over several days. Most of the senior officials appeared and spoke at length, but in the most general and impersonal terms—as people are inclined to do in those circumstances. Then Murray began his evidence and with those superb skills that he had so rarely employed in Australian courts he destroyed nearly all his superiors in the administration. Ballantine, the treasurer, was a drunk: that, he said, was a matter of public notoriety. People will even tell you about the demons he sees when he is raving, Murray told the commissioners. Barton, the head of the British Administration, Murray said, was naturally a weak man who was motivated by personal spite and favouritism. The commissioners may well have been intended to interpret Murray's words as implying that Barton was a homosexual. He undermined the British claim to philanthropy by listing the occasions on which large numbers of Papuans were shot. He wondered why the officers who reported such violence never noted the numbers that they had left wounded. Then almost as an aside he

Sir Hubert Murray

added that the two men responsible for most of the shooting were particular friends of Barton. As a result of the findings of the Royal Commission the Australian government sacked or retired the top of the old administration. Murray was first appointed as Acting-Administrator, then confirmed as Lieutenant-Governor. He came to power hated intensely by many in Port Moresby and regarded with suspicion or reserve by most of the rest of the white community. He outlived, converted, or won grudging respect from all his old enemies. But not all of the white community supported his views, as Penelope Hope explains:

Of course how you regarded Hubert Murray depended on what you were doing in the country. It's natural that the commercial people who were there to make money and get the blacks working for them thought he was absurdly paternal. They didn't think he should place Papuans before them when they were developing the territory: they were putting Papua on the map. His attitude to the Papuans was of course colonial, but you can't blame him for that in that period. Indeed I don't see what other route there was to bridge Papuans from the Stone Age to Independence than the term of paternal care that Murray gave them. But his main contribution

17

Mrs H W Champion (1875–1924)
Ivan, Claude and H W Champion

was to educate the white patrol officers and government servants into seeing Papuans from his point of view, and not as black bastards that had to be kept down and that sort of nonsense.

In impressing his attitudes on the public service Murray had the assistance of a strong and humane Government Secretary, H W Champion. Three of Champion's sons, Ivan, Alan and Claude joined the Papuan service. Early in his career Murray constantly stressed that the field staff were never to fire on Papuans except in extreme circumstances. By the time Claude Champion joined the service this had become part of its tradition: 'We were not supposed to open fire on natives unless we were attacked and in danger of being killed. We joked about it saying, we get killed and then we open fire.' Ivan Champion remembers Murray's determination to intervene on behalf of Papuans:

> When he came round on inspections of the stations he was of course Chief Judge as well as Lieutenant-Governor, but he didn't bother about the ordinary cases, he just took all the cases for native matters. Now courts for native matters dealt solely with Papuans. Resident Magistrates, Assistant Resident Magistrates and Patrol Officers after some years all had power to hear cases in the native

court. They heard many of them when they were out on patrol. Every time Murray came round you had to put out all your station records, all the depositions of every case that had happened since he had last been round. He would go through each case individually. He really constituted a court of appeal because he'd say, 'That man shouldn't be in gaol. That's wrong.' If you happened to be the magistrate who had heard the case, he'd get you in and tell you where you were wrong. If the man was in gaol he said, 'Release him,' and he signed a release. He kept a check on every case like that. He didn't worry about Europeans; they could appeal somewhere else.

Once he was at Buna where Dick Humphries was the Resident Magistrate. Humphries was later killed when Mount Lamington exploded. Humphries had thought that it was time that we had a motor road instead of the foot-tracks and relying on natives to do all the carrying. So he told the natives that they would have to make a road. Under the law they were obliged to keep the tracks clear. But they protested, and when the *Laurabada* came in to Buna with Sir Hubert on board they tried to see him. Humphries asked them what they were doing. 'Well,' they said, 'We want to see Murray about this road work.' Humphries told them to keep away, but one of them got to see Sir Hubert and told him how they were being stopped from talking to him. He immediately went to Humphries and said, 'Pack up your things and be ready to move in twenty-four hours'. At Cape Nelson he told the Resident Magistrate, 'You're going to Buna to take charge.' He sent Humphries down to the west somewhere, and then he sent out a circular: 'Every officer understands that any person whatever may see the Lieutenant-Governor at any time he wishes and he's not to be stopped. If any officer tries to stop a person seeing me he will be dismissed from the service.'

Murray's personal life was lonely and abstemious. He spent most of his time in Government House without his family. One visitor recalls Murray's saddle slung on the verandah: 'it was very much a man's Government House'. Mrs Ivan Champion remembers going there for afternoon tea. The tin of condensed milk was opened and toothpicks placed to keep it clear of ants, and great big mugs brought in for the tea or coffee: 'yes, he didn't have the niceties that we later had in Papua'.

Many found him aloof. Miss Marva Keckwick of the Anglican Mission used to see the *Laurabada* anchor down at the wharf and then watch Murray and his secretary, Leonard Murray, walk up to the mission: 'a very courtly old man, quiet, very reserved'. It seemed to Miss Keckwick that he was interested in people, but his reserve prevented him from talking to them about everyday affairs. By contrast, his grandson, Peter Pinney, remembers being captivated by his talk:

He had this capacity for producing on a very minor key the unexpected which appealed to a child. He would tell simple little stories: vignettes. For instance I remember him telling me how to catch a crocodile. He had a particular method to catch any animal that you nominated. And to catch a

crocodile, he would say, you must first go to a place where crocodiles abound. He always started off like that. Crocodiles abound in muddy places. You must go to a muddy place by a river, taking with you a hammock, a telescope and a very dull book. Also a match box. When you arrive you set up the hammock, you lie down, and start reading the very dull book. And the crocodile, being a curious animal, will see you and come closer and closer. It must satisfy its desire to find out the title of the very dull book. When it is sufficiently close you look at it through the wrong end of the telescope, and it appears very very small. You can then pick it up, put it in the match box, and carry it away to a safe place.

It is hard to grasp just how long Murray remained as Lieutenant-Governor of Papua. In the 1920s he reached sixty-five, and he had to consider retiring. In fact for the next fifteen years in his letters he worried about his pension and how he would occupy himself when he finally left office. When he reached seventy he was still very active. HW Champion used to talk about walking with him from Buna to Kokoda and back, a trek of about sixty miles. On the last occasion old Sir Hubert was finding it heavy going, and by the time they got back to Buna he was holding his side. As he went on board the *Laurabada* he stumbled and someone rushed forward to help him, but he pushed them aside with a quick 'I'm all right.' In 1939 Murray received instructions that in the event of an attack on Port Moresby, he was to retire inland and direct guerrilla activities. He thought this a fine piece of irony. Here he was, seventy-eight years old, being asked to lead a guerrilla force when his son Terence, a professional army officer, had already been retired on the grounds of age.

Murray instituted few reforms. He had an absurdly small budget for a vast territory and he also thought that radical change was to the detriment of the people. The best anthropologists of the time kept telling him that depopulation

Pacific Islands Monthly December 21, 1933

Sir Hubert Murray

Completion of 25 Years of Distinguished Service

ON November 30, Sir Hubert Murray, K.C.M.G., completed 25 years' service as Lieutenant-Governor of the Territory of Papua.

Having been Chief Justice of the Territory since September, 1904, Sir Hubert (then Mr. Justice Murray) assumed the powers of Acting Administrator on April 9, 1907; and on November 30, 1908, he was formally commissioned by the Commonwealth Government as Australia's first colonial Lieutenant-Governor.

In Sir Hubert Murray, Australia possesses a Colonial Administrator whose ability, vision, scrupulous integrity, and rigid adherence to a high code and a splendid ideal has given him a worldwide reputation. In the whole history of colonial development there have been few men comparable with him, for length of service or for the conspicuous success with which that service has been rendered.

In his well-ordered government of the primitive Papuan, and his scientific pacification of the Territory, his method has been that of association and collaboration; his steady policy that of pacification of all the tribes in the heart of the Territory; his fixed principle, the well-being and development of the natives entrusted to his care.

During the quarter century of Sir Hubert Murray's administration, the Territory has been brought under European control. The native population, spread over 90,000 square miles of mountainous and extremely difficult country, has been brought to recognise and to appreciate law, order and peaceful living. Education has been widely spread among them; they have absorbed a considerable idea of modern agricultural methods; and in the settlements near the Government Headquarters they act efficiently as clerks, overseers, artisans, and medical assistants.

The whole period of the Murray administration has been characterised by progress. By the method of association and collaboration, to use Sir Hubert Murray's own words, an administration "tries to preserve the individuality of the natives and to associate them with their rulers in industrial progress and the advance of civilisation generally."

Royal Papuan Constabulary carry Sir Hubert Murray's body 'home' to Port Moresby, 1940.

Translation of speech made at Motu 'masi ariana', burial ceremony

He came among us and saw our lives. Sometimes when he was younger, he hunted and fished with us. He knew us in all our ways. Sometimes when his work was done he met us on the roads. As we came home from our gardens he greeted us . . . There has been only one Governor in our time. He was the best of men. Our children and their children will talk of him . . . He promised us all 'I will not leave you. I will die in Papua.' His words were the words of a true man, for his body now lies in our ground.

would follow interference with village customs. But he won the affection of the Papuan people. They knew that they mattered to him, and they had access to him. Sir John Guise, Papuan politician:

He never lost the common touch. He could move with the princes of the world, but every afternoon he would get his horse, ride down to Hanuabada village, tie up his horse, sit down in the village in his flannel shirt and talk with the elders. Not only that, but he had a Papuan Sergeant-Major of police, Simoi. And anybody could go up to Government House and ask Simoi for an interview. Anyone. So when he died he was the only white man that was given a ceremonial Motuan burial. He was the only one.

Murray finally died in 1940. His last gesture was to refuse to allow himself to be carried ashore from the *Laurabada* to the hospital at Samarai. 'You can carry me when I am dead, but not before,' he told those who offered help.

It was the tragedy of Murray's career that he stayed in office so long. His policies that had been progressive and protective when they had been first introduced or enforced had become discriminatory and negative by the 1930s. A nine o'clock curfew kept Papuans out of the town of Port Moresby unless they were there as servants in white households.

David Marsh, government officer, lists the many petty barriers placed in the way of Papuans:

A native wasn't allowed to wear clothing on the upper part of his body. This was brought in because they tended to leave their clothes on and get wet, and catch pneumonia or skin diseases. A native wasn't allowed to drink. He couldn't go into a picture show with Europeans. When walking along the footpath the native was expected to move aside. We had the White Women's Protection Ordinance which more or less said that if you smiled at a white woman it was rape, and that was the end of the penny section. They also had a Native Women's Protection Ordinance which seemed to say something quite different, and didn't mean much anyway.

There was almost no overt opposition to the discriminatory legislation. It did not occur to most Papuans or Australians that there was anything wrong with heavy paternalism. Sir Percy Chatterton, who first went to Papua as a missionary in 1924, believes that Papuans took it for granted that Europeans lived in a different world and they were not very interested in that world. Europeans on the other hand took it for granted that it was out of the question for there to be any sort of social relationship between the races. Any association, Chatterton says, was on a purely business footing, and consisted of the white boss giving orders to the Papuan labourer. Sir Maori Kiki, Papuan politician and farmer, confirms Chatterton's perception. He spilled his boss's tea into the saucer. His boss took the cup and poured the scalding tea down Kiki's shirt leaving the skin scarred. At the time, he says, he just accepted the punishment. That was the way things were. It was only later that he was filled with hate.

> *I think that the Australians who were here at that time thought they were going to be here for ever. We had to be respectful and by overplaying that we became weak. We became a lot of humbugs. We had no feeling for our country. And it took a while to eradicate that from one's mind.*
> **Sir John Guise,**
> **Papuan politician**

But Murray's attitudes were progressive compared with those of the other white residents of Papua. And it was his policies that helped make Papua more benign than the neighbouring Territory of New Guinea. The white residents were keenly aware of the differences between the two territories. The Reverend Eric Ure, a missionary, says that there was little communication between them. Even on the boats on the way north and south the Europeans from Papua tended to gather on one side of the deck and those from New Guinea on the other. The distinction was carried over into the post-war. The 'B4s', the white community from *before* 1939, used to agree on one thing only: the newcomers were not as good as they were. Neil Desailly, government officer, remembers the spirit of the old Papua:

> The Papuans always seemed to be a little more easy-going—I'm thinking in terms of the government officers. Perhaps the New Guinea officers may have been influenced by the administration they had taken over. They had taken over from the Germans who had a different

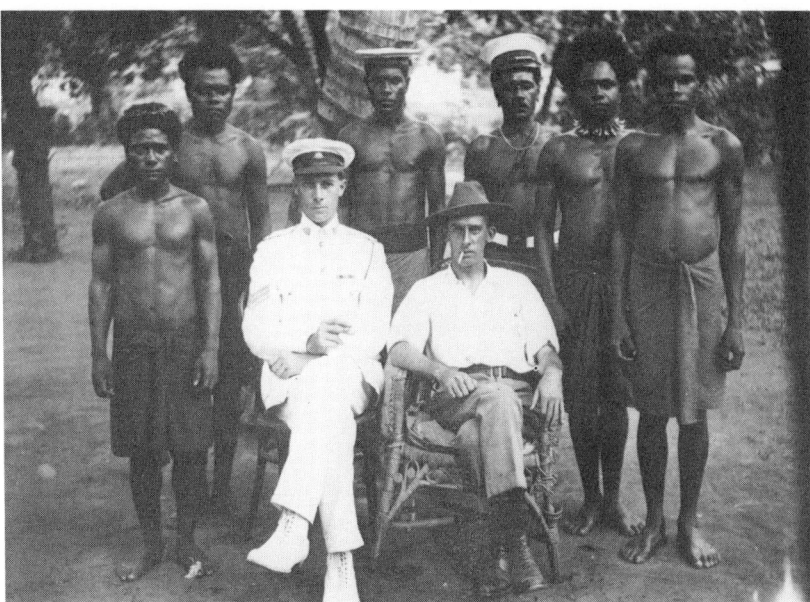

Police masters Sgt Gouday and Pte Pilkington and group of police

approach. In Papua, for instance, it was quite the normal thing at Misima to have a cricket match on a Saturday afternoon in which the government officers would be invited to play. The Papuans all played cricket, and played it very well. They would come up quite politely and suggest that we'd like to join in the game. We'd go down and do our incompetent best. I never saw anything quite like that in New Guinea. I'm not suggesting that there was anything wrong with the New Guinea approach, but there was a slightly different atmosphere. It was a little less sleepy, there was more industry and more production. Papua tended to be a bit of a backwater. There was nothing going on, but there was a reasonable relationship between the people—except that it's been criticised for being too paternalistic.

Sir Hubert Murray had often worried that his replacement would be some retired brigadier or politician who would abandon Papuan interests in the face of aggressive settler and company demands for 'progress'. In fact his office passed to his nephew, Leonard Murray. But his term was brief. In the face of the Japanese advance the civilian administration was swept away in February 1942. The old Papua had gone.

Rev Percy Chatterton

2 The Good Time Before

It's rather a strange thing that when I first came to New Guinea the older indigenous people used to talk about the German regime as the guttaim bipo, *the good time before.*

Cliff Batt, planter

The Germans looked to their colony in north-east New Guinea as a place where they could get a share of the tropical wealth that seemed to be flowing to their European rivals. Compared with the Dutch, English and French, they had come late to the slicing of the melon of the world's colonies. The thickest slices had already gone. Where Britain's Pacific island colonies were among its smallest and most distant possessions, New Guinea was relatively important in Germany's overseas empire. Germany was prepared to pay more for quick development. And, like other foreigners, the Germans saw the profusion of rain forest, the pile on pile of vegetation, and believed that once the land was cleared the plantation crops would flourish. It was an illusion. Their attempts to grow cotton, tobacco, cocoa and coffee on the mainland generally failed. But on the New Guinea islands, at first independent of German policies, the frontier traders changed from buying copra to growing it. On the eastern coast of New Ireland and on the Gazelle Peninsula of New Britain the foreigners found the reasonably flat, fertile and accessible land that they needed for their ordered ranks of coconut palms. Those early planters were of varied nationalities and races: Australians, Germans, French,

Samoans, English and others came for adventure or by accident.

By 1899 when the Germans shifted their administrative capital from the mainland to New Britain the island copra planters were already flourishing. Now supported by the German officials who built roads, stopped the sporadic warfare on the frontiers of contact and encouraged New Guineans to be wage-labourers, the plantation economy continued to grow. In 1911 the colony exported 9000 tonnes of copra and, in 1913, 14 000 tonnes. This was many times more than the total production in neighbouring Papua. The costs were high. White men died of malaria and in clashes with New Guineans. Every year the German annual reports gave a prosaic list of violence. In their last published report for 1913 they noted the killing of a European bird of paradise hunter inland from Madang, a planter on the Ramu River, and the slaying of the Weber brothers who were trying to establish a plantation on Umboi Island. In the last case most of the guilty were said to have been killed in a clash with the police troops and one of the murderers who was captured was 'shot in accordance with martial law'. That probably meant he was shot on the spot—without benefit of any law. Otto Zander's

Government House Rabaul (left)

23

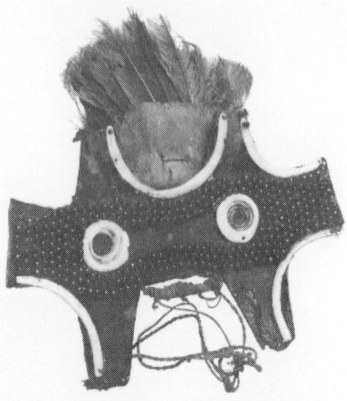

Breast ornament made from teeth, seeds, feathers and vegetable fibres. From the Koiari people, Central Province

THE PAPUAN TIMES.

WEDNESDAY, AUGUST 12, 1914.

The War.

War has been declared in Europe and, at the present moment, all the first-class powers are engaged in a life and death struggle for supremacy. Germany has invaded France, Belgium, and Switzerland, having received a severe check at Leige, a town about 15 miles from the German border in Belguim. Germany is reported to have lost 25,000 men there, and to have asked for an armistice for 24 hours. Austria-Hungary has endeavoured to invade Servia, so far without any success. Russia has invaded Germany, and it is reported that the German fleet was successful in forcing the Russian fleet to retire, after one of her largest battleships had run aground. The British Navy has chased the German ships into neutral waters, and so the trade routes are open for merchant shipping. At any moment we may hear of big battles, both ashore and afloat, and though we have not the slightest doubt our navy will uphold its noble traditions and the honor of our flag, there is no denying that the situation is extremely grave.

father told him the story of the attack on Varzin plantation in 1902. The people of the Paparatava area, although they had accepted compensatory gifts, had bitterly resented the taking of some of their land for the foreigners' coconuts. While the plantation owner, Rudolph Wolff, was away, people said to have been led by Towakira came to trade, a dispute broke out and then sudden violence. Mrs Wolff, her child and a servant were killed and the homestead looted. Wolff returned just as the attack ended and escaped by aggressively riding his horse through the attackers. In the reprisal raid mounted by the settlers many people were killed. Zander says that his uncle 'just shot everybody he saw, be it child, woman or man'. There was no court case. Attack followed by swift punishment was 'accepted then', Zander believes: 'In those days it was a different matter altogether, you know. The indigenes respected you for that. Very much so.'

A memory of German rule as a time of tough predictability was not restricted to just the white planters as Mrs Billy Bourke, the wife of a miner, explains:

One day, after I could understand Pidgin English, I had a talk with a very old native who had worked on a plantation for a German *masta*. He told me how much he admired the Germans. He said that they were very strict, but very very just. He said that they had their flogging triangles for a boy who made something no good and deserved punishment. To his way of thinking that was right. But he didn't quite agree with the friendliness of the Australian *mastas* who put their arms around a native's shoulders and gave him a cigarette and sometimes a beer. He didn't hold with that at all.

The anthropologist, Professor Peter Lawrence, who first went to the north coast over thirty years after the end of German rule found old men who still spoke a little German. They made the same point about German consistency. But 'with the Australians you could never tell. They would kick your backside today and be nice to you tomorrow.'

German scientists visited to observe, collect and classify. Richard Thurnwald did some of the most extensive field work of any of the early anthropologists and the medical researchers included Robert Koch who was subsequently to be awarded a Nobel prize. European museums became rich store houses of Melanesian art. The taking of the artifacts was at the one time an act of pillage and conservation. The collectors did separate the art from the artist and the culture, but had the museums not taken it, then it might have disappeared altogether. The artifacts of wood, basketware and feathers did not survive long in the tropics; and in the face of an imposed peace, Christianity and wage labour many communities were neglecting their old art forms.

Where Port Moresby looked like another dusty tin-roofed north Queensland town, the German stations had the splendour of outposts of a vast and powerful empire. They built homesteads and government offices with an impressive verandahed grace. White coralled walks, shady trees, tiers of steps, and views across harbours and islets all gave Kavieng, Madang and Rabaul a grandeur unknown in the drier, poorer Moresby. The Germans gave themselves the background to a more pretentious and affluent colonial style. It was a time, as one lady recalls, when the men wore two white tropical suits every day, and when the manager of one of the great trading companies could sit at the head of a magnificent festive table and announce: 'Democracy is a heap of dung'. The many Asian and New Guinean servants waiting on the diners would not hesitate in their unobtrusive replacing of plates and refilling of glasses.

But many New Guineans suffered to support colonial elegance—blighted as it often was by malaria, loneliness and violence. By 1913 over 8000 New Guineans were working as indentured labourers on plantations and around the towns and houses of the white community. The death rate was high and conditions harsh. Perhaps a quarter of the indentured labourers died. The German administra-

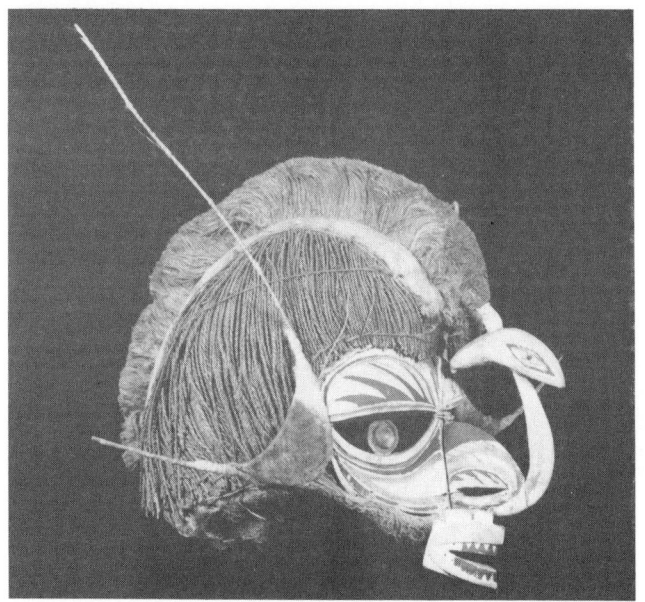

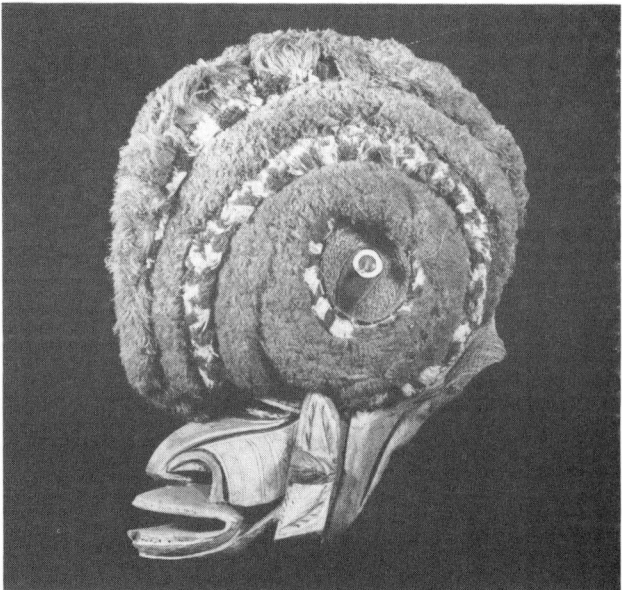

Mask with painted wooden face used in Malanggan ceremonies

Mask of Fatanua variety, used in Malanggan ceremonies, from New Ireland

tion permitted employers to use corporal punishment on their workers when 'they got a bit rebellious'. Rudolph Janke, a planter, remembers:

You could deal with the labour line yourself. You could give them strokes with the cane. You needed something like that because there was no other way of keeping them in order. There were only a couple that had to be kept in order, like children. They never had any trouble with their workers in those days.

Leo Hannett, a New Guinean from the North Solomons, says his people also learnt from another harsh lesson: the Germans imposed peace by a public hanging of those involved in tribal fighting.

At the outbreak of the First World War His Majesty's Secretary of State for the Colonies suggested to the Australian government that if it felt willing and able to seize German wireless stations in New Guinea, Yap and Nauru, it would be performing a great and urgent imperial service. The Australian government and people responded eagerly. Volunteers for a Naval and Military Expeditionary Force were called. Nearly all of the 1500 men came from Sydney. Many had no previous military training. The recruits began enlisting on August 11, 1914, for an unknown military task, they were issued with a uniform and arms, did some basic drill and went on board ship within a week. After a few days of training at Palm Island on the way north the Expeditionary Forces steamed into New Guinea waters. The commander, Colonel William Holmes, wrote to the Chief of the General Staff:

although the work on which I am engaged is of great importance to the Empire and will be of historical value in changing, if ever so little, the face of the map, it will, as far as I can see, be carried out without a shot being fired, a keen disappointment to many with me, who like young foxhounds, would be all the better soldiers if they were blooded.

On September 11 they landed at Kokopo without opposition and raised the Australian flag. A party of naval reservists went inland to Bitapaka to take the wireless station, but 'ran into a bit of strife'. German officers and New Guinean police manning trenches on the Bitapaka road opened fire. By evening the Australians had fought their way through a series of skirmishes to capture the wireless station. They were the first Australians to fight and die in the Great War.

The next day the Expeditionary Force sailed into Simpson Harbour and prepared to take Rabaul. John Fox, who had his first glimpse of New Guinea as one of the volunteers, remembers:

The Papuan Times August 12, 1914

War Scares.

We would like to point out to our readers that, whilst it is only reasonable for the Government to protect life and property in Papua, there is not much fear of an attack at the present stage of hostilities.

There is nothing here to attract German warships, who have all they can do to look after themselves. The wireless here is not of any use to ships, which carry as powerful plant with them, and the destruction of it would not injure Australia in the least. The amount of money to be secured by a hostile raid is not sufficiently large enough to induce privateers to make an attempt to carry it off.

We are of the opinion that if a corps of riflemen is quietly enrolled and taught how to handle their arms and shoot straight—with their position clearly defined and understood by the troops in case they were wanted—is quite enough for present requirements. That guns should be requisitioned for from Australia and mounted, would be a wise cause to adopt. There are plenty of men available to work any guns the Commonwealth can spare.

We would advise townfolks not to be alarmed at silly scares which are bound to happen at a time like this. No ships are likely to enter at night time, and with native pickets properly stationed, no ship can get within forty miles of Papua without being sighted and reported. We again impress upon our readers that there is no real cause for alarm.

New chums from Aussie

The Papuan Times August 12, 1944

WAR SCARES.

Some mild excitement was caused on Sunday last, when a strange steamer was sighted outside the reef, at about 1.30 p.m., steaming towards the entrance. No flag was visible, and acting on instructions the newly enrolled members of the Constabulary hastily assembled at the wireless station.

The Commonwealth flag was hoisted on one of the wireless masts, and about 100 men were armed and ready for any emergency, under the direction of the Lieut.-Governor.

As the steamer entered the harbor the British flag was hoisted and after the vessel had been boarded by the Customs officer, and her identity verified, the force was dismissed at 4.30 p.m.

The inhabitants were aroused at 6 a.m. this morning by gallopers, and the men were told to fall in at the wireless station, an hostile force having landed at Koki.

A force of about 120 men were in readiness for the supposed invaders.

The alarm originated through a canoe and a mission whaleboat landing a few inoffensive persons at Koki, who were immediately recognised by an excitable patrol as armed Germans.

The men were kept under arms until 9.30 a.m., when they were dismissed and returned to town, looking very disgusted.

We were told we were going ashore to take Government House. The major said, 'You know that if you want to make an omelette you've got to break eggs'. One of the Boer War boys replied, 'Well, let's hope you're the first bloody egg!' We landed at dusk and marched up and took Government House with a bayonet charge at daylight. I think it was the first bayonet charge in the war as far as Aussie was concerned. We rushed the gate, got in, but the Germans had disappeared. We were met by the Chinese cook who asked us—with his hands up, of course, as we all had fixed bayonets and nothing to use them on—he asked us if we would like some wine and cigars. Then we celebrated in the good old way at the Governor's expense.

The only opposition offered by the Germans was that on the Bitapaka road. One German, six Australians and thirty New Guineans who had fought alongside the Germans had been killed. The Germans had made a gesture of defence, the Australians could claim a victory at arms, and again the New Guineans had paid the highest price.

In a square bordered by casuarina trees and white bungalows, Colonel Holmes formally raised the Australian flag in Rabaul. The naval band played, the troops sang the national anthem and gave three cheers for George the Fifth, and the fleet in Simpson Harbour fired a twenty-one gun salute. In bad Pidgin English the assembled New Guineans were told that they now had a 'new feller master' and he would 'look out good you feller'. The great imperial change from German to British rule was expressed in the slogan 'No more 'Um Kaiser. God save 'Um King'. After a lot of 'palavering one way and another' the Germans and Australians worked out the terms of capitulation. An Australian garrison, soon to be known as the 'Coconut Lancers', was to run the colony, but they would be the supervisors of a going concern, not the bearers of revolution. They would rule according to German law and the German residents were to be free to run their stores and plantations as long as they did not send produce and funds back to Germany.

At the end of the war the Australian Prime Minister, William Morris Hughes, represented Australia at the Versailles conference. Hughes, claiming to speak for

The occupation of Madang, New Guinea 1914

60 000 dead Australians, was determined to secure north-east New Guinea for his adopted homeland. In a talk recorded for the ABC's *Guest of Honour* program in 1950 the Little Digger recalled his role. Like many other anecdotes in which Hughes gave himself a central part, he may have got the details wrong, but he certainly recaptured a spirit of the time:

> I fought for the mandate over New Guinea and the adjacent islands, control of which was vital to the very existence of Australia as a free democracy. Australia's claim to the mandate was strongly opposed at every step by President Wilson who at last threatened to leave the conference if I persisted in my demands. Lloyd George, then Britain's Prime Minister, summoned a meeting . . . in Paris and told us of the President's ultimatum. Turning to me, he said, 'I want you to understand, Mr Hughes, that I will be no party to anything that will break up the conference, and I want you to understand too that the British Navy will not be at your disposal to keep possession of New Guinea.' All this made me pretty mad, and I said, 'As for the President's threat to leave the conference, all I can say is, that if there was anything I could do to make him leave, I'd do it. As for your talk about the British Navy not being at our disposal to hold New Guinea, you and I, Mr Lloyd George, will go to England and ask the people who own the Navy what they think about it.' And when Lloyd George turned away in anger at my plain speaking, I gave up talking English and told him in Welsh—a fine language for invective—just what I thought of him and of Wilson. In the end Australia was given the mandate and so gained command of a bastion which in the hands of an enemy would almost certainly have meant irreparable disaster in the last war.

The idealism that came with the end of the war to end all wars had not touched Billy Hughes. He had wanted Australia to have outright possession of New Guinea. When he failed to get that, he fought to reduce the power of the League of Nations to supervise Australian rule. There would be no free movement of peoples into Australia's mandated territory: in defiance of American Presidents and British Prime Ministers Hughes

Group of Germans awaiting transportation home, Rabaul 1921

would have no north door to threaten a White Australia. In 1914 the Australians had been generous to the German settlers who were allowed to stay on their properties. But at the end of the war they seemed determined to eliminate all that was German from New Guinea. As one ex-soldier said, the civilian Hun-haters had control of Australian policy. All the German companies were wound up, the German plantations were taken by the Australian Expropriation Board and the dispossessed Germans shipped home. Hughes and other Australians had spoken constantly of the military importance of New Guinea. Privately they were aware of its commercial value and their actions confirmed their eagerness to grasp a prize of war, to get their hands on the assets. The German missionaries were allowed to stay, but the Australian government expected that even the mission societies would now recruit non-German staff.

Australian public servants, many of them ex-servicemen, were embarrassed at the harshness of the policies they had to administer: Kassa Townsend wrote: 'this is not expropriation, this is looting'. Rudolf Janke found it impossible to fight for his property:

I'd never heard the word expropriation before. I never really knew what it meant. But then we soon got to know what expropriation was. They wanted to get everyone out. Everybody was expropriated. So they said to me that I'd have to get out. I said I'm not getting out of this country unless you handcuff me and force me on to a ship. That's the only way I'm leaving this country.

There were a few Australians who wanted me to make an underhand agreement and sign my place over to them. You could save it that way. But I was a bit dubious. They might take it and keep it too. You could never know what you might get caught up in. So we just had to let things go. There were no solicitors. You couldn't get a solicitor to defend you. Nothing. And being ignorant as I was, I didn't have a hope in court. I never had a leg to stand on. I couldn't do anything.

The dispossessed Germans were to be compensated by the German government, the funds coming from the reparation funds that Germany owed to Australia. The effect was that the German settlers were paid in German currency which immediately became valueless in the crazy spiral of post-war inflation. The effect was that many of the Germans could claim 'we never got a penny'.

In the mid 1920s the government sold the expropriated properties by tender. All went to ex-servicemen, some of whom had no experience of running a plantation. 'The sheep and the goats were never sorted out', Bill Seale says. 'I suppose that twenty-five per cent of the people that got properties weren't any good as planters.'

The returned soldiers who went to New Guinea to take up plantations expected a reward, some compensation for the dangers they had faced. They dreamt of a comfortable plantation house with a view across coconut palms to a distant lagoon, and somewhere in the background would be neat huts for cheap, efficient, black labour. In fact they took up the plantations just before the copra prices fell in the Depression. They were often sick with malaria and their labourers were sometimes surly and truculent. They got into debt with the trading companies and soon they were managers on plantations they had once owned.

> *I arrived at the coal wharf in old Rabaul. And I stood there and looked around at all these mountains and volcanoes and things, and I felt small. It made me feel that well, you're only a little man after all. And that's how I felt when I first saw New Guinea. It drew me. I felt that I was going to like the place right from the start, and I did.*
> **Harry Hugo, Territorian**

In spite of the poverty of many planters, New Guinea, unlike Papua, was affluent. New limousines were parked under the shade trees along Rabaul's tarred streets. In contrast few rubber tyres disturbed the dusty gravel roads of Port Moresby. It was just as well that New Guinea had its own wealth for it was expected to pay its own way. Before 1941 the Australian government paid no subsidy to the Mandated Territory of New Guinea and a maximum of $100 000 a year to Papua. Just before the copra industry—and government revenues—crashed in the Depression, the Morobe goldfields came into production. Clive Meares, the Administrator's secretary, says that in 'the worst year we had we finished up with a surplus of one pound'.

The German tradition, the obligation to the League of Nations, the extent of the plantations, the number of ex-servicemen (Rabaul was a suburb of Anzac) and the thriving goldfields all helped make New Guinea different from any other Australian territory. Another difference was the number of Asians. By 1920 there were about 1400 Chinese, 100 Japanese and a few Malays in New Guinea. That was about an equal number of Asians and Europeans. Chinatown at the eastern end of Malaguna Road, the Chinese stores with their conglomeration of goods from bags of rice to toys, the vegetable stalls, the pork butchers' carts, the tailors, the women in broad hats and babies tied on their backs, the babble of languages and the strange foods told Australians that Rabaul was alien. Their first night might even be spent in a hotel run by either Ah Chee or Ching Hing. Their tropical outfits might be made by the Chinese outfitters.

Most of the Chinese had come from the south-east provinces around Canton. At first the Germans had brought them in as indentured labourers, but many of those who stayed came as free men to work as artisans and merchants. James Woo explains how his parents became part of that dispersal of peoples through south-east Asia and into the Pacific:

> My grandfather was a Hakka, the equivalent of the highlanders of New Guinea. My grandmother was from Shanghai. My grandfather moved down to Singapore and married my grandmother there. From Singapore they came to Papua New Guinea under the German administration. They were indentured labourers. My grandfather was an artisan; he was a carpenter by trade. When they landed in Rabaul they lived at Kabakaul and started trading in coconuts. And today my family is still in that industry.

'Chinatowns' grew in all the main centres of New Guinea. The Chinese were seen as intermediaries between the whites and the New Guineans. Territorian Joe Taylor remembers the pre-war divisions between the races:

> We didn't have very much to do with them. They didn't mix into the white society at all. They had their own little

AH CHEE PASSES

RABAUL, Dec. 18.

THE well-known Chinese hotel-keeper, Mr. Ah Chee, passed away on Sunday, December 10, after a lingering illness. He was a most popular host, and was known throughout the Territory for his kindness to travellers and those in distress.

Men all over the Pacific will remember with gratitude the help given them by this notable and big-hearted Chinaman—usually at a time when they were "down and out" and repudiated by their fellow Europeans.

Ah Chee's hotel, in Rabaul, became as famous in the Pacific as the Cafe de la Paix, in Paris—if you stayed there long enough, you inevitably would meet everyone you knew.

Pacific Islands Monthly January 22, 1934

Rabaul Times May 31, 1940

Denied Australian citizenship, the Chinese asserted Australian and British loyalty.

The New Guinea Handbook, 1937

set-up amongst themselves. They were about the middle standard; you could put it that way. But we used to patronise their stores and they were always very pleasant and realised that we were the supreme beings. At least, they let us know that. What they thought amongst themselves is another matter.

In spite of the regulations which limited their opportunities in business and planting, the Chinese prospered. The names of Ah Tam, Alois Akun, Achun, Chan, Chow, Chin, Kwong, Ping, Seeto, became well known throughout the Territory. The Australian administration also enforced very strict immigration rules so that Chinese men could no longer bring brides into the Territory. Partly as a result about a quarter of the Chinese men married New Guinean women. Their children, and those Chinese educated in Australia, had a declining affiliation to a Chinese homeland. When the regulations were changed in 1957 some of the Chinese chose to take Australian citizenship and they were free to expand into the neighbouring Territory of Papua.

There was one other difference between New Guinea and Papua. Perhaps it was the most obvious: Pidgin English was the *lingua franca* of New Guinea. All the long term white residents learnt Pidgin. Some could only shout the most essential orders—*kisim bia, boi*—get me a beer, boy. But nearly all of those Australians who spoke fluent Pidgin still used *tok masta*—the language of the masters. They did not speak the Pidgin that one New Guinean used when he talked with another New Guinean. New Guineans had taken Pidgin and made it their own *lingua franca*. Whites did not have the speed, accent or command of metaphor of the New Guineans, but where the bush New Guinean confronted an alien world Pidgin supplied the white community with an endless source of jokes:

It's very rare to have a hailstorm in New Guinea, but one day we did, and the hail was very, very small, just like grains of rice. The next day I was having people, the Browns, for lunch from up the river. When they arrived Mrs Brown said to me, 'Did you have hail yesterday?' I said, 'Yes, as a matter of fact we did.' And she then told me, 'I have a new house boy, and when he saw it he came racing to me and said, '*Misis, yu kam kwik. Kam lukim dispela samting. Bokis ais bilong Jisas em i bagarap.*' A refrigerator is a *bokis ais*, a box with ice, and that's the only place where he'd seen ice before. When the hail came from the sky he thought that Jesus' ice box was buggered up and the ice was falling on top of him.

Mrs Billie Bourke

Perhaps nothing was so misunderstood by Australians in New Guinea as Pidgin. They often thought that it was a simplified English, something to be used until the 'natives' understood proper English. It was neither simple, nor English, nor temporary. It was another language. The white community was often misled because nearly all the vocabulary was taken from English. But from the 1880s New Guineans were learning Pidgin from each other and using it to cross the many language barriers which divided them. Wherever groups of New Guineans from different parts of the Territory gathered——in labour compounds, in the police and in the towns—Pidgin became their common tongue. By far the majority of Pidgin speakers were New Guineans and they set the standards. White people who thought they were using broken English never learnt the rules of the language. They never knew that there was a Pidgin grammar and they consistently made mistakes in vocabulary. *Pusim* or *Puspusim* means to have sexual intercourse with. *Bokis* can mean the female genitals. This allowed endless fun among apparently docile labourers when a *Misis* was trying to get some boxes shifted.

> *I've been in the Star Mountains just this side of the PNG border and there were people there that were straight out of the bush, real bushies, in every sense of the word. And they used to pick up Pidgin in three weeks.*
> **Jim Leigh, government officer**

When New Guineans became concerned with outboard motors, calculating coffee prices or development economics a new vocabulary entered Pidgin. That was a normal process. All languages are constantly taking in new words as new objects and ideas enter a culture. But English speakers were always puzzled and

The hut in which the Ping family survived Japanese rule.

amused to hear the words of advanced technology in a Pidgin sentence.

A standard white joke was to give a Pidgin term for something strange to a New Guinean. Perhaps the oldest was the description of a piano which was said to be 'one fellow big fellow black bokis suppose you fightim teeth belong em, em e cry out'. Given here in *tok masta*, it was also probably first spoken by a *masta*. The same is no doubt true of a helicopter which was said to be a 'Mixmaster belong Jesus'.

The white community in New Guinea—even those who understood so little of it—took Pidgin words into their everyday speech: *kai* for food, *diwai* for wood or a tree, *haus pepa* for office, *balus* for aeroplane, *tasol* for that's all, *liklik* for little, and, above all, *maski* for it does not matter. But the long-term white residents of Papua were inclined to condemn Pidgin; it was barbarous, 'a frightful language'. It grieved many an old Papua hand when the post-war influx of black and white Pidgin speakers brought their language with them. Some of the Papuan 'B4s' never spoke Pidgin and pretended never to understand it.

3 God's Shadow on Earth

*After all, when you saw a twenty-year-old boy with perhaps five policemen keeping
30 000 warring tribesmen in happy harmony, you were just astounded and thought,
How does he do it?*

Dame Rachel Cleland

By the mid 1960s there was a House of
Assembly meeting in Port Moresby and
Local Government Councils operating
through much of the Territory; but most
villagers still thought of government as
the *kiap*. 'Government' was one Australian
field officer.

The term *kiap* belonged to New
Guinea rather than to Papua. It came from
the time when all white men arrived by
boat, and their boss, whether he was a
naval officer, a trader or pearler, was the
captain. That word 'captain' was corrupted
into *kiap* in New Guinea Pidgin. When
the German and Australian officials began
coming into the villages they too were
known as *kiaps*. Particularly in the early
years there were few *kiaps* scattered
through a vast area of coasts, islands and
rivers. Even by 1938, at the height of
Australia's pre-war administration of
Papua New Guinea, a total field staff of
only 150 men attempted to govern three
quarters of a million people, and about an
equal number of people were completely
beyond or only sometimes influenced by
central government control. In the Sepik
district where over 150 000 villagers had
been contacted, white officers manned
only five posts, three on the coast and two
on the River. It was a government of
isolated points and thin lines of patrol.

Both the British and the Germans had
developed a basically similar system of
administration: the map was divided into
districts each with a district headquarters
and three or four dispersed government
stations. Before 1942 Papua and New
Guinea used different terms to describe
similar systems. In New Guinea there was
a careful hierarchy within the District of
District Officer (DO) at the top, through
the Assistant District Officer (ADO), to
the Patrol Officers and Cadets. In Papua
each Division was controlled by a Resident Magistrate and below him were the
Assistant Resident Magistrates and Patrol
Officers. After the war the New Guinea
terms were applied over both territories
and in 1950 senior District Officers were
given the new title of District Commissioner. Even in the 1960s young Patrol
Officers or ADOs and a dozen police
might have complete responsibility for
the administration of a sub-district with
up to 100 000 people living in it.

The men who became *kiaps* went north
with the same mixture of motives that
prompted other Australians to leave
home, but they were probably more
strongly attracted to the romantic ideals of
adventure and duty on the frontier. John
Murphy, who went to New Guinea in the
1930s, recalls:

A patrol near Wabag (left)

Oh I wish I were
An acting ADO.
Oh I wish I were an acting
* ADO.*
If I were an acting ADO
I'd get more pay than a poor PO,
Oh I wish I were an acting
* ADO.*
So it's hi, it's ho, it's fiddle dee dee
This is what I'd like to be.
Hi ho, fiddle dee dee,
This is what I'd really like to be.

Pacific Islands Monthly October, 1935

I saw two magnificent pictures, one was 'Sanders of the River', very romantic. Hot on the heels of them I saw an advertisement in the local press calling for cadets for the Department of District Services and Native Affairs in New Guinea. It described the job in glowing and adventurous terms, so I thought I'll do one year up there and then I'll come back and go on with second year medicine. Actually I stayed thirty-four years: I didn't go back.

Jim Sinclair, lured by the same ideals, made no spur-of-the-moment decision when he went to New Guinea as a Cadet Patrol Officer in 1948: 'from the earliest that I can remember all I ever wanted to do was to go to New Guinea and climb mountains and explore'. Now, Sinclair believes that historical accident made him a privileged Australian. The field staff who served through the thirty years from post-war to Independence observed thousands of people pass from first contact to nationhood. The 'kids of the modern day' have no similar opportunities for adventure and responsibility: 'there's none of it left any more'.

> He had extraordinary powers, the local kiap. He could put villagers in gaol. He could put me in gaol if necessary. He could fine. He was the liquor commissioner. I certainly know he could bury people, he could marry people, he could impound boats if they came in, he was receiver of wrecks. In fact he was the sexton of the local churchyard. He was everything. He was almost God's shadow on earth.
> **Geoff Elworthy**

By contrast another long-term post-war officer, Jack Baker, remembers an impetuous decision to become one of the 'outside men' of the Territory service:

I was teaching in the north-east of Victoria. For reasons that we needn't go into I had a brawl with the rather conservative Parents and Citizens Association of the school that I was

teaching at. I rode my old motor cycle down to Melbourne and complained bitterly to dear old mother who said, 'Why don't you get away from it all? I saw just the job advertised for you, Cadet Patrol Officer in Papua New Guinea'. She was joking. I applied, was interviewed, and went to Papua New Guinea. With just that much forethought.

When Australia took control of the Mandated Territory nearly all of the men recruited into the public service were ex-soldiers. Some of the Coconut Lancers exchanged their military rank for a civilian designation and kept on with the same work. One of the Lancers was said to have made the transformation from porter at Sydney railway station to District Officer by the accident of war service in the tropics. In Papua, where the entire field service to the eve of the Second World War was still less than fifty men, there were few vacancies and Sir Hubert Murray often filled those with young men who were already working in the Territory. He always seemed ready to take practical knowledge in someone he knew rather than a stranger with high formal qualifications. But from 1926 in New Guinea, and in both Territories after the war, young men entered the field service as cadets. In the village the cadet might be king, but in the public service he was, as one remembers being told, lower than shark's dung.

Before the war the cadets went straight to Rabaul. Horrie Niall, one of the first of the cadet groups, says they had little formal instruction: everybody had enough to do without worrying about six wide-eyed young men who looked all too self-conscious in their white suits and pith helmets. Later a more systematic initiation was arranged. Bob Cole:

We were left in Rabaul to learn as much as possible in, I think it was, about three months. In that time we went to the native hospitals and they showed us everything, from post-mortems to dressings and other first aid work. We went to post offices and we sorted mail and we bagged mail

Pacific Islands Monthly February, 1936

Sunday in Rabaul

and we got it away on boats to see how post offices worked. We went to the police station and learnt as much of the administrative side of police work as possible and we went out to the parade grounds. We saw the Lands Department; we went out with their surveyors and we did surveys around Rabaul. We did a bit of time in practically every department so that by the time we were posted to an outstation we had a little bit of background anyway.

The young men, some away from home for the first time, had more to learn than the details of the job. Bob Cole continues:

> We were quartered in the hotel in Rabaul for the first couple of nights, and Tiger Lil was running the pub. As a young fellow I wasn't drinking so after dinner I just went back to my room. But in the passageway I struck Tiger Lil, and she said, 'Where are you going?' 'Back to my room,' I answered. She said, 'Get back into that bar, and you join the rest of them or else you won't stop in the Territory'. She said, 'You've got to live that way'. And I went back to the bar. You couldn't be a recluse. You had to learn to mix, and you had to learn to take pride in all the banter which they gave you, the chiaking they gave you. Planters had a

go at Government people and vice versa. We had to take it.

After their introductory days in Rabaul the great gamble in the cadet's life was where he would be posted. Ian Downs went to Manus, a gentle introduction to the multitude of tasks that fell to the field staff. Dudley McCarthy, who graduated from Sydney University to find little offering in Depression Australia, went to his first post at Salamaua just as Patrol Officer Ian Mack, fatally wounded with arrows, was carried to the hospital. Even in the post-war young Australians could face a traumatic introduction. Chris Vass:

> I'd been in Laiagam for about eight months so I was still a cadet at that stage. They must have been fairly short-staffed in the Western Highlands—well they were probably short-staffed right throughout Papua New Guinea. But the Patrol Officer who was then in charge at Porgera patrol post had to leave for some reason so I was assigned to go out there. I got carriers and was assigned a few more police to relieve some who were there, and took off west from Laiagam into what was then a restricted area.
>
> Porgera is a very interesting place. It's just over 9000 feet, making it one of the highest patrol posts in Papua New Guinea, and it's in the centre of

'Word always went ahead of the patrol giving the villagers time to prepare to meet the "government" by sweeping the bare earth between the houses.'

precipitous limestone country. A cold, very wet place, it gets a lot of fog in the day so it's extremely eerie. You get the fog with white limestone peaks sticking out of it. There's a lot of heavy rain forest. And when the army came through about a year later they said it was the only bloody place in the world where there were vertical swamps. They were right, too, because they wore out army boots virtually every day, climbing up through the limestone.

So I arrived in Porgera, totally exhausted, as you can imagine, after three days' walking. The patrol post was situated at the head of the Porgera Valley which sloped away very steeply. I'd been there about two hours when I heard this whooping coming up the Valley. The Porgeras have a very distinctive sound they make, a yodel, and it was the characteristic whoop, whoop, whoop of many men coming up the Valley that I heard. Having just arrived, and not knowing the sound, I thought, God, what's this? What's happening? I could hear it gradually getting louder and louder coming up the Valley to the station. Then a party of Porgeras arrived carrying a home-made stretcher with something bound to it. They brought it up to my house, up

the path, right to the front, and deposited it. The government interpreter came up with them. They unwrapped this thing, and it turned out to be the dead body of a woman. I had never seen a dead body in my life before and this wasn't an ordinary dead body. It was a headless woman, and she had a sapling about two inches in diameter pushed right up her vagina so that the top end of it was up near her neck, and just the bottom end of it sticking out between her legs. And the separated head was placed alongside. So you can imagine how I felt: twenty years old, not long in Papua New Guinea, straight from Sydney, never seen a wounded person in my life before, let alone something like that. I'd only been in Porgera about two hours, and it was the first time I'd been on my own in Papua New Guinea.

One way for the young officer to survive—and learn his job—was to work. On most stations that meant going on patrol. An officer, Lloyd Hurrell says, was expected to spend 200 out of 365 days in the bush. Government by patrol was government by inspection. The field officers, unable to speak the languages of most of the people that they governed, were inclined to depend on what they could see. Were the houses well built,

Saturday morning inspection

were the walking tracks properly maintained, was there a proper pit latrine? Word always went ahead of the patrol giving the villagers time to prepare to meet the 'government' by sweeping the bare earth between the houses, repairing and cleaning the *haus kiap*, and the government appointed headman (the *luluai* or village constable) put on his hat of office and got out the village book. When the patrol came into the village the *kiap* was expected to display some imperial formalities: 'You hoisted the Australian flag, the blue ensign, with due ceremony and fixed bayonets, said a few words, and told them what was what'. The patrol officer then checked the village book by asking the people to stand in their family groups while he marked each person's name. Through the book the field staff kept a check on population movements. Lloyd Hurrell: 'You had to look at the women, and if you noticed they were pregnant, you entered that in the book. You didn't do any examinations, but you might question. The next officer when he came would check to see what became of the child. If there was no child he'd put the reason'. The village book had space for notes where the field staff listed instructions that they had given for roads to be repaired or coconuts planted. The next officer then asked whether or not the work had been done.

Leo Hannett, from his boyhood in the village, retains an 'image of the government' as 'a white man in short pants, long socks, with several black policemen wearing blue skirts and hats shouting and ordering people around, and seeing long lines of people being forced to carry the *kiap*'s goods. It was quite akin to a Eucharistic procession'. At the opposite end of the country Ebia Olewale remembers the patrols entering Tureture village. The Australian officer, 'well dressed with shoes and everything', was met by the councillors who walked out to his boat, made a seat with their hands and carried him ashore. The councillors had already inspected the village to make sure that the houses were in proper rows and none of the nepa palm roofs needed re-thatching: they did not want anybody to be fined or sent to Daru gaol. On the day of the patrol no one went fishing or to their gardens; 'we would say the government is coming, we all must stay here'. In the more recently contacted parts of the Sepik district some people, particularly the old, were genuinely frightened of the strangers who brought the new rules. When the census patrol arrived they would hide in the bush and, as Bernard Narakobe explains, the villagers would say, 'Well, he's died or she's died'.

For villagers who were long accustomed to the ways of 'government' and whose

37

daily routine included sweeping the earth between substantially built houses, inspection was no hardship; but communities that were partly nomadic or lived in scattered, leafy huts were likely to find the *kiap*'s orders harsh and even incomprehensible. The absurd was reached when a community actually built a special village where they gathered just to meet government patrols. For the rest of the time they lived as before in family hamlets. In another case recorded by Ian Hogbin, a village kept a carefully fenced cemetery with a patch of freshly dug earth for every death which the *kiap* would eventually record in the village book. But no bodies were put in the 'graves'; they were buried—as they always had been—under the houses.

> *You sort of had a bit of feeling, well, you know, the white man's burden and things like that. Extend colonial influence. Doing some good for Australia, doing some good for the people at the same time.*
> **Sir Horace Niall, District Commissioner and first Speaker of the House of Assembly**

Although in the eyes of the villagers the *kiap* had great power, they might only see him on one or two days a year. Distant villages might be hosts to the government every two or three years. That was only a brief moment of direct rule. As long as they did not go to war or commit crimes against white men they could solve their own problems and pursue their own goals. Language too placed a barrier between the *kiap* and the villagers. An interpreter usually stood between the ruler and the ruled. Sometimes he would modify what was being said, or he might advise the villagers that they would be unwise to tell the *kiap* certain things: he would either not understand or be driven to sudden anger.

Yet there is no doubt that the government officers on their intermittent patrols did constructive work. In fact there has been an ironic twist in the way the term *kiap* has been used. In the 1960s young, radical Papua New Guineans were using '*kiap*' to stand for alien and authoritarian rule. Now some older and more conservative men are looking back to what they recall as a golden time of just, efficient and firm government. They ask for a return of the *kiaps* who brought strong government right into the village.

> *A stern father, but a loving father, this is what we liked to think of ourselves anyhow.*
> **John Murphy, government officer**

One routine duty of the field officer was to conduct courts. After a short time on the job all officers were given power to hear cases in the courts of native affairs or native matters. 'Formalities', Neil Desailly recalls, 'would be minimal'. Courts might be held sitting on a 'stump under a palm tree, or on a log at the side of the track'. The *kiap* would take his place behind a 'patrol table if he had one, or behind a box or something as a sort of improvised bench'. An interpreter and a policeman stood by. When Lyle Hansen first held courts he was conscious of the responsibility thrust on him and surprised that elderly villagers would accept the rulings of a 'young fellow just out of school'. He concedes they might have modified his decision as soon as he left. Sir Horace Niall was helped through many cases by early practical advice:

I had a very uneducated but very sound common sense man with me for two years in Talasea. One of the things he told me was, 'Try and look intelligent, and take advice from the old men'. And I noticed that he, and I did myself later on, heard interminable arguments about court cases on land disputes, smoked several cigarettes, then turned to a couple of the older men around the place and asked, 'What do you think? Oh yes, that's what I think too'. And that seemed to satisfy everybody.

But many disputes were settled without any court hearing. The *kiap* simply listened to argument and recorded a

Waiting for the *kiap*, Kiarivu 1945

decision in the village book. 'Of course', Jim Sinclair says, 'the next time a patrol officer came along these same people might have a go to upset the previous ruling. This was all part of the game'.

It was a simple system of justice, and the *kiaps* were frequently reminded of the need to keep it cheap. Malcolm Mackellar recalled an incident in which bureaucratic austerity imposed strange values. A patrol officer was bringing in a murder suspect. At a log bridge the handcuffed man slipped and his body was quickly swept away. The patrol officer duly submitted his report on the incident. The death of the suspect seemed to cause few problems, but from then on the patrol officer was plagued by a constant stream of demands to account for the missing handcuffs.

The government's concern for its property was transmitted in the villagers. Another story is told of a man on a murder charge being taken to a court hearing. As the jeep turned sharply he made an agile roll out of his seat, crashed down a slope and, in spite of his handcuffs, escaped. An immediate hunt was started. No sign of the man was seen, but after a few days the *kiap* found the battered handcuffs on his doorstep. When the

prisoner was finally recaptured he explained that he knew how much the government valued its goods and he did not want to make the *kiap* angry. The final irony of the anecdote is that the man was hanged. The government was hard to placate.

> *It was a dedicated service. You had to be dedicated. I mean, no amount of money is going to compensate you for being stung by mosquitoes night after night building a road through a swamp or something. You did it because you were dedicated. You were fired with a missionary zeal.*
> **Malcolm Mackellar, government officer**

The *kiaps* in the villages often represented all arms of government: they were concerned with agriculture, medicine and road building. From the earliest times government officers encouraged (and compelled) villagers to grow cash crops. One officer issued seeds to inland people on the understanding that they were kapok and he was introducing a new industry to the area. When the seeds germinated they were found to be paw-

Luluais and Tultuls *Iain*, Kavieng 1945

paw—to the confusion of villagers and *kiap*. But even in newly contacted areas government officers carried seeds to distribute. Denys Faithful remembers that the energetic subsistence farmers of the highlands were always eager to try new crops. In fact new plants would be passed from village to village along traditional trade routes ahead of government influence.

Villagers and *kiaps* appreciated the immediate and obvious benefits of medical work. Gordon Linsley:

When we went on patrol we took a native medical orderly with us and a box or boxes of drugs and medicines. As we went from village to village we took the census. People came up, we recorded what had happened to them since the last visit and then passed them to the medical orderly who physically examined them. They had no option. We didn't say, 'Do you wish to be examined?' They were examined.

When I was in the d'Entrecasteaux area I discovered that there were serious outbreaks of leprosy in the villages simply because that person did not come up for the census. Where

was he? Oh, he was sick. I would then send the medical orderly to see what was wrong with him; and in many cases he was a leper. Yaws was a terrible looking disease. The entire body became encrusted with pustulating scabs; it's a shocking sight. And yet it requires only one or two injections of NAB to cure it. On our census patrols everybody was injected with NAB. The medical orderly had a whole box full of it; and in a few years yaws was completely cleaned up. The medical orderly couldn't treat tropical ulcers because they required hospitalisation. But what happened was the Village Constable was handed a list of people that he had to take to hospital after the patrol moved on. When you got back to the station you checked with the medical assistant whether those people had come in. If they hadn't, you sent a policeman to the village to bring them in. Authoritarian, if you like, but effective.

The cadets who went to the Mandated Territory from 1926 returned to Sydney University for two terms of study after two years in the field. During the Second

World War the School of Civil Affairs operated at Duntroon to train Australians for service in Papua New Guinea. But in 1947 it transferred to Mosman in Sydney where it was re-named the Australian School of Pacific Affairs, ASOPA. A young cadet patrol officer joining the government service did a few weeks induction course in Sydney, went to Papua New Guinea, and having graduated from cadet to patrol officer, went back to ASOPA for more extensive academic training.

> *This is the score on ASOPA*
> *And ever we make it plain*
> *Send not your brave and*
> *   courageous*
> *Send us your weak and insane.*
> *Weak from the red rage of battle*
> *Insane from the lack of the score*
> *Men who'll be useless for ever*
> *But DCs in truth to the core.*
> *Men who've been mucked round*
> *   by Roberts*
> *Pushed round by Cleland and*
> *   Co*
> *Men who've been bled by*
> *   Dwyer*
> *Till they are the lowest of low.*
> *Goodbye to you Charlie Rowley*
> *Farewell to you Victor P,*
> *All that I learnt at ASOPA*
> *Will never make me a DC.*

ASOPA was, at its best, host to productive meetings between energetic students and good teachers. The patrol officers had had sufficient experience on the job to know what they wanted from lecturers in law, anthropology, administration and government. They were quick—sometimes too quick—to tell the staff when they thought that information was inaccurate or impractical. Over the years ASOPA attracted some distinguished staff members. Professor Peter Lawrence, who

himself taught Anthropology at ASOPA, remembers his colleagues:

There were some remarkable men who were dedicated to the whole enterprise. One was the late James McAuley who taught government. He imparted—I've had this from many of the *kiaps* I've spoken to since—a sense of the moral obligation of their position so that it was not just a career, it was almost a vocation with them. And then there was Charles Rowley who was the principal and a person of great humanity and very great scholarship. I think that by about 1968 the Australian administration, which had seemed a bit rough and ready when I first went there in 1949, had become very good indeed. Certainly the bits that I saw were. And it would compare very favourably with administrations in other parts of the old Empire.

The 'academic interlude' at ASOPA was also a time when the men 'from the sticks' searched Sydney for wine, women, and song. Young *kiaps*, fearing that their next posting might be in some thigh-deep mosquito-infested swamp, thought they had better make the most of their days near neon lights. The study, arguments and nights on the town helped give the *kiaps* a group consciousness that was difficult for them to build when they were on their isolated stations.

From 1963 Australian patrol officers were recruited on six-year contracts: the Papua New Guinea field service no longer provided a career.

ASOPA lives on. Having changed its name to the International Training Institute, it has reversed its student flow. It now takes students from the Third World, attempts to increase their skills, and sends them back to work in their home countries.

N.G. PATROL OFFICERS.

NOTICE of a new system of promotion, particularly affecting patrol officers, was given recently by the Administrator of New Guinea.

A Board has been appointed to consider all future promotions to Assistant District Officer and District Officer.

As a general principle, a minimum period of ten years as a cadet or patrol officer shall be served by an officer before being promoted to the office of Assistant District Officer and this principle will only be departed from when exceptional merit of an officer so warrants. Officers will be required to hold a certificate of proficiency as disclosed by examination in law, administration, and such other subject matter as the Administrator may determine.

All patrol officers were notified that the public service regulations were being amended to provide that patrol officers may not be advanced in salary beyond £126 per annum, until they have successfully negotiated a preliminary examination in law and administration, which will be held from time to time.

Pacific Islands Monthly November 22, 1933

4 The Loneliness and the Glory

We were hard, we were tough—we had to be in many ways—and we were foolish.
We did many wrong things. But all told we gave them a sense of justice;
a fair go Aussie.
Sir Horace Niall

A visitor to a patrol post or sub-district office in the days of Australian administration was usually met by a young man wearing a broad-brimmed hat, khaki shirt, trousers or shorts and heavy patrol boots. He had confidence in his skills and fitness for tough bush work. He was a traveller, builder and enforcer of peace. It came as a surprise to learn that only a couple of years before he had probably grown up in the suburbs of Sydney or Melbourne. The *kiaps* were usually immersed in their work. They started the day early and worked till evening. They were on call seven days a week. Bob Cole remembers testing his fellow officers by asking them how much they were paid. Very few could say accurately and some had no idea at all. Their salary was something paid into a distant bank account. There were other satisfactions in the 'sort of welfare role' that they saw themselves playing. Villagers often demonstrated an assuring trust in them. Neil Desailly: 'I've often had people come and say, "Look, I have some money here. Will you hold it and I'll come and get it next week, or next month? It will be safe with you." It just didn't occur to them that we would steal it.'

The *kiaps* came to think of themselves, by training and by the elimination of those slow to adapt, as a special arm of government. 'I think', Gordon Linsley says, 'that we either consciously or subconsciously regarded ourselves as an élite. I'm not putting the arguments for or against it. I don't think it was expressed as arrogance, but just accepted.' But before he reached the point where he felt himself a member of the brotherhood of 'outside men' the young officer had to demonstrate his competence. Cadet patrol officers were not supposed to go on patrols on their own. But Jim Sinclair remembers that in the staff shortages after the Second World War many cadets 'went solo', and sometimes into uncontrolled country. His own first trip out of Wau he remembers as a 'total disaster':

When we were at ASOPA the most useful lectures in my opinion were those given by the late David Fenbury (Dave Fienberg as he was then) on practical administration. He was an experienced field man and knew exactly what the pitfalls were and the sort of advice to give: what boots to buy, the best kind of food to take on patrol, the relationship to have with your police, all that sort of stuff. And he issued us with a lot of very valuable notes. When my first patrol came along I never bothered to check any of that; it all went out of my head.

'. . . met by a young man wearing a broad-brimmed hat, khaki shirt, trousers or shorts and heavy patrol boots'

43

I took off with just about no food, no equipment; I didn't have a bed, I didn't have a lamp. I didn't bother to take a table or a chair. I thought all that was sissy stuff.

Jim Sinclair suffered on that patrol, but it gave him a sharper appreciation of the professional competence that the job required.

> *I think individual officers varied a lot. I am quite sure some thought they were God. Others thought of themselves as being very humble people.*
> **David Marsh, government officer**

Running a station required a wide range of practical skills. Emergencies involving ambushes and flying arrows were of course less frequent than more mundane crises; but the ordinary could still be dramatic. Tony Voutas was eighteen when he was posted to Pindiu on the Huon Peninsula in 1961. He was, he says, an impractical, idealistic 'city slicker' come to live in a palm-thatched house with split bamboo walls and floor. One of the deficiencies of this picturesque home was the toilet: some thirty feet from the house a structure of rough planks and galvanised iron roof was perched over a pit latrine. Tony Voutas:

> One of the problems with pit latrines anywhere, but particularly in the tropics, is that mosquitoes start to breed in them. So never having had anything to do with a pit latrine in my life before, I asked my boss what to do. He said, 'Put a bit of white petroleum down the pit and you kill all the larvae by burning off the mosquitoes'. Rather than go back and get more precise instructions, I wanted to show my capacity to handle the problem. I collected a four-gallon drum of white petroleum and poured an ample quantity of it down the latrine, probably of the order of two gallons. I then proceeded to light a match. Before I could drop the match down the hole this cylinder of flame and excreta came out of the pit, passed

Wooden figure, painted, from Houn Gulf area of Morobe Province

my nose and eyebrows and hair, and went straight into the galvanised iron roof. The force of the explosion, and the fact that it was compressed through a small hole, was so great that it lifted the whole toilet off the pit—me included. Up we went into the air, and landed very shakily back on the flaming pit. Even though my eyebrows were singed and my hair burnt, I had enough sense to jump out of this flaming structure on to safe land, and look back over my shoulder to see the whole toilet gradually sink into an inferno of red flames. It was just three weeks after I had arrived in the country. I was left with this terrible vision of the telegram that could have been sent back to Australia: Your dearly beloved Tony was lost in some kind of action in the sticks of Papua New Guinea.

Ironically for young men who had gone north for adventure one of the hazards of the job was boredom. There was little on the radio to interest them and few made the effort necessary to transport and maintain a library through a succession of bush material houses. If they visited one another, or they joined other members of the expatriate community, they were likely to spend most of their time drinking. The consumption of alcohol may have been related to more than just finding a pleasant way to fill idle time. Neil Desailly suggests that some *kiaps* felt a tension, perhaps unconsciously, arising out of being 'in the midst of an alien culture'. One intelligent and sensitive field officer both took up his spare time and exhibited the strain that he was under by writing his patrol reports in rhyming verse.

Malcolm Mackellar remembers that he and a fellow *kiap* worked out a less mentally demanding way of spending long evenings. Their house with its thatched grass roof and walls was a haven for cockroaches, rats and other vermin that thrive in the tropics. Any attempt to dislodge the pests was next to useless as they were immediately replaced by others that moved into the house unimpeded.

But the rats at least could be sport. After the two government officers had finished their dinner at night the *kukboi* (cook boy) would bring in the coffee, a bottle of port and two revolvers, and put them on the table. Malcolm Mackellar:

We had an imaginary line which went through the middle of the table and extended along the floor to the wall. If you saw a rat which came on your side of the line, you shot it. This was so we wouldn't shoot each other, you understand. And while the rat was on my side of the line it was my game, and as soon as it crossed over the line to the other fellow's side of the room, he could shoot it. The purpose of the exercise was not to start shooting till the rat came on to your side, and to stop immediately it crossed the county line, as it were. We'd shoot one or two rats every night like this.

In these days when people were staking out plantation empires through the highlands a lot of men used to come up from Sydney or Melbourne or somewhere. They'd hitch a ride to the highlands on aeroplanes or trucks or walk, a lot of them would walk. They'd find a suitable piece of land, stake it out, and build a coffee plantation; and some of those large coffee plantations up there now are a result of this sort of selection. One night there was a knock on the door just after we had had dinner, and this emaciated creature stood there shivering with malaria. He said, 'I'm so-and-so. I'm just wandering through looking for land to start a plantation. Could you put me up for the night?' And we said, 'Oh yes, sure. There's a couch over there, you can sleep there if you like. Have you had any dinner?' And he said 'No, I'm too sick. I'd just like to lie down and go to sleep'. We said 'Yeah, OK'. But of course we forgot to inform him of the rat shooting contest. The couch we had given him was in this other fellow's territory. He had just laid down—he couldn't sleep because he had fever so he was staring into space with his vacant eyes—and this rat popped its head out of the wall on my side. I took a shot at it and it ran across the dividing line into the other fellow's territory and he took a shot at it and then it ran under the bed. This fellow was so preoccupied with hitting the rat he just kept on shooting even though it was underneath the bed. The bullets were going within six inches of the poor malaria-ridden guest's face. And after the shooting was over he arose from his death bed and said 'Thank you very much for your hospitality', and walked out into the night.

But where there was only one white man on an isolated station, the loneliness could be intense. Dudley McCarthy remembers that in the 1930s the posts on the middle Sepik had an almost palpable loneliness. It could exert such pressure on some young Australians that they could, temporarily, become another person. McCarthy almost lost the ability to conduct ordinary conversation, a fact more obvious to others than to himself:

I went home on leave. My people lived in the country, in a country town, and I was very fond of them. One day I happened to walk into the kitchen and my mother was having a little weep. She wasn't given to that sort of thing, and I said, 'What's the matter with you? What are you crying about?' 'You,' she replied. And I said, 'Why are you crying about me?' 'Well, you've changed so much.' I said, 'How have I changed?' 'You don't talk any more, the way you used to before you went away.' 'Don't I talk?' 'No,' she said. I asked, 'What do I do?' And she told me, 'You just seem to sit on the verandah and smoke a pipe and look away into the distance.'

Sir William MacGregor in founding the British-Australian field service countenanced neither blasphemy nor immorality. When he found that Robert Kennedy, a Resident Magistrate in the south-east islands, was 'entertaining highly improper relations with native women' he asked him to resign. But MacGregor

Mask, wood face, painted with shell opercula as eyes; 'hair' of cane framework with plant fibres, from New Ireland Province

45

'He brought a travelling picnic.'

did give jobs in the government to men who were already known to be living with village women. Under Captain Francis Barton's more languid administration in the early twentieth century there were probably more relaxed official attitudes. Sir Hubert Murray in one of his many attacks on Barton before the Royal Commission of 1906 claimed that Barton had said 'it was a good thing for an officer to keep a native woman because he thereby learnt the language'. Murray assured the Commissioners that he opposed such relationships, not on the grounds of morality, but because 'if an officer got mixed up with a native woman he inevitably came under the control of her relatives'. Presumably Murray retained his pragmatic attitude during his years in office, but in any case general attitudes within the white community had become less tolerant of Australian men living with Papua New Guinean women. It was not until the 1960s that a *kiap* could marry a Papua New Guinea woman and move into the station residence—without startling either the expatriates or the villagers.

Murray certainly made no effort to secure the 'independence' of his staff by helping them to marry Australian girls. Claude Champion was one officer who was prepared to risk the wrath of senior officials by breaking the unwritten law that Patrol Officers were not to marry unless they had served at least four years. Those who did could expect little from the money-starved administration to help them find adequate housing, stores or transport for their wives. Even in the post-war, Neil Desailly suggests, outstation life placed a strain on a marriage: it was either strengthened or destroyed by the experience. The stress might be all the more intense when the field officer had had few chances to court a girl and the bride had little idea of the sort of life that she would be entering. Mrs Theresa Bloxham remembers seeing young *kiaps* coming back from leave 'down south' with a bride:

The older women who were established used to shake their heads and say, 'You know, they just don't fit'. We would find in the end that the men had gone to Sydney and they'd perhaps gone to a shop and found a nice little shop girl with whom they'd made friends. While the men had been in New Guinea their old friends had been cut off or gone elsewhere, and now one of the first girls they came to they'd asked to marry instead of having an engagement and finding out what the girls' interests were and what their backgrounds were—I don't mean this in a snobbish sense in any way. But the girls came and they weren't satisfied, or they were shy, or they didn't know what to do with themselves. Some of them were overwhelmed with native servants and instead of using a native servant with dignity they were ordering them around all day, telling them to pick up a box of matches or bring a packet of cigarettes and all these silly little things which other women wouldn't think of doing. They were people who had no conversation, really. The young girls would get bored and they would either take to drinking, or they would play cards all day; they weren't even interested in reading a good book. Well naturally the husbands and wives found as time went on that they had no interests in common, unless it happened to be drinking or just socialising. This so-called socialising became a habit; people would get together nightly and just sit and drink. A lot of them just went to pieces. I couldn't tell you now how many of them went away, whether some of them 'went south' or how they ended up. Then they started swapping wives at one stage. There was a lot of fun poked at that sort of thing, but really it was rather tragic.

> *There are of course some people who will say that the* kiap *was a dictatorial, authoritarian, black-bashing autocrat. I won't deny that I personally know some that were that; but they were the very rare exceptions.*
> **Gordon Linsley, government officer**

When a wife came on to an outstation a whole set of customs and relationships changed. Papua New Guinean police, teachers and clerks who might have visited a single *kiap*'s house and talked, and sometimes gone inside to drink, no longer felt free to enter the living quarters. As Trevor Shearston says, they sensed that there was now a barrier; the *kiap* was expected to be 'more of the withdrawn and aloof *masta*'. Perhaps, Shearston speculates, the *kiap* thought that in some vague way he was threatened if Papua New Guineans were in his house. By contrast

the *kiap* who went on patrol with his wife, a baby slung in a basket and a bird in a cage, led a much more relaxed patrol. He brought a travelling picnic to the villages.

Where colonial officials of other nations working in some overseas posts could call on servants with long traditions in domestic arts, Australians in the field service often employed men as servants who had never before been in a Western-style house or even handled a can-opener. Chris Vass recalls telling his novice *kukboi* that he wanted tinned meat, tinned peaches and tinned cream for dinner, and he got just that: meat, peaches and cream all stirred together on the one plate. Similar stories of misinterpreted orders are legion. Lyle Hansen tells a more complex Territory story of *masta*-servant relationships:

I had a *mankimasta* (later they were called domestic servants), and I suspected that he was drinking the whisky. I kept both whisky and rum. I preferred rum. I didn't drink much whisky, only when people came. But I noticed that over a period the level of the whisky bottle had gone down. So rather than just front him and say, you're stealing the whisky, I thought I'd really make the message more potent by playing a trick on him. Each time I noticed that he'd had a swig from the whisky bottle, I'd piss in it and bring it back to its former level. And I did this for some months. I finally thought, well, fair enough, I can't go on treating the fellow like this. He's doing his job, and he considers it's one of his lurks and perks to have a bit of a tipple from the whisky bottle. So I'll tell him the story. I called him up and said, 'Well, you've been caught out this time. You normally have been good, done everything I've asked you to do, and generally been good in looking after the house. But why have you been knocking off my whisky for the last couple of months?' With a most affronted look he said, '*Masta*, I haven't been drinking your whisky. When I worked for the previous *masta*

Skull mask from Rabaul area, East New Britian Province. Acquired before 1897. Human skull over-modelled with resins and painted; beard of plant fibres

Fred Kaad, Government officer

*A young PO I met on jungle
   patrol
His saksak house was one heck
   of a hole.
When he felt blue and
   everything did go wrong
He cheered his heart by just
   singing this song:
Kumul in the tree top
Kapul on the beebop
Kindam in the sea
I knew that I had never and I
   didn't think I'd ever
See a lulai sitting in a tul tul
   tree.*

*(Kumul = bird of paradise;
Kapul = possum; Kindam =
crayfish.)*

he always liked a nip of whisky in his soup and I have been doing the same for you.'

On patrol and in much general work around the station the *kiap*'s most important relationships were with his police. Jim Sinclair: 'It could be a very very close relationship. I think that it was one of the finest things that we had.' The police with their blue serge tunics, heavy belts and 303 rifles were much praised and photographed. In Papua they were the Royal Papuan Constabulary and after the war the title carried across to the combined force: the Royal Papua and New Guinea Constabulary. Recruited from all parts of the Territory, the police for most of the period of Australian rule were given a few months basic training in drill, rifle use, hygiene, basic law, patrolling and general education. Many pre-war police spoke almost no English and were illiterate. For many years sergeant-major of police was the highest rank open in the government service to any Papua New Guinean. Some sergeants, with over twenty years' service to their credit, had initiated at least a dozen young *kiaps* into the ritual of patrolling.

As Jack Baker prepared for his first patrol he found himself under constant instruction from his sergeant: what you take is this and this, don't forget your notebook and pencil. When they arrived at a village the sergeant would say, politely, we will stay here. He would point out the *haus kiap* to Baker and ask if he would like the villagers assembled. If the sergeant thought that the villagers were being less than honest, he would say what had really happened. All the advice was given gently and firmly: 'Why don't you do this? Mr so-and-so used to do this.' If Jack tried to assert any independence he would find things going wrong—to such an extent that he suspected the sergeant had probably directed the disaster. Just to make sure that nothing too alarming happened the sergeant detailed a constable to keep the young *kiap* under constant surveillance:

I could not move without this policeman. It became rather wearing after a while. Occasionally I wanted to get away on my own; I wanted to

think, or I just wanted to walk in the bush. But there was always a policeman. I decided to lose him once. I went down to the river, made certain there was only one canoe, took it, crossed the river, and went off looking for wallaby. I managed to get myself thoroughly lost and had to spend the night in the bush. Next morning the sergeant, with the aid of about fifty villagers, found me, proceeded to shake the finger at me and say, 'You're a terrible embarrassment'.

The best of the Australian field officers were quick to appreciate the work of their police. Keith McCarthy in his book *Patrol into Yesterday* has described the action of Lance-Corporal Anis who rushed to attack ambushing tribesmen near Otibanda. Anis died of his terrible wounds, but his selfless action had saved the others in the patrol. Fred Kaad says that many of the long-serving field staff could point to incidents in which they were saved by the perceptiveness or actions of their police: 'those wily old birds could almost smell trouble'. Kaad himself during the war was suddenly fired on by a Japanese: 'This policeman who had attached himself to me just stepped in front of me and shot the Japanese. But in so doing he was wounded and he could have easily been killed'. The policeman, Kaad believes, saw it as his duty to save the *kiap*.

When villagers watched *kiaps* make decisions in court cases, demand that certain houses be rebuilt, decide to build a road in a certain place, buy new equipment and pay wages to carriers, they had little idea that the *kiaps* worked within laws and regulations. However much the *kiap* might talk about the 'law', to the villagers law was what the *kiap* said. (Not that the villagers thought that the *kiap* was always right or always had to be obeyed. Indeed they would—when certain *kiaps* were well out of the way—fall about laughing at the ease with which they had deceived the 'government'.) But the villagers' ignorance of the *kiaps*' place in the structure of the administration brought problems when field staff began

District officer F N W Shand leads police to hoist the Australian flag, Kavieng 1945.

talking about transferring power to Papua New Guineans. Some village leaders thought that they now had the authority of the *kiaps*: they could imprison, distribute funds and locate roads. But immediately they took any strong action the *kiap* countermanded their orders. In their frustration and humiliation some village councillors shouted that they had been told a lot of lies. Neil Desailly says that he has seen a councillor throw his badge of office on the table and declare: 'You may as well take this thing. It is of no value'. The *kiap* system was at its best in opening up new country: but it was not easy to shift from the *kiaps* to village democracy.

> *I think it was these senior members of the Royal Papua New Guinea Constabulary who more than any other group contributed to the pacification and extension of government control.*
> **Fred Kaad, government officer**

Denys Faithful remembers that when he went to the Western Highlands, Bob Cole, the senior officer at Mount Hagen, invited him and another cadet into his office. After the usual pleasantries Cole asked them why they had come to Papua New Guinea. He listened, filled his pipe and said 'What you young blokes have got to realise is that every day's work you do well is another day towards working yourself out of a job'. Faithful says 'We both laughed politely, but we didn't expect that to come in our time'. In fact the end came quickly. Some *kiaps* were replaced by Papua New Guineans who became the 'outside men' of their own government; and some were replaced by a complex mixture of specialists in agriculture, health and public works and elected councillors and provincial governments. The *kiaps* 'went finish'. For many it was more difficult to fit back into Australia than it had been for them to survive their early days as raw cadets in the sticks.

The *kiaps* were like men returning from a war. They had gone through an experience that they felt had made them different from those who had stayed at home. They had faced dangers and accepted extraordinary responsibilities. Yet their fellow Australians gave them scant recognition. Unlike the returned soldiers, the *kiaps* have no badges and no Anzac Day to remind other Australians of their place in their country's history. They returned to meet many acquaintances and few friends. Even their relatives were dispersed and consumed by other interests. After several years in Australia they were still likely to think of their close friends as other old Territorians. Many of their neighbours with their talk of football and washing machines seemed alien and narrow. If they could not meet old colleagues they were likely to mix with people who might have worked for CSR in Fiji or an oil company in south-east Asia. Others who had lived in the midst of another culture could share a joke, exchange reminiscences and avoid such comments as 'Oh, you were in New Guinea. I know a fellow up there. He's Fred Nerk and he lives in Kuala Lumpur'.

> *He says he knew they were young, but he tried to brief them or give them advice on how to go about things. He tried to be confident in himself so that the young officers would have confidence in him and get that strength.*
> **Translation of Sergeant Gonene, Royal Papua and New Guinea Constabulary**

For many *kiaps* the worst part of returning was trying to find a job. The authority that they had exercised, the skills that they acquired and their sense of professionalism meant little to Australian employers; and they had come back to a contracting job market. The *kiaps* built thick files of rejection letters which politely explained that they were too senior, too inexperienced, or just too old. Few have moved to positions that provide the excitement and responsibility of their old posts.

In houses decorated with artifacts, they value their memories. Neil Desailly:

When I'm feeling nostalgic, it's usually not for Port Moresby or even for Kundiawa when I was there as a magistrate, but for the earlier times, the 'fifties and the early 'sixties. When I think of patrols, I think of the mountains, I think of the sort of work that I was doing then and sometimes I wish that I could move back to that. It was a time of excitement, a time of development, things were moving; you felt that you were really at grips with a situation. I think there was something about the country too. I loved the mountains. I've always liked the bush. I was doing something interesting and exciting and I thought it worthwhile. I was doing it in an environment that I enjoyed. With all the annoyances and frustrations that are inevitably involved in dealing with people of a different cultural background, where there are communication problems and so on—despite all these—I found that I very much liked the people I was working with. There were odd moments when I might feel that I was wasting my time, but they were only odd moments. The total effect was one of a great feeling for people.

After he had entrusted his reminiscences to the tape recorder, one ex-senior officer said: 'Make sure you tell it properly because for many of us the memories are all we've got'.

5 On Patrol

Another time the policeman must have hit the bony slant of the pig's head and the nickel-plated bullet broke into pieces. One native got hit with a piece in his thigh, and another in his upper arm. It just broke the skin and made a bit of blood. Everybody fled—every single one. It took a hell of time to get them back, calling out, saying it was an accident. From then on they thought guns could shoot round corners. They were impressed with the power of the rifle. And peace came over the land with just that old British Army .303.

John Murphy

In much of Asia, Africa and the Pacific colonial officials could rule through local kings, sultans or chiefs. But in Papua New Guinea the political units were small; hereditary chiefs and self-made 'big men' might assert authority over just part of a village of a few hundred people. In this land of families and villages the field officer had to go to the people and that meant he had to walk. The broken, unstable land, the vegetation, the rivers and swamps hindered road-making and prevented the use of saddle and pack animals. Even along the coast and among the islands where government officers could use boats, there was still a lot of walking to be done. And all that the *kiap* took with him had to go on men's backs.

Early attempts by foreigners to travel in the interior ended in disaster. Even gold miners with much experience in the Australian bush were forced to turn back. The flour and other stores that they normally used were soon mouldy, they could not carry their own packs on the steep grades, they became sick with malaria and they were harassed by hostile warriors. By trial and error government officers developed the techniques to patrol. Requiring the combined effort of many people, patrolling was neither simple nor easy. On the track, Sir Horace

Niall says, 'it was just plain hard work: after five minutes you were wet with sweat and you stayed that way all day'.

Efficient patrolling depended on thorough planning. The stores had to be checked and packed: primus stove and fuel, canvas bedding (*bet sel*), tents (*haus sel*), pressure lamps and spare mantles, mapping equipment, ink (in the days before ballpoints), camp oven, water filter, trade goods, spare boots, rice, canned food, medicines ... The cargo varied according to the district, the purpose of the patrol and the taste of the *kiap*. Some goods needed water-proofing or special protection against breakage and all had to be packed into carrier loads not exceeding forty pounds for a single man. Pre-war officers sometimes used wooden boxes supplied by Chinese trade stores and each carrier made a harness from cane and a pad out of his blanket so that he could sling the box on his back. In the post-war the metal patrol boxes 'about the size of a large suitcase' were slung from bamboo poles with a man at each end. The police gathered the carriers from nearby villages. Few men liked carrying, but it was a government duty they could not avoid. At least they were paid and that brought a little cash to some isolated communities; and the carriers had a chance to

The Territory of New Guinea District Standing Instructions 1925

The rate of payment for native carriers will be either 6d. per day in cash or 2 sticks of tobacco per day or trade to the value of 6d per day. In most cases it will be found that in travelling from village to village, the only possible means of payment will be by sticks of tobacco.

51

Bill Bloxham on patrol to Wutung
on Government Schooner 1937–38
Wutung villagers

The Territory of New Guinea
District Standing Instructions,
1925

Instance
A police party is approaching a
village to arrest one or several
members of a tribe reasonably
suspected of having committed
inter-tribal murders. The tribe
throw spears or hold spears in
such a manner as to make the
police, who are endeavouring to
make the arrest, reasonably
consider that the tribe or members
of the tribe intend to throw them.
The police open fire.
Lawful Action
The police are justified in
firing. . . .

travel and make new trade contacts. A
core of men might go all the way with the
patrol, others would just carry from
village to village.

Most patrols were concerned with the
ordinary business of government: taking a
census, collecting the head tax, settling
disputes, checking health, and encourag-
ing the growing of cash crops. The *kiap*
listened to what the people said were their
wari, a Pidgin term that covered any questions, problems or conflicts. Some patrols
had specific tasks: to survey a road, find a
site for an airstrip, stop a tribal fight or
arrest some men to face trial for murder.
Unless it was a major exploratory patrol
or faced special difficulties there were
usually just one Australian, five to fifteen
Papua New Guinean policemen and one
or two medical assistants to be served by
the carrier line. Mrs Theresa Bloxham
remembers her husband's patrol leaving a
station in the Sepik District:

The whole patrol consisted of almost a
hundred people. They set off, snaking
away downhill. I suppose it would take
about a quarter of an hour or twenty
minutes to walk downhill with a load.
I remember feeling absolutely lost and
wondering what on earth to do next. I
stood by the wall of a lookout where
one could see right across the palm
trees to the beach. You could see the
beach road for some miles before it

went into a grove of coconuts, and
then through to the jungle itself. I saw
them snaking away there for, oh, I
suppose it took quite a long time for
the whole hundred of them to
disappear into the distance. And I
concentrated on this until the last
person had gone. I remember seeing
my husband—the patrol officer went
ahead with his group—and I
remember them suddenly
disappearing. They looked almost like
puppets, just characters disappearing
into the Never-Never.

A few police always stayed behind to look
after any prisoners still on the station and
deal with the day-to-day administration.

The first day was usually an easy stage
with early camp. John Murphy describes
pre-war patrolling in the highlands:

. . . thereafter our tents would start to
be pulled down about four in the
morning. The staff would be woken
up and the tents would start coming
down as we were getting dressed
inside. By half past the tents would be
down and rolled up and our breakfast
would be on the folding table outside.
Generally it was pork and sweet
potato and our tea and so on.
Sometimes we made bread on patrol.
Always used a camp oven, the nice
cast-iron things on three legs. Then
we'd be well away and walking and all

the carriers strung out behind us when the sun rose. Mostly we'd be walking above the clouds because they would all have sunk into the valley below. We would walk and gradually the sun would rise, the clouds would pass through us and we would be walking underneath them.

On this particular patrol to Mount Hagen we were joined by groups of people from every little area we passed through. They wanted to travel under the protection of the police. But they came all the way to Mount Hagen with us, 110 of them. There they had great trade in shells and bird of paradise feathers. Never had done that before in their lives.

Well at twelve we'd make camp. Not because we were tired of walking; but we would make camp. We'd encircle the camp with cotton rope and the natives had to keep outside. Inside all the carriers and the hangers-on would cut grass and they'd make themselves little huts. They'd bend saplings over and make little round beehive huts, and they were snug too. Then we'd have some of the people who were from next to this area start yodelling to call the people in. They would watch us from the ridges round about and gradually they'd drift in. Early in the afternoon they'd come in with pigs to sell, string bags of vegetables of all sorts, and so we'd buy our supplies, fresh stuff for the patrol. It gave them time to get in and back to their homes. That's why we camped at midday instead of walking on.

The afternoon we'd spend trying to make friendly contact. Jim Taylor had a lot of pictures from magazines and other sorts of pictures showing life in the rest of the Territory and of other native people, and also other places and Australia. We'd spend a great deal of time with interpreters talking to the people, showing them pictures and all this made a great impression on them. In the evening the *kiaps* were in bed soon after dark. They joked about reading and

re-reading the labels on the jam tins, but the early start, the exhausting walk and constant supervision left little energy even for reading.

The police walked dispersed along the carrier line. They carried guns but no ammunition. 'If', Gordon Linsley says, 'you felt there was a need to issue the police with ammunition, you gave them one clip and strictly forbade them to put one up the breach'. In new country the *kiap* or the police demonstrated the power of the rifle by shooting a pig or smashing shields. (The police might run side bets on the marksmanship of the person selected to do the demonstration shoot.) After one display of how a bullet could splinter a pack of shields, one old man said, 'That's all right for pigs and shields, but this'—and he patted his three-pronged spear—'this is for men'.

Inevitably foot-patrolling was most arduous for the carriers. On long patrols they lumped their packs for day after day, scrambling and sliding on the ridges and wading in the swamps. Ivan Champion has said that when the carriers were staging the stores forward, they walked one thousand miles to advance the patrol by one hundred miles. The carriers were the most likely to suffer sickness or injury. In what was probably the worst case under Australian administration eleven carriers died on Staniforth Smith's patrol in the Gulf in 1911. But most officers were acutely conscious of the welfare of their carriers. Some of them were often recruited from the local gaol. The field staff became admirers of the skill, endurance and humour of their carriers.

The use of aircraft eased the work of the carriers. Early in the post-war, patrols hoping to be supplied by an air drop had to carry a bulky transmitter and wet batteries. Up to twelve men might be needed just to transport the radio. But later, compact, dry-battery transmitters were used. The *kiap* selected a drop site easily located from the air and free of hazards for the slowly circling aircraft. Back at the station the staff checked and double-bagged the supplies. In free-dropped stores the tightly sewn inside bag

The Territory of New Guinea District Standing Instructions, 1925

Patrol equipment as indicated ... will be issued to out-stations;

Tent and Fly, 10 × 12	1
Fly for Carriers, 14 × 16 ..	2
Fly for Police, 14 × 16	2
Hammock (sealed pattern) .	1
Swag Bag for Clothes (sealed pattern)..........	2
Swag Bag for Hammock (sealed pattern)..........	1
Ground Sheet	1
Food Boxes (trade)..........	2
Hurricane Lamps...........	3
Frying-pan..................	1
Saucepan	1
Billycans...................	2
Buckets	2
Stools (folding camp).......	2
Table (folding)............	1
Despatch Box (iron)........	1
Medicine Chest	1
Flag, Australian............	1
Haversack	1
Waterbottle	1
Revolver....................	1
Compass, prismatic	1
Protractor..................	1

Immediately a police patrol enters a native village the Australian Flag will be hoisted outside the quarters of the senior European officer of the patrol. It will be lowered on his departure. During the stay of the patrol it will be hoisted at sunrise and lowered at sunset. . . .

Officers will arrange for an armed guard of any non-commissioned officer (or senior constable) and three constables, together with a constable with side-arms only, to parade at the station or post flagpole at sunrise and sunset. The constable with side-arms will hoist or lower the flag and the guard will present arms as the flag is hoisted or lowered as the case may be.

The Territory of New Guinea
District Standing Instructions,
1925

might burst on impact, but the looser outer bag restrained the spill of rice or tins of fat.

Jim Sinclair who was dependent on air drops on several Southern Highland patrols remembers:

The first thing one would do on the morning of an air drop was make sure that the local people were informed of what was going to happen. Obviously you did not want them wandering over the drop site. Then you would get your police and carriers to set smoke fires around the perimeter of the drop. The centre of the drop site itself would be marked with a cross of a couple of old strips of calico carried specially for that circumstance. Then it would be a question of settling back and waiting. And this could be a very frustrating business. Sometimes I've waited for day after day for the aircraft to come in and because of any one of a hundred circumstances it was delayed. When you're listening for an aeroplane in the bush you start to hear them whether or not they're actually there. But when the unmistakable sound of the aeroplane engine finally burst through, then it really was an exciting business. Generally speaking we didn't have contact between the ground and the air because of the way DCA regulations worked. In most instances it was not possible to talk to the pilot. In other words you couldn't direct him. All of the necessary arrangements had to be worked out before you left. But the first thing the pilot would do would be one or two careful circuits of the drop site to have a look at the configuration of the countryside to see which way he'd make his drop. Generally speaking the pilot would drop away from the camp. The most disastrous air drop that I personally was involved in was the last after a seventy-day patrol in the Southern Highlands. Wind patterns in the upper atmosphere which we simply weren't aware of on the ground brought the pilot to reverse the normal procedure, and instead of

dropping over the camp and away, he had to drop flying in towards the camp. On the first run there was a minute delay in kicking the cargo out and bags fell like a stick of bombs right across the camp and killed two of our people very, very messily indeed. This caused consternation. The local people who were gathered to watch the event all panicked and went screaming into the bush.

In the Southern Highlands virtually all of our drops were made from Norsemen aircraft and from Junkers 52s of Gibbes Sepik Airways. The aeroplane would come in for the first run, the engine throttled well back, almost gliding in, at the critical point the cargo would be kicked out, the pilot would throw open the throttle, the engine would roar into full power and the aeroplane would soar straight up and then around and in again for another drop. Of course this was an occasion for terrific excitement among the carriers and the watching native people. They screamed and yelled with delight as the huge machine would come thundering in, dropping down supplies on to the camp. Then after the sixth or seventh run, when the last of the cargo was delivered, the aeroplane would normally come back as low as possible, the drop crew would stick their heads out of the open window and wave at you and away they'd go. You would send the carriers out to the drop site to gather the food and bring it all back before the store tent. And then there was the exciting business of opening it all up, sorting out all the food, the trade, the bottles, and the packing of it all into the patrol packs ready to move off in the morning for the next stage of the patrol.

In the early years of British and Australian rule, government officers were sometimes involved in bloody conflicts. William Armit in 1900 reported that he and his police killed fifty-four people on one patrol in the Northern District. Similar violent patrols took place in the same

The day broke fine with a few light clouds in the south, and we got away to a good start at six and moved slowly up the water-logged valley (it having rained throughout most of the night) through scattered hamlets and small gardens at first, and then under a limestone escarpment into the bush. The river was crossed and re-crossed, and then at 7.30 we began to climb up the range in between the two arms of the river. The crest of the spur, height 8000 feet, was reached at 8.20 and immediately the crags of a high mountain jutted into view some three or four miles away; but thick grey cloud mist closed us in on all sides. We remained until eleven, but the carriers still had not come up so decided to continue to the main point of descent and await them there. But there was still no descent and we continued to climb through yet another grass clearing at 9700 up to 10 000 feet. The track led through a dreary wilderness of dripping forest and the fantastic shapes of twisted, stunted, moss-swathed tree trunks.

At 12.15 we came out into another clearing. The mist lifted a little and it seemed as though we were out on a spur and had begun to leave behind the main range. Drizzling rain again set in, increased to a downpour. The track was a succession of bogs and quagmires linked by the rivulet in which we trod. At 2.45 we came out into a narrow ledge by a high pointed rock. Breaks in the swirling mist did not show much, but they were sufficient to reveal that we stood on the edge of a precipice. The height was 9000 feet. Light persistent rain again fell as I debated what to do, to camp here or to go on. I determined to go on.

There was no possibility of getting any fires going on this mountain top. The ground, the stunted bush, the twisted trees were sodden. To camp here, therefore, would mean no food and no warming fire and the bitter cold of an exposed mountain top. The rain came pouring down and I had to abandon all attempt at running a true compass traverse. The whole world seemed to be flooded and waterlogged. The rain poured down, the trees shed water, the track was a stream pelting down the steep slope with dangerous slippery cascades where the sudden drops were. And here our proposed camp site was inundated.

We kept going. Dropping down a steep hillside as the rain eased, we saw through breaks in the forest sunlit kunai slopes several miles away, and pandanus forests nearer at hand. At 4.30 we came out into this pandanus area on the banks of a creek, and I determined to go no further. A hundred yards further on were several small huts used for smoking pandanus nuts. And these would provide dry sleeping quarters. The huts were deserted, but there was dry firewood, and we quickly had small fires going and huddled over them, gratefully warming our miserably cold bodies in the smoke of the flame. A native came out of the bush, expressed neither surprise nor nervousness at our presence, and quietly seated himself among us.

At 8 o'clock Hamugwe came back with the tent and my bedding and some of the loads and a hurricane lamp, and reported that the remainder of the carriers were at the creek and camped. Those of us at the huts went to bed as we were, foodless, and I for one got little sleep. Hamugwe came back at 11.30 with some more of the carriers and a report that the seven not accounted for were with Corporal Peme camping in the bush.

Former Assistant District Officer Gordon Linsley's patrol diary of 18 December 1951 written on a New Guinea Highlands patrol

area over the next four years. Some of the early officers used the language of warfare: they wrote as if they were suppressing rebellious tribesmen on the frontiers of empire. In German New Guinea government officers were more inclined to impose their authority with the gun. Even in the 1920s and 30s in Australian New Guinea there were instances of field officers shooting ten and twenty opposing warriors. Against this background of frequent early clashes Sir Hubert Murray and other senior officers demanded that field staff never shoot to punish. Any patrol officer who used his gun now knew that he would have to face a searching enquiry. A tradition of restraint developed. Officers and police became more likely to

When it is necessary for native police escorts in charge of prisoners being forwarded from Rabaul to a district or from a district to another, to be issued with handcuffs, District Officers will be held responsible that such handcuffs are returned with the escort or by return mail.

The Territory of New Guinea
District Standing Instructions,
1925

endanger themselves than use their firearms before absolutely necessary.

When patrols entered areas for the first time, they usually found the people friendly. Jack Baker describes these early patrols as 'gentle exercises in getting to know each other' with the villagers full of curiosity and eager to trade. Sometimes, unknown to the *kiap*, the police would 'adopt' a young boy. After walking out with the patrol the boy would go to a mission school and learn Pidgin. On the next patrol he would act as an interpreter. Based on customary rules of adoption and exchange, the 'lending' of young boys to ease communications between groups was understood widely in the Territory.

> *All officers of the Public Service are granted the concessions of a free weekly issue of Quinine in twelve (12) capsules of five (5) grains. . . . Wives and families of officers are not eligible for a free Quinine issue.*
> **The Territory of New Guinea District Standing Instructions 1925**

Violence could come without warning. In 1957 on his second patrol into a valley a day's walk beyond Koroba, Jim Sinclair suddenly found 'the air was absolutely full of flying arrows coming down everywhere. They simply flashed down out of the darkening sky like raindrops'. When the casualties were counted in the morning five men on the patrol were found to be injured, a villager travelling under government protection had tried to escape and been killed and two of the attackers had been shot and had died.

Claude Champion, attempting to arrest murderers inland from Kikori in the Papuan Gulf, was only too conscious of danger developing:

After several days' walking we heard voices and we saw some women on the track. We caught the women, took them into the village—the long house—and yelled out to the men to come in. We gave the women some calico and a tomahawk and let them go to entice the men to come in. But nothing happened. We yelled and

yelled and nothing happened. The next morning at dawn we heard the shouting of the natives and we looked out and saw, I suppose, 150 natives advancing on us. Two of the men—I imagine they were chiefs—came forward with their bows unstrung. The other natives weren't very far away. They still had their bows ready, and I advised my police: 'Be ready. Put a cartridge in the breech'. (I should say we had the old Lee Enfield single loading rifles in those days. It only took *a* cartridge.) These two natives came up within twenty or thirty feet of me and I walked towards them. I suppose I got twelve feet from them when they both bent down, put their strings on and fired. My cookboy, Naisi, had given me a washing basin which I put in front of my face. I had a .45 revolver and fired at them, but the cartridge was no good. He then handed me his shot gun which was loaded with pig shot in the normal cartridge. I picked this up and the arrows started coming. We hadn't fired a shot. Three police were hit so I gave the order to fire. I myself fired at the closest man. Whether I hit him or not I don't know. But one of them was killed. He was ripped to pieces really so I imagine the pig shot hit him. He—well it's hard to describe—but he was really shredded. The other man got away, and afterwards we found one more dead man. That was the end of the fight. We dragged the dead man, put him against the other one, and put tomahawks, shells and calico as payment for the dead. They couldn't understand it was their fault. After all we were on their property and we had no right to be there. Why should the government interfere? Later I checked with the police and seventy per cent of their cartridges were no good.

That was characteristic of the pre-war Papuan administration: it was strong on principle but it was short on money to support the men who had to implement its policies.

The Territory of New Guinea
District Standing Instructions,
1925

All ammunition is to be kept under direct control of a European officer, and is not to be issued to native police by any person except a European officer, who must make such issue personally. . . . All native police on stations and their quarters are to be searched periodically in order to ascertain if they have ammunition in their possession without authority.

6 Sailo!

When the ship dropped anchor in port she had been heralded by natives on the lookout all up and down the coast who cried out 'Sailo! Sailo!' when the ship was sighted. Every man and woman, black, white or Chinese, made off to the ship because most of them had finished their supplies of grog a week before—or something like that—so the ship became a focus of social activity quite apart from people wanting to get their cargo and their mail and everything else. Steamer day was terribly important in all the little ports of New Guinea.

Brett Hilder, ship's captain

The histories of all countries have been influenced by communications, and in Papua New Guinea location and ease of movement have been crucial in determining the course of many lives. People living close to a road or an airstrip will still be sharply different in the way they look, work and spend their leisure from those living in another village just ten miles away but served by walking tracks.

Europeans first sighted the island of New Guinea in the early sixteenth century, but for over three hundred years they failed to penetrate far beyond the beaches. The foreigners who settled in Papua New Guinea from the 1870s linked their isolated plantations, missions and government stations by boat. Early settlement sites at Samarai, Daru and in the Duke of York Islands were selected because they gave easy passage to the boats. Before the 1890s only the rivers gave foreigners access to the interior.

Papua New Guineans had earlier adapted to the same environment. The travellers were the seamen. The water that separated islands was not a barrier, but a road. The Massim, the Mailu, the Hula, the Motu, the people of the Vitiaz Strait and others spent weeks on their boats exchanging goods and news, and making their names known.

For the foreign community too the boats were more than artifacts for the carriage of goods. The steamers from Australia assured the settlers that they still belonged to a wider world, and that they could, if they had to, escape to milder climates and more familiar cultures. The rhythm of their lives was tied to the coming of the boats. They measured time by them: events were remembered as having happened before or after a boat. The local newspapers recorded in minute detail the movements of boats and of every white person that came ashore or went away. On outstations all demonstrated their concern for the sea link by constantly watching or listening for a boat. Stan Christian, a European Medical Assistant, remembers when no boats came and they went for over four months without mail or fresh stores. But when he was stationed 240 miles up the Sepik everyone on the station had plenty of warning when a boat entered the river mouth.

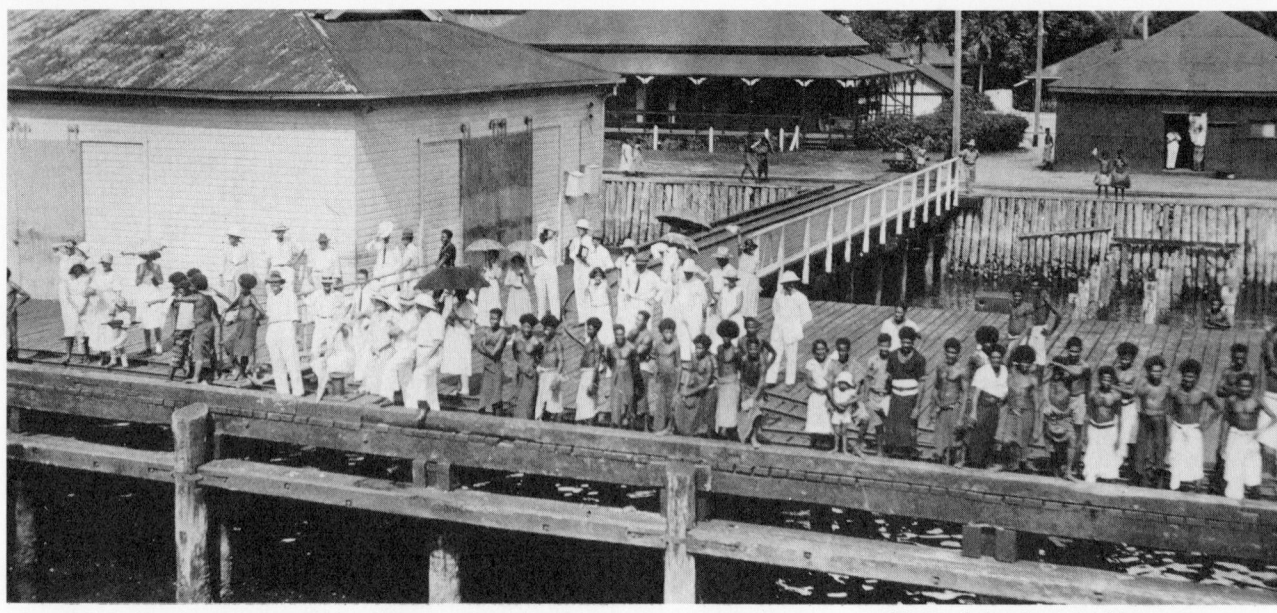

Seeing the *Macdhui* off to Port
Moresby from Samarai

Villagers would begin signalling with
garamuts, the long slit drums, sending an
echoing message up the river in an hour
or two. 'Eventually,' Christian says, 'we
got to the stage where we even knew
which boat.'

Ken Douglas, an island planter, describes the dependence on boats; and the
excitement of one's arrival:

It was very hard to get a ship in those
days to take me out some supplies.
Then I went to Captain Cruikshank,
who was the master of the old vessel
called the *Durour*, a big iron steamer.
And he said, 'Oh, I'll have a stab at it'.
It was arranged that the *Durour* should
call with a couple of months' supplies.
A few weeks went by and of course
the supplies started running
dangerously low. The natives, who
had heard that the *Durour* was coming,
were very excited, and when she
didn't turn up they were getting very
despondent. And all of a sudden one
morning I heard a terrific noise: 'Sailo'
from the beach. You could hear it
running and echoing all along the
beach. They took up the cry at the
local village, a couple of miles away.
You could hear it from there. About
an hour later she loomed up. She
looked pretty big on the horizon, like
the *Queen Mary*. The excitement was
absolutely intense. You could feel it.

Old Cruikshank picked his way
straight into the anchorage. She was an
iron ship and you've never heard such
a clatter as the anchor chain made as it
was being run out; a terrible noise.
You'd think the whole ship was being
shaken to pieces. When it hit the
bottom and everything was quiet a
terrific cheer went up from all the
natives. And I must admit I can still
feel the excitement of it.

Most shipping was controlled by three
main companies: Steamships, WR Carpenters (popularly known from its initials
as Would Rob Christ), and Burns Philp
(or Bloody Pirates). But the settlers'
dependence on the shipping companies
did not mean that they liked them. An
Australian who enquired into the Naviga-
tion Acts in the 1920s reported that he had
never before known such hatred for an
inanimate object as directed by settlers
against the trading companies. It sometimes seemed to the struggling planter
that the companies left his copra to rot on
the wharf, charged him high freight rates,
gave him generous credit for his stores
and then suddenly seized his plantation to
pay the debts. Yet the venom directed at
the companies was not extended to particular managers, captains or ships. The
settlers were only too aware of the hazards
faced by the men guiding boats from one
plantation anchorage to the next. Brett

Hilder, a former Burns Philp captain, explains that their problems were increased by the heavy rains that reduced visibility. Also they worked cargo by day so that they spent the night feeling their way through poorly charted reefs. It led to the expression: any Pacific skipper that says he hasn't hit a reef is a bloody liar. When you did hit one, Hilder says, the important thing was to make sure it was not named after you. You didn't want your disasters commemorated on the charts for ever.

The boat did more than bring mail and stores and take away copra: it was a travelling trade store and social centre. The purser sold everything from a needle to an anchor. And of course the steamer brought liquor. Brett Hilder:

> The ship had no refrigeration. The beer we took was in big bottles in those days. You had forty-eight bottles in a case. Now all the cases of beer were lined up on the foredeck in the sun. You might have fifty cases of beer every time you left Rabaul, and with a bit of luck there were only a few cases left when you got back. When you were invited ashore by the plantation manager for a drink, you had to wait until he got at least one case of beer ashore. The captain of the ship and the manager would then sit on opposite sides of the table with a case of beer beside them and pull out one bottle at a time and finish it off. Hot beer in New Guinea!

Drink brought as many captains to grief as did reefs and sandbars. About half his colleagues, Hilder says, were alcoholics tolerated by a forbearing company. On one ship the captain, chief officer and radio operator alternated periods of drunken insensibility. Inevitably the captain and chief officer miscalculated: one collapsed before the other had re-emerged. That was too much for the second mate—and the company. Both delinquent officers were sacked.

Even in some of the most important island ports there were no cranes, and sometimes no wharves. Improvisation, sweat and luck got the stores to the land, or at least into shallow water. Brett Hilder:

Kilinailau unloading at coconut products wharf, Rabaul, New Guinea

At Salamaua, which was the main port for the goldfields, there was a big open bay with a nice beach running along the shore, and we would have at least a thousand tons of cargo to be discharged on this beach. It was a bit like landing on Bondi Beach with no facilities for getting the cargo away. When I got into the trade there in 1931, when it was pretty new, we took two surfboats, lashed them together side by side, then we had big baulks of timber, about six by six or larger, which we laid across the boats athwartships. On top of that we put hatch covers, and they formed a big square, about the size of a small room, ten by ten or something like that. We could put four of these on top of two surf boats and make a deck, and haul the cargo on to this raft. When it wouldn't hold any more without cargo falling over the sides, it was towed towards the beach. When it grounded in the shallow water the native crew picked up each piece of cargo and threw it towards Salamaua. It landed in two feet of water, one foot of water or six inches, depending on how hard they threw it. Well of course some of these things were crates of galvanised iron, some were bags of sugar, some were bits of machinery, some were cases of beer,

Pacific Islands Monthly August 22, 1933

Hula, Papua 1929

*We were on the second plane
that flew in to Tabibuga strip in
the Jimmi Valley. And I must
say it was hair-raising because
you flew over a very deep valley,
touched down on the edge of the
strip and stopped with your nose
against a mountain. It went
mountain up one side and a deep
valley down the other. You were
just on a little ledge. It was
fascinating because they had
started a school there, and there
were all the school children, all
the people who'd made the strip,
and all the implements which
they'd used to make it. A dance
group sang and danced up and
down the strip. I said to the
interpreter, 'What are they
singing about?' And he said, 'Oh,
they're singing, "Bobby Gibbes
came in. Number One
Government came in. We're the
men that made the strip. We're
the men that made the strip.
Bobby Gibbes came in. Number
One Government came in.
We're the men that made the
strip. . . ." ' They just sang it over
and over again.*

Dame Rachel Cleland

and all these things have a natural distance you can throw them. The crate of galvanised iron usually settled in about three feet of salt water. The bag of sugar might go ten feet, smaller objects would go further. And when the ship had finished discharging cargo over a period, say, of thirty-six hours, and we pulled the rafts back to the ship, dismantled them and prepared to sail, you could look ashore and see what might have been a range of sand dunes growing out of the sea along the edge of the beach. The row of dunes extended for some hundreds of yards; and it was the valuable cargo we had landed. In Salamaua under these circumstances no claims for damaged cargo were accepted. If you didn't like it, well, you didn't ship your cargo.

When Bill Royal washed the first dishes of gold from the rich alluvial of Edie Creek in 1926, he unwittingly set in motion events that changed the history of transport in Papua New Guinea. Edie Creek was six days' exhausting walk from the beach at Salamaua. Every bag of rice, shovel, set of weighing scales and bottle of rum that went into the goldfields had to go on men's backs. But thousands of ounces of gold were being taken back to Salamaua. Edie goldfield was rich enough to support an air service, and just over a year after the opening of the field small

planes were making the flight from Lae to the sloping airstrip at Wau. The first planes were shipped from Australia to New Guinea. Jerry Pentland was there in 1928 when they ran a schooner on to the beach at Lae to unload a DH60X Moth. They laid planks from the schooner to firm ground. Pentland says that in those informal days before any civil aviation regulations were applied in the Territory, they just 'put the wings on it and tinkered around; and I took it up'. There were no weather reports and inadequate maps. Pilots flew according to the rule: No see, no go. But inevitably all were at some time caught in the big build up of clouds that pressed on the north of the ranges when the north-west was blowing and on the south during the south-east or dry season. Bill Forgan-Smith remembers the maxim: 'Fly with your back door open. If the weather was not too good in front you'd keep looking back, and if it was closing in behind, well, get back.' Generally the pre-war aircraft just did not have the power or the range to cross the 15 000 foot mountains to take advantage of the clear weather side.

In spite of the primitive aircraft and conditions, fatalities were rare. The pilots were skilful. As Pentland says, 'They might have drunk a little, they might have been a bit wild, but they were good pilots'. It was not that they never crashed.

(Inevitably George Mendham's small air-line was known after one incident as 'Bendum and Mendum'.) The art was to crash and survive. Forgan-Smith:

> Of course we flew so slowly and you could land in such small places that you could often get away with a forced landing. Engines were so unreliable you learned how to have a forced landing; it was the first drill you learned. Usually if you were going to prang into trees, well tail down so you'd rip the tail off if possible and the nose would drop in. If you looked like you were going to hit something head on, just push full rudder on, left or right, and let the wing tip catch it. The wing tip would crumple up as you hit the side and by that time you'd almost stopped. So it was recognized drills: you just let the aeroplane crumple up around you if you could. A head on crash is no good. You're not to let things like that worry you really. I mean if you do, you'd get out of flying.

So there was another common statement: there are only two sorts of pilots in New Guinea—the skilful and the dead.

With depression limiting opportunities in the rest of the world many hopeful pilots and promoters of aviation compan-ies tried their luck on the New Guinea goldfields. In 1933 more planes took off and landed at Wau than from any other airport in the world. Competition forced prices down and pilots were willing to service the mining camps that spread out from the Wau. Soon there were rough airstrips at Wampit, Kudjiru, Garaina and at Sunset and Surprise Creeks. The missions and the government began to use aircraft as they spread their influence into the central highlands. Then the war accelerated and changed the direction of the aviation industry. It left a litter of wrecked aircraft, more pilots experienced in tropical conditions, and many more air-strips. In 1945 the new war-trained pilots joined the old wood-and-wire men to rebuild the Territory's air services. The planes were about to become the ordinary means of moving between the main centres of the coast as well as in the interior. They did a lot of hard flying as Bobby Gibbes reports:

> We were operating under quite difficult conditions. For instance in Wewak we had no lighting or anything of that nature. I remember my 'forty hourlies', as they were in those days, were done in the headlamps of a jeep by the engineer, and generally I would help him myself. They would have to be done at night because the aeroplane would be fully utilised during the day, and that is seven days out of the week.

The Austers were still 'string and bag', and had to be re-surfaced after a year in the tropics. Airstrips were rough, and radios rare. Gibbes and other pilots became known for their calculated risks. Bobby Gibbes:

> We used to do one trip into Telefomin, and on the way in we'd land at Burui and refuel from a drum which we'd carry with us. On the way back we'd still have a reserve of fuel, and if there wasn't enough in the plane to get us back safely we'd open the door of the Auster, take the cap off the slipper tank, put a hose into the slipper tank underneath the Auster, and with a funnel pour the petrol in as we were flying home. It was a terribly hazardous operation and something that we didn't tell the Department of Civil Aviation about.
>
> The old Dragon when it was fully laden used to lumber right along the Lae airstrip and you had very little underneath you when you went over the end, over the trees. In the event of an engine failure of course it would have been curtains because they wouldn't fly on one motor. The whole way up the Markham valley you'd be climbing hard to get through one of the gaps into the highlands. You would even have to circle to gain that added safe altitude so you could go through one of the gaps. Then the rising terrain around Kainantu was such that the Dragon wouldn't even cope with the increasing altitude of

Guinea Airways Ford tri-motor bogged on Yodda aerodrome at the end of 1941

comparatively flat land because at that height their performance was pretty marginal.

The people on the outstations were full of praise for the Territory pilots. At the same time they destroyed each other's confidence in flying with stories of pilots caught in the dark and reading their instruments by cigarette lighter, or landing with tree tops streaming from the undercarriage. But they did not always act to make life easy for the pilots. Gibbes was once puzzled when his aircraft took a long time to get off the ground at Aitape, and he had to circle to reach even the 2000 feet needed to get into Lumi. Gibbes turned to the mission priest with him:

'Look this aeroplane is heavy. You've got much more than 2000 pounds' or whatever it was I was supposed to be carrying. I said, 'Do you mind if I weigh the load when I get in?' He said, 'No, not at all.' So I weighed the load and we had almost double. I said, 'Father, I'm going to check your scales in Aitape'. 'Oh,' he said, 'I don't use scales. I just lift up each item and estimate the weight and write it on it!'

Just as certain ships are remembered with affection, so are certain aircraft. The Douglas DC3, the reliable workhorse, is the plane most admired by its pilots. Forgan-Smith:

The best aeroplane they've built so far. You could take it anywhere, do anything with it, an old tail dragger; you couldn't worry it. It was built to land on grass strips, so it was in its element when you were doing that. You could get them bogged and get a few natives to lift her out, get going again. It didn't take much. You could get them in and out of anywhere really. You could land them empty at forty-five knots which is fairly slow. I've got them in and out of impossible places—impossible for a DC3 according to what's laid down.

On one occasion he was unable to get into Mount Hagen to deliver pipes needed for hydro-electric plant being built by the Seventh Day Adventist Mission. Day after day the rain would be one or two points over the fifty-point limit for the Mount Hagen drome. Eventually he told one of the missionaries to report forty-nine points. He did. But as Forgan-Smith came up the Wahgi valley he could see the pools of water and rain-washed land below. The airstrip looked like a swamp.

Working on the Rabaul Kokopo
coast road

Jack Bird, his first officer, asked:

'Are you going to land?' I said, 'Oh yeah, they probably only had fifty-three or four points which is not going to worry us'. So I picked a hard spot and came in on a very slow approach and sat down. We only rolled about a hundred feet and we were up to the axles. There was mud from the nose to the top of the tail, red mud. The door opened and the missionary said, 'Well, how was it, Forg? I took the nought off like you said. We had 400 points last night.' I said, 'Jesus, you'll kill a bloke. Christ, I said a couple of points, but God, not 300 odd.' So we unloaded where we were and we got about three hundred natives to lift us out on to a drier patch. We did this three-point takeoff, just opened the throttles and slid along slowly. We were airborne at about forty-five knots, got the gear up and got away. But it had the effect of closing the strip to Dougs for about a year. They had to re-work it. Jeez, it made a mess. Tracks about a foot deep. Highland towns are monuments to the DC3s: they were built largely with what could be carried in the hulls of DC3s.

It is part of the strange history of communications in Papua New Guinea that in many areas air services had preceded roads. In 1940 there was scarcely a road extending more than thirty miles beyond the coast, but by the end of 1953 there was a road from the Markham valley climbing a series of twisting ledges through the Kassam Pass to the edge of the Eastern Highlands. From there it went west across the Ramu-Purari divide, passed through the broad Goroka valley, climbed the Daulo Pass at over 8000 feet, wound down into the Chimbu and on to Mount Hagen. Over 500 kilometres of road had been formed, levelled and gravelled, and drainage canals cut by thousands of Papua New Guineans using little more than picks and shovels. The Highlands Highway was the most spectacular single project of the post-war program of road building. Road, or *rot*, quickly became one of the most used metaphors in Pidgin. A road was a means of getting something. It was an opportunity. But some communities found that they now walked in the dust of foreign owned trucks, and the road was the means by which all the young people left for a different way of life in the towns.

Making the 'rot', Wau-Bulldog 1943

The highland roads were essential to relieve the people from being beasts of burden, to reduce the dependence on aircraft, and to carry the produce of local and expatriate farmers. Ian Downs, who as District Commissioner in Goroka had much to do with planning and directing the road-making, has paid tribute to the Australian supervisors with practical skills. They used forty-four gallon drums, second-hand lift cable from Australia and waste material from the war to build culverts and bridges. But it was the high-landers themselves who did the work; and they were eager to get the job done. Ian Downs:

> We anticipated we'd have to use thousands of people so we had to establish food gardens in the areas where the roads would be built. It meant there would be a lag of three or four months, or sometimes a little more for sweet potato. We started this almost straight away. Then we organised our gangs on very short term work, two or three weeks' work at the most. And we realised that the conditions were extremely bad at high altitude, very cold and sometimes quite dangerous. We were quite prepared to, and did in fact, use gangs of between eight and ten thousand people on particular sites. And eight and ten thousand people making little

carrying baskets and working with spades and digging sticks can do colossal things if they're properly directed.

These were scenes of extraordinary human activity on Australian Territory that few Australians ever knew about.

> *It's very difficult to explain to a person who's never seen a vehicle why they need a road. In fact the first wheels which a lot of Highland people saw were on the undercarriage of aircraft.*
> **Malcolm Mackellar**

By the mid 1950s the *kiaps* were supervising the building of the road from Mount Hagen to Mendi. The people working on the Mount Hagen side knew exactly why they were digging and levelling: they could see the Land Rovers churning up to the roadhead. But the gangs working from the Mendi end had never seen a vehicle, and the Mendi airstrip was too small to allow one to be flown in. Malcolm Mackellar:

> It's very difficult to explain to a person who's never seen a vehicle why they need a road. So it became necessary to show them. One day when I was camped at eight and a half thousand feet at the divide where the road goes down into Mendi a message came from the District Commissioner:

'Arriving on Thursday, walking through to Mendi, please assemble 1000 carriers'. I thought he must have put too many noughts on the message. I thought perhaps he means only a hundred, so I arranged for a hundred carriers to stand by. He duly drove up in the Land Rover which was the normal practice in those days. You'd drive up to the roadhead, and then the patrol would start from there. So he arrived with a few police on board and camping equipment, got out, and said, 'Did you get my thousand carriers?' 'Oh, I thought it was a mistake. I thought you only needed a hundred. I couldn't see what you needed a thousand for.' 'I've got to take this Land Rover into Mendi.' I said, 'Yeah, but there's no road. We haven't built as far as that yet.' 'Well that's the purpose of the thousand carriers. We're going to carry it in.' And I said, 'Well, why don't you pull it apart and carry it in bits and pieces?' 'It's no good arriving with a vehicle in parts. To show everybody along the road why we're building roads, we need to have a vehicle to show them.' So he said, 'Can you supply the carriers?' 'Well, I've got a thousand labourers working on the road. You can have them.' So we gathered them together and he said, 'OK, we're going to carry this Land Rover in to Mendi. Can you do it?' One of the old chiefs said, 'Oh yes, we can do it.'

The way they'd carried things before when they were building roads was to build a stretcher of bark between two posts which two men could carry. So when it came time to carry a Land Rover that was the only way they knew, and we didn't know any different because we had never carried Land Rovers by human portage. They cut down two huge trees and built a platform between them so that it looked like a big stretcher. They drove the Land Rover up on the platform, 500 got on each tree, they went 'Heave ho', lifted it up, and away they went. There was quite

Highlanders working at the Daulo Pass twenty-two miles from Goroka in the eastern Highlands

a bit of excitement seeing them go down the hillside because their idea of going up and down a hill was not to follow the contours. They'd just go from the bottom to the highest point, and when you're going down a hill, you go from the top straight down to the bottom. That's the way they walk across country: it's the shortest way. So that's exactly what they did with the Land Rover. We thought we were going to lose it at one stage when the momentum got out of hand, but they just ran down the hillside, a thousand of them, all running down carrying this Land Rover. When they got to the bottom they kept on running for about another mile until they sort of ran out of momentum. Then they just had a rest and continued. They walked through the bush, the high altitude swamps, the tundra and everything. So they carried it to Mendi that way. It was a dramatic combination of the old and new means of transport.

7 The Boat Came Every Six Weeks

It took three days to get to the plantation. We chugged up the river through the mangroves and then came out on this wonderful open place where three rivers met. We got off the Varoe, *and walked on duck-boards through the coconut trees till we got to the house which was on a slight rise and looked over the tops of the coconuts and out to the river. And I said to mother, 'Oh, this is the most beautiful place I have ever seen'. Mother left one of her most notable silences then said in a very controlled voice, 'Wait till you've been here for six months, dear'.*

Mrs Penelope Hope, daughter of planter, Percival Robinson

Coming from a drought-prone homeland, many Australians were misled by the piles of tangled rain forest and the stands of tall kunai grass. Here, they thought, was a place where anything planted would flourish. In 1906 when the Australian government took control of the Territory a Royal Commission reported: 'the soil of Papua is rich, virgin, and easily worked ... the rainfall is regular and generous, while as a naturally-watered country it stands almost without rival. Streams, ever-flowing, and pure as the sources from which they come, are to be met every few miles ...' But in fact nearly all the Papuan planters struggled. Whatever they could grow, someone—somewhere else in the tropics—could grow cheaper and had less distance to ship to markets. And the Papuan planters always seemed to start too late. They began to develop land for crops at the height of a boom, and by the time their crops were ready to harvest the prices had collapsed. They were the late and the lonely of the tropical planters. Most of them had to add to their income by trading, fishing for shell or recruiting. The experience of Mrs Hope's father, Percy Robinson, was typical of many of the small planters. He went to Ogamobu near Kikori in 1917. As the coconuts were not flourishing in a

rainfall of over 200 inches a year, he decided to replace them with rubber. But no sooner had the rubber trees come into production than the prices crashed in the world depression. He returned to Australia in 1929: 'father did what he wanted to do; he had his pioneering experience, but he didn't make any money out of it'.

The planters that stayed occupied scattered pockets of land along the coast, on the Sogeri plateau, and in the islands. Plantation families were acutely conscious of their isolation from the rest of the white community. Penelope Hope:

The ketch was supposed to come every six weeks with supplies for the household and rice and tobacco and things for the trade store. But it very rarely did, so after about six weeks when we were running short of tea and reading matter and other essentials we'd start listening. There were little creeks running through the jungle and they would magnify the sound of the engines. We got so we could hear an engine for miles and hours. We could hear the beat, and every hornet was an engine. Or a coconut palm, any sound, we'd listen, and try and identify it as an engine.

Then occasionally Sir Hubert Murray's boat, the *Laurabada*, would

The administration's scow-type vessel *Parama* taking aboard passengers and cargo on the Oriomo River in Western Papua

Pacific Islands Monthly August, 1951
Aboard the old *Papuan Chief*

come up on a routine inspection, and occasionally other boats would come in, and the excitement when you saw somebody that wasn't your own family or the people that lived at the government station was out of all proportion.

We wrote letters interminably. We kept going, writing letters and posting them off. When the mail bag came we tipped it out and there were lots of letters and we'd stack them in order of excitement. People would send us books—to get some more reading matter was the great thing. I suppose we were lonely, but we didn't give it a name. If you give something a name it's more real than if you just pretend it isn't there.

On the eastern side of Port Moresby Geoff Elworthy moved into his first small *goru* palm-floored house where a lazy carpet snake lived in the kunai grass roof to keep the rats down. At the end of the day he returned to the house, had a bath, got into pyjamas, settled in the one mosquito-proofed room and

the servant would bring out a bottle of Negrito rum which everybody drank in those days. Nobody ever drank Scotch then. You'd have rum and water, he'd make a couple of savouries, and you'd open a newspaper that was generally six weeks old.

There was not very much radio. I had a radio that I used to get on to the Australian news, but I couldn't always get it with the static. I'd pour myself another rum, read the newspaper, and suddenly it would be ten o'clock at night and I'd have drunk half my bottle of rum. How on earth I didn't become an alcoholic I don't know. I had one chap at one side of me managing a plantation, and he was an alcoholic. He'd go out for two months at a time. And there was another chap on the other side of me, a very, very nice man who'd been a patrol officer a long time ago, and he died of cirrhosis of the liver. He was pretty far gone when I was there. Suddenly I realised that the way I was living I was going like them. So I decided to make a change in my life. I got out of my pyjamas and into long trousers and put on a shirt and a tie. I permitted myself three drinks a night. I set a special time for a meal when I was by myself: I had dinner every night at half past seven. And I found that suddenly things started to run a little better. The house was run with more precision, the plantation seemed to be run with more precision.

Penelope Hope, too, recalls dressing for dinner. But she stresses the practical: after the heat of the day it was a relief to change

Plantation home, Witu Islands, New Guinea

into fresh clothes and have a drink—just one—before dinner.

Isolation brought other hazards. When Cliff Batt's three-year-old son fell and split his lip his wife sewed the wound together with a needle and cotton: they had run out of sutures. Penelope Hope remembers when she started every day with oil of cloves and a chalky substance to make a temporary filling in her teeth. After she finally reached a dentist she had to adjust to the strangeness of breakfasts without the taste of cloves. Her mother's memorable pronouncement was: 'No one should ever come to this country with their own teeth'.

Many pioneer planters went through times of subsistence. They ate sweet potato and taro of course, pumpkin tops, wallaby, pigeon, shellfish and even cassowary and hornbill. The wet hessian sides of the Coolgardie safe kept butter just on the firm side of oil but would not preserve fresh meat. The early kerosene refrigerators, while greatly appreciated, had limited capacity. Mrs Merle Wall says that at Tenekau plantation on east Bougainville she could store enough sausages and other meats for ten days by taking the tops off the ice block trays; but at the end of that time there was still over a month before another boat.

In German New Guinea there had been more land suitable for plantations and the early planters caught the high prices for copra. Some of the New Guinea island planters were able to establish the way of life that accorded with fantasies of white-suited owners on horseback, yearly trips to Europe, skilled Asian cooks, and hundreds of black labourers working diligently among seemingly endless rows of palms. Indeed, when Australians took over after the First World War some ex-servicemen moved into spacious, veran-dahed homes set in lush gardens; but then faced falling prices in the general collapse of world markets in the 1930s. Instead of a nation's reward, they got hard work, debt and malaria. Many of the New Guinea planters of the 1930s or in the years of rehabilitation after the destruction of the Second World War faced the same struggles as their colleagues in Papua. When Norman Sandford went to Bougainville as a cadet plantation manager in the 1930s he had limited space in a large house: someone had chalked on the floor the area still safe to walk on—the rest was rotten with white ants. At Tenekau Mrs Wall had a wood stove, all water had to be carried by bucket, the step up to the door was a stump set into the ground, and the corrugated iron kitchen was attached to the rest of the house by a plank-walk. She reflects:

It was just amazing the way we did live. Our ironing was done by a big old iron that was like a charcoal burner, and it had a chimney. We'd burn coconut shells on a piece of flat iron, scoop the coals into the iron which would heat up, and then we'd do the ironing that way. Our lighting was twelve-volt batteries, and this went for about an hour and a half in the evening, just to give us enough light to perhaps do a little reading and have our evening meal.

As James Seeto explains, most plantation families were on their own; either they made their own entertainment or they left the industry. Penelope Hope says that her mother, a keen bridge player, seized a patrol officer to make up a four whenever she could; and there was painting, drawing, needlework and reading. But lighting was always a problem: carbide and fuel lamps attracted swarms of insects even in the most carefully wired rooms. Mrs Hope remembers:

> You talked, you talked, you talked! And then you talked some more. And had cups of tea at appropriate intervals, and cake. Then you went on to drinks and cheese before you went in to dinner. All the entertainment we needed was to have someone to talk to or listen to.

> *I had a general rule that by seven o'clock in the morning if three things had gone very badly wrong on the plantation I'd agree it wasn't my day. I'd get a couple of lads and go fishing for the day. I'd come back to find that the plantation had generally been run a little bit better than had I been there; and I'd feel a lot better.*
> **Geoff Elworthy, planter**

Regularly a rumour would spread among the bachelors that the next *Malaita* was bringing a bevy of lady school teachers from Australia. It never did, Norman Sandford admits, but there was always the excitement of the possibility. And there were occasional women passengers on the BP steamers; sometimes a few planters would take a schooner down to the Solo-

mons to play tennis; and there were the hobbies of collecting shells, working tortoise-shell and building radios.

On the Papuan coast there were convivial gatherings. Geoff Elworthy:

> At weekends all the plantations would gather together in one house or another. I would generally go to Otomata plantation which in those days was run by a Mr and Mrs Miller, fantastic characters. Cassie Miller was really one of the great ladies of the pre-war of this country, and of the early years after the war. She was a wonderful hostess and a tremendous cook. She was quite a large lady. In 1908 she had been a Floradora girl. In those days to be a Floradora girl, or to be on the stage, you didn't need to be the slim little lass you have today; you had to be rather beefy. I suppose you would call her a big girl; but she had a tremendous personality. The whole district would gather there practically every second weekend. There'd be eight or ten of us. We'd all have our bath (there was a pull-up shower with hot water in it), we'd get into our pyjamas, and all come and sit in the mosquito-proof room and we'd drink rum or gin—some of the ladies used to like gin. It was always with water because there were no bottles of the present-day lolly water. And it was the habit in Papua, I don't know about New Guinea, never to drink after dinner, so you'd do all your drinking before dinner. Consequently dinner didn't occur sometimes till three or four o'clock in the morning when we were all as high as a mob of kites. But it was really good fun. When I look back on it now, those were some of the very happy days of my life. What the cook did I don't know, but he apparently cooked food for about ten o'clock then just kept the fire going and dozed.

Where there were sufficient numbers of white people the informal gatherings were structured into clubs. At the head of the hierarchy of clubs were the Papua Club of Port Moresby, founded before the First World War; the Rabaul Club, started on the same day the Australian civil administration took over in May 1921; the New Guinea Club (it 'opens its membership on a more popular basis'); and the Kavieng Club which began in 1927. But on more remote stations the club was, or could begin as, a modest project of self-help. On the east coast of Bougainville in the mid 1950s the mail runner was given notes to distribute asking for gifts and ideas. After a series of working bees the Kieta Club began to take shape. When the steamer arrived to take out the first big shipment of cocoa the women gathered there while the men went out to watch the loading. An English officer came ashore to visit the Club. Mrs Merle Wall:

> The only lights we had in the Club were what we call sludge lamps. Our children were asleep and the wives were just sitting around with these little wicks burning in tins. The officer had come ashore thinking, maybe, a club, something all lit up. He must have struggled and slipped along the beach in the dark and finally scrambled up the steps. We had made little wire cots, we called them meat-safe cots. They kept out the mosquitoes. This man just looked around, saw the Club, saw the children in these meat-safe cots, and he said, 'My goodness. They sit here in the dark with these little lamps and their children are in cages!' He was astounded. But everybody was very happy because we were comfortable, we had a roof, and we felt on mutual ground. And perhaps most of the wives hadn't seen each other for a year. So this was a very happy time for us.

By contrast the plantations developed in parts of the Highlands from the 1950s were only two or three hundred acres and linked by road. They allowed easy communication. Among a 'very, very marvellous group of people' in the Western Highlands Tom Cole says he was going out to dinner and barbecues two or three times a week: 'and there was tennis and swimming and so forth, and as the situation improved economically people started to put in their swimming pools and build their tennis courts. There were horses and we used to play polo-crosse and so on . . .'.

Even on remote plantations there could be the problem of unwanted guests. One planter found a quick solution. He sent his 'shoot boy' out for some flying foxes. The next morning at breakfast each guest faced a plate of small staring eyes and out-stretched wings amid the terrible stench of boiled bats. They left.

When an Australian family went to live in a plantation house, they also entered a peculiar institution. They seemed conscious of unwritten laws about how the planter, his wife and children should behave. Many of the rules prescribed the treatment of Papua New Guineans. Some of the old pre-war planters said that a *masta* must never speak to a labourer: the white man spoke to the 'boss boy' and he in turn gave orders to the labour gangs. A few of the white settlers were able to accept a string of domestic and personal servants as though to the manner born: they gloried in dominance. Others played the part of the *masta*—they ordered and disciplined the servants—but they were always a little embarrassed or defensive about it. And a few formed effective relationships in spite of the barriers of language, race and unwritten laws.

Malcolm MacGregor explains how taking the job of planter forced him to act according to a very rigid code:

> I would knock off about four o'clock in the afternoon and ride my horse back to my house to be met by my horse boy standing by the front gate. It was part of his responsibilities to wait there for me to arrive. I would get off my horse and throw the reins to him. He took the horse away, unsaddled it and cleaned it. I would walk up the steps of my front verandah and be met by my two house boys who assisted me off with my boots and then served afternoon tea to me on the verandah: white bread sandwiches, as I recall, with a

Breaking cocoa pod, Inus
plantation

pot of tea. I would stay there until about half past five or six. At that time of the afternoon it used to rain without fail for about an hour or so, and I would sit there on the verandah reading and watching the rain. Then I would go in, have a shower, clean up and leave the bathroom something of a mess, walk into my bedroom where my clothes for the evening would be laid out, that is, a fresh pair of white trousers and a fresh white shirt. I would put those clothes on and go back into the bathroom to do my hair to find that the bathroom had been cleaned up in my absence. I'd then sit

down, turn on Radio Australia, listen to the radio for a while, and have a glass of sherry. The tune which signalled the onset of the Radio Australia news was a sign for the house boys to bring in my meal. On the dot of seven I would sit down at my table and have my soup served to me by the boys that lived in the house, one of the guys standing near the table to replenish my water jug when it became empty.

I actually lived in that absurd fashion for the whole of the two years that I was there. That's how the white men ate, if they were married or if they, like myself, were living alone. On the odd occasions when I used to entertain, meals would be very formal; when I was entertained by other plantation workers meals would again be very formal. Of course there was no social contact with the nationals in New Guinea at all. They used to work for us; we didn't mix with them socially. Except that as we lived near Sogeri education centre and there was a fairly good cricket team there, we used to play cricket against them. But that was the only social contact that I recall. That's how life was. I was told how I should behave, and in order to serve my employers well I behaved the way I was taught. Until of course I realised that the whole thing was nonsense.

That careful description of life on a plantation is from the post-war, yet ironically the behaviour described comes closer to the pre-war ideal than most of the toughest of the early planters were able to impose. Not all plantation companies of course demanded such rigid adherence to the role of the *masta*, but when they did they could so easily induce ordinary Australians into behaving in a style alien to that of their countrymen just a few hours' flight to the south. And this was being done when attitudes were already changing on other plantations and especially in the Territory towns.

> *Living on atolls is not the best. Once you've walked around an atoll once you don't want to do it again. I always used to get a little cynical when visitors came out and started getting lyrical about tropical paradises. I said, 'You live here for three months and you'll probably go off your rocker'.*
> **Cliff Batt, planter**

Old planters, having endured volcanoes, floods, mud slips and the ravages of a thousand insect pests, might well have concluded that no human could presume to be *masta*, New Guinea itself always had the power. Mrs Merle Wall:

I went to a place called Palmalmal on the south coast of New Britain by plane, and then I was taken by a little launch to the plantation. People in Rabaul first, at the airstrip and then on the launch said, 'You'll just make it'. I couldn't understand this. I thought, I'm used to rain here in the tropics. But of course when the rain started I knew what they meant. I think that the first month we had sixty inches, and then the next eighty. It rained, the gauge overflowed and we couldn't count the amount of rain. Sometimes it would rain for three weeks, almost stopping at times, and then it was just falling out of the sky again. But we also had our dry period when the weather changed right round to the nor'west. During the wet my husband wasn't able to get the cocoa into the drier. He decided to build a bridge and everyone was terrific. They only had one tractor, there was no other machinery, so they made rope vines and pulled the big logs out of the bush, sixty-foot logs. The wet had started, and all the men kept working with my husband. I'd go down with the children and watch them. They kept singing. They were so pleased building this bridge that they kept working in the rain. They finished the bridge and I think we got two loads of cocoa over it. The rain was coming in heavily and my husband was saying to me, 'Isn't it wonderful! We're right, we've got the bridge finished and the rain is here'. In the morning the people came shouting around, 'Come quickly, come quickly!' We ran down and every stick of the bridge had gone. There wasn't even one piece of decking left. The rain had just come—I think we had thirty-seven inches in thirty-six hours—and of course those sixty-foot logs were swept away like matchsticks.

Foreign plantations have operated in Papua New Guinea for just over one hundred years. Generally they have made money only in the dawn and in the twilight of that period: before 1914 and from the end of the 1950s.

8 Masta – Me Like Work

Recruiting labour was no problem at all because as soon as any planter took up his land and started planting the natives swarmed around. They'd come in all the time: 'Masta, me like work.'

Tom Cole, planter

Plantations depend on cheap labour. In many of the old tropical plantation areas—Malaya, the West Indies and Fiji—the labourers were shipped in from overseas. But in Papua and New Guinea the Australian government insisted that the labourers be recruited from within the territories. Before 1950 the labourers were nearly all indentured. That is, they had signed a contract, or put a mark, or touched a pen while someone else signed. Once they had signed-on they were bound by tight laws. If they left their employer or were insolent they could be gaoled. By the end of the 1930s about 25 000 men were away from their home villages working under indenture on the plantations. They were paid a minimum of five shillings a month in New Guinea and ten shillings in Papua.

In the 1960s there were still over 20 000 men working under a milder agreement system. By then many of them were from the central mountains. They were air-lifted to the coast under the Highland Labour Scheme. Through most of the 1960s the wages for a first-year recruit were still only thirty shillings a month plus keep.

Life on a plantation line was one of the commonest experiences of those Papua New Guineans who left their home villages. For many it was the only way that they could obtain cash. Those experiences may be more important in the history of Papua New Guinea than any economic results of plantation development. The labourers had as much to learn from each other, including a common language, as they did from the Australian owners and managers. Both the white staff and the labour line had to conform to the rhythm of plantation life.

The working day began early. Norman Sandford, who had a 'medical ticket'—he had completed a course in treating common injuries and ailments and meeting emergencies—would be up at four or four-thirty to go down to the 'hospital' to tend the sick and wounded. At first light —'as long as you could see their faces'— the labourers were 'lined' and allotted to their tasks for the day. The white staff might inspect the copra driers before going back to the bungalow for breakfast. The meal over, the overseers walked or rode around the copra, drain or grass-cutting 'lines'. On some plantations the white staff took a siesta after the midday meal, on others they followed the Australian practice of working through the day. In the evening the staff weighed up the copra cut by the various gangs and saw it placed in the driers. Other gangs were

About one thousand men of the Andekelangag and Andauakang clans moved the logs needed to build a bridge across the Muga River. It was impossible to get heavy equipment into the area (left).

Handbook of the Territory of Papua 1912 (below)

COST OF LABOURER FOR ONE YEAR

Food	£6–17–9$\frac{1}{2}$
Tobacco	7–0
Soap	2–7
Laplaps, 4	4–0
Blanket	5–0
Recruiting fee and fare	3–10–0
Return passage	10–0
Fees for signing on and off	6–0
Wages at 10s per month	6–0–0
TOTAL COST	£18–2–4$\frac{1}{2}$

After deducting 52 Sundays, this amounts to 1s 2d per working day.

For domestic service, permission may be granted for the recruiting of male natives over twelve years, who have not attained full physical development. Upon being 'signed-on', the labourer is issued with a box, a blanket, a bowl and a spoon, and then proceeds to his place of employment. . . .

Official Handbook of the Territory of New Guinea 1937

Bosbois (Boss boys) Ono Bio and Oui Aitsi

checked to see if they had reached their 'mark', the work target to be reached for the day. Again in the evening the sores that could so quickly become ulcers were dressed and bandaged. Where Sandford worked on Bougainville the manager, a returned serviceman from the First World War, was so impressed by military order that he imposed army methods on the plantation. The gang 'boss boys' were the equivalent of NCOs, the main 'boss boy' was a warrant officer and the Europeans were the officers. Many plantations worked according to the clanging of a bell; *belo* called men to eat, work and rest. Whatever system was used the planters claim that they worked long and hard. As Helmut Kroenig says, 'You were on duty twenty-four hours a day, seven days a week'. His attempts to reduce the demands on his time were not successful:

Frequently you'd be called out at two or three o'clock in the morning. Somebody would be calling outside the house, 'Masta, one fella boy die finish.' So you'd hop out of bed, go down to the labour quarters and find somebody had fainted or something like that. Eventually I said, 'Look if somebody's died, don't come and tell me in the middle of the night. Tell me in the morning.' So that stopped that until one morning I made roll call and found there was one short. I said,

'Who's missing?' They said, 'Oh, so-and-so, he died.' I went to the labour quarters and he was dead all right. In actual fact he was stiff. I asked, 'Why didn't you come and tell me during the night?' They said, 'Well, you said don't tell you because if he's dead there's nothing you can do.' Which was true, but it gave me a hell of a shock.

Kroenig returned to constant duty.

The Native Labour Ordinance said that the holder of a recruiting licence had to be a man of good character and perhaps the recruiters met that requirement; but they were also tough and resourceful. They had to be. Three were killed by villagers in the 1920s and 1930s. The recruiters joked about themselves as men dodging an axe on the head and a bunk in a Townsville gaol. (Pre-war no white men served gaol sentences of more than a few weeks in the Territory.) Most of the law-breaking by recruiters was just mild deception and they ignored the regulations that said they could not send New Guineans out alone to recruit. But when the Edie Creek goldrush was at its height the recruiters were able to get twenty pounds for a labourer. At that price they were prepared to take greater risks with stone axes and gaols: they used displays of violence to secure labourers. But much of the time recruiting was a leisurely business. The villagers might even explain they were sorry that the recruiter had come at that particular time: they were busy with their own ceremonies. Perhaps if he could come back in three moons then the young men would be ready to *mekim pepa* (sign-on).

On Bougainville before 1942 many planters recruited their own labour from on the island. Norman Sandford remembers that the schooner captain, one of the overseers and about fifteen returning labourers would go on a recruiting trip. Leaving the anchorage they would take their camping gear, stores and trade goods and head off inland along the walking tracks.

> We'd stop about two or three miles short of a village and change into our clean white starched clothes and walk in very much the pukka sahib. We'd set up camp, leave the people to their own devices until they'd finished their work and had their evening meal, and then we would put out our trade boxes and squat down on them. Eventually the chief of the village and his counsellors would come along to pay us a visit. We'd yarn for a while and discreetly hand out a few presents. Mostly in the first instance we'd hand out tobacco because they'd want to start smoking immediately. They used to roll their smokes in newspaper, so we'd give them tobacco, paper and matches. If it looked as if we'd do well in this village better presents would come out, knives and tomahawks. The more it appeared that one was going to get a lot of recruits, the more the presents were pulled out of the trade boxes.

The planters on the Bismarck Archipelago also at first obtained most of their recruits from the islands, but as areas of the mainland were brought under government control the recruiters went inland. The Sepik district with its dense population and few alternative ways of earning cash was rich ground for the recruiters. By 1939 nearly 10 000 men from the Sepik were working outside their home district. Over 3000 of them

were on New Britain and 1500 on New Ireland. In Papua nearly one third of the men were coming from the Eastern Division, particularly from Goodenough Island, and other favoured recruiting grounds were in the West, the Delta and the Gulf. In total the indenture system required the movement of vast numbers of men.

Jack Thurston claims that when he returned labourers to their 'mosquito-ridden' villages in the Sepik, he would have no trouble signing-on replacements. The 'time finish' men, having eaten a better balanced diet, were much bigger and obviously much healthier than their age-mates who had stayed in the village. Their appearance, their talk and the desire of the young men to see the outside world meant that recruits were soon volunteering to go down to the saltwater. From the 1950s the coffee planters were developing their properties in the highlands. Soon hundreds of highlands men were leaving their home valleys to make the request, *'Masta, mi laik wok'*. Many had to hear the reply, *'Sori, nogut wok'* many times before they finally found a minor place in the cash economy.

> *The Papuan shows a considerable aptitude and intelligence in quickly acquiring a knowledge of his duties if explained by practical example . . .*
> *Those employers or overseers who obtain the most satisfactory results from their labourers are men of good character, experienced in working Papuan natives, and who, while maintaining discipline, are humane and just in their treatment. Experienced and properly qualified overseers are an essential in successful industrial development.*
> **(Handbook of the Territory of Papua, 1912)**

Disputes leading to violence, Harry Hugo believes, usually arose from misunderstandings. A village man, uncertain of the white man's laws of ownership or

NATIVE LABOUR IN NEW GUINEA

Should Talasea Be Reopened?

THERE are indications that the problem of securing adequate labour for New Guinea enterprises will become acute. The gold industry is growing and developing, and there is an increasing call in that direction for native labour; and, meanwhile, the recovery of the copra industry is creating a further demand for indentured labour.

The areas to which recruiters customarily resort are not producing a sufficient number of additional recruits to meet the demand. The natives generally are becoming more sophisticated and are inclined to raise their price. Recruiting is more difficult and the higher cost, of course, is being passed on to the employers.

A movement is afoot to urge the Administration to re-open the Talasea district (northern New Britain) to recruiters. When the Nakanai murders occurred in 1926, the Talasea district was closed against recruiting. In 1928, when the Administration wanted labour for Lae and the Markham-Wau road, etc., Talasea was opened to recruiting for a month; but before recruiters could get there the Administration had filled its labour requirements and Talasea was closed again. On one occasion, since, Talasea has been opened, to supply labour to Messrs. Carpenter and Co.'s disiccated coconut industry at Pondo.

The argument of those who want Talasea opened up again is that the Administration in nine years has had ample opportunity to pacify the district and that the very large native population there might now be made available for recruiting purposes. It is stated, also, that the natives are quite willing to accept indentures and that considerable numbers of them have actually offered their services.

The closing of part of the Sepik area and the Mount Hagen area to recruiters has also complicated the situation.

Pacific Islands Monthly August 22, 1935

MANUS BOYS

Strong, Bright Boys available for work as House Boys or plantation labourers in or around Rabaul.

Radio your requirements to K & B before they all go. State what guarantee held.

KRAMER & BURROWS,
Lorungau.

The Rabaul Times June 28, 1940

just testing what he could get away with, would seize a knife or a tomahawk.

Well you had to deal with that. You might be handling him and a mob would decide to join in. So you had to get out the old gun and say, 'Now, look out!' And 'Boom!' just fire one shot into the ground first. That sort of made them blink a bit. Then you showed them where all the shot had gone in the ground and said, 'Look out it's not you that the shot's in.' They were quick on the uptake. And we'd get them down to the foreshore, wait for a boat to come along and put them on it and send them into Rabaul to one of our men. He'd detail them out to the various plantations.

When recruits were taken from newly-contacted areas they were roped together or at least closely guarded on the journey to the coast. There was always the possibility that a nervous man would decide to make a run for home, and the chances were that his traditional enemies would kill him. His home community would then hold the recruiter responsible for his death.

While shipping in New Guinea waters Brett Hilder did some recruiting on the side:

I didn't go looking for them. I just stayed aboard the ship doing my normal job. Natives would come aboard, come up to me and say, '*Masta, mi laik mekim pepa.*' So I'd say all right, stay aboard and be my guests. They'd get fed and I'd write their name on the official form, where they'd come from, what island. The first place I got to which had a government official I would call these chaps up, march them ashore, take them up to the government official and say, 'These men want to make paper.' They had to have a medical examination, by a medical orderly as a rule. One of his tasks was to check that they were over the age of puberty so they had to have a little moustache at the bottom of the tummy. If they didn't have one you'd cut a bit of hair off their head and glue it on there.

That is a traditional recruiter's story. Perhaps it was actually tried, but it's doubtful.

Some areas suffered excessive recruiting. The government tried to protect the worst affected areas by closing them to recruiters, but even so by 1940 there were many villages where a quarter of the able-bodied men were away. This placed a great burden on the remaining villagers who were in effect subsidising the planters by supporting the labourers' dependents. The absence of so many men also helped destroy the old culture. The construction of men's houses, large trading ventures, initiation ceremonies and major feasts lapsed with so many men and so much productive capacity lost to the village. But had the women accompanied the men the dislocation in the villages would have been even greater. Villages would have decayed and there would have been an increase in the number of landless people who had no alternative but to become low-paid wage earners. The ultimate protection of the subsistence villager was always the fact that he could survive without the indenture system. The government officers were right to resist the planters' frequent demands for a permanent workforce.

> *The planter has always been regarded as a controversial fellow in New Guinea, but basically well run plantations did much to introduce a primitive people to another sort of life style. Most of them would pick up the rudiments of Pidgin English in two years. I think planters have never been recognised for what they did in the pacification of New Guinea and in enhancing its economic stance.*
> **Cliff Batt, planter**

The *bosbois*, the black foremen, played a key role on the plantations. Robert Stuart, a Bougainville planter, has explained in his autobiography *Nuts to You* how he was often away from his plantation for weeks on end recruiting and fishing for shell. During that time his *bosboi* ran the plantation on his own, and supervised the clearing and planting of new areas. Even where the planter was always in residence some *bosbois* could exploit the tacit support of the *masta* to assert autocratic power over the gangs of unskilled labourers. Also, some planters deliberately recruited their labourers from different areas so that they could be encouraged to compete against each other at work and be less likely to combine in rebellion against *bosboi* or owner. But most plantation owners and managers at times found themselves in situations where they had to use violence. Harry Hugo puts it most bluntly:

> Now and again you got a bloke that we referred to as a 'big-head'. Well, he had to be taught that he did what you wanted, not what he wanted. I did a lot of boxing in my time and I was never at all worried about asserting myself. Just got stuck right in, bang, bang, and that's all there was to it.

But Jim Hopkinson concedes that at the moment when violence became likely you 'could be as frightened as bloody hell, yet providing you never showed the fright, you had it won: it was all a game of bluff'.

> *It was well known that we caught them a swift clout across the ear if they did something wrong. We also applied the boot to the area where it did most good.*
> **Norman Sandford, planter**

The use of 'a bit of force', 'a swift clout' or 'a boot to the area where it did most good' continued into the 1960s. In fact Rod Collins thinks that the problems of controlling labour increased with the changes in the liquor laws of 1962 which allowed Papua New Guineans to consume alcohol:

> Labour really became hard to control when drink came in. But they all knew the score, and you had to thump them if they got out of control. You only thumped them for a reason, but you gave them a good talking to before you thumped them. You warned them, and if they didn't take any notice, well, you had to take the

law into your hands and give them a good thumping. This was an example that you'd have to set in front of the whole line. They always knew what was coming because they'd all try you, and try you, and in the end you had to do something. You'd mostly thump them with your open hand to make plenty of noise, and sink the boot, but you never closed your hand because it cut them too much, their skin was like tissue paper. You'd just have to do it. One of the thumpings I had to give them, they'd been pinching food from the cook boy, and they all knew this was wrong, and of course if I hadn't thumped them the whole line would have gone beserk and belted them and probably killed them. *Meris* (Marys, i.e. women) were another thing. They were always in trouble with *meris*, and I used to have to belt them for pinching another bloke's *meri*. But I gave that away after a while, too, because it became too common. I've never had much trouble knowing when to thump them and when not to. I only used to do it when it was necessary. And with Hagens and Chimbus if you had right on your side they realised it, and they wouldn't do anything.

Newcomers were instructed not to punish labourers by hitting them on the body. Many labourers had an enlarged spleen from chronic malaria and a body blow could be fatal.

Labour overseers used a variety of arguments to justify the use of force. The labourers respected 'a fighter' because they were recruited from violent societies. The labourers were 'uncivilised', or 'a bit like children', and anyway they were not punished as harshly as many a planter had been chastised by his own father. But the truth was probably that the very system itself depended on the threat or the fact of violence. No system that takes large numbers of single men, works them in gangs on unskilled tasks in which they have no interest and puts them under the supervision of men from an alien culture is likely to avoid clashes. The puzzle, as

The Rabaul Times June 28, 1940

"PLENTY BLOOD HE COME."

Mr. H. L. Kelly appeared for complainant, Geme-Wai, a miserable little urchin from Gaïle, who complained that he had been assaulted by one Emily Hart, of Port Moresby. Geme-Wai, who described himself as "cookey-boy and boy belong carry 'im water," deposed that on Saturday morning he went to the beach at Koki to take his little sister back to his mother, Mrs. Hart having told him to do so. On his return "missis" caught him by the hair and shook him so long and severely that "plenty blood he come long my nose." Also that in addition to the severe shaking the "missis" had struck him on the back. He told her he would go to the Magistrate and she told him to go. Police Officer Hurst deposed that he served the summons on Emily Hart and had admitted to him that she had caught the boy by the hair and shook him, but said that she had not struck him. Emily Hart stated that the boy had left the house at 7.30 a.m. and did not return till 12 o'clock. When he did return she took him by the "little bit of hair" and led him into the kitchen to light the fire. He afterwards came to her and showed her blood on his hands and told her he would go the Magistrate and she told him to go. She did not make his nose bleed. Boys can make their noses bleed when they like. She stoutly denied under cross-examination that she had been in the habit or beating the boy, or that after she received the summons she caught him by the hair and bumped his head.

The Court was satisfied that the assault had been committed and that it was most unjustifiable, and fined the defendant £1, with 3/6 costs of Court, £1 1s. professional costs.

The Court also ordered that the Contract of Service between the boy Geme-Wai and the said Emily Hart be cancelled forthwith.

Papuan Times February 28, 1912

Tony Voutas suggests, is not why there was violence, but why there was so little.

Inevitably there were some Australians who found themselves unable to sustain the role of overseer. It required, Paul Mason says, a ruthlessness, an assumption of superiority, or a special flair for making other people do what you wanted them to do. Malcolm MacGregor was one who found the demands of the plantation system excessive:

One of the problems was that there were many different groups of people working on the plantation, and they tended from time to time to come into physical conflict with each other. I was told that the way to deal with that was to walk fearlessly amongst them as a white man, lashing out from time to time if necessary. And the fact that I was a white man would somehow preserve my safety. I acted on that advice on one occasion and gave a guy in the rubber a clip over the ear only to find that when I rode out of the rubber I was set upon by him and his mates. They took to me with their bucket sticks—long wooden poles about five or six feet long and about three inches in diameter, and perfectly capable of delivering a fairly savage blow. I was struck, as I recall, on the left elbow rather painfully, and wore a sling until the manager of the plantation saw me and told me to take it off; I was not to be seen to be hurt. On another occasion I was supervising the boys when they were cleaning out their huts. From time to time, whether it was because of illness, or laziness, or whatever, you would be defied when you gave an order, and a particular chap took exception to working on this afternoon. I very foolishly gave him a clip over the ear. He reacted very quickly to that by taking out a knife and I sustained a fairly superficial wound to my right wrist. But I think I realised that that sort of employer-worker relationship was fraught with difficulties and was not one in which I could continue to engage.

Dr John Gunther

The anthropologist, Professor Ian Hogbin, who made a report on the treatment of labourers in the 1940s believes that Australians 'in the colonial situation' were more concerned with 'what they called white prestige' than the British. John Waiko, too, says that the Australians imposed their notions of 'white supremacy' over the master-servant relationship. Sir John Gunther adds the importance of basic economics. For much of the time labour was so cheap and so ineffective at pushing for higher pay that there was little incentive to reduce the size of the labour force. Planters who might have replaced one hundred labourers with fifty at a higher rate of pay did not try to do so. The planters' concern was to produce as cheaply as possible a crop for a fickle market. When the prices went up, the labourers took no share of the profit. In that sense, Gunther says, 'exploitation was par for the course'.

Yet in spite of the demands that the plantation as a system imposed on owner and overseer, some people established easy-going relationships with villagers and workers. Mrs Mason speaks of the plantation as a 'little bush manor' with almost a 'family' association with neighbouring villagers. She was, she says, closer to the local Bougainvillean people than she was to expatriates, and she still values the friendships she made with the villagers.

John Watts also points out that the plantation was a place where the people came for medicines and for all sorts of advice and practical aid.

EMPLOYMENT OF INDENTURED LABOURERS IN THE TERRITORY OF NEW GUINEA 1939

Plantations	*20 657*
Mining	*7 162*
Administration Services	*2 190*
Domestic Service	*4 498*
Shipping, Commerce and Industry	*7 107*
Miscellaneous	*61*
Total	*41 675*

EUROPEANS CONVICTED OF ASSAULT ON LABOURERS

1938–39	*24*
1939–40	*15★*

★One European was found guilty of unlawfully killing a native and was sentenced to twelve months' imprisonment with hard labour.

(Territory of New Guinea Annual Report)

On the Papuan coast Geoff Elworthy became interested in land resettlement. In the mid 1950s he went to Malaya to investigate schemes there and returned determined to divide unused plantation land among men who had worked for him for ten to fifteen years. When the Papua New Guinea administration delayed implementing its own scheme he went ahead alone:

I got a private surveyor down and cut up 300 acres of my land and divided it into fifteen-acre blocks. I put a couple of thousand pounds down as a bank for them to borrow from, which they never used by the way, and I chose six, I think, six married people whom I knew well and I thought would make a good fist of running their own plantations. I stipulated that they should clear their land, plant it with coconuts and cover crop, build a house and plant a couple of fruit trees round it. If in two years they had done this, I would then deed the land to them. Well, they trusted me sufficiently to do this and they worked hard, they really did work hard. Of course, the land still being in my name, I was able to go down there and roar gently. Eventually the six blocks were transferred to these people. They've done a remarkably good job with it. One of them a while ago had an income of seven thousand dollars a year. Another one, I got him to Martyrs School. I paid for him to go there and now he is running quite a good business. They have a couple of trucks, a tractor and roller, and they're running the plantation in as modern a way as any European plantation I've ever seen.

I mixed the blocks. I didn't have, say, all Rigos in one area. I put a Rigo man next to a man from Musa, next to a man from Mailu-Domara so that they couldn't form little tribal groups. And things have worked out very well. Then I started up another six blocks. It's a development that I'm very sorry wasn't publicised more because I'm quite sure that many other plantations would have done the same as this. It was very good for the plantation itself because it provided a group of stable people on the boundary who always had passengers, as they're called, they always had visitors staying, so it was pretty easy for them to say, 'Go up and work for the plantation and you can come back here and sleep at night.' So it provided a labour force for the plantation. And that is the other side that I didn't think of at first.

It was my way, really, of saying thanks to these lads who had worked well for me.

Here, too, the plantation that could be a place of rigid divisions run on threats of violence was the benevolent bush manor.

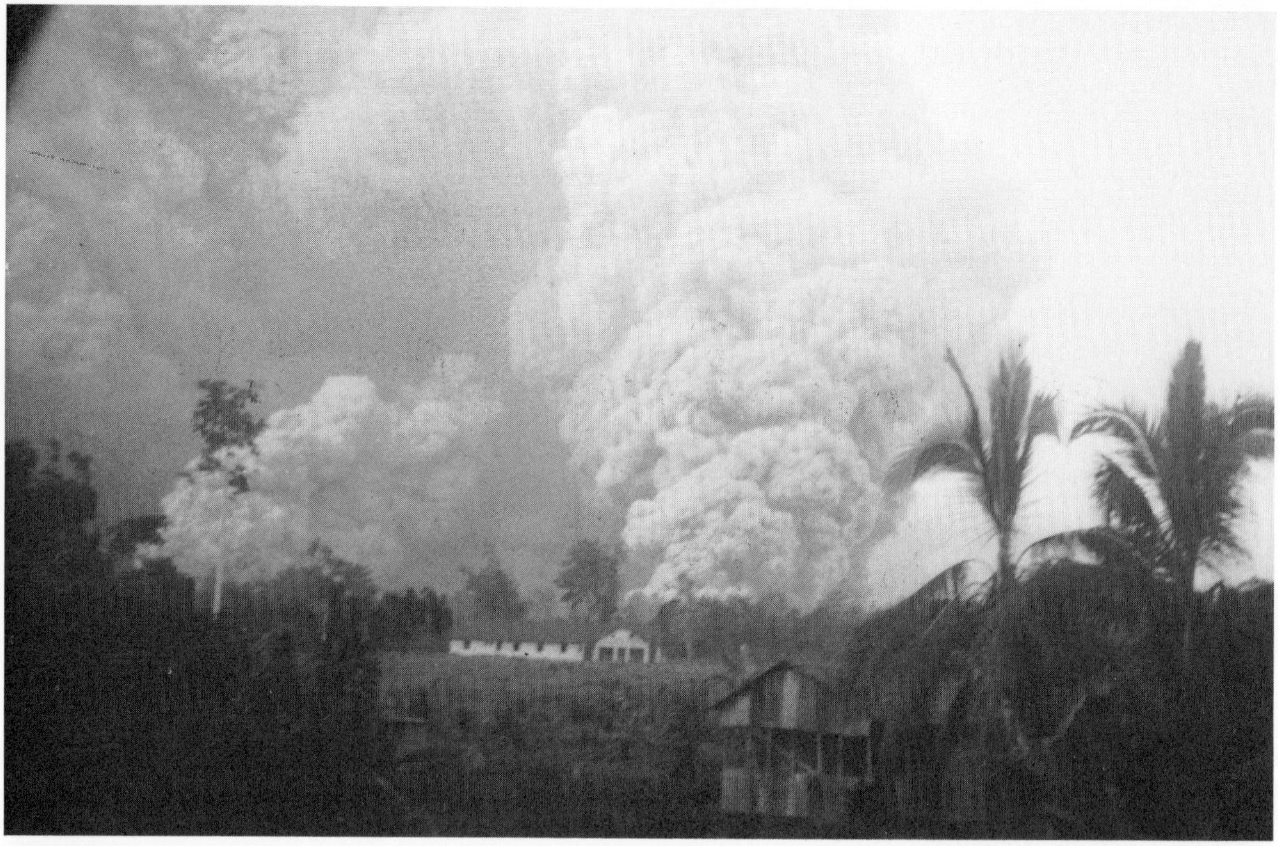

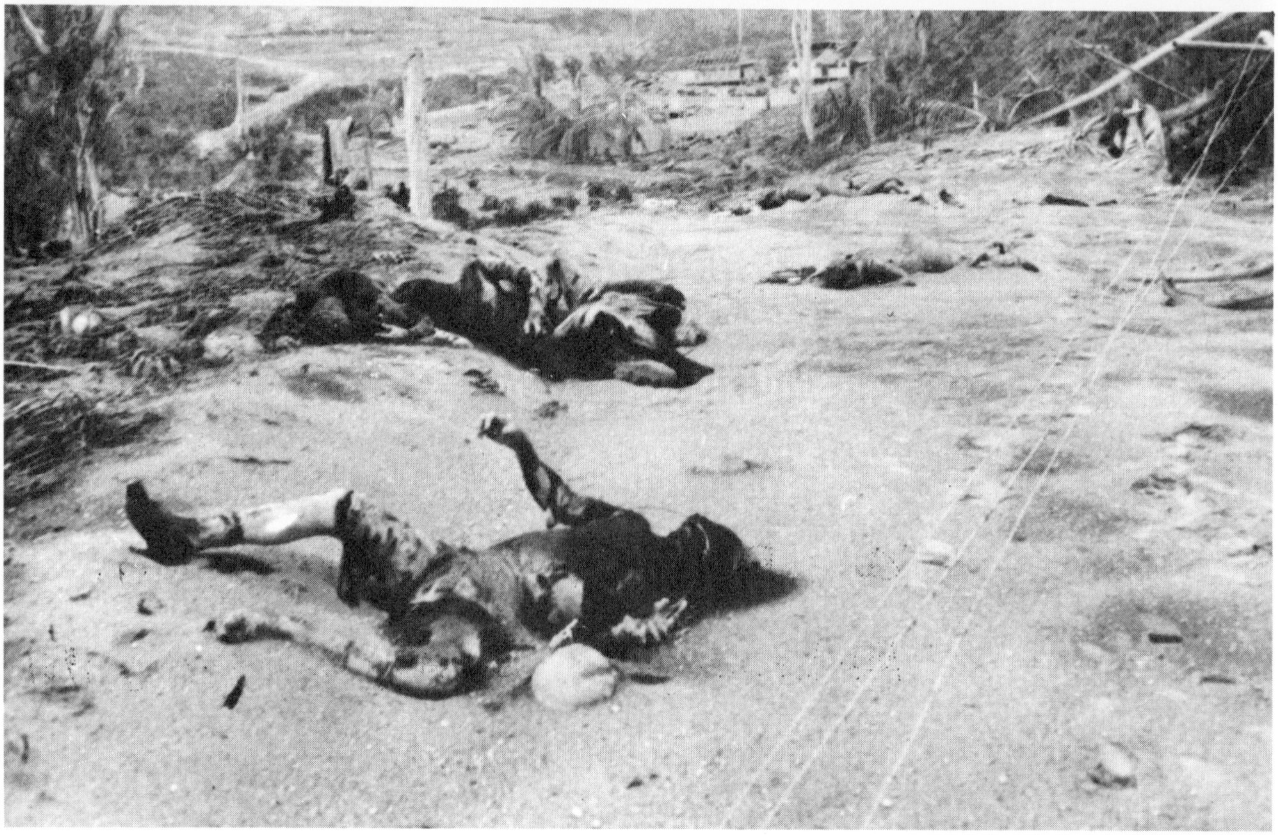

9 The Violent Land

People didn't know it was a volcano. It was just a jungle-covered mountain. Then smoke and flames started up. It went on for a number of weeks. Officials went to inspect it, and said there was no immediate danger to Higaturu. And then it exploded.

Des Clifton-Bassett remembering Mount Lamington

Papua New Guinea is a geologically volatile country poised on the Pacific rim of instability that also affects New Zealand and Japan. The Australian landscape looks like it is the result of slow change, a land made by gradual shifts of sand and silt. Surfaces, long exposed to sun and wind, have been rounded and flattened. But in Papua New Guinea the land has been made by sudden bursts of energy. It has been torn apart, collapsed in on itself, or exploded. Any land free of vegetation is new and raw. It is where a river has changed course leaving piles of silt over a few house stumps, all that remains of a recent village. Or it is a great gash in a mountainside where thousands of tonnes of mud have suddenly slid into a valley carrying all vegetation with it.

It is a land that cannot be trusted to remain steady underfoot. The north and the islands lie at the point where the tectonic plates of the earth's surface thrust over and sheer against each other. The arcs through Bougainville and New Ireland, along New Britain and west along the north coast include some of the most seismically active areas in the world. Hundreds of measurable earthquakes are recorded each year, but the tremors that the people experience are known as *gurias*.

Guria is a word from the Tolai language of the people of the Gazelle Peninsula of New Britain. It was taken into Pidgin English and spread widely. A *guria* could be any sort of trembling, from a person's shiver of fear to a violent heaving of house and land. It was a sign of the old hand, of the long-term Territorian, that he accepted the earth's *gurias* along with sweat, mosquitoes and the wet season. They became accustomed to the slish-slosh of water in the rain water tanks, the wave of trembling running through the trees, the floor boards undulating, the crockery chattering, and, as Neil Desailly observed, the top of the flag pole at Tari whipping through an arc of six feet.

Newcomers were alarmed and then embarrassed when they found that no one else had taken any notice. Theresa Bloxham remembers feeling the floor move, then a picture crashed, and she waited for the sounds of excitement, even the rush to meet an emergency, but there was no response. In fact a violent *guria* could be met with enthusiasm. Eileen Bulmer was sitting on the verandah watching a man building a house when a tremor came:

He was sitting astride the ridge capping plaiting grass on to the roof when this shake came. You could see

Mt Lamington's Nuée Ardente (Glowing Cloud) from the Ambogo valley, March 5, 1951 (top left)

'They just had to disintegrate with time.' (bottom left)

A *masta's* home after the eruption, Rabaul 1937

his whole house sway, and he was completely unconcerned. He said, 'That's it, God, makim savvy'. He just sat there swaying backwards and forwards.

The *guria* could also be misinterpreted:
It happened on a Saturday night at the golf club ball. One lady had a fierce argument with her husband, went home and locked the bedroom door. Much later her husband arrived and camped on the sofa. During the early hours of the night we had a frightful earthquake, houses fell on cars, and wreckage lay everywhere; but the wife stayed blissfully asleep. When she awoke and went into the kitchen there was complete disarray, tomato sauce and jam were all over the place and plates were broken. She picked up the broom and took to her sleeping husband, 'You may have been cross with me but there was no need to wreck the bloody place!'

**Mrs Jean Huxley,
planter's wife**

But *gurias* could shatter the villages perched on the ridge tops. In 1935 violent tremors in the Torricelli mountains of the Sepik District left the ridges broken and fissured. The valleys were filled with tonnes of mud, rubble and vegetation. People were killed by falling timber and buried under mud slides. Food gardens were ruined. In one remote area alone, probably over 100 people died. In the 1930s the inland parts of the Sepik were still largely beyond the assistance of the Australian administration, and beyond the attention of Australian newspapers; the people did their own rebuilding.

There were fewer jokes and more apprehension about volcanic eruption. One of the most widespread stories told by old people in the villages concerns a time of darkness. From the Markham Valley to the western highlands they talk of the black clouds that turned day into night. Ash fell covering houses, gardens and forests with a grey burden. Animals were killed and crops destroyed. The people starved as they waited for their gardens to come back into production. Some of these stories are connected with an eruption that happened about 400 years ago. The distinctive ash layer can still be traced in the soil profile. The many accounts of disaster that are part of the village peoples' oral tradition and the many active volcanoes in the Northern

Province, in Bougainville and along the north coast to Karkar and Manum are evidence of the frequency with which village people have had to experience, and then explain, catastrophe. To recent times they have done that on their own.

On Saturday May 29, 1937, at 4 o'clock in the afternoon Vulcan Island in Rabaul Harbour roared into continuous eruption. There had been plenty of warnings, but few had been able to read them. On the Friday there were quakes and tremors, some so severe they could be heard rumbling in the distance giving people time to grasp for support until the earth returned to its proper tranquillity. Dead fish floated in the harbour and cracks opened in the roads. But as with milder *gurias*, the citizens of Rabaul accepted them. As the chattering crockery stilled, 'You'd say, "Ah, got over that one." ' On the Saturday people went to their siesta, sport or work. Harry Hugo was one of those who had to labour. The *Durour*, which was on the slip, had tilted in the tremors, and its owners feared it would crash through its supports. With a gang of labourers Hugo went to help the captain, 'an old chap called Tom Proctor', and the engineer, another elderly seaman, Fred Northey. They had just started work when one of the labourers called, '*Masta, lookim!*' Harry looked at where he expected to see ocean, and there was the seabed:

> So I sang out to the captain, 'Tom, come and have a look at this'. While he was looking there was another earthquake, and you could see the ocean floor rise another foot. Old Tom, being who he was, a New Zealander and knowing a bit about volcanoes and things said, 'Oh Jesus Christ! Let's get the bloody hell out of this!' And with that he and old Fred Northey made up towards the Kokopo road where I'd put the lorry. And me and the boys we followed them. Young as we were we couldn't catch that pair. I eventually got to the lorry and drove off. I'd just got in to Ah Tam's, which is about five minutes from Rabaul, and there was this loud

bang. We stopped and had a look and Vulcan had blown up. First of all there was a terrific cloud, dark, and then it thinned out to a sort of yellowish white cloud. Then the flames and stones started to appear. At first the cloud blew away from Rabaul ...

Jean McCarthy, newly married, had been in Rabaul a week. She unpacked her wedding dress which had just arrived that morning, hung it on the wardrobe and took her siesta. In mid-afternoon her husband, Keith, woke her:

> People were running and yelling, 'Rabaul i blow up!' But I couldn't speak any Pidgin in those days. We just started to run. First of all we went down to the water, towards the harbour, and then Keith decided no. Cars and people were racing past; everything was in a frenzy. We decided we'd walk across the big football field and up what was called the bridle path to Namanula which was a residential area in the hills behind Rabaul. We had one of our native servants with us, a young Aitape boy called Sumbago, aged about twelve. By five o'clock we had got about half way up when all of a sudden there was this terrible blackout. The soot and ash had blotted out the sun. Everything went black as though it was early nightfall. We turned around and came back into the town, and managed to get to the Cosmopolitan Hotel where they gave Keith a room for the night.

Clive Meares was one of those who spent the night with as many as twenty-five and thirty people crowded into the houses in the hills on the edge of Rabaul. Uncertain what would follow the showers of volcanic dust they closed the doors, put blankets over the fan lights, handed round towels, got buckets of water, and waited. To add to the drama of fire and explosion an intense electrical storm developed around the crater. Samson Patiliu watched in each jagged flash the mass of swirling smoke and the great rocks bursting out and tumbling back into the crater. Trees burdened by ash crashed in the streets.

Terrific Earthquake

Extraordinary Earth Movement on Northern Coast of New Guinea

From Our Own Correspondent.

WEWAK, October 2.

SHORTLY after 11 a.m. on September 20, the whole of the Aitape coast of New Guinea was violently shaken by an earthquake, accompanied by heavy low rumblings.

Houses rocked from side to side, and many crashed. Where Europeans were living, crockery, bottles, etc., were thrown about and smashed.

Parts of the beaches and river-beds sank, whilst other parts rose, the average movement being about six inches. Heavy logs showed markings on the ground where they had slid backwards and forwards for over a foot.

No disturbance was noticeable at all at sea, but the Torricelli Mountains, at the back, suffered severely with terrific landslides. Many hamlets, perched on those pinnacles, were thrown down and destroyed, and created panic amongst the natives. Several casualties, with a small death roll, resulted.

Later, another earthquake of less severity came, followed by many more over the following 48 hours—tremors, with rumblings and shakings, as if the earth underneath was trying to heave itself up.

For over a week, at different periods throughout the day and night, the tremors continued.

This is the worst earthquake experienced here for many years and, as far as the natives can recollect, for about two generations.

Pacific Islands Monthly October 24, 1935

THE
RABAUL TIMES

No.633   Friday, June 4, 1937   Gratis

OUR VOLCANIC ISSUE

WE owe our subscribers and advertisers an apology this week for
being unable - owing to force of circumstances - to publish our
usual issue. It is only due to the great kindness and courtesy of
the Catholic Mission at Vunapope that we are able to issue this
small sheet and right here we wish to record the wonderful work
done by the Mission all through this harrowing period and congrat-
ulate His Lordship Bishop Vesters, and his untiring staff, on the
excellent organisation and display of Christian spirit.

At this particular moment we refrain from commenting on the
possibilities of the future. Even the most usually serene individual
is suffering from the reaction of nervous strain, after the happenings
of the past few days, and his outlook has become distorted and abnor-
mal. Whether the capital of the Territory is to remain at Rabaul or
be removed to some other locality is not a question to be finalised
at this juncture. Both the volcanoes and our mental state must be
allowed to cool off. In a month or so - perhaps more - we can the
better decide such a momentous question.

We must remember this: Rabaul, the Garden City, has disappeared
and there only remains an ugly mud-covered town. It is this drastic
change which is so likely to affect our judgement and make of us
pessimists. There has been no physical panic, but a certain amount of
mental panic. Chins up and carry on! Let hasty decisions be avoided.

Printed at the Catholic Mission, Vunapope and published by
Gordon Thomas, Frisbie Street.

Rabaul Times June 4, 1937

The next morning Vulcan was still erupting; but noiselessly. Clive Meares:

It was very eerie driving down into town with the cars not making a sound on the road. The pumice was about four inches deep. It was like driving on soft snow without sinking into it. It was absolutely quiet.

Even the harbour was covered with a floating blanket of pumice. Small ships could push their way through, but the pumice was the cause of one death. Ken Douglas says that it had banked up between an overseas vessel and the wharf:

Two sailors were going back there one night. One went up the gangway, and the other chap, he was pretty full, said, 'I'll show you what Jesus Christ used to do'. And he jumped off the wharf on to all the pumice. But he must have struck a weak spot because he went straight through. He was never seen again.

A group of senior officials, including Judge Beaumont Phillips, the Acting Administrator, met in the silent town and decided that Rabaul should be evacuated. The people were to assemble at Nordup on the north coast. Jean McCarthy returned to her home:

I took from the house my fur coat, my marriage certificate; I don't remember taking anything else at all. We started to walk again. We got over Namanula, down to the north coast, and by then my high-heeled white shoes had only one heel, and I was hobbledehoying along.

But not all Rabaul's citizens were willing to go. 'A lot of them,' Waiau Ahnon says, 'were just too stubborn. They still love their dear old Rabaul, and they will stay with it even if they're going to be buried with it. I was one of those same blokes.' Ahnon joined in a billiard game on a dust-covered table in the Cosmopolitan. The game continued in spite of the threats of a recently appointed special constable who fired a revolver through the window.

Harry Hugo also joined those in the Cosmopolitan:

We stayed together for the twelve days in which the volcano eventually settled down. It was good, for it was all free grog. I used to drink in those days, I can't now. There was one chappie we had called Morton Wilmot. At this time he owned the Cosmopolitan. We were sitting in a room grogging on, and old Morton used to drink gin. And we lost him somewhere. Next thing he appears. He opens the door, wanders in and says, 'I say, you fellows, has anyone seen the orange bitters?' He had a bottle of gin, a bottle of water and a glass, but he had lost his orange bitters. He wasn't worried at all about the volcano or earthquakes, that was nothing at all; but the orange bitters had to be found. But that's the type of men they were. They were elderly old coves, mostly returned soldiers from the war, and they just didn't care a darn about anything. Real Australians.

In the meantime Brett Hilder on the *Montoro* had picked up the distress call to rescue the more sober citizens:

We altered course straight back to Rabaul and it took us twelve hours to get there. We decided to go into a little bay outside the harbour; there was just a mountain ridge in between the town and the bay. But the chart didn't show an anchorage there of any sort. There were no soundings. We knew it was a fairly clean piece of coast, there were no reefs there that we knew of. So we got the boats ready for loading evacuees. To get the people aboard the ship, in addition to the gangways, we had rope nets hung over the side, very much like landing craft during the war. When we arrived off the little bay of Nordup we steamed in towards the shore and lowered an anchor down to thirty fathoms. We decided that when the anchor touched the bottom (if we weren't already on the beach) that's where we'd anchor. Anyway it touched bottom about a quarter of a mile off the beach, so we just anchored the ship there.

The beach was covered in people who were pouring out of town. There

'the rolling effect of a flood tide'

were some launches and one very nice schooner beginning to take people from the beach. Europeans had first priority. The moment the anchor caught the bottom we dropped enough chain to hold it in position and we lowered all the boats. The chief officer took one launch and I took the other, and we towed a stream of boats ashore. People were walking into the water up to their waists and they climbed into each of the boats as we brought them in. The Government officers had a lot of police boys with them to keep order on the beach. I must say that everybody behaved as though they were just going to work in the morning and going to a pretty dull job too. There was no excitement of any sort, everybody was overawed. They were speechless. Of course they had almost choked to death getting down to the beach because the air was full of ash, so they were all pretty frightened. But all very quiet, amazingly quiet. Almost every person had a bundle of clothes or a little suitcase or kitbag—or a baby.

I think we took something like 200 Europeans aboard; I don't know how many Chinese and something like five or six thousand natives. All this on to one ship that would normally carry fifty passengers. We took them aboard in six hours. We had them standing on every deck in the ship, all the way up to the bridge; we had them in the 'tween decks, but we didn't put any in the lower holds. All these people standing up like cigarettes in a packet, or like on a Sydney bus at rush hour with more people standing up than sitting down. We had the police boys come aboard with them and they kept a gangway clear so we could get up the companionways to the bridge and back. But there was absolutely no trouble, no noise. Everybody just stood like good commuters coming down to the office on the North Shore line.

During the night as soon as we finished loading the people and we'd picked up the boats, we pushed out to sea, drifted down past the entrance to the harbour to have a look at it, and then a few miles further on we waited for dawn to go into an anchorage at Kokopo.

In all about 700 Europeans, 1000 Asians and 5000 New Guineans escaped from the town, nearly all on the *Montoro*.

Besides the un-Christ like sailor, one other European who was trying to photograph Matupit crater, a Chinese trader, and about 438 New Guineans had died. The winds that had at first carried the ash

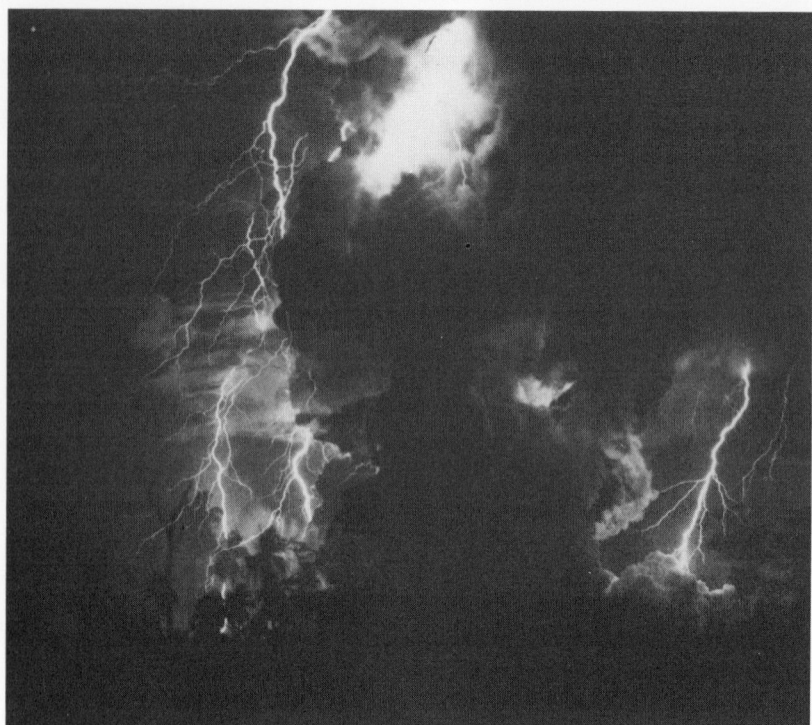

'To add to the drama of fire and explosion an intense electrical storm developed.'

and trimmed neat lawns. Well-known rules regulated all meetings between Europeans, Asians and New Guineans. Now while Matupit continued to smoke, the decision was made to shift the government headquarters. Canberra, Rabaul and the rest of the Territory could not decide where the capital should be, but at least they agreed that they would have to leave the beauty and instability of Simpson Harbour. The old confidence in the place and its ways could not be rebuilt. People kept supplies of tinned food and their cars full of petrol in case they again had to flee. The white women and children were scarcely back before war broke out in Europe. The war in the Pacific completed the destruction of old Rabaul.

Awesome as Vulcan and Matupit had been in 1937, they were but *gurias* beside the sudden ferocity of Mt Lamington in 1951. It was the greatest natural disaster to have occurred on Australian-administered territory. Mt Lamington, rising out of the rich gardening land of the Northern Province, was scarcely thought of as a potentially dangerous volcano, but in the days immediately before the eruption there was increasing rumbling, smoke and tremors. A missionary, later killed in the explosion, wrote that the village people said, 'At night it is like a torch, and we do not understand the sign'. Neither did the white community. They thought the activity was evidence that pressure was being released gradually. On the morning of the eruption messengers carried notes to be read in church assuring the villagers that there was no need to worry.

Just after 10.30 on Sunday morning, January 21, 1951, a paroxysmal explosion released a cloud of intense heat and massive force. The sound of the blast carried for over eighty miles and the dust fell on Port Moresby. Within an area of sixty square miles there was almost complete devastation. The district headquarters of Higaturu, the Anglican missions and schools and many villages were swept by the lethal cloud. The death toll was 3466.

Australians and Papua New Guineans from government, mission, village and plantation combined to shift the severely

away from the town had helped burn and bury the people of Valaur, Tavaua, Letlet and Rapolla. The dead were New Guineans, the mourning was in the villages and the town had escaped, all factors which helped distort the white community's grasp of the magnitude of the tragedy. In fact, in the bungalows the talk was on how few lives had been lost.

> *I was out in the yard. I had Cecil, the baby, on a swing, and I was swinging him. All of a sudden the trees began to shake, and the ground got cracks in it. So I screamed out, 'Mum, what's happening?' She said, 'Come right out to the tennis court quickly and take the baby.' Rabaul had erupted.*
> **Mrs Amy Washington**

The thousands of tonnes of mud and pumice that fell on Rabaul destroyed a way of life as well as a town. Rabaul had been the garden city and the Territory capital. In Rabaul above all places there had developed a way of life that other Australians found strange. It was the town where government officers wore white suits, and black servants prepared baths

injured to hospitals in Lae and Port Moresby, house and feed thousands of refugees, and bury the dead. Ivan Champion:

> I said, 'You've got to bury these today. Bury them in shallow graves it's the only way.' J K Murray agreed, 'It's the only thing you can do.' We camped in the store there at night. I remember this patrol officer coming in, and he said, 'Look, I can't take it any more. I can't.' 'Yes you can,' I told him. 'Have a few rums.' He pleaded with me: 'I just can't take burying these hundreds of bodies.'

Des Clifton-Bassett remembers walking in past the tattered trunks of coconut palms; 'it was a most sickening sight'. Nearly all the bodies were naked, stripped by heat and blast.

Medical Assistant Albert Speer was one of those who worked while the danger of a second eruption was still high:

> The eruption was described by Tony Taylor the government vulcanologist as being like dissolved dirt flooding an area with immense force, immense heat. It had a terrific searing quality and terrific density. The steel flagpole at Higaturu was bent away from the blast. If there had been a recoil action it would have been bent back towards the centre of the actual blast. Taylor describes it as the rolling effect of a flood tide rather than a blast effect, a quick explosion and recoil. The bodies, too, that were lying on their backs had their chest bones broken, the chest cage was crushed with what was apparently a great weight. The corpses were as if they were covered with grey cement. Some in the fringe houses that were still standing were actually seated at their tables as though cement had been poured on them. It was a grotesque situation to witness. We didn't have the time or materials to bury all of these people. They just had to disintegrate with time. It was similar to what you read of Pompeii.

The speed and scale of the administration's response to the Mt Lamington disaster was one of its best actions. Tony Taylor, who risked his life to monitor the volcano, was awarded the George Cross, and others were decorated for bravery or devotion to duty. Nearly all the decisions were made, and the materials gathered, from within the Territory. The 5000 villagers who were forced from their homes and suffered loss of relatives and property were reassured by the response of government officers and volunteers, but they found it difficult to understand why the disaster had happened on their land. Why was it that those particular thirty-five white government officers and missionaries had been killed? Why those sixteen prisoners in Higaturu gaol? Why those ninety Papua New Guinean policemen and their families? And above all, why this terrible punishment of the 2000 Sangara people who were incinerated? And was there more punishment still to come? Bert Speer continues:

> Not many burn cases survived, and those that did were mainly scarred on the back and shoulders. The main ones that I treated were people who dived into a river or creek and their backs were all burnt. The volcanic blast had passed over them, and they had crawled out and come along. The others, the bad ones, were after the eruption; they were burnt in the hot streams. All of the rivers for weeks after the eruption were seas of boiling mud. Whenever rains occurred up on the mountains hot ash and clouds of steam would wash down. This would leave a layer of ash which would be up to two or three hundred degrees underneath the crust. People would just walk into it unknowingly and burn their feet. They had to put logs down and cross on the logs.
>
> It was like a moon landscape. Higaturu station was grey, desolate, hot. When I went up there the heat was intense. You had to take water bottles with you, and they quickly became heated, so you were drinking tepid water and the thirst was terrific. Later on the stench from decomposing bodies was terrible. These were sad scenes and terrible to witness.

10 Moneymakers and Misfits

Shanghai with his walking stick, his white shorts, white shirt and his big straw hat; about eight personal boys walking behind him, one with a case of gin, another with an umbrella, another with a fly whisk, and another with a deck chair. That was Shanghai Brown going to work.

Ted Whitehead, contractor

The white community has been divided into several alliterative categories: missionaries, moneymakers and misfits; or fools, freaks and failures. They are harsh judgments, but there is no doubt that many individualists and 'characters' rushed, escaped or drifted north. Papua New Guinea was Australia's frontier. Travellers could find a zone of free-floating, beyond Australian norms and not yet within another system of tight laws and habits. It was open to those who felt restricted by the uniform white, British, Australian-ness of their homeland. Papua New Guinea attracted the uninhibited and the eccentric, and it tolerated them when they got there. There was Jumbo Degen, a giant of a man who fossicked on the Misima goldfield. He wore just a copra bag and, even when unfrayed, it reached only to his waist. The villagers fed him out of charity. There was one notorious planter who lived on his island like a tolerant agnostic sultan with his numerous Papuan wives and many children. There was Billy the Cook, Nick the Greek, and Frederick Mantle, the ADO in Rabaul, with his distinguished voice and monocled eye. He was matched in Papua by Guy Manning who insisted that every white man call him 'Mister'. It was, he said, essential for his prestige among the 'natives'. Queen Emma, Tiger Lil, Ma Stewart and Mrs Mahony, the Queen of Sudest, have become legends in two cultures. But many of course were not distinguished. They had just rejected, or quietly eased away from, the rules that had bound them in their homeland to settle under the gentle rustle of a sago palm roof.

One elderly Australian who made his home in 'the islands' spoke frankly about how he left a leading Melbourne college: he was caught 'trying to have relations with a young girl from another leading college in the gymnasium'. He was expelled ten minutes later. His father gave him one hundred pounds and told him he had all the world to play in except that small part that was owned and occupied by his father. He went to New Guinea just before he turned eighteen, and he stayed there.

Harry Hugo looks back on a way of life that came close to that idyllic picture of the South Seas as a place of casual, sensual pleasure. It is not hard to understand why some people came and stayed:

I had a boat—only a twenty-five-ton schooner—and twelve boys and myself. We used to wear goggles and nothing else most of the time. If you wanted to put pants on you did. If you didn't, it didn't matter because there

Errol Flynn in his first film *Captain Blood* (left)

91

"Mick" Leahy Returns to New Guinea

Met Errol Flynn, New Film Star, in World Tour

ANXIOUS to get back to New Guinea after a tour of England, Ireland and America, Mr. M. J. ("Mick") Leahy, well-known New Guinea prospector and explorer, arrived in Sydney by the *Monterey* on March 23. He left for Queensland within a few days to visit his father who has been seriously ill, and to join his brother Jim, who accompanied him on his world tour.

In England, Mr. Leahy lectured before the Royal Geographical Society and other prominent institutions, and a summary, with maps, of his explorations between 1931 and 1935 in hitherto unknown territory appeared in the last issue of the Journal of the R.G. Society.

When in America, he left the material for a book with a New York publisher, covering his experiences in New Guinea since 1926 when the Leahy Brothers arrived from Queensland to take part in the Edie Creek "rush." The volume, illustrated by Mr. Leahy's photographs, will be issued by Abbott, McIntosh and Otis before the end of the year. Incidentally, "Mick" Leahy is a photographer of no mean ability, and his unique photographs have been reproduced all over the world.

Mr. Leahy arrived in New York in time to attend the premiere of the film "Captain Blood," starring Errol Flynn, a young Irishman who spent most of his life in Australia, New Guinea and the South Seas. Flynn and Leahy had been friends on the Morobe goldfields and they renewed acquaintance when the hubbub of milling fans, pressmen and photographers had died down after Flynn's outstanding success.

"Errol Flynn arrived in New Guinea about 1930 as a police officer," said Mr. Leahy. "He soon became interested in aviation, then turned recruiter, and finally managed a gold claim owned by Mrs. W. E. Giblin, of Papua. Later he bought a schooner and became a trader, freighting goods and copra. After his boat went on a reef he turned his hand to prospecting. In two years he had won a fair amount of gold, then unexpectedly he sold his claim for £2000 and some shares, and went on a hectic holiday in Australia.

"When his money had dwindled," continued Mr. Leahy, "he and a friend made an adventurous trip to New Guinea in a small sailing boat. Flynn was commissioned to obtain native labour for prospecting syndicates, and after he had made some money he bought another schooner, which was later chartered by Charles Chauvel for a travel film. Chauvel gave Flynn his first chance in films as Fletcher Christian in the Australian production, 'In the Wake of the Bounty.'

"Errol and I laughed and chatted over old times," said Mr. Leahy, "and he wished to be remembered to all his friends in the Territory. He has now jumped into the first rank among men screen stars, and he and his wife are feted everywhere they go, but I cannot imagine Flynn settling down for any length of time—he is too much of a happy-go-lucky wanderer."

Pacific Islands Monthly April 23, 1936

was nobody else around. But we went all round the islands, swimming down and looking along the reefs for trochus and green snail shell. The Japanese used to buy most of the stuff. We went all round the coast and to all the islands—and there were many of them. The people were all different: sort of red-skinned people and some that looked like Chinese, and that was where as a young man you might get a bit of fun. It was the sort of life that any young fellow would love to lead. You were just free all day long, swim all day, no bosses, no nothing. Your own boss. I'm seventy years old now and I'd like to go back to it again tomorrow.

It was certainly better than battling through the grey days of Australia in a world depression.

Perhaps it was the long periods of enforced idleness while people waited for a boat, a plane or a message to come, or the rain to stop. Perhaps the climate induced a lassitude that curbed more active pursuits. Or perhaps it was the absence of television and other devices that competed for people's attention. But, whatever the cause, Papua New Guinea is the home of gifted storytellers. The eccentrics have provided rich material for anecdotes. Malcolm Mackellar:

In the days before government tax came in, several of the missions conducted fund-raising campaigns. For want of a better term the collection was called the mission tax. A mission boat would go along the coast, stop at each village, the missionary would go ashore and ask for contributions. People would give what they could. For each individual this didn't amount to much, but overall it was a tidy sum. One day just before the annual mission tax was to be collected, a bearded beachcomber decided to cash in. He arrived at a village wearing a pair of sandals and a white robe. He stepped ashore to be greeted by the village chief who looked a bit nonplussed. But the beachcomber said, 'I've come for my tax'. 'Well, who are

you?' So the beachcomber explained, 'Haven't you seen the pictures in your church? I'm Jesus'.

The talk soon went round the village that Jesus himself had come to collect his tax and everybody contributed more than they normally did. Having worked his scheme in one village the beachcomber kept going down the coast and collected a fortune. And then promptly disappeared.

A week later the mission boat arrived, the missionary rang the church bell and said, 'All right people, I've come to collect your contributions'. The village headman explained, 'Oh, we've already contributed this year. Jesus came through last week'. The old missionary said with some hesitation, 'I don't think that could be right'. The headman persisted, 'Oh yes, you always said that Jesus would come again. Well, he came all right. He asked for his tax and we gave it to him'. The missionary could hardly deny that there was to be a Second Coming, but even he was tempted to doubt that this was the time and place. He went on to the next village where he heard the same story. The extent of the deception was now clear.

The old missionary didn't know what to do because the people had no legal obligation to pay the tax to the church. They could give their money to anyone. But eventually he went along to the local District Officer and told his story. The District Officer said, 'Oh, yeah,' hummed and hawed, and asked, 'Well, what do you want me to do about it?' The missionary said, 'You should arrest this man, and charge him with impersonation'. 'Well, who's he impersonating?' 'Jesus, the Son of God. He's saying that he is the Son of God.' So the *kiap* said, 'Let me refresh your mind a bit. About 2000 years ago there was a man on this earth who said that he was the Son of God. The local priests complained to the local *kiap*, and that *kiap's* name was Pontius Pilate.

He got himself mixed up in the case, and his name has been dragged through history ever since. If this man thinks he's the Son of God he can—as far as I'm concerned—stay the Son of God. The case is closed.'

Errol Flynn is the hero—and antihero —of many of the anecdotes. In 1927 Flynn, who had just been defeated in the New South Wales amateur boxing titles and recently sacked from his job as office boy, sailed north on the *Montoro*. He was then eighteen. Many of the accounts of his seductions, fights, loans and thefts were embroided, perhaps invented, after Hollywood had helped create another Errol Flynn. In his cavalier autobiography *My Wicked, Wicked Ways* Flynn himself added another layer of distortion to his New Guinea days. But Jerry Pentland was one of those who actually knew the young Errol. Pentland's mining partner, George Arnold, lent Flynn a few pounds to tide him over one of his many moments of insolvency. When returns from the mining claim declined old George wrote to Flynn in Hollywood suggesting that he repay his debt. Flynn sent back a signed photograph, but no money.

Jim Leahy had the distinction among old Territorians of knowing Flynn both in New Guinea and in America:

He was a very unscrupulous man. I can remember Paddy Leahy saying, 'Look out for that bludger, he'll eat anything and take anything.' He was a happy-go-lucky fellow who'd steal anybody's wife or dog. It didn't matter whether the wife was black or white or what she was. In 1936 when Mick and I went on a world tour we both saw him. He was married to Lili Damita then and he came out and met me and took me through Universal Studios. I can remember him telling a story of Papua New Guinea in the studios. The bulk of it was that if you walked out of your camp you were likely to get a spear, if you walked down the road they were firing arrows at you and everything was hair-raising. When he came back to me he said, 'How did I go?' I had

In front of Ma Stewart's Pub in Wau, 1932

actually been on a trip out to the goldfield with him and he'd mentioned something about that too, highly exaggerated. 'Oh', I said, 'I thought you went very well. I didn't know it was like that.' And he said, 'That's the kind of bullshit they like'.

Flynn finally left New Guinea in 1933. Two years later he made his first successful Hollywood film, *Captain Blood*. In small movie houses and at outdoor screenings the white residents of Papua New Guinea looked on the flickering swashbuckler who had already played many roles for them. They had seen him as the jodhpur-clad fop, the pub fighter, the failed planter and miner, and the laughing, engaging scoundrel. They met his appearance on screen with cries of, 'Where's my money, Flynny?' And Eric Wien, the fighting dentist from Wau, got the greatest laugh when he demanded a credit on the film for repairing Flynn's splendid teeth.

In spite of the fact that the white community applauded exaggerated masculinity there were always some women who flourished in the frontier conditions. One of the most famous and loved was Mrs Flora Stewart, always known as Ma

Handbook of Papua and New Guinea 1958
Wau Hotel, 1931–32

Stewart. She had lived in Port Moresby, Samarai and Salamaua before she became known Territory-wide as the proprietor of the Wau pub. The large bar room with its billiard table in the corner was the social centre of the goldfields in the early 'thirties. There Ma Stewart, tough, generous and resourceful, presided over the drinking, arguing and brawling. Her daughter, Ela Birrell, remembers two regular customers who always drank steadily together, but with pauses for fights. One would take his teeth out, plonk them on the bar, and the other would whip out his glass eye and put it down. Ma would intervene: 'No fighting in here, but if you step outside I'll hold the lamp.' Out they would all go, Ma would hold the light, they would fight, come back in, replace teeth and eye and carry on with the drinking.

In 1936 Ma opened the first hotel in Lae, the Cecil. With the rest of the town it was destroyed by the war, but Ma with her persistence managed to be the first civilian white woman allowed back into the Territory. She re-opened the Cecil in rooms taken over from the army. Andrée Millar says that you could never claim to have slept alone at the Cecil. Long barrack-styled rooms were divided with sheets of three-ply that reached neither to the ceiling nor the floor. On one occasion Mrs Millar was certainly not alone:

I woke up in the night and I thought, 'Oh, good God, a *guria*, an earthquake'. The bed was heaving around. Half asleep, I went to step out of bed and put my foot on this damn thing and it was a pig. It wasn't an earthquake, it was a pig under the bed.

Darcy Williams says you could tell all the blokes that were at the opening of the Cecil. A character by the name of Walkie Talkie (from his habit of incessant conversation) wired the stainless steel bar to an old aircraft generator and put a few volts through everyone's elbows whenever they relaxed on to the bar. From then on all regular customers drank with their elbows stuck out square from the shoulder. Fights, pigs or electrocution, Ma continued her rule at the Cecil: 'She was a great lady'.

While many of the strangest characters were beachcombers or planters, recruiters, traders and miners in isolated areas, a surprising number of engaging eccentrics held posts in the government service. In apparent contradiction of public service concerns for correct procedures and orderly promotion by seniority, the Territory administration seemed to tolerate people of strange habits.

Dr John McInerney was one of several Territory doctors whose exploits are rapidly passing into legend. A Sydney University graduate, McInerney served in

the commandos and trained as a para-trooper. In war he was more concerned with killing than curing. In the post-war he went as a government medical officer to the Sepik District. A wild, hefty, impetuous man, his character was sometimes in conflict with his undoubted skills as a surgeon and physician. Although once both character and professional training came together: he felled a man and then immediately performed the emergency surgery to save him. McInerney was constantly disappearing, getting caught in some improbable escapade, reappearing for a spell of frontier doctoring **and then** again entangling himself in what **would** become the basis for another Doctor John story. He chased rumours of a gold strike to the interior of the Sepik District where he was involved in a shooting war with aggressive villagers. He suddenly appeared on Horne Island in Torres Strait where a beautiful woman caused him to invent numerous reasons to keep him away from his patients. When Rusty Phillips knocked on his door to get urgent treatment for Fred Bannigan, he hit Rusty on the jaw, and then had two patients in the hospital. Graham Taylor was dependent on McInerney for supplies and when the Doc flew over as just a speck in the sky Taylor was justly annoyed. Confronted by Taylor, McInerney said blithely, 'Didn't you get the butter? I tossed some out'.

Perhaps butter cascaded out from 10 000 feet to land among some startled villagers, or to add alien compost to the jungle, but it did not do Taylor any good.

The aircraft that gave McInerney his mobility was also the cause of his death. Bobby Gibbes:

Old Vanimo was a very nasty aerodrome. He took off downwind in what I would have considered an overloaded aeroplane without an airspeed indicator. He didn't bother doing his straps up. Undoubtedly with the wind coming from behind, he sensed that he was going faster than he was when he got out over the water. He did a split S turn and speared straight in. He knocked himself out. He was actually drowned while the other two clambered out safely. He did some extraordinary things. He liked dogs more than people, I think.

The *kiaps* have been subjects and raconteurs of some of the most memorable anecdotes from the Territory's rich gallery of humanity. Graham Taylor:

One of the great *kiap* characters of my time, who had best be nameless, was a legendary figure in the Sepik area; he spent a lot of time at Angoram. A great big chap, he was tremendously overweight. He was a prodigious drinker and eater. It's said that his favourite trick was to invite somebody

THE CUP THAT CHEERS.

During his absence from his ship Peter Garland evidently passed away the dreary time by imbibing not wisely, but too well; but resented the soft impeach-when hauled before the Court, and pleaded not guilty. Police Officer Hurst deposed that Peter was undoubtedly drunk, and couldn't walk a chalk line if he tried, and also that it would have been an utter impossibility for him to pass the Wowsers' Club test of sobriety by clearly articulating "preliminary ultimatum," or, in other words that he was unsteady in his gait and could not articulate clearly. Peter Tornaros, the commander of the "Merrie England," also deposed that Peter was in a "drunken state" when arrested. Peter admitted that he had had a few drinks, but in his opinion was not drunk. He thought the prosecutions were spite on the part of Captain Tornaros.

For his little jollification Peter contributes 11s. to the revenue.

The Papuan Times February 28, 1912

to dinner, and after the meal while they were sitting around having coffee, he'd just pick up the unfinished leg of lamb, and with a penknife, he'd just sit there and steadily pare his way through the joint. After dinner!

He had a Japanese bugle, which somebody had found in the jungle, nailed to the wall of his living room. Because he was so big and so ungainly, he used to crash through all the dining room chairs that anyone ever got for him, so he had a special chair built. It was like a great royal throne, and he used to sit in this. Underneath his right arm, screwed to the chair was one of those little rubber horns like you have on a kid's pedal car: the sort that goes 'Pomp, pomp' when you squeeze it. He had this positioned so that it nestled just under his armpit. From the rubber horn a length of garden hose ran to the Japanese bugle on the wall. When he wanted service, all he did was press his arm in, and you'd have this 'Pomp, pomp' on the wall. From the kitchen there'd be 'Yes sir'; he'd call out 'More beer' or something; and his servant would come rushing in with the beer or whatever.

When he became ill 'from excesses of one kind or another' the local doctor told him to eat less quantity and more quality. His next order therefore listed a case of carrots. The storekeeper, naturally incredulous, decided that the message was garbled, and despatched a case of claret. The gross *kiap*'s reputation was more persuasive than any written instruction.

Australian Ministers for Territories in Canberra and various Lieutenant-Governors and Administrators in Port Moresby and Rabaul set down policies; but the villagers came into contact with people, not policies. And when they think about their years under Australian rule they may well remember *mastas* of gargantuan appetites or of various wild eccentricities. Historians will have to accept that some of the most improbable stories told by Papua New Guineans about their recent rulers are true. Perhaps government and farce are never far apart.

In the early days of Australian administration in the Western Highlands Cadet Patrol Officer Chris Vass went to his first posting at Laiagam. He was twenty:

I arrived there one evening to be met by the Assistant District Officer, a man by the name of Denys Faithful, a real character who had actually spent most of his time in the Sepik District before being posted to the Western Highlands. But he had a reputation which I'd heard of even in my short time there. People were saying, 'My God, you're going to Faithful's station. Half your luck!'

So I arrived and was met by this man with a big, bushy moustache. Not a very tall man, but fairly wild looking. He showed me around the station briefly, and showed me to my house which was a peculiar sort of place. It was the only timber place on the station, everything else was built out of bush materials: grass roofs and plaited walls. But this timber house was perched up on the side of a hill and it was pink. Some character at some stage had painted it bright pink and it had a grass roof. So I was ensconced in this and left to my own resources. Faithful had just said 'Right, off you go, Vass. You're sleeping in there. Come down later on this evening and we'll have a few grogs.' I went off, cleaned myself up, had a look around the house, and went down to start what turned out to be the first of numerous drinking sessions with Denys Faithful. We sat in his lounge room, which was a very large room, and the centre piece was a magnificent fireplace, the sort that Faithful was renowned for throughout Papua New Guinea. He was the master fireplace builder. Every place he went to, he always made sure that if there wasn't a fireplace, there was one shortly afterwards. And in Laiagam he'd built this magnificent affair. This particular night was cold, as it was every night in Laiagam because it was just over 7000 feet.

By 10 pm we'd been drinking quite

solidly for some time; the two of us sitting in the middle of this vast room with the fire blazing away, and on the nearby table there was one of those old portable record players. Faithful had only one record. I think from memory it was a Trini Lopez record, and there's nothing worse than Trini Lopez when he goes on and on and on. He's bad enough once without hearing him repeatedly. Faithful would put this record on, and play it over and over again. After you'd had a few grogs I suppose you didn't mind.

So we were there at ten o'clock, Trini Lopez was going round, and my head was going round and round, for I was young and not used to that sort of drinking. I happened to glance across to the fire and noticed what seemed to be a flame leaping up from the wall adjacent to the fireplace. I said to Faithful, 'Denys, I think your house is on fire.' He said, 'Oh, don't worry about it. Have another drink.' I proceeded to have another drink, looked again, and the wall was definitely on fire—the flames were starting to leap up the wall. I said, 'Faithful, the bloody house is on fire.' He replied, 'Don't worry about it. Sit down and have another drink.' I said, 'My God, man, the whole bloody house'll burn down!' He sung out, 'Kalabus!' That's the Pidgin word for prisoner. At that stage it was common practice throughout the Highlands for each Government officer to have prisoners working in his house and around the garden. This poor prisoner leapt into the room with a red laplap

on, nothing else, took one look at the wall, his jaw dropped about five feet, and his eyes stuck out of his head. Denys just said, '*Mekim dai paia!*' which means 'put the fire out'. Of course Denys hadn't moved from his chair at this stage; he was still sitting there with drink in hand, and so was I, on his orders. The *kalabus* dashed out of the room to get the bucket and he made enough noise to wake the dead so that the whole police detachment and half the station came down to the house, and there's water flying everywhere, there's flames all over the place, and in the end the whole wall dropped out into the night. In the meantime Faithful hadn't moved from his chair, Trini Lopez was still yodelling away, the record was still spinning around, and I, under instructions from the boss, was still sitting in the chair next to him drinking grog. Finally the fire was put out, the station calmed down, the fireplace—that magnificent edifice—was standing in the middle of a vacant wall, Faithful was still drinking, and we were sitting there looking at the stars. I don't know whether it was a typical night in Laiagam, but it was the sort of thing that one came to expect from Faithful. My first week in New Guinea. I thought, my God, what have I come to, what is this?

Moneymakers and misfits are both misnomers. The eccentrics did not make money, and if the misfits didn't fit in Papua New Guinea, then at least they were less constricted and met fewer disapproving sniffs and stares.

THE WHISKY THEY ASK FOR AGAIN

KING GEORGE IV SUPERFINE SCOTCH WHISKY

Pacific Islands Monthly July 19, 1934

11 Wife and Missus

We went to Kikori where it rained and rained. Everything became mildewed. The food was ghastly, all out of a tin. About the only fresh food we had was bacon. We had a ship, if you could call it a ship, a little schooner, that came once in six weeks. There was no other communication. By the time the food arrived, our crate of potatoes would be nothing but skin and cockroaches.

Mrs Claude Champion, wife of government officer

The first white people to settle permanently on the Papua New Guinea mainland came as a family. In 1874 the Reverend William Lawes of the London Missionary Society, his wife, Fanny, and their son arrived in Port Moresby. They moved into a four-roomed verandahed house, and when the ship that had brought them sailed, they were a cultural island with the hills of the Koiari and Koitapu peoples behind them and the beaches of the Hanuabadans before them. Later Mrs Lawes was to be praised for setting Papuans what was called 'an admirable object lesson in family living'. That was her expected role and she paid a high price to play it. Her second son was the first white child born in Port Moresby. Eighteen months later, wasted by fever, he was the first white child in the cemetery. Mrs Turner, the second white woman to settle at the mission station, was forced to leave after a few months and she died before the boat reached a cooler climate. Mission women, as wives, teachers, nurses and nuns, continued to be one of the main groups of foreign women in Papua New Guinea: but the largest group was always those defined by the census takers as 'wives without gainful employment'. Many were to know the harrowing trials of Fanny Lawes as they tried to bring up their families in isolated bungalows.

Mrs Elsie Champion's daughter was born prematurely in Port Moresby. When the baby was nine months old Mrs Champion left 'Port' to set up house at her husband's station at Ioma on the Mambare River. In 1930 Ioma still retained its reputation gained in the 1890s as the 'white man's grave', the place where many miners and government officers had died of spears, axes and malaria.

I went to Samarai. From there I caught a small boat. I had to sleep in a tent with Ivan on the bank of the river, and the sandflies were shocking. This dear little baby scratched all night, I scratched all night, and she cried all night. In the morning we started off against a flood in a canoe with an outboard motor. We went up for about a day, and then had to come back to where we'd started from. So we had to walk. Of course I wasn't prepared for walking as I had shoes with high heels. Ivan cut the heels off. We carried the baby in a pram, but we covered it with a net so that the leeches and sandflies wouldn't get her. I was covered in leeches, and every now and again Ivan would burn them off with a cigarette or a match. It took

'A Sunday afternoon stroll in the jungle was part of the routine.'

five days to get to Ioma with the baby. Feeding her every three hours.

We used to camp at night. As we came to a village one night I heard this terrific coughing. Living on a plantation you learn a lot about medicine because you've got to be your own doctor. And I knew this cough. I said, 'That's whooping cough. We can't stay here.' Ivan said, 'Well, where can we go?' I said, 'We've got to go somewhere, sleep in the bush, but we can't stay here. How far did we go then, Ivan?' 'Two or three miles.' Anyway we eventually arrived at Ioma. The sad part of that is that after about the third day my little girl developed a high temperature. She got so ill we had to come back again. Of course we floated down the river in no time. We got back to Samarai where we had to wait for a boat to Port Moresby.

And there weren't many boats. Then in came the *Laurabada*, the Government boat. I was so delighted. Leonard Murray was the captain then, and he was also the Lieutenant-Governor's secretary. Don't forget that Leonard Murray had known me since I was a little girl. Mr Atkinson from the Resident Magistrate's office went down and said to Murray, 'Elsie Champion's here and she's got a little baby who's very sick. They want to get to Port Moresby quickly.' He said, 'I can't take her.' Mr Atkinson asked, 'Why not?' Murray said, 'I'm not having napkins hanging all over the deck of the *Laurabada*.' And he refused to take me. We had to wait for the next boat. She was a very sick girl for many years.

Sickness, and the fear of sickness, were constant worries for women with young children. Before they had access to modern drugs and advice by radio, the women could do little to combat illness. The medicines recommended by the Government Medical Officer, Dr Walter Strong, in 1912 were not likely to give an isolated mother confidence in her capacity to meet an emergency: carbolic acid, boric acid, tablets of zinc sulphate, turpentine liniment, bluestone, quinine, Dover's powders, Easton's syrup, Livingstone rousers (whatever they were) and so on. They were a mixture of the helpful, the harmful and the useless. The quinine was recommended not to prevent malaria, but to combat the disease after the patient had already developed fever. Old Territorians still believed, or comforted themselves with the assertion, that rum gave protection against various tropical ailments. Blackwater fever, probably a complication of malaria, was a mystery to the doctors. They advised giving the patient a dose of salts and making him sweat. In general the population had to learn to live with fever.

Amy Washington remembers the pre-1914 family passing through successive bouts of malaria:

The fever was terrible. Terrible fever. There'd be six of us, all in bed at once. Mr Riley, the missionary, had some medical experience, but he really wasn't a doctor. He used to give us Warburg tincture tablets, but they had to be taken with brandy which I hated. It would make you perspire. I remember that from tossing my head from side to side, my long hair got into a great big mat. Dad said, 'Look, there's nothing for it, mother, but to cut it off.' And I cried and I cried. So my elder sister came in with a bottle of methylated spirits, a comb and a brush. She said, 'Don't you worry, Ame, I'll get the knots out.' She sat, it must have been for two hours, and she unmatted all of that hair.

During Amy Washington's childhood there were two qualified doctors in all of Papua.

Along with contributing to the civilising mission by administering a model household, white women on outer stations and plantations were expected to minister to the sick. At Ogamobu Penelope Hope's father 'lined' the plantation labourers, allocated the fit men to their tasks for the day, and sent the ill to report to the house. There 'mother, received them attired in a most beautiful

Amy Washington's family portrait

Japanese dressing gown with purple storks on it'. She treated men with tooth ache, 'mumps, sore heads, upset stomachs and snake bite and anything else with impartial hands'. Her bluestone topped with a white bandage was particularly popular.

When Joe Bourke was mining out of Wau before the Second World War, his labourers, unaccustomed to the cold wet of the mountains, were vulnerable to pneumonia. Mrs Bourke remembers sitting through many nights looking after plasters and proffering egg nog and brandy. If a man died the government officer would demand to know why he had not been transferred to hospital, although in many cases transport was difficult, and by the time the illness was apparent the labourer was already too sick to shift.

But into the post-war, Australian women experienced their most intense anxiety as they tried to nurse their own children through crises. Marie Skinner:

My child got tetanus from working down in the gardens. He liked to go down there with the native women. He only had a small cut on his finger, but we were alerted to the symptoms because a week or so before a young

patrol officer had died with tetanus in the Eastern Highlands. When David started these symptoms my husband got on to a doctor on the coast, but our weather was so bad we couldn't get a plane in. We just had to hang on the phone and follow his directions. He had one actual spasm of locking the jaw, and the doctor said, well, in so many hours you'll know whether your treatment has been satisfactory; if it happened again, that was it. We just had to wait it out. At that time, too, I was in this little house, and I had about eight people there who were stranded waiting for an aeroplane. I was trying to feed and look after them, and I had this terribly, desperately sick little boy.

Even in crisis, the women sustained their other role of running an orderly household.

The white women were always a minority. By 1933 there were still only 1382 in all of Papua and New Guinea. Even in Rabaul and Port Moresby there were more white men than women and outside the main centres there were nearly three men for every woman. A succession of outstanding women advanced their careers while working in Papua New

Pacific Islands Monthly July 19, 1934

The New Guinea Handbook 1937
Patrol officer's house in Buna

Guinea: the anthropologists Margaret Mead, Hortense Powdermaker and Beatrice Blackwood, and the naturalist Evelyn Cheesman. Beatrice Grimshaw, the writer of innumerable romantic novels, was a long-term resident of Papua. There were always four or five women on their own running plantations, including properties isolated in the islands and on the Fly River. Apart from the many women working within the missions, the most numerous group in paid employment at the 1933 census were stenographers and typists. And as there were only forty-four of them, they just exceeded the number of women who were patients in hospital. Defined in terms of her relationships with various other people the white woman was overwhelmingly the wife, mother and *misis*. In spite of their scarcity white women were not always encouraged to come to the Territory. In fact the pre-war administrations sometimes did their best to keep young brides at a distance, preferably over a thousand miles away.

Marie Skinner, after two years of separation from Ian, her patrol officer husband, arrived unannounced at Madang in 1939. As war had just been declared in Europe the District Officer had the power to send her straight back to Australia before she saw her husband; and he tried to do just that. Mrs Skinner evaded his order by arranging for a New Guinean to take her by canoe to one of the islands in the Madang Harbour until the boat had sailed. Eventually the District Officer offered her accommodation with the gracious words: 'It's been used by dogs and kanakas, but you might be able to do something with it.'

A bride's problems in establishing a home were often compounded in Papua New Guinea. Jean Ashton remembers coming over a rise and seeing her house for the first time; with its high thatched roof 'it stood out like a cathedral'. But the grand exterior was just about all that she had. She had to hand sew material and weight it with sand to cover the empty spaces where doors should have been. At least they had a place for their one possession, a double bed mattress. Her husband, Des, put planks across four occasional tables to make a unique sixteen legged bed. Des also found a rusty army stove in the bush to replace the stone and clay construction that Jean had at first used. Even the metal stove had its deficiencies: 'The handle on it was so old and rusted I had to keep a big stone beside it. I'd hammer the catch up, peer inside the oven with a torch, and then hammer the catch back again.' When their neighbours, a plantation family living half a mile away, bought a refrigerator, the Ashtons could arrange a change of diet:

We asked them if we could set a jelly and put it in their refrigerator. We'd sit on the verandah, late in the afternoon, and send our cook boy with a note to the Priestleys, saying please give him the jelly. Then we'd watch him running down the hill, disappearing to cross the river at the bottom, then coming up the other side. We'd be sitting there poised with our spoons ready, waiting to have the jelly. That was our only cold food for nine months.

In her attempts to obtain variety from tinned foods, Jean Ashton spent a year's housekeeping money in the first four months. But even where cans were plentiful, there could still be problems. In the immediate post-war Mrs Elma Holmes was able to buy cases and cases of tins, but they had no identifying labels, just army code numbers. It was a culinary lottery in which she sometimes drew whole cases of dried egg powder, tinned parsnips or quinces. They challenged the most inventive of cooks.

> *Living on a plantation for a woman can be quite idyllic. In my case I was only twenty-six miles from Madang, on a beautiful setting, right on the Bismarck Sea, a large house designed for the tropics, letting all the sea breezes through, somebody to look after the house. It was really an idyllic existence.*
> **Mrs Jean Huxley**

Women who were able to bypass disapproving government officials and live on outstations still had to face long periods without their husbands. The wives of government officers in particular had to endure many months of separation. Mrs Theresa Bloxham had only just arrived at Aitape when her husband had to leave on patrol. Unable to speak Pidgin and apprehensive in a strange environment Mrs Bloxham had a revolver and an empty house:

> I got into bed and thought I would have an early night. I tried to read and that was hopeless. Every sound

Theresa Bloxham on patrol

worried me. I felt under the pillow for the revolver. I thought, shall I cock it or not? If I cock it, it will be ready, but isn't it too dangerous? I wondered, would it shoot through a wall? I couldn't be sure whether a bullet would go through a wall if it went off by mistake. In the end I decided not to cock it. It was about ten o'clock, and I was just feeling that I could settle down, when I heard a thumping sound coming along the verandah; the slap, slap, slap of naked feet. I heard the rattle of a rifle, and a voice call out, '*Misis kiap? Yu stap?*' It was quite silent for a time. I thought, I wonder who this is, and then I realised it must be the boy who is looking after me. I called out, 'Who's that?' He said, '*Mi Buka, man bilong lukautim yu.*' He was quite happy that I had spoken to him, and he marched off. I could hear his footsteps disappear. Well, this is very good, I thought, he'll be there till morning and no one will come near me. But at midnight when I had actually fallen asleep, the footsteps came again, slap, slap, slap along the verandah and the thud of a rifle: '*Misis? Misis kiap? Yu stap?*' I was beginning to feel rather doubtful about this going on. I put the light on and it was midnight. I thought, good heavens, I'm not going to get any sleep at all.

Houseboys at work

Away he went, apparently he was satisfied. I rolled about restlessly and eventually sort of dozed, woke up and dozed. Two o'clock, he came again. He came every two hours, solemnly. I didn't know how to explain to him that he mustn't keep coming to wake me up. So it was ten o'clock, twelve o'clock, two o'clock and four o'clock. I finally woke up just as the light filtered through the blinds. I thought, thank heaven for that. Out of bed I got, and just as I went to the bathroom I heard this sound again. It was six o'clock. He'd come again, and couldn't find me this time. I heard a voice in the distance, but didn't take much notice. I thought it was the boys who had come back to the house. Well, the poor boy was frantic. He got hold of every boy he could find; he got Sambun, he got the *mankis* (youngsters), to rush through the house to try to find out where I was. I hadn't realised the reactions that had taken place, and how frantic my poor watchman was. To get out of their way, I took myself off and shut myself in the bathroom. Of course this made the situation worse. It wasn't until they came hammering at the bathroom door, which was even worse as far as I was concerned, that they found where I was. The

policeman was not satisfied until he heard my voice. I had to talk to him through the door. That was my initiation into that sort of living.

It was also, Mrs Bloxham says, just one incident among many as she became accustomed to her New Guinea home.

The Papua New Guineans most white women came closest to were their servants. In fact, many women rarely had a chance to speak to a Papua New Guinean who was not an employee. But the largely unwritten laws about avoiding sexual excitement and how best to deal with servants stopped many white women from ever knowing Papua New Guineans as ordinary people. Before the war when servants were paid only ten shillings or so a month an ordinary household might employ four men: 'you'd have your cook and your laundryman, and then you'd a couple of others to do the general household chores'. Into the 1960s wages were still only three pounds a month plus housing, food, clothing and tobacco.

Where the servants were efficient, they allowed the *mastas* to develop a privileged way of life. Mrs Phyl Linsley:

You didn't have to run in and out of your kitchen, so you spent a lot of time setting the table as nicely as you could with all the best crockery, silver and crystal. If you wanted the boy to bring in the next course you had a little bell that you could ring, and so the empty dishes were taken out and the next course brought in. It was gracious living.

Coming from Australia in the mid 'sixties, Amirah Inglis noticed that there were very, very few women who put the argument that as they would not employ a man to do their work in Australia they wouldn't be having a servant in their house in Papua New Guinea. She also noticed how most houses were exceptionally clean and tidy; the result of the labour of others. Gladys Stevens recalls that every day servants put polish on the board floors and rubbed them with coconut husk till they had a mirror sheen.

> *In the early days at Rigo my wife was rather concerned at the fact that we didn't have a silver butter knife. We ordered butter knives to be sent, but we still didn't use them. One was put on the table each evening, but we would simply use our bread knives. Phyl didn't want the boy to think that we didn't use the butter knife, so she would religiously get it and scrape it over the butter.*
> **Gordon Linsley**

But many women were unable to direct their servants efficiently. 'There were always the people' Marie Skinner says, 'who thought nothing of hitting them, or yelling at them.' Andrée Millar found that she had to spend a lot of time in careful explanation and demonstration. If she still did not get the task done the way that she wanted, then it was case of learning to like it the way the servants wanted it, or doing it herself. It was pointless expending energy in anger and frustration. Few white women realised, Ian Hogbin suggests, that Papua New Guineans did not like being domestic servants. They did the work because they needed the money, and being in the house was preferable to the few other manual jobs available. Although the plantations and mining fields demanded far more labourers, domestic service was a common experience of many Papua New

Guineans who entered the cash economy. In the 1930s there were over 5000 men working as household servants. Little wonder then that even in the smallest coastal village it is often possible to find a man who talks of having worked for a *misis* or *sinabada* (Motu for white woman) as his one-time boss. One irony is that in the district known as the home of the most efficient servants, the local term for a lazy woman is now the same as for a white woman.

It sometimes seemed that the one thing all white women in the Territory had in common was stories about servants. They varied, of course, in the way they told them—sometimes with understanding and occasionally with scorn. Nearly all the stories involved misunderstood instructions. The man told to starch the shirts put starch in handkerchiefs, singlets and underpants as well. The waiter instructed to serve the suckling pig with a lemon in the mouth and parsley behind the ears duly appeared with the pig held aloft, a lemon in his mouth, and parsley. ... Ginnie Williams recalls that her mother told the 'boy' to catch a *kakaruk* (rooster), pluck it and put it in the refrigerator. He did. And her mother was later startled to find a cold, featherless, but very alive, chook in the refrigerator. Shirley Taylor also illustrates the gap between order and response:

> I'd mixed up some milk, and because there were no fly wire screens on the windows or anything like that I decided I needed something to cover it. I said to the boy that was in the kitchen to get me a cover. I said it in Pidgin, *laplap bilong susu*. I was amazed to see him walk towards the bedroom, and he came back bearing a bra! *Susu* can mean a woman's breast as well as milk, and this was his interpretation of a cover for it.

In the 1960s the domestic servants freed some 6000 foreign women to take paid jobs. Some went to air-conditioned offices and specialised shops, even boutiques; but earlier the wives were often uncertain just what they should do. Andrée Millar:

> If you liked the social round of

Pacific Islands Monthly February, 1951

Servants' quarters—they preferred to have separate accommodation.

women it was a tremendous life. There were morning teas every morning and usually afternoon teas, and a couple of afternoons a week you'd play mahjong, or there would be a bridge four. Sometimes you'd go out to bridge at night as well. It was just an endless round of utter chit chat actually, and it got on my nerves.

Mrs Millar broke the cycle of trivia to become one of Papua New Guinea's best known horticulturalists and plant collectors. She established a more productive relationship with the environment than almost any other Australian.

Dame Rachel Cleland who lived for thirty years in post-war Port Moresby while it grew from frontier town and ex-army camp to national capital, believes that no simple descriptions cover the variety of lives led by Australian women in the Territory:

It depended entirely on the women. You got people who tried to reproduce as nearly as they could the suburb they came from in Australia. They were frightened to step outside of that. Others came with a sense of adventure and wanted to go and do things and see the country, and get to know local people and visit villages. So you got all sorts. For a woman life is what she makes it. I mean the CWA in Moresby, for instance, was a very big thing. They had to raise money so they had their staff at home to run the house and do the washing up, and they spent their time raising money by turning on morning teas every day. And they did the washing up! They all got together and enjoyed it, but I always used to tease them and say, really, you do love washing up, don't you! They ran pre-schools, using themselves on a roster as voluntaries, and they became Girl Guide leaders. They played a lot of bridge and golf and things like that. The ones that liked acting.... People really made use of the fact that they had someone else to do the housework, and then did the things they'd always wanted to do.

Tinned parsnips, liquid jelly, cockroaches and gracious living were all part of the life of a *misis*. By the eve of the Australian withdrawal it was an experience over 10 000 Australian women had known in Papua New Guinea.

12 Growing Up

I remember being called out about two weeks after I'd been at school. The boarding mistress came down and said, 'Now, little Miss Hopper, you're not in the jungle any more, and we do wear clothes at ladies' schools'.

Jane Hanson

On the eve of the First World War just one hundred white children lived in all of Papua. There were only eight in that two-thirds of the Territory west of Yule Island. Vulnerable to malaria and dysentery and other childhood accidents and ills, many had a precarious hold on life. Amy Washington, born in 1897, was a survivor. Her father, Alexander Henry Symons, was first appointed a sub-collector of customs in the old British New Guinea service in 1896, and he rose to be a Resident Magistrate in Sir Hubert Murray's administration of Papua. Theresa Symons followed her husband through his various postings from Daru in the west to the islands of the south-east. As her family grew Mrs Symons developed the practice of giving the oldest daughters full responsibility for the new babies. 'Rosie,' Mrs Washington explains,

> she reared Moresby. I remember getting on the sailing boat when Mother was going over to Cooktown to have Muriel. Moresby was about fourteen months old, and the baby was due in a month's time. Rosie was sitting on the hatch, and she had to feed and do everything for the baby. She had long black hair, and Moresby would not go to sleep unless he was holding one of her plaits.

When Alexander Symons was appointed to Bonagai on the almost deserted gold-field of Woodlark Island, Amy at fourteen took care of her baby sister Ena. She bathed, dressed and fed her; went for walks with her on Sundays; and when Ena caught dysentery and died within three days Amy suffered the anguish of both a sister and a mother.

Mrs Symons, already four months pregnant when Ena died, left to go to Samarai for the birth. As Alexander Symons was away on patrol in a whale boat the three children remaining at Bonagai were left partly in the care of neighbours and partly on their own. They waited anxiously for the return of their mother, standing on the verandah of the residency and peering through a telescope to pick up the speck of a boat on the horizon beyond Entrance Island. At last mother arrived with a new son:

> Oh, it was a beautiful baby. The next morning when she was bathing him in the bedroom she called me in. She finished bathing him, dressed him and gave him his food. They'd give them condensed milk. And she said, 'Hold out your arms, Amy.' As I put my arms out I said, 'What, Mum?' She said, 'Now here's a baby for you to look after.' From then on I looked

Misima, c1920

after Cecil. Cecil and I are the only two left out of a family of ten.

The oldest daughters were not to marry innocent of the rigours of childcare.

Even in the 1950s and 1960s Australian women in isolated areas faced an anxious time through pregnancy and their children's early years. The rapid increase in the number of Papua New Guineans trained as medical assistants, the *liklik doktas* as they were called in Pidgin, reduced child mortality in the villages. But health care equal to that available in an Australian town often depended on luck of radio communication, fine weather, an aircraft and a willing pilot.

When Ancie Shindler feared she would miscarry, a plane came in to Kainantu and took her to Lae, and then she travelled over rough roads in a jeep to the hospital. The matron met her with, 'Well, if you weren't losing it then, you are now!' On a second occasion she was at Aiyura. The New Guinean Medical Assistant at Kainantu sent over a morphine tablet which her husband dissolved and injected into her arm. It immediately ballooned with swelling. A plane came into Kainantu but the pilot refused to wait while Mrs Shindler was brought to the airstrip on a stretcher:

He said, 'I'll go to Hagen and be back. If you want me, put up a smoke signal.' So I was carried down to the airstrip to a little shed we had there. Tom and Jack Fox built a great big fire as soon as they saw the plane, they put up this tremendous smoke signal, but he flew miles away, we could see him. He didn't even fly over our place which was a landmark for the planes because of the house—a big white place—on the top of the hill. At Kainantu Ian Skinner said, 'They're waiting for you'. And he said, 'Oh, no, somebody else is coming for them'. Well nobody came for two days. Then they only came to take my father-in-law out. He was on holiday and it was a plane that he had arranged. They'd argued in Lae, and nobody had wanted to come in, apparently.

Mrs Shindler had had her second miscarriage.

Before the birth of her last child Marie Skinner attended the local hospital in Mt Hagen. As she sat on the rough benches in the dirt-floored building wondering what her mother would think about her choice of prenatal clinic, two young New Guineans arrived at the door with a donkey. The Australian doctor took a glance and told his assistants to get the man who had been leading the donkey, bring him inside and take his temperature. The young man was brought in, sat down and a thermometer put in his mouth. After a brief nod towards the thermometer the doctor said, 'Put him in ward three.' At this the young man protested vigorously, and finally communicated the basic message that it was the donkey, not him, that was in need of medical care. The incident did little for Mrs Skinner's confidence, but she was more concerned about when to make the decision to fly out to the coast for the birth. Rough flights through storms, or airstrips closed in bad weather, could mean disaster: 'That was the sort of thing you had to put up with to have a baby at that stage'.

The white child that survived could become a centre of attention beyond that ever created by the most doting of relatives. In 1953 Jean Gibbes took her daughter, Julie, home; she was the first white child to come into the area. The villagers

> literally fought each other to carry her basket up to the house. They found out she was a girl, and that disgusted them a bit; they didn't see why we would have bothered really. But anyway we put her in a basket in the bedroom, and they all clamoured to see her. For about a week we had a file—it was like the tomb of Lenin— shuffling past to see Julie.
> She was always a little girl who smiled a lot, and she sat, propped up with pillows, just as if she was holding court.

Fifty years earlier Amy Washington was herself the centre of a curious crowd. Her father, then stationed at Daru, had gone by boat up the Fly River to hear court cases. Amy waited on board until her father called one of the men to bring her ashore:

> I was dressed in a print dress, black ribbed stockings, button-up boots, knickers, petticoat, and on top of the dress, a pinafore, with big tucks and frills. And I had a big, lined mushroom hat with ruched muslin round it. This boy put me in the boat and carried me up the bank, and I went over and stood near Dad. The women just left the court case and came over. Well! My skin, you see, I had white skin and all these clothes. The natives just didn't understand. They were asking and

asking about the dress, and they were very interested in my hair. The top was in a plait, and that plait went into another. I had very long hair, down to my waist. So Dad said, 'Now look, girl, let your hair down!' I said, 'Dad!' 'Let your hair down.' I had to take two bows off. The natives fingered it, squealed, and clapped their stomachs. They'd never seen a white child before, never. They touched my face, and I thought, 'Oh, dirty fingers, I'll have to wash my face.' Then they looked at my legs. And I didn't take a bit of notice. Dad said, 'Pull those stockings down.' So I pulled them down, and I never heard such squeals of delight. The court case just had to wait till they had their inspection of me. But I got upset then, of course. So Dad let me sit beside him for a while till he'd finished the cases, and then he took me back to the boat.

The layer upon layer of clothes worn by Amy Washington were a part of that mesh of cooler climate fashions and values that the white community carried with them. The Symons family went to great lengths to obtain the clothes that they wore with pride and discomfort:

> When we were in Daru, we'd go to Thursday Island. My Mum was very clothes conscious, and she'd have her clothes made there. She was always well dressed, even in a place like Daru where there was no one to see her. We got our boots at the T Boot Company in Sydney. We'd get a shipment out. Dad and Mum, Rose, Tess, Herb, Amy, Moresby and Muriel, we all got our shoes at the T Boot Company. Nowadays I don't know what you'd say about our clothes, but for us they were beautiful. We had the best of material, all tucked with torchon lace and insertions and lovely little pearl buttons, and always long sleeves; you never wore short sleeves. Long sleeves with a buttoned cuff. The girls wore skirts and blouses. The skirts would be heavy material, beautifully gored, so many gores in the skirt, and lovely silver belts. The

The Pacific Islands Monthly October 24, 1935

belts were made with engraved discs joined with little links. And me, I lived in beautiful pinafores. I think now, of course, people wouldn't do it, but in those days you'd wear your dress for three or four days, and then you'd wear the pinafore on top of it for three or four days. But you were always spotlessly clean. And we all wore button-up boots. Oh, we were always beautifully dressed.

By the 1950s white children wore few clothes. They were growing up just as healthy and less restricted than their age-mates in Australia. Often they were living in homes where both parents were away at work, where there were no grand-parents to offer cautionary advice; the Papua New Guinean servants were reluctant to be strict so they could have a surplus of freedom. They might also have a false sense of their own importance; just by being white they were of the rich and powerful. Paul Mason, whose parents owned Inus plantation on Bougainville, could range over a wide area. The only white child within a five-mile radius, he was immediately recognised by villagers who always fed him and cared for him. With five or six 'reasonably close' friends he went swimming and fishing during the day and perhaps eel-catching at night. It was only as he became older that he noticed his parents' slight embarrassment as he came into the house trailed by his 'shirtless' friends. Soon he was avoiding his parents and sneaking his friends into the kitchen where they could all eat. Jane Hanson, who also grew up on a plantation, remembers similar easy mixing with local children before she went to school. Even stark differences were then of little significance: 'At Christmas time you'd have a great big stocking and be very excited that Santa had been. And they had never heard of Santa. You'd just show your ordinary toys to them and they'd be just as excited because they knew they'd play with them with you.'

As a school girl Anne Whitehead had two worlds:

I went to school in Wau for two years. For all intents and purposes I

was living in an English village, and certainly as a young kid of eleven or twelve I had very little understanding or desire to know what New Guineans felt. I was in a very insulated, closeted little environment. That's in one way. In another way, I lived out a sort of dream world based on a kid in the tropics. My dream world came from the comics of the period which were Tiger Girl, Sheena, Queen of the Jungle, Diana, the Phantom's lady—all these kinds of people were my heroines. So I was very conscious of myself living in a tropical country where there was a native population, though it was a very overlord air I had about it all. I was master of the jungle and sailed through it. I used to act it out. I had a grass skirt when I was eleven (I had no breasts at all) and I'd rush into the jungle and imagine I was swinging from vine to vine.

But Anne Whitehead also found complexities in her relationships with local children. She was suddenly forbidden to play with her one close New Guinean friend. Some of Anne's dresses had disappeared and they were found in her friend's village. The New Guinean girl who had been her companion in reality and fantasy never came to play again.

By its repetition the routine of the white child in the Territory came to have an ordinariness. Yet it could be outside the experience of all other Australians; and it was often the Papua New Guinean 'nanny' that brought a difference to the Territory childhood. Jane Hanson remembers the New Guinean woman, Betty, who bathed them in the evening, dressed them, 'then we would go downstairs, have dinner with my parents and listen to the ABC serial or the late children's hour'. Usually their mother put them to bed and listened to their prayers. But the next morning again it was Betty who got them up and dressed them. Jane remembers her protectiveness; and out of her closeness to them she influenced the language that they spoke and the customs they acquired. Her brother had a particularly strong relationship with Betty:

He didn't speak English until he was
about five years old; he only spoke
Tolai or Pidgin. He called her
'Mumma', and my mother was 'Mrs
Hopper'. He used to come up to the
house as if he was a sort of baby
servant and say, 'Mrs Hopper, me like
some kai kai now', and things like that.
But my parents didn't mind at all
because he'd spent most of his time
with Betty, and she was his 'Mumma'.
One day the house in Rabaul caught
on fire and my younger brother and
sister were asleep. Instead of saving
anybody else, the nurse came up,
smashed all the windows, went
through the fire, grabbed my little
brother only, and ran out with her
piccaninny. But everyone else had to
find their own way out. She alerted
them of course, but she just wanted to
save him.

School brought more differences for
the Territory Australians. In the 1930s
there were just five government primary
schools for white children in all of Papua
and New Guinea. The small school at
Kavieng had only fourteen pupils. The
children on out-stations had to take correspondence courses run by the Queensland
Education Department. After the war
there was a rapid increase in the number
of primary schools for Australians, the A
schools as they were called. They were not
exclusively for white students, but nearly
all the students were white. Most Papua
New Guineans went to T schools—the 'T'
stood for Territory. The A schools taught
according to the New South Wales or
Queensland syllabus. But Australian children living away from the towns still
depended on correspondence. The lessons
could force a sudden separation from
village playmates. Jean Ashton remembers
starting her five-year-old daughter, Lyn,
on a correspondence course:

after the first week she got a bit tired
and said, 'Oh, don't let's play school
today, Mum, let's play something else'.
Meanwhile all the piccaninnies would
be sitting outside in the sandpit
waiting anxiously for her to come
back outside to play. So it was a bit
hard to get the message across.

But the big break for the child, the parents
and companions came when it was time to
go to high school. In Port Moresby, Lae
and Rabaul the administration maintained
secondary schools staffed by Australians
and teaching Australian courses. To assist
Australians in the rest of the Territory get
their children to high school, the government met part of the cost of sending a
child south to boarding school. Families
that would not normally have sent their
children to private schools did so, either
because they had access to no other
schools or to take advantage of the gov-

ernment's largesse. By the 1960s over 1000 white students were taking the free fares and the subsidised education in Australia. From 1954 about twenty scholarships a year were also offered to selected Papua New Guineans to pay the complete costs of their joining the student exodus south. The 'native' scholarships were introduced against the opposition of those angry members of the white community who always denounced such schemes as 'premature'. Black and white mothers now had in common the dread of separation with their eleven and twelve year old children: 'it was something that sort of hung over our heads all the time'.

> *You'd open the plane door at Port Moresby, and the heat would come tearing at you. All these poor little kids would be sitting there in their formal serge tunics, trying to seek out their parents among the myriad of parents' faces, and trying to get off the tarmac and out of their clothes.*
> **Jane Clarke**

Having observed the annual separation of parents and children at Territory airports, Marie Skinner vowed that she would never go through that anguish, but she did. And now she declares she would never go through it again:

> after they had gone, it was very hard not to think about them all the time. I used to say my children just lived in my head. It didn't seem to matter what I was doing. If I stopped to think, there'd be a child in my head all the time.

Although, as Jan Sinclair remembers, parents could learn new facets of their children through letters, they missed so much of the passage from child to young adult. Particularly for women whose husbands were absent on long patrols, it was a return to the loneliness that they had known in the early years of their marriages. In compensation they tried to concentrate a year's experiences into the six weeks' Christmas holidays.

The school year began with specially scheduled flights. Anne Whitehead:

It wasn't as terrifying as it might sound for a twelve-year-old kid because others were doing it too. The great day came and you got into an old DC3 with bucket seats along the sides, the sort you see paratroopers getting into in old films. It wasn't pressurised so as you went over the Owen Stanley Range at about fifteen thousand feet kids were being sick everywhere. I remember all the way, hopping down to Townsville, kids would be sick into their sick bags the whole time, and lunch was a cardboard box with a couple of sandwiches and an apple. They didn't trust air hostesses on these flights: they had tough stewards who acted like orderlies in mental hospitals and pulled kids into line. We didn't have any adults with us, but we booked ourselves into a hotel in Townsville. The following day we went to the railway station and got into this train, rattling along on the Queensland three foot six gauge up to Charters Towers, an incredible trip past great ant hills, and, as you got near Charters Towers, great mullock heaps. I remember arriving at night; I think there were only about six of us on the train. We were all terribly new. Someone from the school met us at the station and took us to the school, though all I remember is absolute horror as I was taken through this dormitory of mosquito nets. There just seemed to be hundreds and hundreds of mosquito nets and sleeping bodies beneath them. It was just a nightmare.

It remained a nightmare through the first six months during which she was 'wretchedly homesick'.

Jane Clarke's introduction to school at Toowoomba was to find herself suddenly deserted. Only later did she learn that her mother was no more capable than she was of enduring a protracted goodbye.

A few Territory children settled quickly to the new routine, but for many it was a difficult period of adjustment. They sat apprehensive through the formality of long, crowded school assemblies, faced the inevitable teacher remark, 'Now you're not in the jungle any more', and learnt to conform to the bells which determined all behaviour, even such natural acts as when to talk. Then it was time for the return flight. Seasoned travellers avoided those aircraft crowded with uninhibited teenagers. Jane Clarke:

> We had uniforms for travel which comprised a serge blazer, full tie, shirt, serge skirt, thick grey seamed stockings, gloves, and a going-out hat. The school rule was quite simply that until you reached your destination there was no getting out of uniform. There were several boarding schools in Toowoomba and I suppose all together there would have been about thirty girls and boys from New Guinea there. They would bus us up to Brisbane. The airlines used to put planes on at two or three o'clock in the morning. There were thousands of kids flying north for the holidays. They used to put on these ghastly flights because there were no parents there to get cross if you were off-loaded, and kids didn't make a fuss. In those days they used to fly Electra jets which took four or five hours to get there. We all used to sit at Brisbane airport because we had no money—everything at boarding school was done on account, and so you just didn't have any spending money. You'd arrive in Brisbane about one o'clock in the afternoon, and sit with masses of other kids, all equally uncomfortable in their serge tunics. Then they'd fill the plane absolutely crammed, chocka full. The first thing everybody did was light up cigarettes because you were out of school and there was nobody to check.

They stepped into the intense heat of Jacksons Airport, found their parents, and quickly changed into the clothes that the parents had brought with them.

The children themselves realised that they were maturing in isolation from their parents: their voices broke, they shaved, they wore long pants, and they negotiated the purchase of their first bras.

Jane Clarke continues:

> I remember writing home and saying, 'Dear Dad, I need to buy a bra, could you please give me permission to do so.' My father wrote back, 'What for? To smuggle sweets into the school?' And I said, 'Dad, look, I am now thirteen, you haven't seen me for a while, and I've got news for you, things have happened here.' My mother was on tour in New Guinea at the time, so she wasn't there to answer the correspondence which I now read with much hysteria with my father about how I needed a bra and could he kindly not discuss the situation; I just needed it. Eventually he said, you can have one. Then we went into the whole thing again. If you needed one, you needed three.

The sequence was repeated when at fifteen she decided that she would like to wear mascara to a school dance.

> *I used to consider myself as a Papua New Guinean, and I didn't want to have anything to do with Australians. I just wasn't interested in them because they didn't belong to my perception of the future.*
> **Paul Mason**

In the post-war many Australians went to Papua New Guinea newly married. They had their families in the Territory. But in middle age they resettled in Australia. Their children were 'Territory kids'. They were conscious that they were somehow different from other Australians, but few felt that they were Papua New Guineans; that it was right for them to take citizenship in the country where they had grown up. They have had to accept that they are a different sort of Australian.

At school the Territory kids' differences with other Australians were simple matters of being able to speak bits of other languages, having black servants, and not knowing about shearing or trams. But as adults they search for more subtle influences that make them conscious of a distance from other Australians.

13 Into the Highlands

We only had five rifles and a few men so I kept moving. We started to travel at night too, and we'd get into whirlpools. We still had a hurricane lantern left. My raft was in the lead, and I'd have this lantern so the others could follow me. One night another crowd of natives came off in canoes, and several of them jumped aboard my raft and tried to steal a tomahawk. We pushed them off. We went on . . .

Ivan Champion

From the 1870s, missionaries, adventurers, miners and government officers made frequent attempts to penetrate the interior. Some died in the attempt and some returned to claim success. Three at least wrote books of the fantastic sights they had seen: cavalry mounted on yellow and white striped ponies, giant apes and peaks that made Mt Everest a pimple. They were men with more imagination than bushmanship. Their claims might have won brief acceptance in London, New York or Sydney; but not in Port Moresby or Madang. There it was generally believed that as you approached the centre of the island the mountains became higher, the country more broken and the population more sparse. The centre beckoned the explorers and adventurers, but not those who wanted souls to save, people to govern or land to farm. That vast tract of land, from the Markham Valley in the east running over three hundred miles to the Dutch border and beyond, was one of the last mysteries for the map makers of the literate world.

By the 1920s white men had four routes to the edge of the highlands. In the north-east they could attempt to climb out of the broad Markham and Ramu Valleys; in the north-west they could go up the Sepik; in the south-west they could follow the headwaters of the Fly and Strickland; and in the south they could leave Kikori and look for the source of the massive rivers that muddied the waters of the Gulf of Papua.

In 1926 Charles Karius and Ivan Champion, two field officers of the Papuan administration, set out to cross from the upper Fly to the Sepik River. They were trying to cross New Guinea at its widest point. Like many other expeditions, its success depended on the ability of its leaders to get information from people who were meeting white men for the first time. Ivan Champion was twenty-two when the expedition started:

We left Port Moresby in the ketch *Elevala*, went to Daru, picked up carriers there, pushed 500 miles up the Fly and then started off to cross New Guinea. We still hadn't got into the mountains; we had to take our stores another hundred miles or so by winding track before we made a dash across the mountains. So you adopt the relay system. You have thirty or forty men, the carriers, twelve police, and you make a camp in the bush. You carry your rice, the main food, forward three or four hours and make another camp. Then those carriers go back the same day to the first camp so

The Early camp at Wabag

Jack Hides, *The Papuan Courier*
August 21, 1931 (below)

The attack came sooner than I expected. At dusk, standing near the flap of my tent, a carrier a few feet away from me, I heard a rattle of arrows on the ground and the woodwork of the houses. I saw the carrier fall with two arrows in his body. I hurried to his assistance, and after drawing the arrows, assisted him to cover. The arrows had ceased by then and no further volley arrived. Right throughout, quietness had reigned; there had been no shouting from the attackers, nor was there a sound to disclose their whereabouts. The arrows had arrived from a point about a hundred yards distant and above the camp.

Examining the wounded man I discovered that one arrow had entered the back, just below the shoulder blade, and the other had passed through the right leg, above the knee, and through the penis. The wounds are clean and, although slightly painful, will not incapacitate him to any great degree. I bathed the wounds in boiling water with a solution of permagnate and applied Iodine.

Posted a strong guard. Once during the night an attempt was made to break through into the camp, but the strict watch maintained by the guard warned me in time to scare them off.

A halt during an expedition . . .
Colonel L F S Hore, Sgt Gouday

Wooden hand drum from the Sepik
River area, East Sepik Province

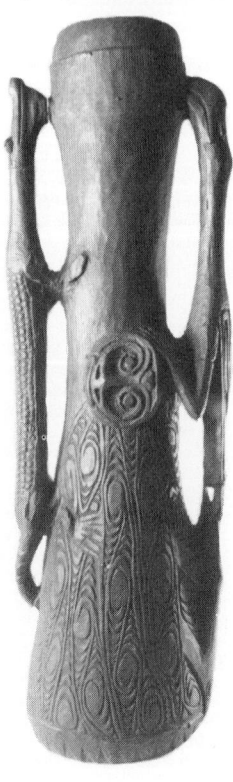

thought, 'I'm not going back. I'm going to disobey orders'.

The natives used to come down to the camp, and I started to pick up their language. I used to get a stone, put it on the ground, and I'd say, 'stone'. This would go on for a while before they'd say something. Then I'd know that's their word for stone. Then I indicated the river. 'Wok, wok,' they said, and I realised that meant a river. I kept on. I'd say, 'Palmer', and finally I got 'Wok Luap'.

Champion, by gradually building up his vocabulary, was equipping himself to ask specific questions about tracks and rivers. Eventually the people told him that they came from the north-west, close to where, Champion suspected, the Sepik took its rise. Having divided his small party of five police and eleven carriers, Champion set out for Bolivip, the people's main village. The men they traded with along the way were still using stone and one man who was given a tomahawk attacked a tree with the chipping movement that he was accustomed to using with a stone adze rather than employing the full swing of the axeman. After crossing a range at 7000 feet their guides brought them down to the Bol, another tributary of the Fly. The next day the small party entered Bolivip:
They made a tremendous fuss of us. They wore great cassowary plumes and their dress was the penis gourd, these great things, and the women wore little grass skirts. A fellow came out looking like a biblical character with his black beard and his cassowary plumes. He clenched his fists in front of him, linked his little fingers, and pulled them apart to make a clicking sound. They kept shouting 'Num seno, num seno'. I learnt it was 'My friend, my friend'. After, my police used to call them the num seno taudia. In Motu taudia is people. We camped there, and I had little knives and they rushed those. I bought food, taro, and they kept bringing taro in and gazing at us. When I took my hat off they just gasped, they thought it was part of me.

they won't be eating the food at the forward camp. And so you go on and on, a slow drag. We finally got into the mountains at the base of Mount Blucher on the headwaters of the Palmer, a tributary of the Fly. We couldn't speak to the natives we struck. They were all primitive, nobody could speak to anybody. It was all sign language.

At the base camp on the Palmer Karius said, 'Well, I'm going to see if I can cross that range. You stop here'. He went off, I've forgotten how long he was away, came back and said, 'Tremendous mountains, but there's a river flowing that way, and I think that it's part of the Sepik'. 'No, it's not,' I said. 'You haven't gone far enough.' I was the map maker. Karius was a remarkable man, he never got down-hearted, but he had no geographical sense. He had an extraordinary way with natives and never upset them. That's why he was chosen. He said, 'I'm on the Sepik where Dr Walter Behrmann [the German explorer] shows it flowing north-east. So I told him, 'No, you're not, it's impossible'. 'Well,' he said, 'I'm going to make a dash.' 'You'll have to go back down the Fly with the worst of the carriers that can't do the trip and some police.' Off he went. And I

Then the old fellow lined up a lot of women and he kept pointing to them. I thought, My God, what's going to happen now. Then he brought a little boy about ten years old, very light skinned. He grabbed my hand, put the little boy's hand against it and pointed out the similar colour. He pointed to the sky and he pointed to the boy. Then he made a sign, was I born of woman? He seemed to make out the boy came from the sky somewhere; and I learned after that they'd found him, and taken him in.

Champion had been the first white man into other villages, but this was the first time he had been so far beyond the frontier of contact that the people had not even heard of white men. Throughout the next day he questioned his hosts about a great river on the northern side of the towering ranges. But they appeared not to know of it. Instead they led him to the mainstream of the Fly and mimed warnings against the cannibals who lived further west. As they sat round the fire one evening they suddenly realised where Champion wanted to go: the Wok Takin. The Wok Takin, that was the Sepik. Convinced he could now find a track across the mountains Champion turned back down the Fly. Where the river was still a torrent he and the police risked launching rafts, but they were wrecked on the second day. On rebuilt log crafts they took a month to drift downstream, often travelling at night behind Champion on the lead raft with their one hurricane lamp. While they were still beyond the area of government control villagers tried to loot their meagre stores, but they were able to push the pirates overboard. At the first plantation on the river they met Karius on his way to look for them. Caught in jagged limestone country at the head of the Strickland, he had had 'a terrible time'. Despite the rigours of their trip Champion and Karius were eager to go back. In Port Moresby both were relieved to hear Sir Hubert Murray say 'You can try again'.

For the second journey they recruited more carriers, choosing the tough wiry

Ivan Champion

men from the D'Entrecasteaux Islands in the east and long-term prisoners from the Port Moresby gaol. Assisted by an opportune flood they got their boats higher up the Fly then rushed their carriers through to Mt Blucher without the time-consuming relays. The local villagers recognised Champion, but they explained that there was drought and they could not again be generous with their taro. Karius, noticing the people's lack of enthusiasm, said to Champion, 'My God, I hope you're not leading me on a blind track'. Ivan Champion:

Anyway, we got to Bolivip, and I saw the old chief, Tamsimara, again. We carried a big adze with us so we could hollow out canoes. I said 'Wok Takin,' and he shook his head: no Wok Takin. They weren't going to take us. I pointed to the adze, and in sign language told him, you take us to the Wok Takin and this is yours. After a lot of talk they said they might go. Next morning when we were all ready to start nothing happened. Nobody wanted to go. I brandished the adze and tomahawks and things, and all of a sudden he gave the word. He and six or seven others rushed out of the village, 'Come!' Away we went. After a couple of hours they said 'Up there'. Up this great mountain; it looked perpendicular. They had a

Openwork engraved board, from Tambanum East Sepik Province. Such boards are thought to have been used for display of head-hunting trophies.

Papuan Patrol Officer's Narrow Escape

From Our Own Correspondent

PORT MORESBY, July 26.

KNOCKED down and surrounded by 60 armed natives in the Kagua Valley area, Papua, on June 16, Patrol Officer Ivan Champion saved his life by shooting one of the natives as he was about to fire an arrow from a distance of five yards. The native was killed, and the others ran into the jungle.

With two carriers and a native constable, Champion, who is in charge of the Lake Kutubu police, was travelling about half a mile in the rear of the main party.

The natives emerged from the jungle as he was crossing a creek. One of them grabbed his rifle, and he was knocked to the ground. Several arrows which were fired narrowly missed him. Champion rejoined the main party, which searched unsuccessfully for the natives.

Attacks were made recently on two previous patrols in the district, but the natives scattered when rifles were fired.

The native who was killed came from Iawi village through which Champion had passed previously.

Pacific Islands Monthly August 15, 1939

Wooden mask, engraved and painted, from Saparu Village on a tributary of the Yuat River, East Sepik Province

track, but only they could see it. They only had bamboo knives and stone adzes, and you couldn't see where they marked their tracks.

Stretching forward to find handholds, they hauled themselves upward. At the first ledge Tamsimara made a sign for Champion to sit and rest. As the young Australian and the old villager waited together one of the D'Entrecasteaux carriers, scarcely any bigger than his forty-pound pack of rice, slung his load down and said in Motu 'Phew! Ten bob for all this! Phew!' That was his comment on the carriers' pay, ten shillings a month, the same as that for the plantation labourers. On they climbed through the scrub and moss-covered 'devil country'. In spite of the frequent rains they could rarely find water for it all disappeared into the porous limestone. One night they were reduced to squeezing the moss to find a few droplets to cook a little rice and taro. Finally, after a rainy night, they set off into

a very dirty, misty morning. We came out on to a grass patch, and there was old Tamsimara standing on a rock and he says, 'Wok Takin, Wok Takin, dim, dim dim. . .'. There it was flowing in this great grass valley in front of us. I remember all the carriers coming in and saying, 'Rabaul River! Rabaul River!' Where we'd come from there was a very small population, but here was the smoke from many villages.

Tamsimara led them down into the valley. Over the next day he contacted the Feramin people who gathered to inspect the travellers. Tamsimara made speeches explaining how the strangers had come to Bolivip, made friends and presented him with steel tools. He scorned the miserable amount of taro that the Feramin had so far provided and asked them to be more generous in gifts and guides. But the Feramin were also suffering a seasonal shortage and the expedition was forced to open its precious rice packs. Champion and Karius were unable to persuade the northern peoples to provide guides, often forcing the expedition to spend days on short rations finding their way through the formidable Sepik gorges. Champion's

knee, injured on a limestone outcrop, became infected and eventually disabled him. The carriers, their loads long since consumed, now carried Champion on a stretcher made from his canvas bed. Two policemen took two hours to manoeuvre the stretcher over a swaying lawyer cane bridge, high over the Sepik.

After a fortnight Champion was able to walk and they were through the gorges. But the river which had picked up in volume was 'still a terrific pace'. Champion was confident of his skills as 'a water man':

I said 'I'll raft this river.' And Karius, he was a bit wiser, said, 'No, you can't. But if you like to try it, you go with nothing.' We had two or three police from the Northern District who were used to rough rivers, torrent rivers, and we made one raft and got on it. We'd only gone a hundred yards and it just went over and over, and there we were in this boiling cauldron. I lost my glasses. I was hauled out by the corporal, and we all got ashore, about five of us. Karius had gone on ahead and we caught him up. The police had lost their rifles. That hurt them more than anything. A policeman without his rifle. They were absolutely ashamed. When we joined Karius he said. 'I told you so'.

Battling sickness and starvation, they came through sago swamps to the point where they could safely launch rafts. They thought that they were still 300 miles from the nearest government station of Ambunti, but almost immediately they encountered

natives in canoes coming up the river. They were talking about something going 'boomp, boomp, boomp, boomp'. We couldn't make out what it was. We thought they must be talking about the Germans twenty years ago: 'boomp, boomp, boomp'. We started off escorted by these natives. It was late afternoon. Suddenly we shot around a bend and there was the boomp, boomp; there was the *Elevala*, the ship that had taken us up the Fly. They'd sent her round and

PAPUAN EXPEDITION—
A Progress Report

In the middle of December last Mr. Jack Hides, A.R.M. of the Papuan Administration, and Patrol Officer J. O'Malley left Port Moresby by the "Vailala" with native police and carriers in an attempt to penetrate the unexplored country between the headwaters of the Strickland River and the great Purari River which rises in Mandated Territory of New Guinea and flows southwards across Papua to the Gulf.

The expedition sailed across the Gulf of Papua to Daru, in the Western Division, and from thence journeyed up the Fly River to Everill's Junction. In the "Vailala" they proceeded up the Strickland River to Douglas Bend, over 100 miles from the junction with the Fly. The party with their stores and equipment were then transferred to canoes and slowly made their way up the Strickland. After several weeks' journey by canoe the party discovered a large river flowing into the Strickland from the east. This was named the Rentoul, presumably after Mr. Alex Rentoul, who was Resident Magistrate at Misima Island when Jack Hides was A.R.M. there.

As this river flowed from the direction in which their course lay, Mr. Hides decided to follow it. After 40 miles by water, hampered greatly by floods and rapids, the party disembarked, and in the middle of February were about to make a long trek overland through absolutely unexplored territory to reach the Iago River, north-east Delta Division, and later journey down the Purari River to the coast. The party appeared then to be making satisfactory progress, and if all continues to go well news should be received at the end of May that the expedition have attained their objective thus bringing credit to the Papuan Administration, and fresh laurels to the intrepid young leader for his daring feat.

The Papuan Courier June 7, 1935

Tree house on the upper Fly River

into the Sepik. The captain of the *Elevala* said, 'I've been here three weeks waiting for you people. I was going tomorrow, giving you up for lost'. That was the end of the journey. We never fired a rifle in anger, and we never got an arrow in anger. One of our carriers died while we were making our rafts; that was the only loss we had on that trip.

On their two patrols Karius and Champion had been in the field for eleven months. They had conformed to the highest ideals of the Papuan service. They had taken risks rather than use force; they had shown great skill as bushmen; and they paid generous tribute to their police and carriers. But they had missed the broad and densely populated valleys of the central highlands. Missionaries and miners climbing out of the Markham were the first foreigners to look on the intensely gardened highland valleys. In the meantime Papuan officers kept cutting tracks across the blank areas of their maps. Their expeditions were so modest in cost and equipment, and so extravagant in time and human endurance.

In 1935 Jack Hides and Jim O'Malley walked for five and a half months from the Strickland River through the Southern Highlands to the Purari. From the third month the members of the patrol, almost exhausted and with few goods left to trade for food, were forced to fight off attack after attack by angry tribesmen. And, like Karius and Champion further west, they had to cross the limestone barrier on the way in and again in the south on the way out. The bare-footed police called it 'the broken bottle country'. But Hides had had the reward that all the frontier men dreamed about. When they first broke through those desolate and cruel ranges they had looked on a land that was beautiful in itself and everywhere marked by the works of a numerous and industrious people. Hides savoured that moment:

as we looked excitedly northwards, O'Malley and myself stood spellbound gazing at a scene of wild and lonely splendour.

Below us, on the opposite side of the Ryan [River], a large lake lay on a platform of the divide, while the Ryan itself was seen to emerge from a deep gorge about two miles to the northwards; and beyond the gorge, gold and green, reaching as far as the eye could see, lay the rolling timbered slopes and grasslands of a huge valley system. On every slope were cultivated squares, while little columns of smoke rising in the still air revealed to us the homes of the people of this land. I had never seen anything more beautiful. Beyond all stood the heights

A *ravi* (Kaimari village Gulf Province, Papua) where only single men sleep.

Sago-making in Kaimari

of some mighty mountain chain that sparkled in places with the colours of the setting sun. As I looked on those green cultivated squares, of such mathematical exactness, I thought of wheatfields, or the industrious areas of a colony of Chinese. Here was a population such as I had sometimes dreamed of finding.

Papuan Wonderland,
(pub. Angus & Robertson)

I will always regret the shooting of this native, for I knew his people had looked upon us as invaders, and I had been prepared to risk a lot to save them from their fear. But the ambush had been thrust upon us so quickly . . .
Jack Hides,
Papuan Wonderland

Jack Hides was restless, romantic and courageous. Born in Port Moresby, he joined the government service at nineteen. After the Strickland-Purari patrol of 1935 he left the public service to lead a

disastrous and exhausting search for gold on the Strickland River. He died soon after his return to Sydney. He was only thirty-one.

With Jack Hides at the small Port Moresby school for white children had been the three Champion brothers, Ivan, Alan and Claude. All joined the Papuan field service. Six years before the Strickland-Purari patrol, a youthful Claude Champion had gone north to the edge of the Southern Highlands. He just missed being among the first foreigners to see those heavily populated valleys. With Assistant Resident Magistrate W B Faithorn in 1929 he had crossed the Murray Range into the Samberigi Valley. While coming down the Erave, a tributary of the Purari, Champion asked a policeman to climb a high tree on a northern ridge. From his eyrie the policeman saw a vast valley smudged by numerous columns of smoke indicating a dense population. But Faithorn decided that he had neither the authority nor the resources to divert the patrol. The chance was missed.

In 1937 Claude Champion was given

another opportunity to penetrate deep into the Southern Highlands. With George Andersen, twelve selected policemen ('the men to get you out of trouble') and over one hundred carriers he went by canoe then relayed stores to Lake Kutubu. Established the year before as the only government post in the highlands, Kutubu was a police camp on the shore of a twelve-mile stretch of water 'of unfailing serenity'. From Kutubu Champion and Andersen patrolled into the Tari and Wage valleys:

> That was a six weeks patrol and it took us to some of the places Hides had been to. At one of the places on the Wela where he had a terrific fight, killing a lot of people, the men greeted us with bows and arrows; but they made signs that they didn't want any 'boong, boonging'. We put our rifles down, and eventually the natives put their bows and arrows down, and we gave them some shell. We call it *mairi* shell; it was a gold-lipped shell. We gave them some of that, and they went off and got food. That's how we made friends with them.
>
> Some days later we crossed a very high mountain. As a matter of fact it was the coldest night I have ever spent in my life. When I say crossed, we couldn't cross, we got caught at eleven thousand feet. Andersen and I were going up with the police hitting the carriers, not belting them with sticks, but hitting them with open hands to keep the circulation going. We knew once they stopped, they'd die. Eventually we got them into camp at eleven thousand feet. It was limestone country and no water; but we could hear a creek right down below, and there was a hole big enough to get a bucket down. We lowered the bucket and got enough water to cook the carriers' rice and our food.
>
> The next morning we didn't get up very early. The natives built fires to keep themselves warm. We set off about nine o'clock, and that's when the trouble started; the yodelling came from everywhere. Hides had warned us about the yodelling: if they start to yodel, watch your step. When we got down into the valley, into the long spear grass, we came up against their long trenches dug for defence purposes. They're about ten feet deep and about nine feet wide. They were for protection against other natives. Anyway we got into a big clearing, and these thousands of natives surrounded us with bows and arrows, yodelling, and all ready at the draw. But my native cook boy, Naisi, who played the mouth organ very well indeed, came and sat down and played. I was at one end of the carrier line with some police; Andersen was at the other end. The natives had never heard anything like this in their lives. They just stood stock still and put their bows and arrows down. I said, 'Naisi, keep playing, keep playing!' One of them heard the name 'Naisi', and he ran up calling, 'Naisi, Naisi!' They all dropped their bows and arrows and just sat and listened to him. Personally, I think he saved the whole party.
>
> When I returned from Lake Kutubu, after seven months very strenuous patrolling, I was tired and haggard, but I had to write a report. It had to go into Port Moresby where, of course, it was read by Sir Hubert Murray who said to the Government Secretary, 'What a wonderful patrol Claude did. But isn't it a shame he spelt exorbitant with an aitch!' I thought that after seven months in the field he might have found something better to say.

In communication with outsiders Murray praised his field staff for achieving so much with so few resources, but he was never likely to unbend sufficiently to express enthusiasm directly to the men themselves. Murray's restraint seemed part of the austerity of his government.

In the ten years after Karius and Champion had crossed from the Fly to the Sepik, Papuan Government officers had mapped the general outlines of the Southern Highlands; but in the north more dramatic journeys had been made.

UNKNOWN CENTRAL N. GUINEA

Papuan Reconnaissance by Air

AN aerial reconnaissance over the newly discovered territory in Central Papua will be carried out almost immediately by Mr. Ivan Champion and Mr. Jack Hides.

It is reported that a Guinea Airways machine will be used, and that the object of the flight is to enable Mr. Hides to point out to Mr. Champion the leading features of the country which Mr. Hides penetrated last year and which Mr. Champion will pass through during his forthcoming exploratory patrol (referred to in the December issue of the *Pacific Islands Monthly*).

Mr. Hides, after extended sick leave, left for Papua by the *Montoro* on January 11. He has not yet recovered his health but he was glad to comply with the wish of the Lieutenant-Governor (Sir Hubert Murray) that he should make available to Mr. Champion all possible data which might assist Mr. Champion in the contemplated patrol.

This aeroplane reconnaissance, as far as we know, is the first of the kind that has been attempted over this difficult and practically unknown terrain, and the result of the flight will be awaited with much interest. If it should prove to be a practicable method, it probably will be used extensively in the future in securing accurate knowledge of the remaining tracts of unknown Central New Guinea. In this connection it is worthy of note that just across the border, in Dutch New Guinea, large modern aeroplanes are being used in a preliminary examination of that hitherto unknown territory.

Pacific Islands Monthly January 24, 1936

14 The Promised Land

That was a terrific experience. When we walked in, I'll never forget, it opened out like a beautiful picture. It had rained the night before, and everything looked so fresh and so beautiful. Beautiful mountains either side. Looking up the valley from where I was there was Wilhelm over 14 000 on one side, and Kubor on the other side, that was a bit over 14 000. And this great range, you know, right along, and looking up this beautiful valley. You can imagine it.

Dan Leahy

The highlanders had never been completely cut off from the lowlanders. They had met to trade and fight at various points. The villagers of the upper Markham Valley had called the people who lived high on the escarpment 'the hawks': they were like birds of prey who watched and then launched sudden raids. But there were some villagers in both the valley and on the slopes who were trading partners so that the shell and clay pots of the lowlands could pass into the mountains. The foreigners were to use these traditional routes for a slow, then a spectacular, penetration of the highlands.

From the time that they built a station at Kaiapit in the Markham the Lutheran missionaries were looking further afield. Much of the early exploratory work was done by black evangelists but by the end of the 1920s Leonhard Flierl, Wilhelm Flierl and George Pilhofer had travelled beyond Kainantu. They were well into the Eastern Highlands. By that time, too, gold prospectors, such as Ned Rowlands and Helmuth Baum, were working on the streams of the highlands fringe. The easy riches of the Wau goldfields had now gone and the miners still working the old field decided to finance an expedition to test the new country in the eastern highlands. Two young but experienced miners and bushmen, Michael Dwyer and Michael Leahy, carried their hopes.

In 1930 Leahy and Dwyer went looking for the headwaters of the creeks shedding the little gold then being won in the Kainantu area. Without realising it they crossed the watershed dividing the upper Ramu from the tributaries of the Purari. Following the south-west streams, Mick Leahy recalls, they walked into 'the thickly populated wide open grass-covered valleys and ranges of what is known as the Goroka Valley'. In May Leahy and Dwyer had left the known edge of the highlands and emerged on the Papuan coast in July. They had walked right across New Guinea. Starting on the Dunantina where it is only an inch deep they had followed the main stream through its various changes in name along the Bena and Asaro Valleys, past the junction with the Wahgi, and finally on to the Purari. Leahy and Dwyer had had only sixteen New Guinean employees, and no other support. Sir Hubert Murray, with another characteristic understatement, said that it was 'a good piece of bushmanship'. Central New Guinea had now been cut by two exploratory lines: Karius and Champion had crossed from south to north in the west, and Leahy and Dwyer from north to south in the east.

Girls from Mount Hagen (left)

Cane and bark cloth face, painted, from Muru Village near Orokolo, Gulf Province

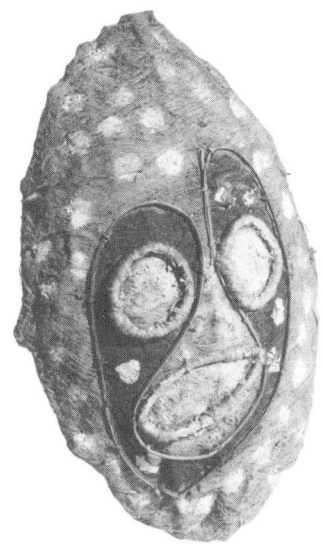

The prospectors were determined to get back into the highlands. Mick Leahy explains:

> The reason we were so anxious to get back in there again was that when we were following down the Purari we found areas of backwash where huge goannas were picking the bones of decomposed bodies of natives that had floated down the Wahgi, Benabena and Asaro. That gave us the idea that the country evidently flattened out, and of course when you're looking for gold in New Guinea, the idea is to get above where the streams race down the mountain sides and get up into the highland country where they flattened. There was a good chance that any gold shed into the streams would be still there, similar to the gold in Edie Creek above the Bulolo River.

The prospectors followed a line of inference: the bodies indicated a dense population, high populations were most likely in open country, streams deposited gold where they slowed as they came on to high plains.

> *Early in 1933 we left our base, Dan and Charlie Marshall and myself, crossed the Asaro River, climbed the range to 8200 on the other side, and camped on top. From there we travelled approximately east then turned back west again, and from a divide near what is now Mount Elimbari, a very prominent triangular shaped limestone mountain, I looked in to what is today the Wahgi-Hagen Valley. Lost in the haze of distance and, as far as the eye could see, thickly populated.*
> **Michael Leahy**

Engaged by New Guinea Goldfields Limited to locate dredging prospects, Mick Leahy, now joined by his youngest brother Dan, returned to the highlands. The Leahys pegged a claim near Bena. It gave a poor return; but the Leahys could use Bena as a base to push further west. On their return from a reconnaissance of the Asaro a curious and courageous young man joined the expedition. Mick Leahy:

> We picked up Namu from the village of Sirupu. Our ambition had been for a long time to pick up some of the younger native boys and take them with us wherever we went, to learn Pidgin and eventually to become interpreters. The natives were all very shy, of course, and very much afraid of handing themselves over to us. However at Sirupu two of the young natives decided they would come with us in the morning—by sign language, the head on one hand and the eyes closed indicated that they would sleep, and then in the morning a few beckoning motions and pointing in the direction we were going. But one of them got cold feet at the last minute and Namu only was game enough to say 'Well, I'll go'.

After a few hours on the track Namu himself began to have doubts about his decision. But by that time the expedition was moving through the land of his enemies; if he left the protection of the foreigners he would almost certainly be killed. Reluctantly the Leahys tied Namu to some of their New Guinean labourers. Other villagers along the track now assumed that Namu was a prisoner being led to some terrible fate: it became all the more important that Namu be returned free and healthy through the area.

At the newly opened airstrip at Lapumpa near Kainantu Bob Gurney put the apprehensive Namu into a small moth aircraft and flew him to Lae. At Henry Eekhoff's store Gurney

> fixed him up with a red laplap, a white singlet, a huge empty twenty-five pound flour tin full of all sorts of odds and ends, two bottles of sea water to show how much salt (their most prized item of trade) was available down there, and some long hairs out of a horse's tail to show them how big the pigs grew.

On the walk back to his home Namu took the lead, telling everybody of the marvellous world that he had entered. From then on the Leahys had trouble keeping back

A saltwater expedition, Bougainville, March 1917

'the multitude' wanting to travel with them. They adopted the plan of walking with a crowd until they came to the clan boundaries then

> selecting some of the young bright natives and shooing the rest back.
> After months of travelling with us and seeing what we were doing they knew we were only looking for stones in the creek, and they were quite happy. We told them we were looking for a certain stone that we wore in our teeth. I happened to have a little gold in one tooth, and they quite appreciated the human decoration point of view. They learned Pidgin very quickly, and in time, through one, two or three interpreters, we could practically speak to the whole of the valley.

As the Leahys found out, it was easy enough to find a guide who would direct them around 'all his relatives to show us off like a circus', but they travelled more efficiently and safely when they had someone able to stand on a prominent point and shout that the foreigners were peaceful people just looking for bits of rock to put in their teeth. That was, Mick Leahy concedes, a message beyond human understanding, yet it seemed to satisfy the immediate curiosity of the crowds of 'fantastically arrayed' highlanders that gathered about the camps.

To avoid the long walks into Lapumpa, the Leahys decided to put in their own airstrip at Bena. Using digging sticks and bare feet the local people cleared and levelled a 'long, flat hogback ridge'. The strip was ready and the four signal fires lit on Christmas Day, 1932. Bob Gurney came over, dropped Christmas cake and 'a little Christmas cheer', then risked a landing. With continued support from New Guinea Goldfields and supplies landed at Bena, the Leahys extended their prospecting deeper into new country. All the time they were developing the techniques of greeting and co-existing with local people that became standard in highland exploratory patrols. Shells, steel axes and knives were given as presents or traded for pigs and sweet potato. A rope was erected around the camp as a symbolic boundary. This guarded against pilfering and a rush attack from the volatile crowds. On one of their prospecting trips early in 1933 Mick and Dan Leahy and Charles Marshall, the surveyor, stood on the divide near Mt Elimbari and gazed on the greatest of the highland valleys, the Wahgi. The haze of a hundred village fires and vast areas of orderly gardens were set in a frame of spectacular mountains.

On their way back to Bena the Leahys met Jim Taylor. From the mid 1920s government officers had been taking patrols out of the Ramu and Markham

Men of Mount Hagen

into the edge of the highlands, but it was obvious that occasional visits would not bring the numerous highlanders within Australian rule, and neither would they prevent violence between villagers and miners. In 1932 Jim Taylor established the first permanent government station in the highlands at Kainantu. Now Michael Leahy suggested that they combine forces for a major expedition: the Leahys had to secure the support of Major G A Harrison, the general manager of New Guinea Goldfields, and Taylor had to obtain authority from Rabaul.

Infected by Michael Leahy's enthusiasm, the necessary blessings from superiors had been given, the stores flown in, and the carriers assembled before the end of March, 1933. Leahy and Taylor planned to make more effective use of aircraft than on any previous patrol into new country. Both men made reconnaissance flights west from Bena. They arranged to have a temporary air strip ready in the Wahgi a fortnight after they left Bena, and then another further west at Mount Hagen. Unlike the leaders of earlier exploratory patrols Taylor and Leahy had a clear idea of the country they were entering, they could pick up fresh stores

right in the heart of the area to be patrolled, and they could get sick or injured men out in an emergency. But it was still arduous work done at little cost. The government allowed Taylor ten pounds only to pay for his reconnaissance flight, and the expedition fed itself by trading. The sixty New Guinean carriers did not lump the forty-pound packs of rice and tinned meat that had exhausted their predecessors, but the trade goods that would be exchanged for food. The poverty of government spending was in contrast to the magnitude of the work that the Leahys and Taylor had undertaken. Jim Taylor:

> Then began one of the greatest experiences of my life. I was quite a novice at this time as far as the highlands were concerned; Mick had had great experience. We felt that we were about to take part in some very great discoveries and looked forward to life with bounding heart.

On March 28 'the combined party left Benabena and headed out over the range into the promised land'. In the middle Wahgi, well beyond the range of any of their interpreters, they located the site for an airstrip. Mick Leahy continues:

we levelled it off in this draught board shaped garden country. The ditches had to be filled and stamped down to harden them as best we could. For a start things looked rather bad. These were essentially spear people with great long spears and three auxiliary prongs about two or three feet from the main end. The idea being that if they missed with the main point, one of these side spikes would jab. I never did like spears, spears are a quick jab weapon, and we decided to establish a spear park for anybody coming along to see us. They put their weapons there, just outside the fence.

When the people looked most tense Taylor went forward with placatory gestures. Mick Leahy recorded the incident in a series of photographs that capture the quiet assurance of Taylor and the turbulence of the warriors torn between trying to destroy or befriend the unknown. The intruders also had to prepare the people for the arrival of the first aircraft:

Jim Taylor, adept at making noises like aeroplanes and waving his arms around like a propellor, did quite a good job. Every day, of course, there were literally hundreds of them collected outside the camp, viewing everything. These were fine, big, bearded men, big strong fellows, so strong and confident of their fighting prowess that their women and kids always came along with them, a sure sign of their cocksureness of their fighting ability.

On the day appointed, with a pair of binoculars, I sighted the plane afar off and we pointed excitedly. As the hum from the engine grew into a roar they began to show all sorts of signs of fear. The plane circled over the area to spot our signal fires, and as it came lower they began to go down on their knees. By the time the plane circled round, landed at the bottom end and started to taxi up to where the multitude were near our camp, they were right down on their knees. Some even flattened out on the ground. When Ian Grabowsky, the pilot, who is

about six foot six, dressed in a white flying suit with a white skull cap and green square-shaped goggles, stepped out of the plane, they just groaned and really flattened into the ground. However we persuaded them back on to their feet, led them over to look at the plane, feel it, and see that Grabowsky was just like one of us.

When the probing hands of the highlanders discovered Grabowsky's genitals, they were assured that he was indeed some sort of human. To Grabowsky's consternation, another fifty hands sought confirmation.

The expedition continued west. Where they could they walked straight ahead, sometimes accompanied by over a thousand people. At the border of their clan lands the crowd would halt, but men standing on the ridges would be yodelling and calling to neighbouring communities. If the patrol approached new peoples from the direction of their traditional enemies, it might be met by ranks of apprehensive warriors. Dan Leahy:

Then it would be very tricky. You'd have to dodge a few arrows occasionally before you could get in. But we had a big dog with us, he was a half bull and half cattle dog. He was fierce looking, but very intelligent. If a fight started, he'd rush in. Well, they'd never seen such an animal. It was like a lion let loose among our people. They had only skinny little dogs then. Nine times out of ten they'd go for their lives. Then we'd dash into the place and get a few of the old people that couldn't get out. We'd make friends with them, shake hands, give them little presents and tell them to sing out that we weren't going to fight them. They'd see that we were nothing like their enemies, and then one by one they'd come back.

On the outward journey, Taylor says, they were rarely met with hostility. Some people, believing the foreigners to be spirits, were 'stricken with awe' or passed into 'ecstasies of delight':

Some of us were recognised by the people as having recently been

Wooden figure, engraved,
from Milne Bay Province

amongst them but having died. Two children identified me as their father and they walked in silence, each holding one hand, as I passed through their particular area. People as far as Hagen thought we had come from above, and so did the people further west, but the real difference was that the people on the eastern side had some respect for spirits, whereas further west they despised them.

The white men had come as angels, but, Taylor adds in quiet irony, 'I don't know if they think so now'.

From a base at Mount Hagen the patrol moved out into the Jimmi Valley in the north, and south to the Papuan border. Jim Taylor:

> I had in my mind that ours was a noble task, and that it was our duty to bring the *Pax Australiana* to these people. Mick and his party were primarily, of course, interested in prospecting, but they were just as interested in native people as I was, and I was just as interested in the prospecting as they were. We got on very well together, all of us in the camp, and it could not be otherwise with Michael Leahy in a camp. His attitude to native people was one of his outstanding qualities. I always remember the first time I went into a camp of his; it was like coming out of an office into fresh air. He gave orders in a manner that wasn't customary in New Guinea in those days. He might want to find something that he had misplaced, and I can hear him now saying, 'Iwunga, I wonder where I put that saw? Would you have a look?' 'Yes, *Masta* Mick,' he'd say, 'I think you left it down there behind the wheelbarrow. I'll go and have a look.' That wasn't normal speech between master and servant in those days. There were many good employers in New Guinea, but none that created this attitude in the camp in which it was like a brotherhood. In those days, too, an employer might make a mistake and give a severe dressing down to a fellow and discover later that he had made an error. The normal attitude of those days was that a European should never admit an error. There was nothing of that about Mick. Mick might be very angry with a fellow and discover he was wrong. If it was Iwunga, one of his most notable boys, Mick would say, 'That matter this morning, I was very angry, Iwunga, but I'd just like you to know I've discovered I was wrong and I'm sorry. There's the trade box, take what you like.' Iwunga would go to the trade box. He could take something worth ten pounds. Mick would say, 'You've got what you want?' 'Yes.' 'What did you take?' And Iwunga, almost with tears in his eyes, would say, 'I have a pipe, *Masta* Mick, thank you.'

In that tribute Taylor demonstrated his own generosity as well as Michael Leahy's enlightened attitude to his fellow men. Taylor and Leahy consciously avoided imposing the rigid racial divisions of the coast: they wanted the highlanders to come under Australian rule without humiliation.

All of the early government officers, miners and missionaries who walked through the highlands were impressed by the vigour of the cultures that they encountered. They came away feeling privileged to have met peoples who were proud, industrious and volatile. Jim Taylor:

> It was an agricultural society. The basis was the material things, the food production. Of course they had a deeper magical life which I couldn't judge in those times, but I should say it was a rich primitive life. But there were certain very great limitations to it. They were warriors—on active service more or less perpetually; but not within each clan. Groups had quite a pleasant and charming life. They had marriage ceremonies and funereal feasts and their entertainment, but there wasn't much travel outside their own immediate area. Few had travelled more than five miles from their homes. There was trade—a great

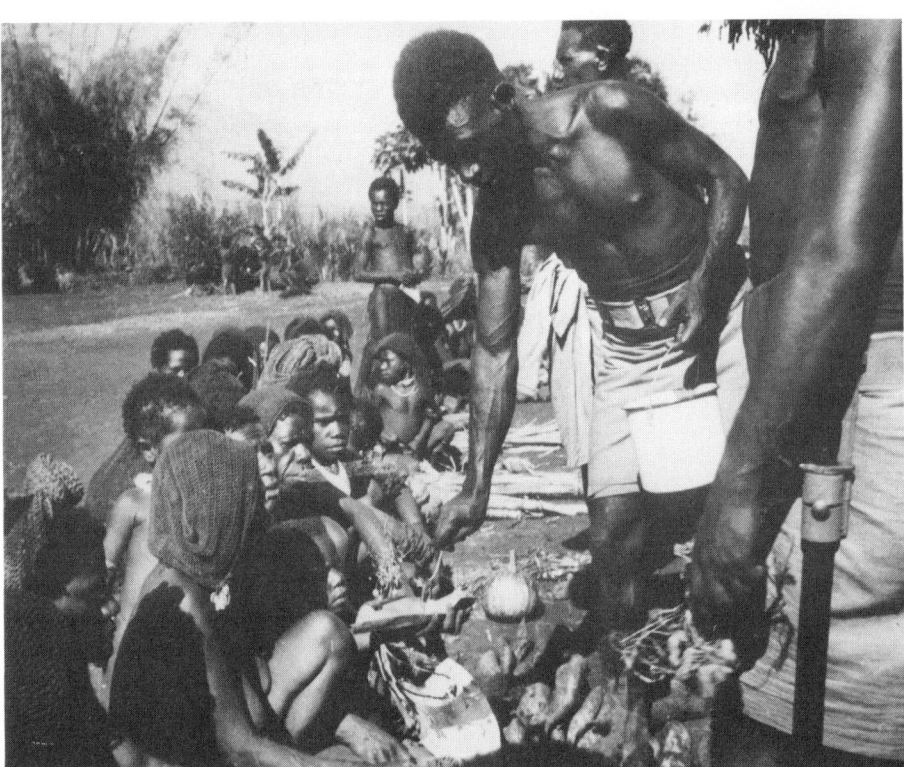

Police paying for the patrol's food with salt

trade—through extensive mercantile systems. For instance, the exchange of Hagen axes for salt. But it was much like the silk road from China to Europe in the Middle Ages: no one knew actually where the goods came from. Each community, I should say, felt that they were superb and the centre of the universe.

It was, Taylor says, like walking through a mediaeval society.

The return to Bena was difficult and in the Chimbu the patrol was in immediate danger of being overrun. The attitude of some peoples had changed from awe to truculence and contempt. Several times the police fired over the heads of threatening hordes and twice Taylor had to shoot to kill threatening warriors. But in general the expedition had been, as Taylor explains, a triumphant progress into the heart of the highlands:

We were out seven months, most of the time travelling. We met thousands of people, covered hundreds of square miles of country. There were some arduous days, but most of the journey was through green and pleasant land. Not the rugged and rough terrain of forested New Guinea, but through gardens and meadows and native tracks and hamlets and copses and happy people wearing flowers. We liked the people and liked the country. Some time later Mick said to me, 'Jim, good country, good climate, good kanakas. Too good to find gold in.'

Taylor and the Leahys had been responsible for the conduct of the first meeting between tens and thousands of people and the first foreigners to penetrate their valleys. They were the carriers of pervasive changes in the government, in the economy, in the relations between people, and in the very languages of the highlanders. No detailed search had been made to select men with special skills to carry out that extraordinary task. It was just fortunate for Australia's reputation as the administering nation—and for the highlanders—that the men who led the pioneering patrols were sensitive and restrained. Part of that restraint came from the fact that they had confidence in their own skills in the bush and in their ability to control the first contact situation.

Leahy was always more restless and impatient than Taylor. And later he was to

129

Carved wooden post, with bird and 'human' figures, painted, from New Ireland

be more concerned that the outside world should recognise his achievements. That concern took him to London and the Royal Geographical Society. As Jim Leahy remembers:

> We had managed to make a few bob out of gold mining, so we decided we would see the world and see the Royal Geographical Society. It wasn't all that easy to get into the Society because we didn't have any introduction. But anyhow Mick exploded, and accused them of being phoney: it didn't matter what you did, if you didn't have somebody to introduce you, you couldn't get anywhere. So a very fine old admiral named Goodenough took us under his wing and said, 'We'll investigate everything you have done.' And not only him, but a few others came good when Mick got his bog Irish up.

Michael Leahy addressed a special meeting, the Society examined his maps, and in 1936 presented him with the Murchison Grant for his explorations of central New Guinea.

The exploratory patrols of Taylor and the Leahys in 1933 were not followed up by the New Guinea administration. But adventurous missionaries moved into the Chimbu and Hagen areas, and prospectors were still keen to test new country. In 1934 Tom and Jack Fox, tough identical twins, spent nearly three months walking hard west of Hagen. Their report that they couldn't find enough gold to fill a tooth dampened the enthusiasm of the miners. But the area to the west was still unknown to the cartographers. In 1938 the government returned to advance its frontier. Jim Taylor was selected to lead another major expedition west and north-west to the Dutch border. With Taylor was medical assistant C B Walsh and patrol officer John Black.

The Taylor-Black patrol of 1938 and '39 was the best equipped pre-war government expedition. It was the first to carry a radio transceiver and to be supplied with air drops. But its success still depended on the ability of the men on the ground. Although Taylor aimed to use the established techniques of travelling with the co-operation of the local people and exploiting their knowledge of their homelands, the patrol was moving into some of the most difficult country in Papua New Guinea. The party divided with Black leading his group to the headwaters of the Strickland. Soon he was in the 'fretted limestone', the sharp-edged honeycomb, that had tortured Hides, Karius and Champion. The sparse population was unable and unwilling to supply large amounts of food. After a fortnight crossing the flooded Strickland, Black moved west to Telefomin, and then, united again with Taylor, went south to the tributaries of the Sepik:

> At the headwaters of the May River we were attacked by the Mianmin people. We had camped on a razorback ridge and although we called out during the night no one came to see us. But they did come at dawn the next morning. A fighting party surrounded the hut that the Waria police had made. The Waria were, you know, good reliable blokes. They couldn't get out because there were all these armed people who shot and killed one of the carriers. A man called Kunjul was shot with a big bamboo-bladed arrow like a huge carving knife and he bled to death. Anyhow the Warias drove them off. About an hour later they attacked on one side of the razorback. One man got within twenty feet of me with a big shield. I must admit I was cowardly enough to take shelter behind a big square medical box. Standing up alongside me was a little cook boy who shot the shield bearer with a shotgun. Eventually we drove them off. Now about ten minutes later they attacked from the other side of the ridge and they were driven off too. Apparently they didn't synchronise their watches properly because the obvious idea was to have the two attacks together. We had done nothing to those people that they could blame us for, but the reason for the attack possibly was that we had

come from their tribal enemies' country, from Telefomin.

The Taylor-Black patrol was the last of the epic patrols. They were in the field for over fifteen months. Soon after they got back to Rabaul war broke out in Europe and their reports won little public applause. In fact their maps now had a military value and senior government officers thought it best to keep quiet about some of their findings. Taylor and Black had cut lines across the last big blank on the map of Australian-administered territory. In their use of radio and aircraft they looked forward to the methods of the post-war officers who would complete the work. John Black's return from the May River to Wabag, a constant walk of three and a half months, had met the standards set by the best of field staff: he had shown endurance and bushmanship and he had not fired a shot to kill or injure.

Today roads wind through the mountain passes and disappear where the dark green of the coffee groves and the white tops of the kunai grass merge in the haze. Towns and supermarkets are built on the valley floors that only fifty years ago were unknown to the outside world. In 1981 Jim Taylor and Dan Leahy were still living in the region that they had first entered in 1933. Dan Leahy:

The only way I can describe the vast change that's gone on is to say that I've lived in two ages; the first one about 4000 years ago, and the present one, the modern one. That is what the change has been in the highlands.

But Taylor, the Leahys, the Foxes and many others who walked into the highlands in the 1930s were changed by that experience as much as the villagers.

15 First Contact

In the Samberigi valley the natives had never seen a European before. They were so amazed at the colour of our skins. When they came down out of their stockade they licked their fingers and rubbed them against our white skins, and looked at their fingers, thinking, well, what's that? They looked at the police: the same colour as they were. They just couldn't make it out. From then on we were really good friends, and they helped us in every way possible. They were easy to get on with as long as you didn't interfere with their gardens or their women. If you interfered with either of those, then you'd had it.

Claude Champion

In the years of Australian rule in Papua New Guinea over one million people were brought under the influence of the central government. Because of the nature of the country and the small scale of the village political units, the process had to be repeated over and over again. Even in the islands of New Britain and Bougainville in the 1930s there were still isolated communities beyond the reach of the Australian administration. In 1942 the Australian coastwatcher, Paul Mason, encountered people in central Bougainville who had never met a white man. From their mountain homeland they could look down on the world of the foreigners and they had heard of the war: they asked Mason whether he was 'English' or 'Japanese'. At that time nearly one third of the people on the mainland took no orders from any outside authority. It is an extraordinary fact in the history of Australian government in Papua New Guinea that Australia's rule was imposed so recently on so many people. For most Papua New Guineans the coming—and the going—of Australians as rulers has been within living memory. For some communities Australian administration was so brief that it is more accurate to say that they experienced an interruption rather than enduring a period of foreign rule.

Government officers in the 1890s sometimes thought that their job was to assert their superiority over turbulent tribes. They wrote of 'teaching the natives a lesson', and any community showing signs of independence was condemned as 'arrogant' or 'cheeky'. But the process of contact was never just one way. There were always courageous and restless individuals in the villages who were prepared to take risks to go and meet the outside world. Government officers going into some areas for the first time were met by men who had made their way out through enemy territory to sign-on as plantation labourers. Some communities sent representatives inviting government officers or missionaries to come and see them.

A patrol entering new country would move cautiously. Often the 'oldtime policemen' would be the most experienced members of the government force, and, as Des Clifton-Bassett found when he was working out of Telefomin, they would take the initiative. Rather than have the *kiap* at the head of the column the corporal would suggest, '*Masta* you stay back there'. Two policemen would scout ahead to make sure that no ambushes were set on the narrow track. *Tambu* signs, sticks placed across the track,

The dance festivals of the Gulf were destroyed. Photo by F E Williams, Government Anthropologist, Karena-Orokolo Area prior to 1940

FRIDAY, JULY 20, 1951.
BANIR TAURI PATROL

ARMED BANDS THREATEN ATTACK ON EXPEDITION

"AFTER a while Yagi passed word that a large band was following the party and other police reported that houses through which we were passing were filling up with armed men. It looked as if the people might have decided to stage some show of force ..." Such dramatic incidents highlight this, the second instalment of Patrol Officer J. P. Sinclair's report of a 31-day patrol of the Watut, the Banir, and the headwaters of the Tauri.

We started to move at that roughly follows the ridge (the Tauri headwaters came). As a result of Mr. Hurnoon. The patrol line was a 1'2inched at least 6,000 feet—in sight. A great many off-trell's visit I made an excellent long one and visibility, that hard, tough going. Camped (agax seen from this point, first contact and obtained a by the thick mist, poor k-Vuf (at 110 p.m. after a tiring and The guides were afraid to go out of food.

South Pacific Post July 20, 1951

Double-ended dance wand, engraved and painted, probably from the Trobriand Islands, Milne Bay Province

were a warning to travellers that they were entering an area that the local community felt it should defend. On the approach of the patrol some peoples retreated into the bush. 'It might take days' Bob Cole remembers. 'It was just a matter of shouting, calling, sitting down and leaving presents, and eventually they'd come in, sell food, and then we'd start to talk to them.' Jim Sinclair found a similar response when he was patrolling from Koroba among the wigmen. After they camped early in the afternoon

> the interpreter would stand on the perimeter of the camp and yodel to the people 'Come, come, come on in, the government's here. We want to talk to you. We want to buy food'. This was repeated over and over. Curiosity, if you were patient enough, almost always resulted in somebody coming in to find out what all the fuss was about. I used to be careful to get permission to cut down trees and to pull out the grass to thatch a hut.

But, as Ian Skinner observed, in other parts of the highlands the people would be waiting with a pig ready to kill and a mass of sweet potato:

> there would be singing and dancing, and it was a great day for them, as it was for you. You usually found yourself well and truly covered with pig grease where they all patted and admired you. Some of the greeting ceremonies were a little unorthodox. When you were greeting a man you revered or a friend, you clutched him to your bosom with your left hand round his back, and hugged him to your chest while you tenderly caressed his testicles with your right hand. There's a funny story there. When the first American nurses went in in slacks they were given this greeting, and the people found that things weren't quite as they should be. It was done very gently and there was nothing aggressive about it.

But without the presence of trouser-clad army nurses, there was only one moment of awe. David Marsh: 'You only shock them once'. Jim Sinclair tried to preserve

calm by persuading people to sit down: 'the physical act of sitting, and getting whole groups to sit in the camp, in my experience, was three quarters of the battle. You would very seldom have any real trouble then, even if there were no women or children there'. But where a crowd of excited, armed men crowded about a minority of strangers any incident could provoke a sudden change of mood. Dudley McCarthy:

> We got into this village and we knew they were very edgy. They wouldn't be parted from their weapons, and they were very frightened. A scuffle broke out between a policeman and a group of villagers through some misunderstanding, and suddenly they panicked, they stampeded, there's no other word for it. I was just sitting back on a chair, alongside the ADO, and suddenly I was flat on my back with all these people charging over me. They disappeared down the mountain side.

The process of bringing about a quiet meeting had to begin again.

> *We had some difficulty in arriving at this particular village because the paths were strewn with sharpened bamboo blades. They're like razor blades. They were hidden amongst the grass so that if one blundered on to the stakes it could be very, very unpleasant.*
> **Dudley McCarthy**

At the first meeting the government officers made few demands They tried to say who they were, that they represented 'the all powerful Queen, if you can describe a queen' and instructed the people that they were to cease fighting. Through interpreters they tried to convey the complex idea that they were not then judging the rights and wrongs of those engaged in warfare: they merely insisted that it stop. To enhance their standing the *kiaps* exploited their technological advantage. They looked for a dramatic and simple cure of an illness, demonstrated the power of the rifle and gave other less awesome displays. David Marsh thought he was most effective if he took out a file and sharpened an old steel tool that might otherwise have taken its owner many days to hone with a piece of rock. Very quickly the villagers would start to argue about the terms of trade. On the first day they might have accepted one shell or a razor blade for a string bag of *kaukau* (sweet potato) but on the second or third they might be demanding two blades, or something different altogether. That, Marsh says, was a significant step, for the villagers were both accepting the foreigners and testing the extent to which they could be influenced.

Once a community was accustomed to the presence of the 'government', the patrol officers began a village book. In it they recorded people's names, their relationships to each other, notes about customs, the names of men with influence in the community, and what actions they had taken on their visit. The book was given into the care of the government-appointed headman, the *luluai* in New Guinea and the village constable in Papua. Sometimes the villagers would weave a special basket to protect the *buk* from rain and dirt. About a year or eighteen months after founding the station at Koroba in the Southern Highlands, Jim Sinclair says that they began appointing village constables. Each man 'had a cap of office, a leather belt, a handcuff chain, a sheath knife, and that was about it'. In earlier times they had been given a *dabua*, a black shirt and laplap, and a pair of handcuffs, but no key. If the village constable put the handcuffs on a man then the accused had to go to the government station, explain his predicament and have his hands released. The fight leaders appointed as village constables near Koroba were men of real authority in their own communities. Although at the end of five years 'most had not the faintest idea of their function' within the Australian administration, they were, Sinclair believes, effective points of contact between *kiap* and village.

Young Australians who were among the first foreigners to meet new groups of Papua New Guineans were involved in strange and affecting events. In the 1930s John Black had one such experience:

In the Enga country I was on the top of a mountain one morning getting bearings when a little family group came up, a man and his wife, and some children including a boy of about twelve or thirteen. They thought I had just stepped out of the clouds, on to a tree and climbed to the ground. Later on we found that the Enga people believe that some sky people are light skinned. They thought there'd been some strife in the sky, we'd come down to earth, and we were accompanied by some of their dead; our natives were the dead returned to earth trying to find their loved ones. This old chap, I remember, rushed away and got a little pig and some vegetables. Then he cleared a patch of grass and suggested by signs that I demonstrate a take-off. I made signs to the young boy, what about joining me and coming with the patrol, which he did. He remained with us for another eighteen months. He saw the aircraft flying at Wabag, and he saw what he thought to be sky people in the aircraft. But he still used to say from time to time in a loud voice what a good ghost I was, although he must have seen all the evidence that I was a human being. He was saying it when he could speak Pidgin.

Knowing nothing of the white men's home country or why they had left it, and seeing none of their women, the young man was left with the only plausible explanation that his own culture could provide.

Neil Desailly was involved in a different sort of encounter. A previous patrol passing through the area had been forced to fire over the heads of the people. Now Desailly had moved back, camped in the area, and waited, hoping that the villagers would eventually make contact. They gave no sign of coming in

so I went for a walk. As I often did, I took a couple of policemen and an interpreter. I was walking along a little

April 17: In camp—established a cleared patch of ground below the main camp for natives to gather—they started to arrive at 6.30. Very few women in sight—the men carried in the bags of food but this may be because they were unwilling to let their women come to the camp.

"Spent the day in trading, talking and gathering and checking information. The best contact to date.

"Found that a very acceptable payment for small amounts of food was tufts of hair from my two blue cattle dogs—all through the area the natives were amazed at the size, build and colour of these dogs. Their own are invariably wretched things.

"Natives informed me that they would cut up my dogs' hair very finely and mix it in the food given to their bitches. This would cause the next litter of pups to be born in the image of my own dogs. . . . Camped.

South Pacific Post July 20, 1951

Wooden figure with engraved and painted designs from Buka Island, North Solomons Province

David Marsh

Wooden figure, engraved, from
South Cape of Milne Bay Province

track when a young man stepped out of the bush about twenty yards in front of us. He was unarmed, he was looking very, very troubled, and he was perspiring. He just stood there. I walked up to him and said something in English which he didn't understand, of course; but it was meant to be reassurring. He picked up a handful of clay and smeared it on his face and chest. Now I'm still not sure precisely what he meant, and the interpreter wasn't either because he had only a smattering of the language. But the whole feeling I had was that he was saying this is my ground, this is my place, emphasising that we had no right there and he did have a right there. The ground was his, and he belonged to it and it belonged to him. It was quite an experience. We stayed there for a while, unable to communicate very well. I think we gave him a small present to reassure him, and I went on my way. The next day a small group came down and eventually we traded for sweet potato. But I often think of that young man. It must have taken a great deal of courage to step into the track of these grotesque strangers and act out that sort of statement.

One wonders if the young man's own community had a means of recognising and rewarding his bravery.

Chris Vass was another patrol officer involved in recent contact. It was the fulfilment of a fantasy that had helped take him to Papua New Guinea in the first place. About four days' walk out of Porgera the patrol camped opposite a cane suspension bridge. A whooping noise came echoing down the hills and half a dozen men with 'inverted icecream cone wigs' emerged from the bush, crossed the bridge and stood at the edge of the camp. After much gesturing and persuasion from the interpreter who spoke a related language the men crept into camp. Before they left the wigmen invited the patrol to visit them:

The next day we crossed the river, climbed up the hill, and came into the clearing where these people were living. They had obviously removed the women and children because they still weren't sure of us. They had a house up in a tree, a huge communal house, quite different from all the other people in the area. The house was to accommodate all that particular clan group. We sat down with them, and they showed us some of their implements. They were intrigued with the things that I had to show them, a steel axe which they had never seen before, an electric shaver which I got out and demonstrated on one of them, but the thing that really intrigued them was the aerial on the radio. I turned the radio on, and of course the sound coming out of the box fascinated them, but far more intriguing was the aerial coming out of nowhere. They just could not comprehend how three feet of aerial could come out of six inches of space. They sat there for hours afterwards pulling the aerial up and down. I gave them steel axes and they gave me a couple of bone daggers, beautiful things, which I've still got. They told me they were made from the legs of men killed in battle. After three or four hours they brought the women and children in.

Some time after Vass had demonstrated the power of his rifle by shooting two pigs they explained that a spirit in a tree was destroying their crops and generally harassing the community. Could he shoot it? Not wishing to appear either unco-operative or ineffective, Vass put a shot through the tree. On a second patrol a year later he was greeted by enthusiastic people who showed him the dead tree. Vass savours the thought that he is probably the only *kiap* to have killed a tree with a single shot.

Missionaries were contacting Papua New Guineans along the coast before the colonial governments arrived, and they continued to be the first foreigners into many areas. French Catholics, German and American Lutherans, English Congregationalists and Australian Methodists

brought diversity to the meetings of cultures. Miners and recruiters, too, continued to move in front of the government in some places. Even in the 1930s miners and local communities, with no language in common, were sorting out their different needs for food, labour, land, women and trade goods. But in nearly all first contact situations other Papua New Guineans stood between the villagers and the foreigners. Papua New Guineans from other areas were always there guiding, interpreting and sometimes directing the meeting.

In November, 1953, Patrol Officer Gerald Szarka and Cadet Patrol Officer Geoff Harris were patrolling out of Telefomin in the far west. When the two officers were separated by several hours walk the Eliptamin people attacked, axing to death both Australians and two New Guinean policemen. Szarka was thirty years old and Harris twenty-one. The Eliptamin had no idea that their attack would bring a response from so many foreigners with such great powers to punish. The incident was a late reminder to the field staff that they were often close to violence.

In an ambush or a rush attack there could only be a hectic scramble for survival, but equally worrying for a government officer was the situation that developed slowly. An officer had to decide at what point he would use his gun. When he was mapping in the Southern Highlands in 1937 Ivan Champion was involved in an incident that moved gradually to violence.

> *If there's someone in the crowd that's got malaria and got a headache, whack some Aspro into him, even if it's a double dose. You get rid of his headache. And it has a surprising effect on people; you've got some strength that they haven't got.*
> **David Marsh**

As he moved down a ridge a policeman warned him that when he turned his back young men were aiming their bows and arrows at him. Champion instructed the policemen to fire if the warriors looked like they were going to release their arrows. They held their fire, but became increasingly aggressive, prancing about and brandishing their arms. The rest of the patrol were still over two miles away. Although Champion believed that an attack would come, he feared that any threat of violence on his part would provoke a mass attack. Just then two old men came forward, and taking Champion by the wrist led him into a creek bed:

> I turned round and there was a chap standing above, a fine young man with bow and arrow. He let fly

From Orokolo, Gulf Province

Wooden basket work, with two
figures and four hooks, from
Yuarma on a tributary of the Yuat
River, East Sepik Province

the fish line fence around their camp on a 'narrow hogback ridge'. In that thickly populated area many people were soon pressed about the camp, 'fine, big, up-standing men with distinctive head-dresses'. They were very aggressive, shouting their peculiar chant, abruptly cutting it off, then uniting to break the silence with a deafening roar. Those that had brought sweet potato to trade threw it over the fish line. They did not need payment, they told the interpreters, because they were soon going to have all the trade goods for themselves. Michael Leahy:

I wrote in my diary: 'Everything is all right here, but there is one big-mouthed bastard parading up and down outside the camp, twirling his stone axe, and I am quite sure his remarks are not at all complimentary'. While I watched him, he raced away through a lane in the crowd up on to a little knoll overlooking the camp and broke off the peace sign, a small leafy twig, the universal sign in this country of peace, and waving it over his head he threw it on the ground and stamped on it. He then dashed down the side of the ridge and reappeared a few minutes later with three spears, two in one hand and one poised in the right hand. He screamed out to the mob down below who opened a laneway through their packed mass right on to our fishline fence where Iwunga, the old boss boy, was at that time guarding the line. I said to Dan, 'Look out, here he comes.' As he raced down the hill I stepped out to stop him if I could. But at the same time I wanted to be quite sure that the multitude understood exactly it was a matter of kill or be killed. If there's one thing the primitive New Guinea native understands it's war; it's kill or be killed. I almost left it too late for a stopping shot and was forced to hit him in the stomach, the biggest target. The first shot hit him, and as he went down another quick shot lifted the top of his head right off, which of course horrified the multitude. But

knocking my hat to one side. I turned to him again and he was aiming another shot. I held up the rifle and hesitated. I thought, 'You've seen this rifle,' but he didn't stop. He started to let go, and I fired. I hit him right in the chest from fifteen feet away. I can always remember the astonishment in his eyes, and over he went.

The crowd's shock at the shot and the death of the man gave Champion the initiative, allowing him to take their arrows and order them to unstring their bows. The incident disturbed Champion who had spent over a decade in peaceful movement through hundreds of miles of country that was not previously known to white men:

I wanted to go through my whole patrol career without ever having to fire a rifle. I failed there and I was very cut up about it. In fact when I got back to the camp on top I felt physically sick. I'll never forget the astounded look as he was hit in the chest. I couldn't miss. I gave him a chance, but he kept at it.

Michael Leahy, who survived a severe wound in an ambush, was given notice of violence in another attack. In 1934 he and his brother Dan were prospecting near Wabag in the highlands. As usual they set

not sufficient to stop my boys shooting. There was a round of shots and I screamed, 'Finish, finish, finish. Him that's all like killim you me'. To which the old boss boy and the other Waria boys said, '*Nogut, nogut masta. Dispela olgeta i laik kilim yumi*'. (No, they all want to kill us.) They showed me our fishline which had been progressively moved in until we were going to be easy victims to a stone axe raid. However the killing of their leader stopped all further hostilities. Before they had gone a hundred yards we called them back again, patched up what wounds we could, and then asked them through our interpreters what the hell did they mean. Some of the old men said, well, we thought you were going to be dead easy. We didn't think those damned things you were carrying would go off like that.

The next day the highlanders, apprehensive but friendly, escorted the prospectors from the area. The speed with which foreigners and villagers re-established communications was characteristic of many brief, violent confrontations.

In spite of the restraint shown by many field staff and the skill that they gained in anticipating responses, the gun was important. In the last resort it was the gun that gave the foreigners their advantage in power. It is impossible to travel far in Papua New Guinea without meeting a community whose history has been changed by rifle fire.

The villagers' reaction to early patrols was often determined by the values of a particular Papua New Guinea community and by internal politics unknown to the foreigners. The Binandere were a strong and warlike people occupying the north coast of Papua. When Captain Moresby arrived on their shores he came from the direction of their enemies. The Binandere, as John Waiko explains, could not allow strangers to come unchallenged on to their land. They attacked and Moresby shot one of them. That initial encounter, John Waiko argues, helped determine subsequent relationships between the Binandere and white men.

The Binandere waited eleven years to pay back the attack by Moresby. In 1895 they killed George Clark, the leader of a team of Queensland prospectors. But the miners and government officers then combined in a punitive raid to shoot and gaol many Binandere. Again the balance of the dead was against the Binandere. Even those Binandere who went to work for the foreigners felt the obligation to seek revenge. A Binandere policeman serving with John Green, the government officer, plotted the retaliatory attack. Green, an unusual man, spent a long time with the villagers learning their language and trying to gain their confidence, but that could not save him against the Binandere's deep sense of grievance. When warriors armed with spears and axes had surrounded the station, the policeman went to Green. John Waiko, himself a Binandere, continues the story:

He asked Green, who was up on the rafter of a house that they were building, if he could have his revolver. He said he wanted to shoot some pigeons perched on a low branch. Green, probably wanting to lunch on pigeon, gave him the revolver. As soon as he got it, he threw it into a creek and gave a signal to the warriors. They beat their drums, sang their war songs and massacred the whole government force except for a few of the police. They took the bodies to the village, and lined them up to make sure that they equalled the number of Binandere who had been killed. Then they cut the bodies, cooked them and ate them. And one of the famous stories is that a warrior thought that Green's boots were part of the white man's leg. He started eating them, and when he found the small nails, he thought these were bones—until somebody told him about his mistake. But the point I want to emphasise is that the way the Binandere responded to the intrusion of the whites depended on that initial contact.

On the very eve of Independence there were isolated communities still making that initial contact.

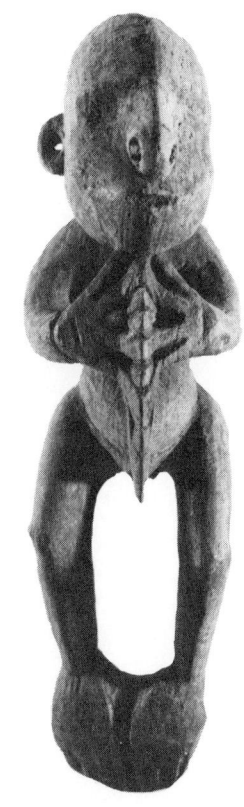

Wooden figure, female, *kangabungdimangu*, from Kraimbit village, Karawari River, Sepik Province

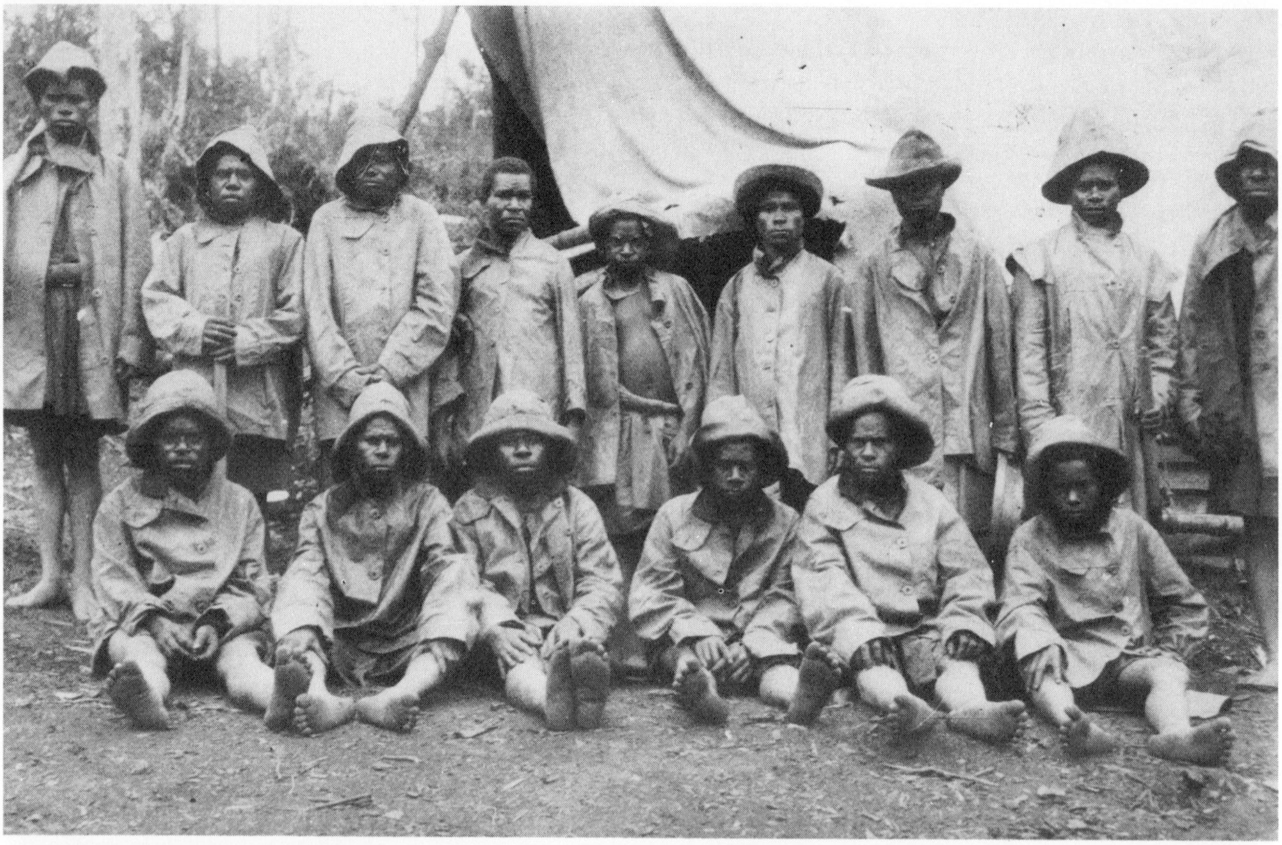

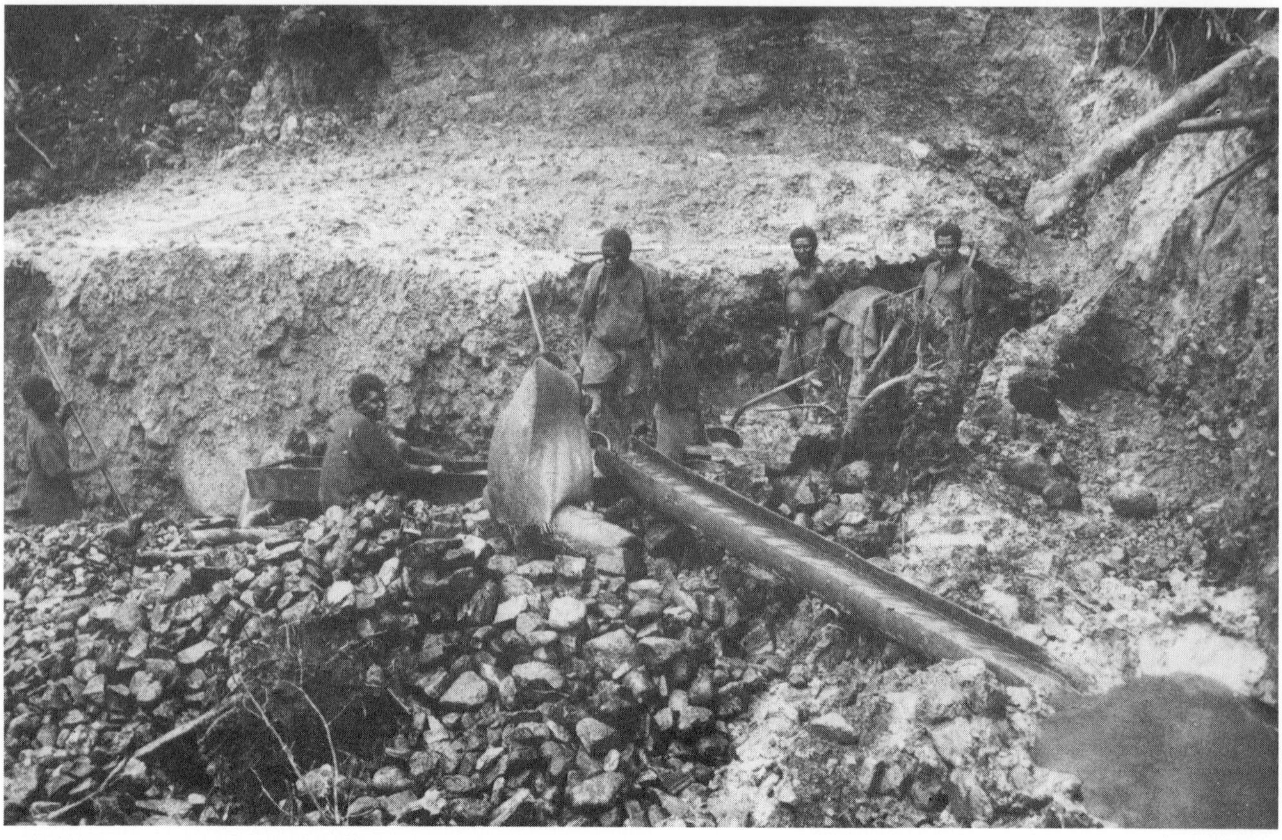

16 Gold!

*In the early days there was nothing in the way of lodes and reefs, as they call them;
it was all box and dish or sluicing, sluice boxes. You shovel the dirt in, the riffles in
the boxes catch the gold. The water coming in through the box or a flume washes
all the stones and the sand away, and leaves the gold stuck in the riffles. That's how
you catch it. And then you wash up at night. Might wash up fifty ounces, might
wash up five or six. But it was only worth two pounds six an ounce then. Now the
same gold would be worth about four to five hundred dollars. There's a lot of
difference. Between eight dollars and eight hundred. Eight dollars! Eight! It's not
laughable, it's cryable. We had to work hard, too, to get that eight dollars.*

Bob Franklin, miner

From their earliest sightings of New
Guinea, Europeans assumed that somewhere in the interior they would find
gold. The ruggedness of the mountains,
the denseness of the vegetation, the very
secretiveness of the interior, seemed to
convince them that those ranges that they
could see from the decks of their ships
concealed a great treasure. Prospectors and
miners were the foreigners most likely to
go beyond the beaches. But the first pay-
able gold was actually discovered in the
islands of the south-east, on Sudest,
Misima and Woodlark. In the 1890s small
fields were opened on the mainland on
the Gira River and on the Yodda near
Kokoda. In 1910 most miners shifted
south to the Lakekamu. All the early gold
discoveries, all the small fields and dis-
appointments, had been in Papua. Then in
1926 Bill Royal tried the alluvial in Edie
Creek, 7000 feet up on the slopes of
Mount Kaindi and six days' walk from the
beach at Salamaua. Fifty years after the
first hopeful miners had gone inland from
Port Moresby, they had at last found the
big one.

Old miners who had spent years chasing elusive pennyweights on minor fields
were among the first to stake claims on
the new Morobe goldfield. Within
months they had taken out more gold

than they had seen in years of bending
over the sluice boxes. Norman Sandford,
going north from Cairns, saw them after
days of hard celebration: they were
trundled back to the ship slumped in
wheelbarrows. Young men from Australia joined the rush. Michael Leahy was
one who gave up his job in Queensland to
take ship to the Mandated Territory:

In Rabaul we ran into an obstacle. We
heard that we were required to have
sufficient money to ensure a return
passage rather than becoming a charge
on the administration of the Territory.
We overcame that by pooling our
resources into quite a respectable sized
roll of currency, and as one came out
of the Government Secretary's office
he handed it to the next chap going in.
The same roll eventually got us all the
necessary permit to proceed to
Salamaua.

Perched on a narrow peninsula on the
south of the Huon Gulf, Salamaua was a
crude settlement littering a beautiful setting. As the 'jumping off place for miners
going to Edie Creek' it offered the services of a Burns Philp and a Carpenter's
store, a 'primitive hotel' and a straggle of
miners' shacks along the beach. Bob
Franklin remembers the way that he
acquired his 'residence':

Indentured mining labourers
wearing their sou'westers (top left)

A 'team' putting in a sluice box on
one of the workings at Edie Creek
(bottom left)

EDIE CREEK HOTEL

6000 Feet Above Sea Level

Come and Rest at Mount Kaindi

Healthy, perfect climate in
New Guinea's greatest goldfield
Wonderful scenery by road from
Bulolo and Wau

Miss. A. Allan,
Proprietress

The Papuan Courier January 23, 1942

The bloke at the pub said 'Well, you need a house to sleep in'. I said 'Yes, I'll want a house'. So he said 'I'll get you a house built for four pounds, good house'. Native materials, of course, *saksak* (sago leaves) and bush poles. Four pounds. Not bad. You wouldn't get that now, would you, in Sydney town?

As a meeting point of the hopeful on the way in and the successful or disappointed on the way out, Salamaua developed, Bert Weston says, as a 'unique community':

A lot of them were returned Australian soldiers from World War I so there was a strong sense of mateship. The hotel was the rendezvous, all the time, day and night. It even sported a billiard table in a rough tin shack. Drinks were served in the primitive goldfields way of putting the bottle on the bar. You helped yourself. You paid each time that you had a drink, but you filled what you wanted. The barman said that he won in the long run because the miners tended to pour a good noggin first, but as they got drunker they'd taper off. I saw on one occasion forty miners down from Edie Creek to meet the boat, breasting the bar, bottles of spirits and beer from one end of the bar to the other. One well-known character, Normie Neal, who was manager of the Day Dawn mine, got up on the end of the bar and ran along kicking all the bottles off. He just said, 'Set them up again!'—which cost him forty pounds for the shout.

The Depression was just around the corner and men went up from Australia looking for fame and fortune. They'd get off the boat at Salamaua, go into the pub and it was on for everybody, liberty hall. They'd get talking to a successful miner who was down. They used to come down to meet the boat to get a bit of fresh meat and so forth. Next thing the chap would be given a claim. These miners would peg out more than one claim and under the regulations they had to

man them within twelve months or forfeit them. Well, they'd have this claim crying out to be worked, so they'd say to the chap, 'I'll give you a claim to work and a couple of boys'. That was the start of a fortune for quite a few fellows.

Mick Leahy had no such easy introduction to the goldfields. Without labourers, he carried his own pack. One optimistic member of the party had four mules, but once they left the level going of the coastal strip the miners had to take over the mule packs. Stranded with useless mules and no carriers, Leahy heard that the miners at Edie were about to ballot for claims. Leaving the main party, he and a companion, Jack Logan, pushed ahead to the Bulolo River, then climbed a further 3000 feet up to the cold, mist-shrouded Edie Creek. Leahy won a claim, one hundred by two hundred feet, but without stores and labourers he could not mine. When he fell ill with malaria his very survival was at risk. Camped in a lean-to at 7000 feet, he realised that his life as well as his livelihood depended on pushing back to the coast. He struggled down to Salamaua to rest and to recruit labourers.

> *Eight days to go in and four days to get back. Up and down. No roads, just native tracks. Rough shelters at night to sleep under. And it rained all the time.*
> **Bob Franklin**

In Australia the miners took pride in themselves as workers; they were the independent diggers. In Papua New Guinea they were employers and *mastas*. They were dependent on a gang of labourers. A miner could not stay on the goldfield unless he had stores, and all cargo had to be carried on Papua New Guinean backs. The lone miner could not clear the vegetation, move the overburden, dig the water races, and put tons of alluvial through the sluice boxes. That needed a team of perhaps ten men. The carrying and labouring on the goldfields was often extremely hard and coastal men were strangers in the cold, wet country of the

Old mess hut at Edie Creek showing the warden's quarters, the courthouse and police headquarters in foreground, 1929

mountains. Returning labourers told stories of the harsh life and 'Kaindi', as they called the goldfield, became a place for workers to avoid. But the diggers had to get labourers.

They could, as Bert Weston explains, approach the professional recruiters, Clem Hendry and Gregor McDonald, on the beach:

> You bought, as we used to call them, slaves. You'd buy native labourers from them at about ten pounds a head. Otherwise you had to gird up your loins and head out into the blue into the mountains, up the Markham Valley or around the coast—and recruit them yourself.

But, as Bob Franklin found, recruiting could take a lot of hard talking. Although he told the villagers all that he thought they wanted to hear and was generous with trade goods, he found the people were eager for him to move on, sometimes offering him 'one stupid looking bloke' just to get rid of him. Bert Weston:

> Having done the rounds of the villages, you'd eventually set off down to the coast, an eighty-mile tramp. This was the time when some of the more unscrupulous recruiters used dog chains and padlocks. Every night they'd chain the boys up because the further they got from home, the more homesick they'd get, and they'd try to break back. Eventually you'd get them down to Lae and take them by pinnace across to Salamaua for signing-on. Once they got across the water they couldn't break back, they were trapped.

The New Guinean labour clerk checked that each recruit was issued with a wooden box in which he could keep his personal goods, a laplap, a blanket, an enamel bowl and a spoon. Each man then said that he was willing to work, the '*masta* was a good man too much', and they put their thumb print on the contract:

> The boy did regard this as binding. Once that print went on, you had them. They seldom deserted or played up. They were paid six shillings a month, three shillings in their hand at the end of each month, and three shillings deferred.

The first task of the labourer was to carry stores. 'They'd kick off with fifty pounds.' The rough track, the rain, 'nothing but rain', and the flimsy shelters at night were not the only hazards. In the early days on the field the villagers in the Kaisenik area expressed their resentment against the intruders by 'picking off the stragglers'. John Fox says that they had to keep an armed miner at the end of the line to guard the last carrier from being 'kaikaied'. If the labourer stayed on the carrier line he was twelve days on the

Goldfields Aerial Transport Service

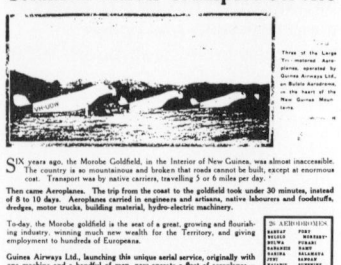

Three of the Large Tri-motored Aeroplanes operated by Guinea Airways Ltd. on Bulolo Aerodrome, in the heart of the New Guinea Mountains.

SIX years ago, the Morobe Goldfield, in the interior of New Guinea, was almost inaccessible. The country is so mountainous and broken that roads cannot be built, except at enormous cost. Transport was by native carriers, travelling 5 or 6 miles per day.

Then came Aeroplanes. The trip from the coast to the goldfield took under 30 minutes, instead of 8 to 10 days. Aeroplanes carried in engineers and artisans, native labourers and foodstuffs, dredges, motor trucks, building material, hydro-electric machinery.

To-day, the Morobe goldfield is the seat of a great, growing and flourishing industry, winning much new wealth for the Territory, and giving employment to hundreds of Europeans.

Guinea Airways Ltd., launching this unique aerial service, originally with one machine and a handful of men, now operate a fleet of aeroplanes—including three very large tri-motored monoplanes—and employ 80 Europeans and a numerous native staff. Their aeroplanes run on fixed time-tables from Lae, Salamaua, Bulolo, Wau and Port Moresby, carrying passengers and freight, and maintaining regular communication between 26 aerodromes.

New parties of Prospectors are constantly springing up new country, pushing steadily into the almost unknown interior. They make camp, and clear an aerodrome, and, within a few days, Guinea Airways' planes are arriving with supplies. This pioneering work goes on ceaselessly. Guinea Airways, with their unique experience, skilled personnel and modern equipment, are ready and waiting to operate wherever they are needed.

GUINEA AIRWAYS LTD
LAE · SALAMAUA

The Pacific Islands Monthly
August 22, 1933

---

track before he was back in Salamaua. In that time he had consumed much of the load that he had started out with. Franklin estimates: 'You had to have roughly sixteen boys to keep four working on the goldfield'.

> *I was up to my knees in water and slush, and I was hoping to God there was no gold there. I asked old Jim Scobie what it was like. He was a good hearty drinker like the rest of them. 'Well', he said, 'the only way I can describe the place is, it's Madman's Gully, it's Flyshit Creek.'*
> **Jim Leahy**

Edie Creek, the centre of the richest alluvial area, was 'full of old miners, good old hardy types', men that Jim Leahy remembers having names such as 'Yukon Smith and Klondike something else'. Bert Weston:

> They lived a pretty rough life. It was 7000 feet up which, even in the tropics, is bitterly cold. Most of them built a primitive hut out of flattened biscuit tins—they were large tins—and whatever timber they could scrounge. Most of them had a fire going all day. Rum was the main beverage. Everything was inflated in price. A handful of nails cost an ounce of gold. Of course gold was only worth about eight dollars an ounce. Rice was the main food for the natives, tinned meat for the miners. The classic thing to do was to pull all the labels off so you didn't know what you were getting each day. You might be having tinned tripe or you might be having sausages.

The labourers had no chance of a surprise with their *kaikai*.

Jim Leahy soon learnt the truth of Mark Twain's definition of a good goldmine: it was a 'hole in the ground owned by a liar'. But some men were washing fortunes in Edie's dull-coloured gold. With an experienced team of labourers, a miner could sit in his hut, stroll about and yarn, then wander back to his claim in the evening to clean up the day's takings. Mrs Billie Bourke:

Did you hear about the old fellow with the glass eye on the goldfields? He got pretty bored just standing there watching the natives shovelling alluvial through the boxes. So he said, 'See this eye of mine, I'm going to put it on this post. Don't you dare stop working, it will watch you, and it will tell me when I get back if any of you have been loafing.' But after they had been working for a while, one of the labourers crept up behind the eye and put a tin over the top of it so they could all sit down for a good laze.

That was a standard story told about many plantations and goldfields. In their turn the labourers had their stories and laughed at the *mastas*. But on Edie the labourers were often on the losing side. By 1930 over one hundred had died of dysentery and another sixty were dead from respiratory disease. Others had been killed on the track in clashes with local villagers. In the early days on Edie conditions were as tough as they had been on the earlier goldfields. Like other frontier settlements, Salamaua, Wau and Edie were places of excitement, brutality and memorable camaraderie. Ela Birrell, who was on the Morobe field as a young girl with her mother and hotel keeper, Flora Stewart, speaks of the miners as trustworthy, generous and callous. When one died the hat was passed around and funds sent to any surviving widow or children. But Ela also remembers a funeral at Salamaua's flat and water-logged cemetery. The rain poured down as the miners stood around, some still in their pyjamas and many suffering the after-effects of a prolonged wake. To the astonishment of the drenched mourners, the coffin suddenly emerged from the saturated grave and floated seaward. The miner who had had been reading the service said, 'Oh bugger you. If you can't wait, read it yourself'. The miners retired to the hotel, leaving the dead man's son to decide how to discharge his duty to the wandering coffin.

On another occasion Ela Birrell and her mother visited the miners at Edie:

We sent out word to invite all the miners to come to Jim Scobie's place.

We took our cooked chicken with us, and all sorts of food. In those days the roads were like—well, they weren't roads, they were bush tracks. Of course it sounds dreadful now, but every man who had his own boy had given him the name of a car, 'Buick' or 'Ford'. When they wanted to go home, they would call for their 'car', and the boy would piggy-back them. We were shocked about this, but it's true. They would have broken their necks because they only had little mountain tracks to go on. Anyway we invited them along to join us and everybody had to do an item. Jim Scobie was very shy and he went behind the 'house cook'. We said, 'What are you doing, Jim?' And he said, 'I'm broadcasting.' He sang his song, but we didn't look at him.

Mother made pufftaloons. They're fried scones and you have them with golden syrup. Of course, the miners, not having any home cooking for so long, thought this was absolutely heaven. Then everybody washed gold. It was a fantastic holiday for me. There was no way they could give children lollies or anything like that, so everybody gave me a nugget. I had a Champion Ruby tin full of nuggets from all over the country.

It was hard for the fourteen-year-old Ela to return to school in Australia, and equally hard for her companions to believe the stories she told.

By November 1926 there were 219 miners and 1324 New Guinean labourers on the Edie Creek field. Recruiters began to range more widely to get the urgently needed labour. Weston, pushing into newly opened country beyond Kaiapit, a 'place no good' where 'man i savvy fight too much', was ambushed in a narrow valley. As the regulations required, Weston's party was well-armed. Dodging arrows and shooting whenever they saw a target, the recruiters withdrew. Weston killed one determined club-swinging warrior: 'I pistolled him in mid air'. Many of Weston's labourers were wounded, and Weston himself was doctored by his 'cook boy' who used his teeth to extract an arrow shaft from his boss's rump and then filled the wound with Friar's Balsam.

As the easy alluvial on Edie was worked out, the miners too began moving out into new—and dangerous—country. Four miners—Naylor, Clarius, Baum and McGrath—were killed in the early 1930s. Jim Leahy recalls the attack on his brothers when they were 'prospecting in the Kukukuku country':

In the middle of the night my brothers were attacked. Mick got a hit on the head with a stone club and Paddy got a few spears in him. This was a few days away from civilisation. They were able to defend themselves and win the fight, then they managed to get back and get attended to.

Paddy was enjoying, but retarding, his recovery by drinking heavily. Under threat from Mick, the other miners agreed not to supply Paddy with alcohol. But the next day when Mick arrived they had all obviously been 'on the booze'. There was a temporary halt in consumption as the miners waited for a labourer to make the fifteen-mile walk to Bulolo to pick up another supply. The 'cargo boy' was on a bonus calculated according to the speed of his trip. Jim Leahy:

In record time the boy came back with a case of Dewars. Mick said, 'Who owns this?' And they all said, 'It's not mine, Mick'. And Paddy, who was very full, said, 'That's mine'. Mick said, 'Right'. He ran down to the creek, pulled the top off the case, and bottle by bottle he smashed them on the rocks. I can always remember my brother Paddy coming home and telling me, 'That bloody Mick. I said, "Well, leave the last bottle". Mick said, "The last bottle!" And he went bang. There wasn't a bloody drop left.' The miners were all standing about with their mouths open, parched, because they'd finished all the drink the night before. And here's the poor boy who'd run up and back to get the case only to see it wrecked.

At least the runner was paid his hard earned bonus.

The Pacific Islands Monthly
August 15, 1939

Aircraft quickly made Morobe different from any previous Territory goldfield. By the end of 1927 four airlines were operating between Lae and Wau. Freight prices dropped, but there was still the problems of carrying stores up the last fifteen miles and 3000 feet to the claims on Edie. Fred Deckert took much of the burden from the mules and New Guinean backs by cutting the chasis of a truck and reconstructing a special, narrow vehicle. Although Deckert's truck lost something in stability and elegance, it could negotiate the narrow ledge that passed for a road. To the miners taking the truck, it became 'dicing with death with Deckert'.

There was a casualness, too, in the way the miners used the aircraft. Bert Weston:

Gold was carried in a most haphazard manner. At one period I was in Lae acting as beach manager for an aircraft freighting company. A miner would come down from Edie Creek with perhaps 500 ounces of gold in a tea tin. The fellow would drop his gold, perhaps on the pilot's seat or anywhere, and go and get sozzled. He'd think no more about it. There'd be no freight notes, dockets or anything. But when the plane arrived at Lae the next morning, I'd have a look, and I might find half a dozen lots of gold—in tea tins, tobacco tins, and some very carefully sewn up in little canvas parcels. I'd throw the gold in a box under my bed until the launch came across from Salamaua, eighteen miles away. I'd just put it into a wheelbarrow, and tell the boy to take it down to the beach and put it on the launch. I've had as much as three thousand ounces under my bed, labelled in the most casual way. Two lots came down once from a chap in white woollen socks, just tied up at the top. Written on one sock in indelible pencil was 'BP from Scotty' (Burns Philp from Scotty). There was never any instance of it being lost. It all got there by divers means, passed on from hand to hand, everybody trusted everybody else.

Over thousands of years creeks had washed gold from the slopes of Mount Kaindi. The Bulolo Valley had become a massive deposit of silt, gravel and fine gold. It was too poor for the individual miners. But for a company with the capital to install dredges capable of treating millions of yards of alluvial in a year, the Bulolo was a rich field. It was, as one mining engineer said, 'the world's most important placer deposit ... since Klondike'. The problem was to move the dredges, the hydro-electricity plant, the workshops and the town to house the mining community from the beach to the Bulolo Valley. The Bulolo Gold Dredging Company made the bold decision to shift everything by air. That decision put New Guinea on the frontier of aerial engineering. In 1931 Guinea Airways carried nearly eight times as much freight as the combined airlines of the United States. Flying Dr Dickson's Baby Austin car from Lae to Wau was simple compared with the heaviest of the dredge parts. Bertie Heath was one of the pioneer aviators:

A typical day started at half past six in the morning. The planes were loaded overnight. If the weather conditions were good you took off and if they weren't you might have to wait for an hour or two. You'd get the thing in, the cranes would unload it, you'd get back again, and by that time another plane was loaded and you could step out of one into another.

At Bulolo the plane taxied up to the crane which lifted the cargo straight from the plane to its position on the dredge. One of the Junkers trimotors made nine trips in a day and all the freight planes were expected to make thirty flights a week.

The biggest of the dredges weighed nearly 4000 tons. Shifted piece by piece, they were assembled by teams of riveters, many of whom had previously worked on the Sydney Harbour Bridge. First the barge was built, launched, and then the massive super-structure constructed. When the power was turned on, the bucket line, the winches, and the tumbling of hundreds of tons of rock released a cacophony of screeching and thumping.

Eventually eight dredges were gouging their way through the valley.

A special town was built at Bulolo to house the mining staff. Physically and socially Bulolo was a sharp contrast to the egalitarian crudity of early Salamaua and Edie. Andrée Millar:

> We had three kinds of houses. Type 1 was for the general manager. Type 2 was for the next layer and Type 3 was for everybody else. The life really depended on the people themselves. If you were a snob, you didn't ask people in Type 3 to visit, and if you weren't, you all mixed, and you got on. But you had some funny incidents where people thought they couldn't have you to tea because you lived in a Type 3 house, or when somebody in a Type 3 was invited to tea by the general manager's wife and she thought all her Christmases had come at once. It never seemed to worry the men very much, but it did worry the women. I think it was because they didn't have enough to do. In Lae, Port Moresby and Madang there were jobs, serving in stores and all this kind of thing before local people took them over. But on Bulolo there weren't. Everything was company.

The dredges kept churning after the war broke out in Europe. Production reached a peak in 1940 when over 180 000 ounces were taken from the Bulolo Valley. Bulolo Gold Dredging was by far the most profitable company to work in New Guinea before the war. In the ten years from 1932 it made a profit of $32 000 000. Then suddenly the Japanese were in Rabaul. In March 1942 they took Lae and Salamaua, and seemed poised to push inland. Amid confusing reports of Japanese troop movements, the Australian commander of Kanga Force decided that the Japanese were about to break into the Bulolo Valley. In fact the Japanese did not make their move for another four months. But the order was given to destroy all assets. Bob Franklin:

> I burnt Wau down, with two others. We were out in the middle of the night with nothing. The army didn't give us a box of matches even. We were told to go and burn the place down. We'd get a nice house going up in flames, get a cane-bottomed chair alight, and use that to burn the next house. By the time you got across to the next place, the chair would have gone out. You'd try to go back into the house, but it would be too hot. You ever try to burn a town down? Don't try. Anyway we did a good job. Only one house didn't burn.

Bob Franklin saw Edie in its earliest days, and he was an instrument and a spectator when the Morobe field was destroyed.

Although the dredges gouged into the Bulolo alluvial again in the post-war, they never reached their pre-war significance; and the old drama of the industry was gone. The number seven dredge still stands where it finished up, at the head of the Bulolo Valley. Like a rusting dinosaur it sits in a patch of brilliantly green grass surrounded by the heaps of mullock and rubble it tore from the river bed.

17 The Good News

A lot of things have been taken from us, and they are now in Europe. The missionaries considered them to be bad ... And of course they have their scientists to study our culture. What about our future generations? How will they study their own culture when they have been deprived of their own things?

Michael Somare

When the new nation of Papua New Guinea adopted its constitution in 1975 the people pledged themselves 'to guard and pass on ... our noble traditions and the Christians principles that are ours now'. They also declared that their nation was established under the 'guiding hand of God'. One hundred years of work by Christian missionaries had clearly had a profound effect. But the early attempts to make converts were not successful. In the 1840s Catholic missionaries went to the islands of Woodlark and Umboi. They laboured for eight years through malaria, semi-starvation and rejection before they finally left the islands and the graves of their colleagues. In 1872 the London Missionary Society settled South Sea Island Christians on the south coast, and in 1874 the Reverend William Lawes built his station in Port Moresby. The next year the Methodists began work in the New Guinea islands. Permanent mission work had begun on the coast ten years before either the British or the Germans set up their governments.

By 1890 the major Protestant missions in Papua had defined their spheres of influence. The government enforced their separation by the neat device of not letting a mission take up land outside its own sphere. The LMS sought souls on the south coast, the Anglicans worked on the north-east, and, as the Reverend Percy Chatterton says, 'a good hefty range of mountains in the middle prevented us from running into one another'. The Methodists made their base in the islands of the south-east. The Catholics, who said they were not bound by the agreement, generally accepted the 'comity of missions'. They moved through the LMS on the coast to the hinterland north-east of Yule Island.

In 1901 the Reverend James Chalmers, the Reverend Oliver Tomkins, nine Papuan Mission students and two other Papuans went ashore on Goaribari Island in the Papuan Gulf. They were killed and eaten. The incident, a rare case of one of the commonest events in stories and cartoons of the South Pacific, generated world-wide interest. Government officers in punitive raids shot many Goaribari. Three years after Chalmers was killed a young Englishman, the Reverend Ben Butcher, arrived to take over the LMS station at Daru. His colleagues advised him not to go into the Goaribari area and Sir Hubert Murray warned him: 'those Goaribari men are as wild as hawks'. But he got his chance when he met a Goari-

Catholic mission, Nissan 1949

From the *Nupela Testamen*, The New Testament in New Guinea Pidgin

GUTNIUS BILONG JISAS KRAIST

Matyu	*I*	*Raitim*	*Mt*	*11*
Mak	*I*	*Raitim*	*Mk*	*120*
Luk	*I*	*Raitim*	*Lu*	*188*
Jon	*I*	*Raitim*	*Jo*	*303*

WOK BILONG OL APOSEL   *Ap 383*

Good News, or *Gutnuis* in Pidgin, is the Gospel.

Sister Mary Martha Kettle

bari man who had been away to work on a plantation. The man was now stranded. To get home he had to travel across the land and water of enemy peoples. Taking the young Goaribari man on board, Butcher sailed west. In an interview with James Peter of the ABC in 1972 the Reverend Butcher, who was born in 1877, recalled how, as they felt their way in through the shallow waters, canoes kept putting off from each village so that soon they

Sister Mary Martha Kettle:
There were four sisters in the first group. Three of them are buried in New Ireland. One of them said that they had sago as a kind of porridge for breakfast, sago pancakes for dinner and sago balls for tea. In the end they were given a choice: if they wanted to go back to Thursday Island, they were free to do so. They said no, and they went inland, into the Mekeo, up the river. I remember the sisters saying they were bereft of everything. They didn't have mosquito nets, nothing; they had no idea what they were coming to. But they just hung on and hung on. Many of them died, died with blackwater fever mostly. But they stuck it out, and now we've spread out everywhere through Mekeo.

were being followed by a tremendous crowd of shouting men who were all armed with their bows and arrows. I made my way past the people where Chalmers was killed to where this man had his home. And there we anchored. I couldn't get near because it was very shallow water off the village. So I went ashore in one of their canoes. There was great excitement; but having brought back a man they had thought was dead gave me an introduction. As we went ashore the men collared me and my one boy who was with me. They were shouting something and we could only make out one or two words which were like words in the language further west. Among the words was *zapia* which meant 'kill', and we were thinking that we might be killed when we got ashore. But when we got ashore I was taken up to the big house crowded with men. The place was full of excitement. I saw a dead pig lying there and I knew then that the killing referred to the pig and not to us. The pig was presented to us as a gift, a token of thanksgiving for bringing back their man.

For most missionaries, malaria and lack of regular nourishing rations were more likely to be lethal than the people they went to convert. When the Roman Catholic church set up permanent stations in Papua, it had faith but little material support. The first sisters of the Daughters of Our Lady of the Sacred Heart went from Thursday Island to Yule Island in 1887 when the mission was still struggling through its 'very, very hard beginnings'.

Unlike some Protestant missionaries who gave a part of their career in the church to mission work, many Catholics went with little hope of ever seeing their homeland again. Theresa Bloxham:
Across from Aitape we had a reef with a number of islands on it. The biggest island was Tumleo. The others were Selio, Ali and Angel. On the island of Tumleo six sisters had been dropped. They had been there some considerable time when I went to Aitape at the beginning of 1937. They ran a native hospital, and they lived

Hula Mission Station, Papua about 1916

entirely on their own and relied on supplies dropped off by the shipping which came through at three or four monthly intervals. I was quite oblivious at first that these women were there and I would have given anything to talk to the sisters. In two years I never managed to get over there. They were never taken from their island. I imagine they stayed there until they died, because that is what happened with most of the missions in the case of women. While I knew that they were doing a tremendous job I felt angry....

The Reverend Eric and Mrs Ure ran the LMS mission on Daru pre-war and like missionaries everywhere learned to make the best of what they had. The need for improvisation had now replaced the fear of starvation. Mrs Ure:

I needed to know how to cook sea birds' eggs, turtles' eggs, dugong, turtle and bush pig. And there weren't any books to tell me any of these things. Fortunately there was a woman on the station, the wife of the head pastor, Maggie. She was a marvellous person. She had been cook girl to James Chalmers when he was there, and eventually she lived in the house in which we lived. She taught me how to take the mud crabs, boil them and take the meat out, and those nice red shells, and all the lovely things that you can mix together and turn into a very attractive dish. She taught me how to cook dugong. It needed an awful lot of boiling; it was better minced unless it was very young. The turtle meat was strange. At first it looked like veal, but if you cut it it jumped, the nerves were all still alive, and when you put it in a pan as likely as not a piece would hop right out. I tried to set jelly while we were out there, I was just longing for a bit of jelly. I was told that I could set it overnight, but who wants jelly for breakfast?

Inevitably the mission house was the centre of a culture as well as of a religion. Although the Anglican missionaries at Dogura lived on token salaries they sustained 'a certain formality for meals'. Miss Marva Keckwick:

We maintained a standard, or we tried to, for meals and for entertaining. When we had visitors there would be clean tablecloths, table napkins, and nicely polished silver—which was old and battered generally. And so was the china. But we always tried to maintain that standard. It wasn't easy. It was tinned meat, unless you got a bit of fresh fish; a certain number of tinned vegetables, apart from a rather monotonous diet of sweet potatoes,

Reverend H J and Mrs Short and
Giro Paulo, Hula Mission Station
about 1916

pumpkins and greens which were generally pumpkin tips. We did as much as possible in training the Papua New Guinea children to keep a nice outlook on domestic life.

The missionaries succeeded in educating some Papua New Guineans in the social arts of the Western middle class. Visitors who have taken afternoon tea with the local pastor have been the wondering beneficiaries.

The missionaries were also deeply involved in formal education. Virtually all the pre-war schools for Papua New Guineans were provided by the missions with little government assistance in Papua, and none in New Guinea. But when a missionary first went among a community he had to convey what writing was before he could attempt to teach it. Ben Butcher, sitting in the long house with the skulls of the slain dangling above him, would take down words phonetically. The people, looking over his shoulder, were unable to associate the strange marks with the sounds. The moment of comprehension came suddenly:

I was building a house on my station and some of these wild fellows came in to see what we were doing. They were wandering around and I wanted a tool that was up at my house on the hill. So I picked up a sliver of wood that one of my helpers had just adzed off a log and with my carpenter's pencil I wrote on it what I wanted. I called one of these men and told him to take it up to my wife and it would tell her what I wanted and he would bring it. He looked at this piece of wood and then he looked at me as if I were making a fool of him. I had a job in explaining I was quite serious. Very reluctantly he started up the hill and all his fellows were sitting there, sniggering and laughing. It looked so silly to them for a big man to be carrying a little piece of wood up the hill. After a while I saw him coming down. He'd gone up very slowly, but now he was coming down in leaps, down the hill he came. He had the tool in his hand, he gave it to me, and then he rushed off with the piece of wood and showed it to them. 'Look,' he said, 'look what this man has done. I took this piece of wood and he made it talk. I took it up the hill and it talked.' Now that was the first realisation they had of what writing might mean: making things talk. And from then we went on.

Butcher translated the gospels so that they might read in their own language; but he was interested to see that immediately, and on their own initiative, they exploited the 'gift of the written word' by sending letters to each other.

Within the missions there were always arguments about the extent and nature of the churches' involvement in education. Some missionaries thought the schools should be just a means to save souls: the students should be taught reading only because that was a way for them to learn more about Christ. But that was less than many Papuan New Guineans expected. Win Herry, a training school supervisor, remembers his early schooling as

mainly hymn singing, bible reading and some drawing of pictures of early Christians, and all about Bible people. The teachers were not qualified, but just village pastors or missionaries who had no formal education. I am very critical of the policies even today. They are not trying to advance the people, but are influencing members of a Christian church to remain with that church and do various jobs for it.

John Waiko recalls a different characteristic of the village mission school that he attended on the north coast. The Papuan teachers wrote English words on the board and the students had 'terrible difficulty' trying to pronounce them. The teachers would

really punish us. They would pull our ears or bash our heads against something. I remember one occasion when I didn't comb my hair. I got up late from sleep and I had my wash and the bell went. So I came to the classroom without combing my hair. And this teacher got up and said, 'Well, why haven't you combed your hair?' He really got me and bashed my head against the wall. This was the way in which they were teaching us hygiene and smartness.

Olive Dixon says that at her station there was a practical reason for imposing rules of cleanliness before beginning lessons on reading, writing and 'simple arithmetic':

They wore a leaf in their armband that had a very strong smell. When there were about fifty or sixty of them in a fairly small room and it's very hot, you could imagine what it was like. So the first thing, I sent them

down to have a swim; that was my first lesson in hygiene, getting rid of this smelly thing that they were wearing. They did a lot of dancing at night, and goodness knows what went on there, and sometimes they'd come in with their faces painted, and I'd try and get them to clean it off if it was objectionable, but not otherwise.

At higher levels in the mission schools John Waiko encountered an Australian woman who invited students into her home where they talked, read and felt at ease. It was a significant experience for young Papua New Guineans at boarding school suffering their first separation.

> *I came up very anti-missionary. I thought what right had we to go and change these people's beliefs; but, golly, you've only got to go around and see the way the missionaries live, the self-sacrifice, and the way they are respected by the local people. The reason they are respected so much is because nearly all speak, not Motu which government officers learn, but the language of the district. Also they are often in the same area for twenty or twenty-five years, and so they are part of the scene. The other thing I've always observed about missionaries is that they're happy, sparkling-eyed people with a gorgeous sense of humour and remarkably little dissension between them. The ecumenical spirit was very active in Papua New Guinea long before Pope John.*
> **Dame Rachel Cleland**

In the post-war the government declined to subsidise mission schools primarily concerned with religion and teaching in the local language. Les Johnson, the former Director of Education, concedes that there was a case for teaching in the vernacular, assuming a later change to English. But he argues that it seemed impossible to provide adequate written materials in hundreds of different languages. He also wanted to avoid the situation created by some of the missions where they had the Bible and text books printed in one language, and then imposed them on a neighbouring community. That was making a 'foreign vernacular'.

With their long commitment to caring for the body as well as the soul, the missions were from the start important in providing health services. Even when the government rapidly increased its expenditure on public health in the post-war Sir John Gunther estimates that 'at least fifteen per cent of all the medical work' was carried out by mission staff. Hetty Warner was one who entered a mission with the specific aim of caring for the sick. Although not a Christian she attended a church meeting at which a call was for missionaries. Later, while absorbed in the prosaic task of cleaning the bath, she decided that she would serve in the mission. Before going to the Territory she qualified as a nurse. Accompanied by a locally trained nurse and a 'medical boy' she went on patrol by foot and canoe:

> I remember going to one village and nobody was there. I had a little hand gramophone, so I put it on and in no time they were all crowded around. I was able to give injections and quinine because of the gramophone.

Although she 'loved the nursing', she faced many strange situations:

> We had one man who was mauled by a wild pig. We put twenty-three stitches in him. He was very brave too, because my anaesthetist wasn't there, so I had to treat him without an anaesthetic. He stood it all.

When an epidemic of influenza raged through the station she and a fellow sister worked for a week without taking their clothes off. As they sat down to an evening meal feeling absolutely exhausted, a nurse called to say that one of the babies was taking fits: they worked for another five hours. They explained their capacity to keep going with the observation: 'Somebody at home is praying for us'.

The missionaries came to change beliefs and much Papua New Guinean art, as elsewhere, was associated with matters of the spirit. When the missionaries changed one, they inevitably affected the other. But other foreigners also aimed to destroy parts of the old cultures. Recruiters, traders, planters and government officers were all agents of change. Nor were the Papua New Guineans just sitting in their villages waiting to be acted upon. They were as eager to go out and meet the outside world as other villagers in Ireland or Italy. But the missionaries were the most obvious agents of change because they preached the need for change and some of them in moments of zealousness burnt irreplaceable objects of Melanesian art. Encouraged by missionary advice reported by Stephen Takaku as ' "That is rude, that is no good, that's against God" and all that crap', the villagers themselves ceased many of their old artistic practices. Sir Maori Kiki and Percy Chatterton agree that along the south coast of Papua Samoan pastors were sometimes the cultural aggressors. Holding chiefly positions in their own society, they assumed the right to act in a lordly way towards the villagers. Kiki regrets in particular the fact that the Orokolo abandoned their dramatic festivals with their *kovave* and *hevehe* masks, and destroyed the *hohao* boards, objects of art and 'sacred to our people'. Michael Somare points out that it was not just the practices that disappeared, but the cultural record as well. Ironically what the missionaries condemned was being packed and shipped to Munich, the British Museum and the Museum of Primitive Art in New York where it was displayed and admired by members of the missionaries' home cultures. In some cases missionaries themselves were the collectors.

The missionaries measured their success by their ability to change Melanesian religions. By their calling they could not tolerate all of the people's spiritual world; but they varied greatly in the way that they laughed at, ignored or respected the villagers' beliefs. Ben Butcher:

> I never treated their religious ideas with even a smile. I reckoned that these were sacred things to them, very real, and I treated them as that. It was often their beliefs that helped me to give them something further. I

remember sitting in one of their great houses and there was a figure of Iriwaki above my head; Iriwaki, one of the great ancestral spirits. Iriwaki was a great warrior, and always there at the entrance to the great house was his figure with a bone dagger in its belt, and bow and arrow and things like that. Iriwaki was the god of war, and yet he was more than that. I remember sitting and asking the people things about him. I said, 'Do you know anybody who belonged to Iriwaki?' 'Oh yes', they said, 'there's Meriwaki, that's his brother.' 'Ah, well', I said, 'what about his father?' I was amazed when they said, 'But we don't know his father. We've never heard of him. Iriwaki and Meriwaki, yes, but never his father.' 'Ah well', I said, 'I knew his father.' That immediately intrigued them that I should know someone related to their Iriwaki and Meriwaki. I began to talk of God; and at once God became real to them.

Butcher was not of course according validity to their religion; he was, in a sense, exploiting it. But it is also true that missionaries who spent thirty and more years among a particular community acquired more knowledge and respect for a Papua New Guinean culture than any other foreigners. In a strange twist, some missionaries have become guardians of the old village values against what they see as brash, secular modernism.

An old, but basic, question that all missionaries eventually face is: Would the people have been better off had the missionaries stayed at home? Archbishop David Hand answers that it is unjust to separate the missions from the rest of foreign influence. As Papua New Guinea could not forever remain isolated from foreign penetration the question really is whether the missionaries should have entered the country as part of the flow of people, goods and ideas. Papua New Guineans, Hand suggests, had to sink or swim in the modern world and the missionaries have worked to help them swim. He is also strongly critical of those Westerners who believe the Papua New Guinean was once the Noble Savage.

Mission critics under that romantic delusion should see how much of traditional life and society was ruled by sheer fear of upsetting the spirits of the ancestors, sheer fear of sorcery and witchcraft, sheer fear of evil spirits which could cause sickness and death; vendettas, paybacks, fighting. Well the whole thing just falls to the ground.

But Ben Butcher, interviewed in his ninety-fifth year, was not so confident:

I wonder. I think their life was better then than it is now with the vast evils that have been introduced; though I don't know. It's so difficult to say which is the better, or what would have happened. The fighting was always there, and yet it was under control. They would always have had their promiscuous intercourse. But they wouldn't have had their drinking. I don't know. You can't say that it would have been better or worse. Who knows? I remember I was in a village in Papua, a lovely, lovely little place in my part of the country. I'd gone in to have a talk with the people. I was just sitting in the great house, and the men gathered round, and the women came in with only one or two children. 'Oh', I said, 'I want to see the children too. I'd like to see them.' 'But', they said, 'there aren't any children.' I said, 'What?' 'No', they said, 'there are no children now.' And here was a village depopulated by our introduced disease. It was a terrible thing and it came as a great shock. I spoke to the Governor about it, and he sent doctors from Port Moresby to see what could be done and they gradually brought it under some control. That's what I saw with my eyes. Now I don't know. You say, would they have been better without us? I don't know.

In his lifetime Butcher had passed from the confident assumptions made by Victorian Englishmen of their superiority in arms and morals to an old age of sensitive uncertainties.

18 The Mission Rush

Some missions will not baptise a man if he's got more than one wife, and traditionally of course they've got two or three. I've known one man who had seventeen. They are told that they won't go to heaven where all the pigs and kina shells and the marys and the kau kau and all the good things of life are. The majority divorce their wives; they get rid of them. This upsets everything. There's the children and all sorts of things to be taken into consideration. But this particular chap, from a remote area, had three wives and they wouldn't baptise him. The solution was simple: he just killed off two. He could see nothing wrong. He could now be baptised so he could go to heaven. Well, where do you go from there?

Ben Probert, government officer

The Lutheran and Catholic missionaries began work on the north coast of the mainland before the end of the nineteenth century. By the 1920s both churches were employing missionaries from Europe, the United States and Australia. They brought with them a variety of attitudes and cultures. A visitor to a mission station was never sure whether he would be greeted in the accents of the American mid-west, South Australia, Holland or Germany; and he might enjoy the incongruity of sitting down in one of the world's remotest corners to enjoy a meal owing much to French provincial cuisine and French vineyards. Conversation at the table might be conducted in Pidgin, the only language that the white men held in common. But on all established mission fields most Papua New Guineans were converted by other Papua New Guineans. The Lutherans made special use of the black evangelists. The home villages gave the evangelists some support, but generally the New Guinean missionaries showed great self-reliance as they led the advance into the Eastern Highlands. They were also moving well ahead of government officers until miners and *kiaps* made their epic patrols in the 1930s.

Robin Radford, who lived at Kainantu on the eastern edge of the highlands and researched the work of the frontier evangelists, says that the New Guinean missionaries came into the area, negotiated with villagers for the use of local land, and then planted gardens which would later sustain them. The Kate-speaking evangelists were almost as alien to the highlanders as were Europeans. Redford quotes Gapenuo, an evangelist, who wrote in his diary of the way in which the Wampur people perceived the black missionaries:

> Our dead ancestors seem to have come back again, making their living quarters among us. With their big ears (by which he means hats) they cover their heads. They have big wings covering their whole bodies (referring to their laplap and jacket). In the day time they go around, but in the night time they seem to hide in their water basin like eels do.

The Kate missionaries survived threats and rejection to wield great influence as agents of a religion that they had made their own.

Soon after Mick and Dan Leahy and Jim Taylor walked into Mount Hagen in 1933, Mick Leahy wrote to Father William Ross: 'This is a fabulous country; a vast population, a beautiful climate, in fact this is the real New Guinea'. The next

Lutheran Mission Church, Kundiawa Chimbu (left)

Sunday morning at Vunapope, New Britain

year Father Ross made the thirty-eight day walk from the Ramu River to Bundi, crossed into the Chimbu and travelled west to Hagen. Employing hundreds of highlanders and working long hours, the missionaries soon built large stations at Mingende and Hagen.

The Catholic ventures into the highlands were not without cost. After a dispute over a pig, the people of the Chimbu gorge killed Father Carl Morschheuser. A fortnight later they attacked Brother Eugene Frank who died of arrow wounds in Salamaua. Father Ross stayed on in the Western Highlands for forty years. Born in New York, he was heavily bearded, short in stature and full of aggressive energy. Dan Leahy:

> I tell you he was a real missionary. He had nothing. Everything he had, he gave it away. Some old native dying somewhere up in the mountains would sing out for Father Ross and he'd walk all night to get to him.

Like all foreigners in the highlands in the 1930s Father Ross went armed. Dan Leahy continues:

> All the missionaries carried guns. Lutherans, Catholics, everyone. They all had guns, and good ones too. The Lutherans had some of those Mannlichers and Mausers. You had to have a gun.

In fact for a time the Australian government refused entry to miners and missionaries unless they carried adequate means of defence.

Father Ross himself was more inclined to joke than apologise for his gun-carrying:

> Father McEnroe, veteran missionary from Port Moresby, decided to come to Wau across the range, following the Bulldog Trail. While he was in Wau the Guinea Airways pilot told him about Mount Hagen. He said there was a priest there and why didn't he come in and see. So he arrived just about the time we had word Brother Eugene had been killed. I was here alone and Father McEnroe stayed with me. We were walking up to Kuta one day and he was wearing a crucifix. Over in Papua, apparently that was the way they used to greet the people: they'd show the crucifix and the people knew immediately that this was a missionary. He was doing that here, and I said, 'Father, you're wasting your time. This country is not like Moresby. I always carry my revolver, and I show them that. It's a life insurance if you want to say it. That's all it is.' He was a bit shocked at the time, but after a few days here I think he realised that there was a lot of sense in that.

On other occasions Father Ross demonstrated both his courage and his faith in something other than guns. Jerry Pentland recalls flying in police and an Australian government officer to the Mount Hagen 'drome while Father Ross 'in white surplice and carrying a bible and a polo stick' walked backwards and forwards between hundreds of armed and jeering warriors, random spears flying overhead.

When Australia took New Guinea under mandate from the League of Nations in 1921 she guaranteed freedom of religion. She gave that pledge again in 1946 when she accepted the United Nations Trusteeship Agreement. Those commitments reduced the likelihood that any Australian government officers would limit the movement or the actions of any missionaries unless they were involved in the most blatant abuses. One cost of international and Australian concern for the fundamental right of freedom of religion has been, Sir John Gunther suggests, 'too many missionary organisations'. Most of the new churches sponsored by small groups in Australia and America are, Sir John says, 'grossly fundamentalist' and 'uneducated'. Where the old spheres of influence had once reduced conflict there is now intense competition in some areas. Archbishop David Hand: 'It has become a bit of a riot. I believe in Goroka now there are forty-six different churches within a radius of a mile or two of the town.'

> At Tari in the Southern Highlands all the missions were sitting within a two and a half mile radius of the station. They sat there for months waiting for the gun to go off.
> **Sir John Gunther**

The increased competition was most intense in the post-war as each new area of the highlands was opened up to foreign penetration. Dan Leahy:

It was like a mission rush. A gold rush had nothing on them. The Catholics would come in and the Lutherans would sit alongside them, or vice versa. And there was a lot of missionaries now, all these new-fangled ones. I don't approve of them very much because they've got all these silly ideas. The people that don't know much about it get a bit confused as to all the missions.

In extreme cases the mission advance guard camped on the boundary line waiting for the minute when the government *Gazette* cancelled the old restrictions. In 1962 Chris Vass was the officer in charge of Porgera station in the western highlands. He was in the centre of an area about to be declared open, and the missionaries were poised on the starting line:

On the appointed hour they took off and the great race began towards Porgera. They got within a few miles of the station and I got a telephone call from the Assistant District Commissioner to say that when they arrived I was to send them back because they had taken off a week before they should have. So with great glee I said to them, 'Back you go fellers. It's not de-restricted till next week.' They all had to turn around and get out of the place.

Then the next week the same performance came on again. It was amazing. I think the Seventh Day Adventists got in first, maybe it was all the vegetarian diet. They got in a bit ahead of the others and proceeded to take the prime position at the end of the airstrip for their church. The Catholics, I think they might have come in last. I don't know whether that's usual for them, but they got a place some way off the patrol post to set up their mission. The Lutherans got a site fairly close to the airstrip, so they must have been fairly good in the race. The other people that did well were one of the minor Protestant religions that came in just after the Seventh Day Adventists and got themselves a choice position just off the station.

The Anglicans, Archbishop Hand says, avoided the scramble for souls, but they have not been free of competition. The new missions have moved into the areas of the established churches, sometimes proclaiming as sinful the dancing and *kundu* drumming that had long been incorporated into the normal services of the older missions. Revivalist movements have further divided villages and clans. Archbishop Hand:

> I'd be the first to recognise there's a place for what is these days called the charismatic renewal in the church, a certain degree of Pentecostal re-emphasis on the work and presence and power of the Holy Spirit in the life of the church and all this. But when you get groups that come in and completely upset people, get them almost mad with emotionalism, and when the emotionalism wears off and there's no solid basis to it, then the last state of that man is worse than the first. These sorts of expressions of religion seem to me to be not religious but hysterical, psychologically bad, and therefore not in the best interests of the society.

Ben Probert, a government officer, has been critical of the hysteria engendered by some religious movements. Confronted by people who were neglecting their gardens, and falling down and frothing at the mouth, he told them bluntly 'that Jesus Christ was a worker, and they'd got to work'. But he found little support from the missionaries who thought the people privileged to have experienced so intensely the power of the Holy Spirit.

Peter Lawrence did anthropological fieldwork in the Madang District where there was a dramatic misinterpretation of the way the foreign religion worked:

> About 1961 when the Catholic Archbishop from Alexishafen was going through a village the *luluai*, who was an ex-catechist at the mission, came to the Archbishop and asked would he sacrifice a black rooster, a *blakpela kakaruk* as they call it. The Archbishop said why should he do that? And the *luluai* said, 'Well, we want you to kill the rooster and sprinkle the blood on the village to cleanse it of its sins.' The Archbishop replied, no he couldn't do a thing like

that because it wasn't a very nice thing to do. The *luluai* made a signal and a man, as the story was told to me, came running, stood in front of the Archbishop and the *luluai* and stretched his arms out horizontally in the form of a cross. The *luluai* then got a very sharp bush knife and cut the man's throat. It emerged in cross-examination that what this man believed was that the Europeans had the world made right for them, with plenty of cargo and all the good things, by the sacrifice of Jesus Christ, the white Jesus. Now what they had to do was to sacrifice a black Jesus and then the same would happen for them.

Other, more casual, observers speak of the missions' excessive talk about the fires of hell and the pressure on the villagers to contribute to church collections: 'They used to put a four-gallon drum in a village with a slit in the top, and say now next time we come around we want that filled with marks—that's shillings.'

Steve Collins who went to the highlands at the age of nineteen to work as a lay Catholic missionary left after six months, disillusioned by the 'great competition' between the churches and the way that Papua New Guineans used the missions for their own purposes. He was sceptical that there were many real conversions: but the evidence that the missions have been having considerable influence on the behaviour and beliefs of the people is substantial. In 1966 government officers took their first comprehensive census. People were asked, 'Which mission do you belong to, or, do you follow the beliefs of your grandfathers?' Ninety per cent named a particular mission and another three per cent said that they were just generally Christian. Only seven per cent said they followed the religions of their ancestors. The Papua New Guineans had claimed to be more Christian than the white community. At least for the purposes of identification Papua New Guineans have an extraordinary allegiance to Christianity. The rate of acceptance of Christianity is all the more outstanding when it is remembered about

New church at Rabaul, 1948

one third of the population only came into contact with missionaries after 1945.

Although the missionaries often claimed that they were different from the rest of the white community, in fact they have always shared many values. In early times that meant that they believed in the superiority of their race as well as of their religion. Noel Levi, a New Irelander and Minister for Foreign Affairs and Trade in Sir Julius Chan's ministry, says

> I could never forget a Methodist missionary that we had in my particular area. After church there were the usual handshakes. Then immediately after that a bowl of water was brought across for the missionary's wife to wash her hands. Looking back on it now, I see nothing ruder than this action. She could at least have been more discreet and gone off behind the house or something. But to insist that a bowl be brought to her there . . .

Neville Threlfall, who has been both a missionary and a historian of the mission, found that the people in the pre-war had come to accept that the 'European was always dominant', and that the white missionary would act as befitted his race. One of the New Guinean pastors told the Reverend Threlfall 'not with rancour':

> when the missionary wanted to ask me a simple question, he stood on the verandah and I stood on the grass at the foot of the steps and we talked. If he wanted me to help him for a long time with translation we went into his house, and he sat on a chair and I sat on the floor.

The older pastors told Threlfall that later they found it embarrassing when the young, post-war missionaries expected to be called by their first names: the pastors had never called any Europeans by their Christian names.

Where the old discrimination lingered into the post-war it angered young, educated Papua New Guineans. Leo Hannett, Premier of the North Solomons Province:

> In Rabaul there used to be two masses, one for blacks, and one for white, mixed race and Chinese. In those days some Papuans used to think of themselves as somewhat closer to the white man because they were slightly whiter and they could make furrows in their hair. I have seen a Papuan try to go to a European mass, and be chucked out by the priest. For me that was a vivid shock to see what the church was in the books and what it is in reality.

At least some of the missionaries have been broadminded enough to take pride in the fact that the most sensitive and articulate Papua New Guinean critics of churches were trained in the missions.

'Most Papua New Guineans were converted by other Papua New Guineans.'

The tradition of conflict and cooperation between God and Caesar was extended and replayed in Papua New Guinea. Sometimes the *kiaps* resented the influence that long-serving missionaries wielded in the villages, but the limits of the authority of church and state were often tested on apparently minor issues. Trevor Shearston:

A patrol officer built a bridge across one of the rivers near Mendi. It was essential for the mission because the river was a real rager. The policeman who supervised most of the work was a Sepik and he fancied himself as a bit of a carver. When the bridge was finished he carved a couple of posts on each side of the river. One was a man and one was a woman so he carved a great big penis on the man and a great big vagina and breasts on the woman because that was the way carving was done in the Sepik. When the missionary heard about it he came hurrying down and put some sort of a grass skirt around the male and female figures. The patrol officer came along and removed the grass skirts; and the missionary put them back again. I don't know whether it was the missionary himself or perhaps a Papua New Guinean pastor who eventually chopped off the offending penis. The patrol officer really got quite angry about the whole affair and went up to the mission and told the missionary to leave the bloody thing alone, that was how the bridge was going to stay. 'Leave the bridge as it is. OK? It's the government's bridge, you've got no right to touch it.'

While senior government officers readily acknowledged their debt to the missions for much education and health work, some conflict was inevitable on out-stations where *kiap* and missionary were the obvious representatives of separate systems of law, advice and patronage.

Different missions have taken different stands on whether to engage in business. The dilemma facing the missions is expressed by Gunther: either they obtain profit from business ventures or they suffer financial stringency. Archbishop Hand concedes that the Anglicans 'have been poorer than the other major churches' partly because they have generally kept out of plantations and trading ventures. The Anglicans, he says, have only run stores where there has been no alternative means of bringing such services to isolated communities. The Methodists have gradually moderated their early opposition to business. Neville Threlfall:

The first Methodist missionaries in the New Guinea islands had no policy of business involvement, but simply devoted themselves to preaching, teaching and related work. Some commercial developments which came later grew from the needs of the church. For example they were producing religious literature, it took a long time to get proofs back from Australia, and they set up their own printing press in 1908, just a small press to handle their own work. They found that other people in the area wanted printing done, and so a commercial side developed until by now our printing press is still running and handling far more commercial work than religious publications. The plantations grew mostly in association with church training institutions. They planted gardens and coconuts to supply food for the students. If there was spare land they planted more coconuts so that money would be coming in as the palms matured. Some of these plantations grew so big they provided funds for church work and gospel expansion in other areas.

But soon, Threlfall says, ministers and teachers were spending so much time debating questions of maintenance and investment that they set up a company with hired staff to run the various church enterprises. All profits still return to the church, but the missionaries' time is no longer absorbed in the everyday problems of directing complex businesses. The Lutherans too have established companies to control some of their ventures, making every effort to allow Papua New Guineans to hold positions that enable them to direct policy.

The Catholic missions have probably the greatest range of business ventures. To support their spiritual and welfare services the Archdiocese of Rabaul has developed great capacity to produce and sell in the secular world. The general manager of the Archdiocese, Father Tim O'Neill:

> We build all our own boats. We keep about fifteen of them, anything from a thirty-footer to a ninety-footer, for transport, for taking supplies to and from headquarters to the outstations. We also run metal workshops, automotive engineering, marine engineering, furniture making. They are not very lucrative; if they pay their way we are quite happy about them. Then we run a few plantations and sawmills and timber businesses, and that is the financial support of all the work that we do for religion, medicine, education, social work and the economy. If we can produce it here, we don't believe in going around with a cap to poorer people overseas. There are many missions more unfortunately placed than we are. We give employment to about 2000 people, and we are able to support ourselves.

But once missions engage in business they become entangled in problems of employer-employee relationships. Educated Papua New Guineans who have criticised conditions of workers in foreign-owned companies have been equally critical of the missions. Leo Hannett:

> Christianity was very much the handmaid of the West. When you go into plantations you see very little difference in how the Catholic church runs its plantations or how the manager treats the workers from the kind of treatment that is meted out on the plantations of Burns Philp. Workers are treated in a very inhuman way; the same kind of salaries. Theology doesn't seem to come out very much on the plantations, or the concept of brotherhood, and so on.

The problem for the churches has always been that if they provide higher wages they immediately draw the wrath of employers who claim that the church exploits a privileged position to break established wage levels and bankrupt small businessmen. And of course if the churches pay out more, then they have less to invest in welfare and preaching the word of God.

While the missionaries—for good and ill—have shared many of the assumptions of the rest of the white community, they have been less inclined to take from the country where they labour.

163

19 You Had to be Firm

I think that the Australians thought that they were going to be here for ever. We had to be respectful, and by over-playing that we became weak; we became a lot of humbugs. We had no feeling for our country; and it took a while to eradicate that from one's mind.

Sir John Guise

Australia's management of Papua began in the golden age of colonialism when the British Raj was at its height and the right of the European to direct the destinies of millions of indigenous peoples was un-questioned. Even in the 1920s some of the most respected anthropologists were still telling their students that there were inherent differences between the races. Indeed, they said, the peoples of the earth could be put on a scale with white men on the top descending through various Asians to the black hunter-gatherer com-munities on the bottom. When that was the assumption of the experts it would be absurd to expect the ordinary white set-tlers or government officers to deny that they were 'the lords of human kind'. Nor could anyone have predicted the speed with which the intellectual and political bases of their assumed superiority would be shattered. Within their working lives Australians passed from being *mastas* to being foreigners in the same land. It was a transformation which placed a strain on individuals and complicated all relations between races.

In their rhetoric, the Australian nation-alists of 1900 prized three things: their country would be white, egalitarian, and distinctive. They took those ideas with them when they crossed Torres Strait—and they found them full of contradic-tions. They were conscious of their race, but at times they wanted to joke and slap black backs. They wanted cheap and obedient workers, but they did not want to claim privileges of wealth and birth. They were characteristics of the Europe that they had left behind. They wanted to rule, but they did not want to be seen as representatives of an imperial power.

They also carried with them a record of their experiences with the Aborigines. From the start Australians talked as though they had to make up for their past sins: the Papuans would not lose their lands, they would not be sold alcohol and they would not be allowed to die out. Also there were white men going north who had already tried to settle racial disputes with guns. As one of them said publicly in 1906, the best thing to do with warlike Papuans was to 'disperse them'. And by that he meant shoot them.

Most Australians went to Papua New Guinea with the best of intentions, but poorly equipped intellectually and by ex-perience to establish good race relations. Few could bend their starched white suits.

What John Black calls the 'master-servant, yes sir no sir, *taubada* business' overlay the belief that change had to be gradual. All 'natives' would be advanced

'We rolled them smokes.' (left)

'The Colonial atmosphere was degrading both to those in charge and those who were governed.'

slowly and uniformly; there would be no black élite lifted above their fellow villagers to challenge the *mastas'* hold on all positions of wealth and power. By the 1920s and 1930s the distinction between the races was sharp and fixed by regulation. Sir John Guise, who was born in 1914, remembers:

> Discrimination was tough. We had the quarter-to-nine whistle blowing, curfew at nine o'clock, and anyone caught a minute after nine would have to serve a gaol sentence of two or three months. You had to run for your life at a quarter to nine to get back to your quarters because if there was a group of Europeans walking along the street you could not pass in front of them. If you did, and if any of these Europeans wanted to report you as being rude, well, you'd had it.

The regulation which prohibited Papuans and New Guineans from wearing clothes on the upper parts of their bodies had been introduced to protect them from pneumonia and skin disease. But a custom that had been benign in origin had become a means of putting pretentious blacks in their place. Some white officers would rip the offending shirt off in a dramatic gesture of dominance. 'The colonial atmosphere' Ian Hogbin says, 'was degrading both to those in charge and to those who were governed'.

There was, Tom Flower argues, much talk but little substance in stories of 'boong bashing and ill treatment of boys':

> You had to be firm with them; you didn't have to knock them about. But you would stop their tobacco or their bully beef. Often they had a go at me, and I had to look after myself, which I was able to do in those days. I was supposed to be able to run native labour. I was firm, I was fair. People say, you exploited the natives, and you did this and that. I never found, or very seldom found, it necessary to crack them or manhandle them. But I treated them as natives.

Flower says that he ensured his men were well-housed, fed and paid; and 'if I thought a boy was worth it I'd foster him and then make something of him'.

Yet in spite of the apparently strict separation of the races and the legislative ordering of relationships, many Australians found they were constantly altering their attitudes to the people that they ruled. Billie Bourke:

> You go up there and you feel extremely sorry for them because they're underprivileged and childlike, and you spoil them terribly. Then you suddenly realise you're being shockingly imposed upon, and you become very very stern and strict. Then as the years go by you mellow

because you have to live in harmony with people no matter where you are in this world, and that's the easiest way to do it. The first two years you are searching, but after two years you think, 'I know what makes natives tick.' I was up there from the start till I came away in 1962, twenty-five years, and after that time I'd realised I knew nothing at all about them. They were too complex.

Differences in culture and the belief that it was necessary to maintain a position of authority stopped some Australians from even attempting easy communication with people who spent years in the same house or office.

Sometimes there was a sudden demonstration of cultural differences. Gladys Stevens had one servant for many years, but one day his father died:

They smoke the dead, then they sit them up in caves, and they stay there forever. Takes a week to smoke them. Finally he came back, but in the meantime I had put on another boy. He took a very dim view of that. He was a very good boy too, very clean. He wanted to know what this other man was doing there. I said, 'Well, you've been away a long time.' So he told me all about smoking Papa and what they had to do. He said, 'You raus—that means get rid off—You

raus this man or me cut im throat. I said, 'Oh, you can't do that.' 'All right,' he said, 'Me cut im throat. This place, me long time me stop along this place work along you. Me work true. Me work good. Now this man, this no place bilong im, e place belong me.' Anyway he put on a dreadful act, so I had to get rid of this other boy.

That was a case where the *misis* found herself making concessions to Papua New Guinean values and assertions.

Even where close friendships developed across the racial divisions in the pre-war, the Australians still, in Guise's term, 'radiated a paternalistic outlook'. Among other Australians they may have adopted the common stance of superiority to protect their own names, but even in private, Guise says, Australians would still be patronising. John Black, known as one of the progressive officers of the old Mandated Territory field staff, explains the difficulty of establishing effective relationships:

You had an upper class and a lower class, accentuated by racial difference. To most Europeans, native society became an underworld, and only a few of us had the privilege of getting a glimpse into it occasionally. Now for that reason I preferred to be, especially on a long trip in dangerous country, the only European. If you get two Europeans they form a little club, a little enclave of Australia, and they don't know what's going on. You've got to get down and know the people that you're dealing with, and think in their terms. If you can do that you can become a leader of them. If you get hoodwinked by the notion of white prestige, which generally meant that you were allowing yourself to be regarded as a fool by your native people, you were stacking the odds against yourself.

But John Black's position within the government demanded that he communicate with Papua New Guineans as a leader, not as an equal.

Dealing constantly with white men and women who expected subservience,

Correspondence.

Papuan Times March 13, 1912
Sir John Guise

(To the Editor of the Papuan Times.)

Sir,—If you could spare me a space in your valuable paper I would to draw attention to the present state of affairs in the swimming baths.

In some parts of the world we have mixed bathing, and in others there are hours appointed for males, and hours appointed for females, but, in no other part of the world have we swimming baths erected by public consent, and with public money, where natives are allowed the use of the baths allotted to white people.

On Monday evening, a number of men, hot and weary after a hard day's toil in the sun, went to the baths to refresh and cleanse themselves. Arriving they found the baths in possession of a number of Port Moresby ladies and a number of Hanuabada and Hula ladies.

The white ladies objected to the white gentlemen bathing, but welcomed their black sisters in a "true spirit of Christian charity."

This, in the presence of natives, was a direct blow to the prestige of the white race.

It is in fact, the placing of a black gin on a higher plane than a white man.

Unless we uphold the dignity of the white race we shall have a state of things worse than South Africa, and these very same ladies together with the authorities, will be well-thrashed with the rod they have made for themselves.

We don't want this kind of mixed bathing, i.e., black and white, and we must have some provision made for the people whose only leisure for recreation is after 5 p.m. every evening, and Sunday, a day which the ladies have presumptiously and "unselfishly" taken to themselves.

Papua is a man's country. The male far out-numbers the female, and must be recognised.

If mock modesty must divide the time to be devoted to bathing, let it be in the same ratio of male to temale.

The bath is causing a great deal of ill-feeling, and no little personal feeling, so trusting due notice of this admonition will be observed by those concerned, and by those in authority.—Yours truly,

FAIR PLAY.

The Papuan Times March 20, 1912

Papua New Guineans could develop a debilitating cringe. Sir John Guise recalls: 'We had to be respectful, and by over-playing that we became weak; we became a lot of humbugs. We had no feeling for our country; and it took a while to eradicate that from one's mind'. His voice fixed by a recording made in 1953, Guise himself provides evidence for that observation. Just returned from London where he had served as a member of the Royal Papuan Constabulary and New Guinea Police Force contingent at the coronation of Elizabeth II, Sergeant John Guise was interviewed on the ABC. He was fed questions which determined his answers: 'there must have been a great deal of excitement ... You must have been very proud to be representing your people ...'. And he gave the expected answers in a quiet, fluent, respectful voice: 'We were very proud ... Yes Mr ...'. The two interviews, recorded twenty-seven years apart, are an evocative demonstration of the way situations enforce patterns of behaviour. What would have startled most Australians in the 1950s would have been any suggestion that Papua New Guineans in the presence of white people were consciously playing a role. And it was a role that the Papua New Guineans despised.

> *You couldn't even smile at a young lady. If any Government official noticed that you were becoming fond of any young Australian girl, then brother, you'd had it. You could go up for a charge under the White Women's Protection Ordinance.*
> **Sir John Guise**

The legislation controlling sexual relations between black and white reflected the fears and prejudices of the law makers. In the 1930s a white woman committed an offence if she consented to have sexual relations with a New Guinean who was not her husband. A New Guinean who attempted to have carnal knowledge of a consenting white woman could be gaoled. The Act said that it was to prevent the 'defilement' of the white women. In Papua anyone convicted of the rape of a white woman was to be hanged and even attempted rape could bring the death penalty. Other offences against white women could be punished by whippings and long gaol sentences. Papuans were told that the White Women's Protection Ordinance was the strongest law and that white women were 'sacred'. In 1934 a Papuan was hanged for the rape of a white girl. In their fear of sexual attacks on white women many of the European community showed themselves to be an insecure minority, full of fantasies about a majority that they neither understood nor trusted. 'Some of the nicest people', one government officer said, 'had a definite siege mentality'. They were consumed by the belief that 'blacks have a lascivious desire for white women and must be kept completely and utterly away'.

White men seem to perceive attacks on white women as threats to their power, property and virility. The anxiety in white women may be deep and barely conscious. Amirah Inglis:

I found in myself a fear of black men that I didn't know existed in me. It was so deep I was shocked to discover it in myself. Black men must have come to be threatening figures. I got over that initial fear. But then it seemed very interesting and strange to me that when you walked down the street in Port Moresby in 1967 Papuan men would get off the footpath as you went past. Men would keep themselves away so as not to touch you. In the market, for example, where people normally jostle each other, nobody would touch you. They'd keep well away.

Those personal experiences eventually prompted Amirah Inglis to write *Not a White Woman Safe*, a study of the passing and application of the White Women's Protection Ordinance of 1926.

While white men spoke of guarding their women as their 'sacred trust', they did not allow the Native Women's Protection Ordinance and similar legislative restraints hinder their easing the white man's burden by casual encounters with village girls. 'You had to be careful that you didn't let the white man down', Harry Hugo says, but 'taking a native girl and sleeping with her was not letting him down; just one of those things, nature'. It was not a case of 'rush in and pick up the first mary you came across', Harry explains, but rather of getting to know the girl and 'well nature's nature, isn't it; black, white or brindle'. But Jim Hopkinson says that other men preferred less romance and a more direct transaction. They went into the village and said to a man, 'Me like im piccaninny mary bilong you. How much money me must throw away long buy im piccaninny mary bilong you?' Having settled for, say, half a bag of rice they made their payment and took the girl.

> If you and I were married
> tonight, dear,
> All our kids would turn out black
> and white, I fear,
> I want kids like other beaus,
> Not like a set of dominoes,
> Black girl, bye bye.
> So I'm packing my grip, I'm
> saying toodledoo,
> Like a Bondi tram, I'm shooting
> through,
> Black girl, bye bye.

Pre-war few white men formally married Papua New Guinean women. It is a distinguishing mark of Australia as a colonial power that government officers did not marry the women that they ruled. In the earliest years of Australia's administration some frontier traders legally married Papuan women, but between 1924 and 1940 no white man legally married a local woman in Papua. After the war there was a gradual change. In one year from April 1967 forty-five out of the 310 officially registered marriages involving Europeans were inter-racial. That was still only fourteen per cent, and some were unions between Australian men and Asian or mixed-race women; but it was certainly a significant difference from the norm of twenty, or even ten, years earlier.

Dame Rachel Cleland claims that the government 'looked down on' or 'stopped' informal relationships, but that there were 'quite a lot of marriages. And they were happy marriages. They were accepted and the offspring were accepted and the wife was accepted. I just took things as I found them'. Other members of the post-war white community were less tolerant. Ian Boden:

Those who did marry Papua New Guinea girls were going against the established society as far as the people who worked in the administration were concerned. The more senior ones amongst them were apt to say, 'Oh well, so-and-so's gone native'. You found yourself well and truly shunted off the social register. I would estimate that when I got married, or when I announced my intention of getting married, that I probably lost about fifty to sixty per cent of my European contacts. One of the aspects of such marriages that people tend to overlook is that this type of reaction was from both sides of the fence. If you had a number of Europeans who were offended by the concept of black-white marriages, you also had an equal number of Papua New Guineans who were similarly offended for different reasons.

Yorky Bott, too, has no doubt that when he married a 'local' that he was 'looked down upon' and 'My wife was kicked out of the Girl Guides'.

Although marriages between black and white were relatively few there was substantial mixed-race community in Papua New Guinea. Generally these were the children and grandchildren of mixed-race parents. In Rabaul the mixed-race people tended to live in a particular area and developed their own sense of a belonging to a group. Yorky Bott:

The mixed race community when I first came here lived out at Rapindik Tip. It was called in those days 'creamy land'. A mixed race was part Ambonese, part Filipino, part Indonesian, part Chinese and part European from way back. They were a conglomeration.

Many went to special mission schools where, Rudi Zander says, 'we were brought up Western style. We were really taught Victorian style. You know, sit up properly at the table, eat with knife and fork and not with your fingers, and all this sort of thing.'

By 1960 perhaps a thousand mixed-race people lived in Port Moresby. Formal and informal rules continued to force them to have a separate identity. They had their own clubs and sporting teams, but it was the liquor laws that most obviously made them declare their separateness: whites could drink, mixed-race people had to have a permit, and Papua New Guineans were not allowed to drink at all. From the early 1960s formal regulations changed. The Australian administration said that there would only be two groups of people: migrant and indigenous. The mixed race could either apply for Australian citizenship or they could call themselves Papua New Guineans. The informal pressures to be distinct were still there. Rosa Petch:

> I've always thought of myself as being a Papuan. I think I'll always think of myself as being that. Because 'in between' sort of sounds ... 'in between!' The no-where people, being in between. You're not sure whether you want to go one way or the other. Most of the time we went out with the Australian guys. They were more fun. I mean most of them knew where to take girls, and most of them had cars. You could go for a drive around, go to the movies, and if there's a dance on they take you dancing. They do all the spending. We just sit and be ladies.

James Seeto solved the legal question of identity by taking Australian citizenship, but that has not altered how he feels or how others regard him:

> I have been in a lot of situations where I am not a Chinese; I am not a Papua New Guinean. In my early days of wanting to become an Australian I was instigated by this feeling that whenever people think that I am some benefit to them, whether it's Papua New Guinean or Chinese, they will regard me as one of them, but when I am no benefit to them they regard me as not one of them. And I tell you, you have to be a mixed race to know what it feels like. But I get hurt more from the people of Papua New Guinea when a situation gets to where you have to have an argument, and they abuse what I am. Because I feel that I was born here and I should without hesitation be regarded as one of them.

Many of the mixed race believe that in order to prosper they have had to pay the cost of denying part of themselves.

By 1940 there were nearly 2000 Asians in New Guinea, nearly all of them Chinese. From the beginning of their administration of the former German colony the Australian government strictly limited all Asian immigration: white Australia was imposed on black New Guinea. James Woo:

> The Chinese knew discrimination in the full sense of the word. Take for instance young Chinese men. If they wanted to bring their wives from Hong Kong or China they put in an application. From experience we know that when the authorities sight the application, the first thing they look for is the age of the woman. If she was of childbearing age the application would automatically be refused. Sure it was all right to bring in your old mother who was sixty or seventy years old to die in peace in this country, but they did not allow us to bring our women folk in so we can expand our families.

With the main importing and exporting business and town retailing dominated by the big firms, the Chinese traders became merchants to the villagers. Being in closer contact with New Guineans they were also more likely to be targets of envy. Sally Hansen defends her kin:

> The natives always had a grudge about the Chinese because we were the moneyed people. Most of the people you talk with say that the Chinese robbed the native. Maybe some of them did, but all that I know really worked hard, twenty-four hours a day.

The Chinese have money, but through hard work.

The white community (when not in competition with the Chinese) saw the Asians as supplying special services and being part of that exotic background which constantly told them they were living in a place of alien fascination. Mrs Stevens:

Lovely people. There were so many of them, in one store after another. And very cheap, especially the beautiful tablecloths and the linen, and all that sort of thing. And the weddings—their weddings last two days. They have a huge dragon, and before the couple are married they light the tail, and bang, bang, bang, bang all the way up the tail. The hospitality, it's just marvellous. The Chinese food . . . of course they can cook. We'd go to engagement parties and dance and laugh. I find the Chinese people very nice. Gracious and charming. The women are just ladies; they're lovely.

The brief social encounters were a long way from the situation conveyed through former District Commissioner Bill Seale's remark: 'Generally the Chinese were second class citizens; let's be quite honest about it'. In Rabaul where the divisions between the races were most rigidly maintained, the three races had separate schools, hospitals and places to be buried.

In 1957 the Chinese were offered Australian citizenship. Some Chinese, born in Papua New Guinea and educated in Australia, immediately took Australian citizenship; other Chinese hesitated. The decision was particularly difficult for those who were part New Guinean or retained strong ties to a Chinese home-land. They did not feel that they were Australians or that they were wanted by Australians. James Woo:

I am a second generation Papua New Guinean. Like my parents I have great feeling for this country. I thought of applying to be a citizen of this country at one stage; but I saw that the legislation was loaded against us. There is a clause in the constitution that places a moratorium on certain things

They met as comrades.

we can do. For instance we may not be able to own land for the first five years, or certain types of businesses for eight years. It took us a long time to be given the privilege of Australian citizenship, and we prize it highly.

The Chinese community has travelled a strange track through German New Guinea, second class accommodation in Australian New Guinea, to citizenship in either Australia or Papua New Guinea.

The war was a massive disruption to the old pattern of race relations. In January 1942 the Japanese South Seas Force swept ashore at Rabaul. Soon 300 000 Japanese were in the New Guinea islands and on the north coast. As the Allies responded, over a million servicemen moved north, fighting or staging through the Territories. Papua New Guineans suffered greatly, travelled further, handled more cash, tried new jobs and met a variety of foreigners. The Australian troops knew nothing of the old *masta-boi* relationships and they rejected them when they found them. Other Australians had wanted to convert, rule or employ Papua New Guineans. The troops in the base camps wanted nothing more than a photograph, a yarn or a coconut. Front line troops met Papua New Guineans as comrades-in-arms and as carriers. They formed a bond that was sentimental, but strong and based on events that left sharp impressions. Fred Kaad:

'They carried me.'

Legends often grow out of truth. If it hadn't been for the Fuzzy Wuzzy Angels, then I suppose eventually we might have won the war, but we certainly wouldn't have won it in Papua New Guinea. We would have been pushed back off the island and had to fight on Australian soil. They were the people who not only carried out the wounded, but carried in the food and ammunition.

Men of the 39th Battalion who did the early fighting on the Kokoda Trail speak of a debt in terms of compassion rather than of logistics:

—They carried me. I got wounded at Gona. I couldn't describe ... They were so kind. Wonderful men.

—It was never known for a stretcher to be deserted.

—You stayed with them for warmth. Rode in the trucks with them. We rolled them smokes.

—You can't describe love. And we loved them.

Several times in recorded interviews Australian ex-servicemen used the term 'love'. It was almost certainly not a normal part of the vocabulary that they used to describe their relationships with any men or women.

Sir John Guise was involved in an incident that bound men together:

I was sent out to rescue some Australian soldiers that were on rafts between Goodenough Island and Cape Frere. Two very seriously wounded Australian soldiers; very very young, I would say around seventeen. They were mortally wounded. You could smell them; gangrene had set in. Both of them lay on my lap, one here, the other there. They asked me, 'Brush my hair, please'. So I brushed his hair, and they were crying. They were talking about 'Daddy, Mummy'. It was very sad. I knew they would not live. As soon as we came through East Cape they held me, both of them held me. They were finished, dead. One could not help but feel that I was like them and they were like me. Just ordinary human beings. I mean the friendship was bound, if I may use that term, on the battlefield of blood; and if friendship is bound on the battlefield then it's difficult to eradicate. This is exactly what happened when Australians and Papuans and New Guineans fought together, died together, suffered together. And no force in the world can smash that friendship.

Jack Boland, another member of the 39th Battalion, places the relationship of the troops and the Papua New Guineans in context. His unit had arrived in Moresby several months before the Japanese attacked through Kokoda. They first met Papuans as conscripted labourers:

Whenever we were with these people, at the base camps and so forth, our cooks would prepare lunch, and if there were twenty or thirty or more natives working, we'd always have them come down and share our food. This was, quite frankly, frowned upon by the local white population. They considered this to be not the thing to do at all. They were quite disgusted, and I believe they made protests.

There was a local picture theatre in Port Moresby that had two showings a week for the natives only, and the rest of the time the natives were not permitted to go. We soon made a change to that. We said if the picture theatre was going to be open, it was open for natives as well as troops. That was after the white people had departed in a bit of a hurry after the first air raid.

The white residents, Boland says, blamed the troops for 'spoiling' the Papuans, but, Boland argues, 'we were rewarded for spoiling them. If we hadn't treated them the way we did, well, we'd have been left for dead when we really needed them'.

Sir John Guise adds a final comment on the changed perception of the Papua New Guineans:

I think the attitude of the Australian soldiers, together with American soldiers, made a tremendous impact psychologically. Because here we saw a different type of white people who were friendly, who shared things with us. There was no paternalistic outlook from them, you know. And when the coloured Americans came along, the negroes came along, we said, 'Well, we didn't know that a black man could be a captain, a black man could be a colonel, a black man could be a major'. This had a tremendous effect, it made us think that the brown and the black person were just as good as the white people, and that the white people, the brown people and the black people were all equals.

While the war had been a time of terror, hard work and harsh overseers for many Papua New Guineans, it had also enabled many of them to see that the world might be different. But it did not give them the means to make it different.

20 Across the Barriers

There were very few people who really saw the people of Papua New Guinea as what they are and what they have become. It was a great shock to a lot of people to realise that they were human beings, just as smart as we are and just as capable of giving and taking friendship.

Andrée Millar

In spite of the thousands of soldiers, the deluge of *materiel*, and the destruction that came to Papua New Guinea from 1942 to 1945 much of the 'time before' survived. Papua New Guineans who worked or fought for the Allies were paid the old pre-war rate of ten shillings a month. Many of the Australian soldiers who directed Papua New Guineans to labour or carry were enlisted from the pre-war Territory white population. They did not spend their time praising the Fuzzy Wuzzy Angels. The Australian New Guinea Administrative Unit, or Angau, which looked after civil affairs, was initially drawn from the pre-war government services. The most humane of the government officers, who had valued the strong paternalist tradition in the pre-war service, found it difficult to enforce tough war-time decisions. They were now doing what they had previously been trying to prevent. David Marsh remembers: 'You recruited them under pressure and you escorted them under pressure till you got them so far from home that they couldn't turn back'. In some areas every able-bodied man was taken. Neither they nor the people left behind in the villages knew what they were going to or how long they would be away. Government officers, aware that the troops in the forward areas were completely dependent on the carriers for survival, were forced, Lloyd Hurrell says, to

> use a little extra effort and probably a little more force than persuasion to get people, who were sometimes reluctant to carry. It was fairly common to clout somebody with the open hand. But very few people struck with the closed fist or anything of that nature. But a boot in the backside, yes, or a clout over the ear with the open hand; or quite a common one was to grab them— they've got a lovely head of hair to do this with—to grab them by the hair and shake their head.

The conscripted villagers were the same men lauded for their devotion to the wounded. And the evidence is that they earned the praise.

Out of the war and the planning for the United Nations came a general belief that there should be a new deal for the colonial peoples of the world. Also Australians felt that they owed a debt to the Papua New Guineans who had come to their aid when they were most threatened. The Australian government promised to end the old indentured labour system and provide better welfare services. Colonel J K Murray, a Professor of Agriculture and a

'Boong Train'—the diggers used the term sardonically, affectionately. They were only too conscious of their dependence on the carrier line (left).

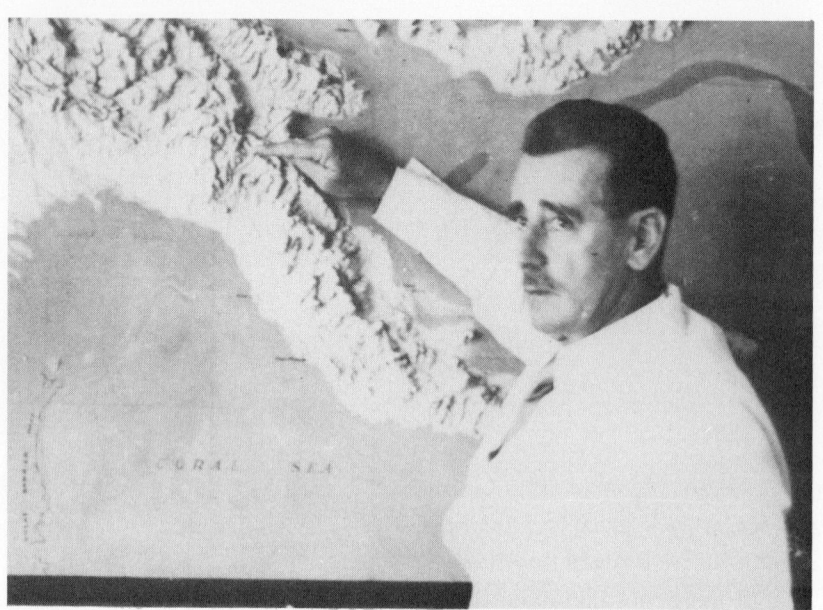
'Kanaka Jack', J K Murray, post war administrator

give after the war was based on the fact that if you want a healthy plural society, you've got to have mutual racial respect, equality before the law, and equality of opportunity. That's the ideal; and we were trying to get a little closer to it.

Early after the war John Black was given an indication of the opposition to change in a conversation with Judge Phillips. Although a defender of New Guinean rights under the law, Phillips found it inconceivable that the 1930s' division between the races should not be maintained into the 1950s.

Change was slow and uneven. An Australian who had left Papua New Guinea in 1938 could have returned to many places in 1958 and seen no difference in the old *masta-boi* relationships. But one place where change was most obvious was on the sporting field. Tom Huxley:

gentle, aloof idealist, was appointed the first post-war Administrator. Fred Kaad:

He had the 'temerity' of doing such things as inviting local people to Government House for afternoon tea. And even later inviting them to lunch. That sort of attitude towards local people didn't endear him to those who felt that local people had their place and Australians had theirs. Something like the serfs and the barons. There is no doubt Kanaka Jack, and I use that term affectionately, broke those barriers in no uncertain way.

Others sneered when they spoke of 'Kanaka Jack'.

In the post-war administration many of the senior posts were held by men from the old separate Territory services. Many had little sympathy for those who wanted the government to press ahead with mild reforms. In fact they would have been happier to return to the old order of the 1930s. But a few *kiaps* from the 'time before' were committed to change. 'There was,' John Black says,

Taylor and myself, and I can think of Keith McCarthy. The *Pacific Islands Monthly* wrote about the long-haired socialists trying to turn Papua New Guinea into an anthropological zoo. It at least illustrates that there was developing another school of thought. The sort of advice we were trying to

The first real change in cricket came when we took three native cricketers to Rabaul from Madang. We weren't very well received in Rabaul. But a bloke named Bill Washington who owned a plantation just out of Rabaul was an army mate of mine, and he said, 'You know, you mightn't have done the right thing, but it's going to happen. You'd best send the three boys out to my plantation.' I said, 'No, we brought them over here to play cricket, and if we can't get them accommodation like the rest of us we won't play cricket'. Arthur Brown who owned the hotel in Rabaul said, 'Well, that's a fair enough bloody argument. I'll give them the bridal suite—on condition that the three of them sleep in it!' So we went on the field and a chap named Charlie Bates who was captain came to me—I was captain of the Madang team—and he said, 'What's this? You've got a couple of boys playing with you?' I said, 'Yes, three, Charlie.' 'Oh well, it's going to happen I know,' he said. 'I just didn't expect it.' Charlie opened the batting with a bloke named Foley who was another to become a District Commissioner, and one of my boys from Samarai bowled both of them out for about three runs. Bowled Charlie Bates for a bloody duck first ball.

As Sir John Gunther says, some white cricketers admitted that they opposed integration because if Papua New Guineans played they would have been unable to get a game. That might have been selfish, but it was not racist.

Sir John Guise, a gifted sportsman, began his playing career at a time when almost the only occasion when the different races met on equal terms was on the cricket field:

> I always enjoyed playing against a white team. Here I saw the opportunity to use my cricketing powers to bash them for sixes and fours and cut them through the covers and swing them to leg for sixes; and I enjoyed every bit of it. Because here I showed them plainly on the field of sport I was superior to them. Though during working hours of course I had to be a servant, on the field of sport I showed them I was their master. I was getting my own back.

Bill Gammage played rugby union in Port Moresby in 1966 with Aduni, an integrated team drawn from the students and staffs of the Administrative College and the University of Papua New Guinea. While Bill agrees that sporting teams were among the first groups to cut across racial divisions he is sceptical of the extent to which friendships made in the teams continued away from the sport. He points out that John Kaputin, one of the first non-white rubgy league players to break into first grade in Port Moresby 'faced a lot of trouble'. John Kaputin:

> I always accepted the view that as a Papua New Guinean I was a footballer. Say they want to give it to you, as a footballer you say, OK, it's your turn. My turn next time. When I was playing, probably the references to my colour and the sort of things that they said hurt me more than the physical contact. But I always maintained my cool rather than lose my temper because if they are psyching you, you

John Kaputin

Jack Karukuru and Brian Amini at rugby practice

can psych them back by being passive, or you can just get up and smile back.

The pervasiveness of old attitudes was demonstrated on sporting fields in the way that white people continued to hold positions as captains and coaches when the outstanding players were all black.

Those Papua New Guineans who went south on scholarships to Australian secondary schools encountered a different range of inter-racial attitudes. Jack Karukuru speaks of 'fond memories of going as far back as Goondiwindi' to stay with 'school mates' and go horse riding and 'shooting roos':

> When I look back over it now I realise that I had fears that everybody was my enemy. But when I got to have school friends and they took me to their homes and I met their parents and was made to feel almost part of the family, then that fear disappeared without my knowing it was disappearing.

The shock for the young Papua New Guineans was when they re-entered their own country. It was an experience that Noel Levi never wants to repeat:

> You live in an Australian school, you are part of the community, you become less conscious of the colour of your skin. But as soon as you arrive at Jacksons Airport you realise straightaway you are different. You

THE AGE, OCTOBER 19, 1968

A Papuan writes a book

Proud of his people

KIKI: Ten Thousand Years in a Lifetime. A New Guinea Autobiography, by Albert Maori Kiki (Pall Mall, $3.50).

David White

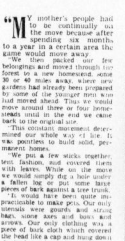

Mr. Kiki.

"MY mother's people had to be continually on the move because after spending six months, to a year in a certain area the game would move away.

"We then packed our few belongings and moved through the forest to a new homesite, some 30 or 40 miles away, where new gardens had already been prepared by some of the younger men who had moved ahead. Thus we would move around three or four homesites until in the end we came back to the original site.

"This constant movement determined our whole way of life. It was pointless to build solid, permanent homes.

"We put a few sticks together, tied, fastened, and covered them with leaves. While on the move we would simply dig a hole under a fallen log or put some large pieces of bark against a tree trunk.

"It would have been quite impracticable to make pots. Our only utensils were gourds and string bags, some ares and bows and arrows. Our only clothing was a piece of bark cloth which covered the head like a cap and hung down the back nearly to the ankles.

"In a sense it was the war with the neighbouring peoples, the constant watch out for enemy activities, the 'payback' expeditions, the preparation of weapons that provided the major content and excitement of our lives. I have sometimes been asked by Europeans whether there was any way of breaking the vicious circle of revenge and counter revenge and arriving at some kind of peace. I think we still on really want peace because we enjoyed fighting ...

"When the enemy killed a man and left his body unmarked we would not touch the one we would pay back for enemy action off, we too had to cut off the head of our victim."

This was the existence which Albert Maori Kiki led in rugged hill country in the island of the Gulf District of Papua for almost all of the first 10 or 11 years of his life.

Now, less than 30 years later, Mr. Maori Kiki is the secretary of the Pangu Party, which is seeking home rule for Papua-New Guinea.

In the past few years he has naturalised, qualified as a pathologist, worked as a welfare officer and helped organise the Territory's first trade union.

In Fiji he learned some other imperious lessons. He first became aware of the poverty among some of the Indians there. He was also drunk alcohol, at one unsuspecting stores and cinemas and thus became acutely aware of the discrimination which then existed in Papua-New Guinea.

And he first learned of taboo snakes — an experience which immediately made him reflect on the lot of his half-brother who was recovering ten dollars a month as a self-taught carpenter.

He returned to the Territory, married his intelligent and understanding wife Elizabeth, and worked as a pathologist.

Remembering his Fiji experiences he helped found the Territory's first trade union which negotiated a minimum wage for Port Moresby workers.

Albert Maori Kiki had made up his mind to stand up for his people and he was already making enemies among conservative Europeans.

After a brief contact with an anti-Administration group, he sought an appointment as a welfare officer.

In 1964 he returned to Port Moresby to gain his adult matriculation at the Administrative college.

He continued to work for the Administration until he helped found the Pangu Party last year and resigned to become its full-time secretary.

Unfortunately, Mr. Maori Kiki's autobiography is rather slumpy and superficial on the past five years or so and is in fact, inaccurate on some points.

One would also wish for something deeper than the bland optimism which he expresses when discussing his country's future in the last few pages.

But it does make clear that this determined man has fought against discrimination when he has encountered it and has striven to move his country towards self-government in the face of opposition.

The Age October 19, 1968

---

are not allowed to go into the section reserved for white people. You get second preference.

As Noel explains, the impact on the students was all the greater because it was then inexplicable and they were unable to express the turmoil they felt. Their treatment as lesser beings in their own country was then so accepted, so much part of the norm, that they could not even feel hatred. Shirley Taylor remembers the irony of seeing two Papua New Guineans returning from Queensland with their tennis racquets strapped to the outside of their cases. But they were excluded from the one court in their home district.

> *There's no use pussyfooting around. We did believe we were the superior people; that was just accepted. We liked them, we looked after them, and we valued them, but they were primitive people and we were the master race. There's no doubt about that.*
> **Lloyd Hurrell**

Much of the mass of discriminatory legislation of the 1930s continued into the post-war. It was only from the end of the 1950s that Australians passed from paternalism to partnership, and then to concede that the country really belonged to Papua New Guineans. In the revolution of status from *masta* to foreigner nearly all the obvious changes came in the last few years of Australian rule. The old regulations preventing Papua New Guineans from wearing clothes on the upper part of their bodies went early; the curfew and the penalties for being absent from quarters changed in the mid 1950s; and the separate censoring of films for Papua New Guineans ended in 1962. Practice sometimes lingered after the law had gone. In the 1950s the laws that required separate seating in places of public entertainment were repealed; but in the 1960s few Papua New Guineans were assertive enough to take the most comfortable seats. According to Ian Stuart the authorities avoided the most obvious racist insult by erecting two notices at Ela Beach in Port Moresby. One said 'European Swimming Beach' and the

other, 'No Dogs Allowed'. Again the beach remained the preserve of whites long after the notice had rotted or been destroyed.

By the early 1960s Papua New Guineans, many of whom had been educated in either Fiji or Australia, were challenging petty discrimination. Sir Maori Kiki remembers going with a group into the food bar at Port Moresby's Top Pub and asking for soft drinks. As was the normal practice at the time they were served in plastic cups; glasses were reserved for whites. They demanded glasses; but as Kiki admits: 'in those days you could not win'.

Soon they were winning concessions. Noel Levi:

When we started our training in Port Moresby in 1961 as assistant patrol officers a group of us fronted up to the Papuan Theatre one night and the manager said, 'Look, you know we can't let black people into this theatre'. We insisted, so he said, 'If you go in, and anybody asks you, you can tell them you're mixed race'. And we said, 'We aren't going to tell anybody we're mixed race. We are Papua New Guineans, and that's all there is to it!' We argued on, and eventually he let us in.

Older Papua New Guineans were disturbed by the changes which upset what they had come to accept as the proper ordering of human affairs. Mrs Peg Ashton says that when her daughter brought a New Guinean school friend home 'my cook boy was horrified. He almost refused to serve this boy lunch; he wasn't used to waiting on another native'. On another occasion the Ashtons entertained a United Nations Visiting Mission:

After dinner we put on some music, and this rather tall American Negro asked me to dance. He said, 'Ah, Mrs Ashton, this takes me back to my student days in Vienna'. And I was enjoying it too; he was a marvellous dancer. But the next morning my cook boy, his arms akimbo, looked me straight in the eye and said, '*Misis*, who was that kanaka you were dancing with last night?'

A Seventh Day Adventist campaign against alcohol in New Guinea

The law which prohibited Papua New Guineans from drinking alcohol was the focus of much debate and resentment. Then on Friday November 3, 1962, the law was changed, and amid loud expatriate predictions of doom and disaster thirsty Papua New Guineans surged through the pub doors for their first legal drink. Optimistic Papua New Guineans, Gunther explains, proclaimed by gesture, 'Here we are, pot of beer in our hand, and we're just as good as you now'. But within a few days the white drinkers had withdrawn to exclusive sections of the bars, and soon the hotels were building separate bars where dress regulations were used to maintain the old racial divisions. The battle had to be resumed. Bill Gammage recalls the day in March 1966 when he and some University students 'cracked the Boroko hotel' beer garden:

> We went down to the hotel, I ordered a round of beers, a jug and some glasses, and was served. Then Tony Siaguru went over. He came back and said, 'They won't serve me'. So he and I went back together and I said, 'What seems to be the trouble, mate?' The Papua New Guinean barman said, 'This man's not properly dressed'. In fact Tony was dressed better than I was; he had sandals on, I had thongs. I said, 'Oh, that's rubbish.' So the barman got the manager who said,

> 'He's not properly dressed; I can't serve him.' And I said, 'But I've already been served. This person is quite respectably dressed and behaved.' Which was true. In the end the manager accepted it, and Tony was served. Thereafter Papua New Guineans were allowed to drink in that bar. That would have happened sooner or later anyway, but it was a tremendous feeling to be there when it was happening.

Such incidents confirmed the fears of conservatives that the university would be a centre of subversion.

Change came more slowly outside Port Moresby. In Rabaul Don Penias found that convention and dress rules still maintained a strict segregation in the late 1960s. As a member of the ABC staff he moved in a group that was largely unconscious of differences in race, but as soon as he entered some places he was acutely aware that he was an outsider:

> We used to go around into the white man's bars and have a beer. And they used to have smorgasbord lunches. You walk in, you stand in line, pick up a plate, and fill it with whatever you want. But you had this feeling that there were people always watching. White people were looking at you because you would be the odd one out. You were the only black in that

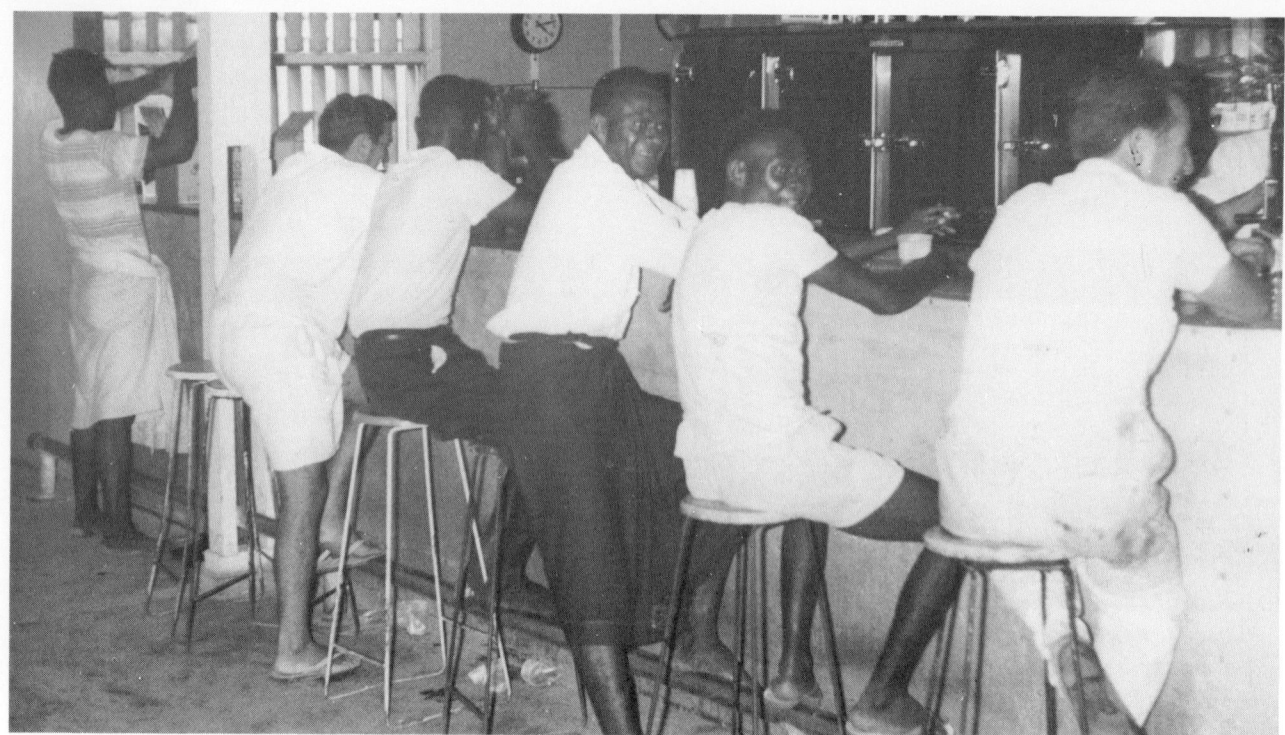

At first the rule was that shoes must be worn in the bar, but the rule didn't last. Bare feet and betel nut are now accepted.

line, and somehow they felt that you were invading them. You could feel in your body that they were watching.

In a deliberate attempt to break the old attitudes Penias and others went into bars which pretended to exclusiveness. Inevitably there was trouble and some of them spent nights in the lock-up. Penias now speaks without anger of those days. The expatriates who have stayed, he says, are 'easy to get along with' and those who thought that 'they had the whole of Papua New Guinea to themselves' and would always enjoy the services of a *manki* (young boy) to take orders have left—or changed.

In 1961 the first formal marriage was celebrated between a white Australian woman and a Papua New Guinean man. Some members of Port Moresby's white community publicly condemned the marriage and privately wrote cruel, anonymous letters. Three years later there was still only one such marriage and the appearance of the couple in the street continued to cause people to nudge and stare. Even when nearly all formal discrimination had ended and it was accepted that Papua New Guinea would soon be an independent nation, sexual relations

between black men and white women remained the basis of much talk, fear, prejudice and fantasy. Many white women found their lives restricted: they looked out through windows covered with 'boy wire' to deter prowlers, they did not drive at night in case the car broke down, they did not wear shorts and they would not allow the domestic servants to wash underclothing or make the beds. But a few behaved as they would in Australia. Dame Rachel Cleland:

I'd walk about the roads at night without any fear. I still do. Things did happen. But I said the wonder was that there's not more attempts by native men to get their own back with all the interference that went on by Australians with village women. But there was very little of it. I think they were very forbearing.

And, Noeline Shaw says, there were white women who took the initiative to cross sexual and racial barriers:

Everybody met at the Lae Club at a quarter to twelve. The women drank along with the men. It was a very artificial life. A lot of the women had affairs because their husbands were away for a long time and they had a choice of who they wanted to have an affair with. There was plenty of company available. A lot actually had affairs with natives, with house boys, basically because they were in the house all the time, they were there, and the women got to know them. They talked about it very openly. Most of them were silly, they were ageing quickly, and they found that sex was a necessary part of their lives. If there didn't happen to be an available *kiap* around the station, well, the house boy was the next best thing.

In her research Amirah Inglis did not meet any white women who spoke of sexual relations with their servants, but she did of course hear of such cases. She offers another explanation:

It's a great place for male beauty. I remember one day I was sitting doing some work in the library and I looked out the window, idly, and there was a chap cutting grass. All he had on was a laplap round his middle and nothing else. He had beautiful brown skin, and he was very fit; no flabby pot belly. I am sure this is what turned the heads of the young white women with the university students. There were a tremendous lot of very gorgeous, fit young men.

As Amirah Inglis points out little has been written about the attraction felt by foreign women to the 'lovely young males'.

> *Women had to be extremely careful about the way they dressed. The natives were very sexually attracted to women's legs: you never wore shorts, you never wore slacks.*
> **Noelene Shaw, nurse**

The hazards faced by young black and white bodies attempting to come together were still real. While John Waiko was at school one of the Papua New Guinean students and a staff member's daughter were attracted to each other. They were discovered together and the next morning the teacher brandished a gun before the assembled students threatening 'I will shoot with this gun whoever comes to touch my daughter'.

Although sexual relationships ran the full range of human preferences little has been said in public or been published about homosexuality. An Australian male says that homosexuals were largely left to lead their own lives 'as long as they didn't race around the landscape obviously trying to seduce the natives' or parade as 'an obvious trissy queen'. Homosexual relationships were tacitly accepted as long as they remained within certain limits:

The boundaries were that the person concerned had to be recognisably an adult, much more so than would be true in Australian or European society. The relationship could exist between a European and, say, his domestic servant. That was fairly common, and acceptable. It was seen as one of the solaces for the white man's burden. Another form of relationship existed between Europeans and Papua New Guineans where the son of some adult known to the European would be brought up by the European and given many advantages. The relationship between the European and the young man was tacitly recognised by the parents, and by society in general, but nobody said anything because the advantages were seen to be all for the young guy who was being educated, housed, clothed, fed, whatever. There was little reaction on the part of Papua New Guineans against this kind of relationship. If anything it led to humour rather than to condemnation. It was thought to be mildly amusing that the big white master would dally with a young gentleman rather than many of the available young ladies who'd cheerfully have gone to bed with him at any time. It was just thought to be yet another of the quaint peculiarities of the European. The relationship was seen to be something that the child, or rather the young man, because they were never really children, that the young man of say high school age would ultimately,

Saturday afternoon scene in one of Rabaul's two hotels. Only one European was drinking in this bar when the photo was taken. But it certainly doesn't seem overcrowded.

NEW GUINEA DRINKERS DON'T HAVE IT SO GOOD

From a Port Moresby Correspondent, and AAP-Reuter

Twelve months after the introduction of liquor to P-NG natives there are growing complaints in several areas about drinking conditions. People in both Rabaul and Port Moresby say that the towns have too many native drinkers and not enough bars to hold them.

RABAUL has two hotels and the Rabaul Town Advisory Council says it ought to have a third, together with licensed restaurants to cater for natives. The council has also suggested that storekeepers should be able to sell single bottles, for many native drinkers, who have to buy a carton, use all their wages and often drink the lot in one sitting anyhow. Wives and children go hungry.

Tolai women have recently marched through Rabaul in protest against the drinking conditions. They said their men folk should be taught how to drink intelligently or else they should be banned from drinking.

Rabaul police have had to crack down recently on methylated spirit drinkers and some suppliers have suggested that the spirit should be adulterated by the addition of quinine before it is sold.

In Port Moresby, which has three hotels for a population of 35,000 there has also been a request (to the Liquor Licensing Commission) for another hotel.

Sittings of the commission have recently helped to bring many native drinking problems into focus, and shown many Europeans throughout the Territory that the drink problem is not as simple as it might first have looked when prohibition was lifted in November, 1962.

The commission has heard applications for extra liquor outlets in large urban centres, aimed mainly at giving the native population greater access to alcohol.

During these sittings groups of native women have demonstrated against greater availability, and have demanded the reintroduction of native prohibition.

Police have told of increased "tribal brawling", increases in petty thievery, and attacks on police.

Missions have warned of the demoralising effects of alcohol on their converts.

Far Ranging

Police Commissioner Normoyle says, although serious incidents during the past year or so have been rare, the social effects have been far-ranging.

The basic wage rate in the Territory's urban centres is about £3 a week. A native base rate labourer or houseboy faced with the upkeep of a wife and two children plus a liking for alcohol has found the problem in many cases almost too much for him to bear.

In some cases wives and children have been neglected, essential items of clothing for families are just no longer available, and sometimes the wives and children have been forced to return to the villages so they can get enough to eat.

Pacific Islands Monthly February, 1964

if you like, grow out of. It was assumed by the parents that this relationship would exist up to a certain time and that then the young man would marry, have children and lead a perfectly normal life. And in the vast majority of cases this is exactly what did happen. But the benefits to these young men who were involved in relationships of this kind were very real. Indeed there are quite a number of people holding senior posts in Papua New Guinea today who are the product of this type of situation.

The white community was a strange mixture of much hectoring about proper behaviour, and much toleration of those who behaved differently.

By the 1970s marriages between Papua New Guinean men and white women were still rare, but they no longer incited either outrage or intense curiosity. Barbara Lepani married in 1972. As an educated white woman with a critical and independent attitude to her own culture she was aware of the difficulties she faced by becoming the wife of a Papua New Guinean. She saw herself

> moving into a society that was based on kinship where the demands on the wife were those of serving and looking after vast numbers of men and cooking food, and not having strong opinions about politics or economics. When we went to the Trobriand Islands we stayed in my father-in-law's house which at that time was being occupied by a chief. The custom in the Trobriand Islands is that women may never walk in front or behind a man if he is seated. As the women cannot be taller than him they have to get down on the ground and crawl past. Or they have to call out and ask the man to stand up. If there's a chief in the house this becomes critically important, and even men have to bend over in front of the chief so that they're not taller than him. Well, I felt very awkward. I was a feminist, I saw myself as a Marxist, and I didn't know how I could adjust these positions with having to bend down

in front of a man just because he was sitting. At the same time if I didn't bend down then I was being a typical colonial and not acknowledging another culture and its rules. So how could I reconcile these two positions? In the end I would bend over. I never ever crawled across the floor because I found that just culturally impossible to do. I bent low at the waist and thought this is a polite gesture.

> Another situation caused the most difficulty. I had been a rebel in my own culture and disobeyed all the rules in a search for honesty. When one wanted to go to the toilet one could say, 'I'm going to the toilet' instead of 'I'm going to powder my nose'. Now I suddenly found myself in a culture that, according to the books, was one of the most free cultures in the world: it had no sex taboos; it was famous for its sexual freedom; but I discovered that going to the toilet was a major exercise in cultural diplomacy. If I wanted to go to the toilet then I had to do so in such a way that no one knew that's what I was doing. I had to disappear in a subtle way. There were no toilets to go to, but there were certain parts of the bush where one went. I found it very difficult as a prominent large white lady to melt into the distance when I was in a crowd of completely brown people who were watching every move I made. So that used to put me into enormous confusion.

> One of the biggest problems for me was that I felt completely and utterly incompetent at the sorts of things that village women do. I'd come from a culture in which I was extremely competent, relying on verbal skills to manipulate situations, to suddenly enter a culture where none of these skills were at all useful. People were very polite in a way that my own culture wouldn't have been if they were in my position.

The surprise is not that many such marriages have ended, but that some have flourished.

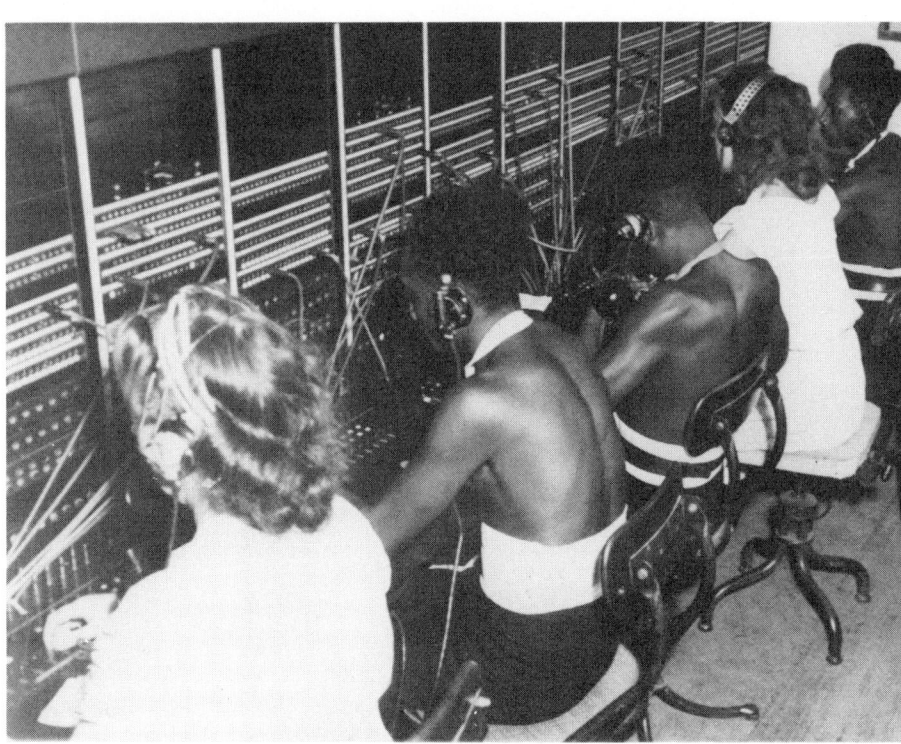

Sharing skills and space but not pay

When white Australians and Papua New Guineans met, skin pigmentation was only one of the markers of difference. In any one situation other factors were more likely to be more important: levels of education, wealth, political power, and the distinctions between master and servant. But through one hundred years of meetings across these barriers personal friendships have been made, and common experiences have tied Australians and Papua New Guineans together. Anio was Jack Baker's personal servant for fifteen years. His children and the Baker children grew up together. Some time after he left Papua New Guinea Jack was able to bring Anio to Queensland to visit the caravan park that Jack now runs. It was the illiterate Anio's first trip outside his homeland.

> The only aspect of life that Anio found impossible to adjust to was the sight of me emptying a hundred garbage cans each morning around the caravan park; he just could not watch this performance without lying back against a post and laughing his head off. I found this very hurtful, and I also found hurtful the fact that he declined to assist in any way with garbage clearance!

The story, and Jack's telling of it with infectious humour, are evidence that the relationship between the two men has long since passed beyond that of master and servant, or of white and black.

Sir Maori Kiki suggests that the bonds between Australians and Papua New Guineans are more than just an affinity in particular and exceptional cases. There is a general bond:

> There's a closeness, you know. Say for example you find an Australian in somewhere like Bangkok and there is a Papua New Guinean walking in, the Australian will spot him. He has never seen him before but he will know he's a Papua New Guinean. And when you talk to him, he will expect you to talk like an Australian. 'That's a bloody Papua New Guinean! Hey, you Kanaka, where do you come from?' And the Papua New Guinean will look at him and say, 'Kanaka! You are Australian, you bastard, where have you been?' I have experienced it myself. Plenty of people have said this. You feel you know each other.

If Papua New Guineans and Australians feel that they know each other, then that is a considerable achievement.

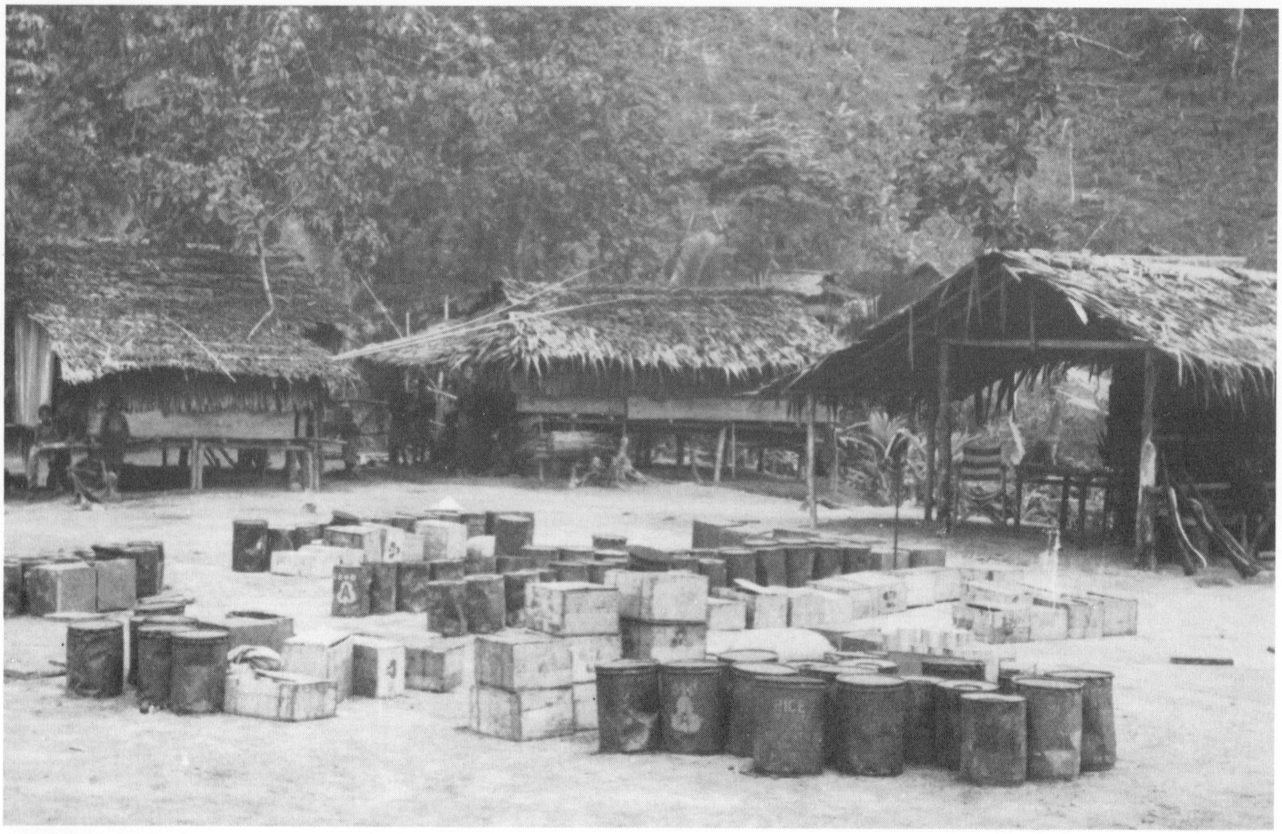

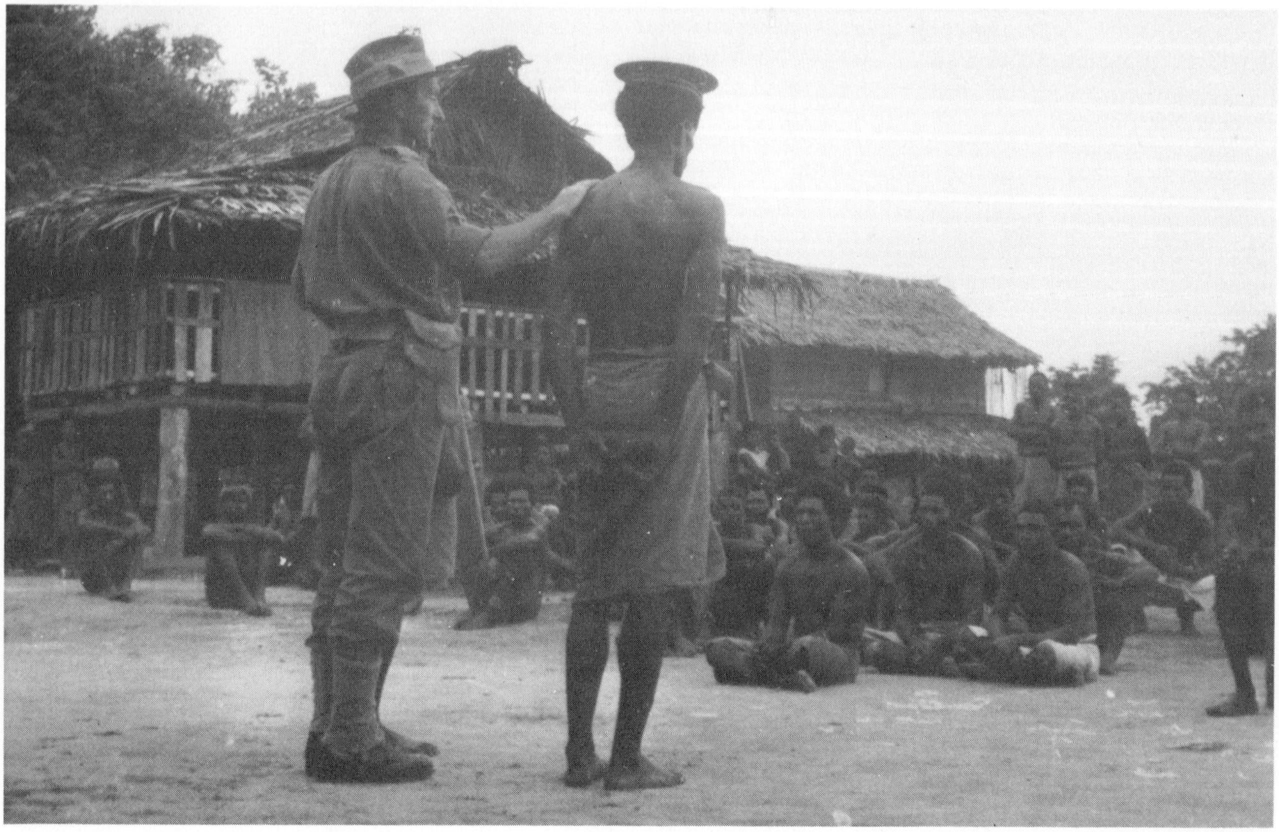

21 Courts and Calaboose

Melanesian systems of justice depend a great deal on compensation for those injured. This compensation was vital. Really, vendettas could be avoided if the compensation was big enough, but it never was. Of course people were too proud to bring tribute, that would concede dominance. And so killing resulted.

Ian Downs, District Commissioner

One of the basic functions of the frontier officer was to impose a new system of justice. If the government officer could not establish a superior system of law then a major justification for his intervention in the lives of the people had disappeared. Inevitably then, colonial governments and their agents were sensitive about their role as the carriers of new laws and of new ways of settling disputes. A problem in Papua New Guinea was that the traditional political units were so small. There was no centralised system that the colonial authority could take over and modify. It was a case of imposing Western law over an infinite variety of subtly changing local customs and values. The process had to be repeated over and over again. The Australian field and legal officers did not oversee the work of sultans or chiefs; they themselves determined innocence or guilt, and decided on the appropriate punishment. And in the Papua New Guinea village, as in other communities, many legal decisions were also political decisions. The prestige and authority of individuals and clans were determined by rulings in cases about land, assaults, sorcery, marriage

settlements and in a hundred other cases where it was not just one person being ordered to make amends for one clearly defined crime.

Through most of Australia's rule there were three levels of courts. At the lowest level were the *kiap* courts, in the middle were the District Courts, and at the top was the Central or Supreme Court. The field officers heard the vast majority of cases. '*Kiap* justice' Jim Sinclair says, 'has been severely criticised, particularly by academic lawyers, and no doubt it was rough and ready justice; but it was justice and it was ready.' Many of the summary cases coming before the *kiaps* were offences under the 'Native Regs': the Native Regulations in Papua and the Native Administration Regulations in New Guinea. Other charges were usually laid under the Queensland Criminal Code which had been transposed north. As the Regulations had a subtle nominal variation from one Territory to another so did the *kiap* courts: they were the Courts for Native Affairs in New Guinea, and the Courts for Native Matters in Papua.

The *kiap* courts were a mixture of the ceremonial and conversational. The flag

A cautionary tale: instead of distributing stores (top) supplied in wartime to his fellow villagers, a *luluai* called Bumbu kept them for his own use. He was caught, demoted and Bill Bloxham swore in a new *luluai* (left).

185

POLYGAMY TABU—SO NATIVE KILLED HIS WIFE

From Our Own Correspondent
RABAUL, July 2.

THERE was much criticism and bickering at the beginning of the year when the N. Guinea marriage laws were amended to make it impossible for a native to contract a European or Christian marriage. In introducing the bill, the Government Secretary (Mr. H. H. Page) said that the majority of natives were not able yet to understand the obligations of matrimony.

In the Supreme Court last month, an interesting case showed the significance ascribed by natives to marriages made according to mission rites.

A native, Sangar, was charged with wilfully killing his wife. He explained, as his defence, that he wanted to take another woman as his spouse, but having been married by a missionary was unable to do so. He told the court that he solved the problem by murdering his wife!

Sangar was sentenced to death.

Pacific Islands Monthly August 19, 1936

was raised, the police and the interpreters stood by, and 'you'd put a table out in front of the house kiap and if it was hot and you'd prop up a sort of big umbrella, or get under the shade of a big tree'. Although those men who had gone through the two-year diploma course at ASOPA had what Jim Sinclair calls 'a comprehensive and solid law course' the instruction from the 'senior fellows', Bob Cole says, was the simple direction 'to be firm and fair'. Where possible they arbitrated rather than laying specific charges. Neil Desailly:

Nearly always if there's a little bit of incentive to do so people would arrange some sort of compromise themselves. My place would be to say, you have in this community certain men who are of standing, who understand your ways, who are involved in this sort of thing all the time. They should be able to assist and advise you. Use them. The *luluai*, the *tultul*, some other village leader, is here, sit down over there, under my eye, and discuss it. If they were highlanders they usually had axes with them, and I'd insist that the axes be left out of reach, parked over at the side somewhere. And discuss it they would. They'd argue, they'd orate, and carry on for hours quite often. Usually they did reach, if not a consensus, at least some sort of agreement. Always with the underlying threat: If you can't settle it then I must. It's my duty to. And if I make a decision of course that will be supported by the full authority of the government. Sanctions will be applied and I will make sure that you do what I say. Maybe it would be better if you decide on something because perhaps nobody will like what I decide.

Law through directed discussion was, Desailly concludes, 'almost a standard procedure'. Lloyd Hurrell agrees that they often said 'now you fellows get in and settle this yourself', but that ultimately the kiaps 'stole' the villagers' powers to make their own decisions; 'there were probably too many court cases held and it denuded

the powers of the village as a village organisation'. Leo Hannett puts the same criticism more sharply: 'It was a one-man show. If the kiap said he was guilty, well, he was guilty.' Even if the people knew that the decision was unjust, Hannett says, they did not believe that they had any right of appeal.

The most common cases involved land, women and pigs, 'they're the three'. But, as Ian Downs pointed out, 'Melanesian systems of justice depend a great deal on compensation for those injured'. Village communities were practised in gauging the payments needed to 'straighten' common wrongs. A field officer who was prepared to listen to the people could usually find out what they believed was reasonable payment and then sanction the handing over of the money or goods. The problem for younger members of staff was to judge the point in village discussion when it was appropriate to intervene and enforce an apparent consensus. Chris Vass:

People might come in with a matrimonial problem. You'd first hear the husband's story and then the wife's story for about half an hour, and make some sort of decision that you thought was reasonable. It probably was fairly reasonable when looked at through European eyes, but it may not have been the best solution for them when you took into account the enormous complexities that are involved with marriage in their society. The ties between husband and wife had far reaching effects between clan groups. Moneys and goods that were paid for brides, gifts that were given to brides, were passed from clan to clan and had an important meaning to ties between the clan groups. But quite often young Australians didn't appreciate these things. They might have sat down for an hour or two to listen to the people; but really that wasn't enough. Talking to people later on I learnt that problems like that would have taken many more hours, if not days, to have been solved by the people themselves.

Bernard Narakobi is more harsh: 'I think the Australians' understanding of the

KNUCKLE-DUSTERS TABU.

From Our Own Correspondent,
RABAUL, Nov. 3.

A NEW regulation has been published, which is an additional clause to the Regulations under the Native Administration Ordinance, 1921-1927.

It is now an offence for any native to have in his custody or possession, without lawful excuse, any knuckle-duster, or other article of a similar nature.

Under the same regulation it is an offence to carry, without lawful excuse, any razor or razor blade.

The penalty is a fine of £5 or imprisonment for six months, or both.

Pacific Islands Monthly November 22, 1933

Judging a man who has been accused of theft.

customs of the people was not very deep. Basically they regarded the people as savages, and if they were gentle they would qualify that term by calling them "gentle" or "noble" savages.'

The *kiap* wore all legal hats. He was arresting officer, prosecutor and magistrate. 'As a magistrate' John Murphy says, 'we took no notice of ourselves as a police prosecutor'. The distinction may well have been lost on the accused. Bill Bloxham recalls a sequence of demanding and confusing roles that the pre-war *kiaps* could be called upon to carry out:

I went in with my squad of police to apprehend this murderer. The murderer resisted arrest and was shot in the arm by one of my native police. He was then brought back to the government station at Marienberg where there was no doctor or medical assistance. I patched him up until he was fit for trial. Then in the District Court I committed him for trial for murder in the Supreme Court which sat in Rabaul. In my function as head gaoler I then took him into custody. For him to be transferred from one gaol to another as head gaoler I had to sign a series of documents authorising the head gaoler in Rabaul to take over. As a protector of natives I then had to put in an informal report explaining the degree of civilisation where the

crime had been committed and any other relevant facts. After trial in Rabaul he was sentenced to death, brought back to me, and I had to supervise his execution as the officer of the sheriff. He was taken to the place where the crime was committed and hanged from a tree before an assembly of all the local chieftains. I might say that headhunting and murder had been quite common in that part of the world, and as a reminder of the power of the government and what it could do to people that offended its code, the rope which was used to hang him was cut into sections about eighteen inches long and a piece was handed to every chieftain from that area. That was a grim reminder, but I think that it paid dividends in the long run.

Another Sepik officer, Kassa Townsend, who gathered 2000 people to witness one hanging wrote that 'It was the ultimate demonstration that the Government meant the warnings that it gave; that the Government was "strong".'

In the 1930s there were only two judges in New Guinea and one in Papua, although there Sir Hubert Murray, still remembered by some Papuans as 'Judge Murray', could preside over cases before the Central Court. Where there were so few professional magistrates individuals

Saturday morning inspection

could have a marked effect on the conduct of the law. Mr Justice R T Gore had first gone to Papua in 1924, and he was still taking cases when Tos Barnett met him in the 1960s:

I am very glad I arrived in time to see him in action on circuit. Before the war he used to do the circuits on horseback, leaving Port Moresby and heading off into the mountains. He really knew a lot about the country and the people, and had long ago put aside most of the niceties of legal procedure that some of the more recent judicial appointments brought with them from Australia.

One case that Tos Barnett recalls concerned an old man who had been charged with murdering his daughter. The girl had reneged on an arranged marriage with an older man thereby causing all kinds of problems, including recovery of the bride price. The prosecution alleged that the father had killed her, and then thrown her body into the river, but the defence made effective use of technical medical evidence which suggested that the girl was alive when she entered the water. Tos Barnett:

Judge Gore acquitted the man. Very reluctantly. Then he called all the headmen and lined them up at the back of the court. The defendant, a very strong character, was still there looking at him. And Gore just got

stuck into them. This enormously large white man with a red robe and a bald head thumped the bench and said, 'Look, I've been coming here for years and years and years, and I have told you people that these practices of selling your young daughters in marriage have got to stop!' And he thumped the table again. He said, 'Now look, I know you did it, but I've got to acquit you, I've got to let you go free. But you are a dirty old man. Now get out.' The fellow sank to his knees, burst into tears, and crawled out of the court house. The line-up of old fellows at the back stood quivering.

There was a place in Queensland, Judge Gore wrote in his reminiscences, where the crows flew tail first to cool their backsides: he longed for the facility of the crow, he said, when he sat in his robes in many of the Territory's cramped court houses. It was the policy of the Supreme Court to take justice to the people. Even in the remotest places the judge sat in 'full criminal court rig of scarlet robes and grey horsehair wig'. The full court party, the judge and his associate, the counsel for the prosecution and the counsel for the defence, usually arrived together, the judge inspected the police guard, and entered what might be a humble building. Tos Barnett:

We would stand in our gowns and we'd bow to the judge as he came in.

'If it please your Honour, I appear for the defence'. And we would refer to each other as 'My learned brother', and 'Your Honour'. The full procedure, the full laws of evidence, were applied just as if it was in Australia. Occasionally, if it was right up in the sweltering Sepik, some of the judges would say that it was quite all right if we felt like taking our robes off, and then we'd just do it in shirt sleeves.

Nick O'Neill suggests that the formality of the court was never such as to frighten people, and Bernard Narakobi, himself a lawyer, sees virtue in legal display:

Ceremony is one of the most important parts of our culture. Symbolism, mystery, the power of God. These things become identified with mysterious symbolism. Wigs really added to the aura and the mysticism that was associated with the white man's law.

Sir John Minogue was a strong advocate of taking the court to the people. Appointed a judge of the Supreme Court in 1962, he was Chief Justice from 1970 to 1974. He points out that many highlanders who attended the court wore vastly superior wigs and the setting was often not one to inspire awe:

The case would be called on and the charge read in English. It was then translated into Pidgin if it was on the New Guinea side, and into Police Motu if on the Papuan side. Then, dependent on the language involved, it would be translated once again into another language through another set of interpreters into what we called the 'place talk' of the area. Indeed I recall one case in Wewak in which we had twenty accused. This was the first case heard from the area. They had been brought down from the May River, up near the West Irian border. We had to have four interpreters, and as might be expected the case collapsed in confusion, we couldn't get through to them. In the early days we sat in grass huts, and I can recall in Kundiawa up in the Chimbu area

sitting in a round grass hut with bare earth floor and being bothered by wandering chickens under my feet as I was hearing a civil case. A poor fellow involved in the case was carried in on a stretcher, being a quadriplegic. The chickens were scratching under his stretcher and on the court floor as the case was heard.

The dignity of the court, Sir John suggests, was compatible with chooks.

The Australian courts were consistently confused about how to deal with sorcery. For Papua New Guineans sorcery had a reality that the courts could not accept. Nick O'Neill appeared for the defence of several people charged with the murder of sorcerers. Once in the Milne Bay area

a woman was sick. A man who claimed to have killed twenty-nine people through sorcery came to her place and threw leaves in the window. He then got in his canoe and rowed away. Her husband gathered a couple of friends and they chased him. They believed that if he started a fire and blew smoke in her direction she would die; that was the next and final process in the magic. So when they caught him they killed him. Under our law provocation as a defence would not apply because there was time for their passions to cool. Self-defence didn't apply because he hadn't really done anything which was a direct and immediate threat to this woman in our perception, in our law. Insanity didn't apply because perfectly sane Papua New Guineans believe in sorcery, and that's the view that's been established in Africa and elsewhere by colonial courts. So these people were found guilty of wilful murder.

In that case the judge gave light sentences of three years. But, as O'Neill argues, the problem had not been solved because the people believed that the killers should not have been gaoled at all. If, on the other hand, the courts gaoled sorcerers they were in effect confirming the power of the sorcerers to harm people.

Another source of persistent confusion arose in the sentencing of men found

UNLAWFUL KILLING

N.G. Miner Gets Two Years' Gaol

From Our Own Correspondent
RABAUL, Feb. 4.

GEORGE CHESTER, a prospector who has been working on the Lower Dunantina River, in the Purari district—one of the most isolated areas in the Morobe goldfields—came before Chief Judge Wanliss on January 17, charged with unlawfully killing a native. Accused pleaded not guilty.

The evidence was that of an incident which might happen at almost any mining camp in the Territory. The assault took place at the end of the day. Koluve, the deceased native, was controlling the water that was running into the box, when the daily wash-up was taking place; he allowed too much water to flow, with the result that gold and concentrates were washed into the tail-race, and much was lost. The accused, incensed at the boy's action, according to the evidence, lost his temper, and assaulted the boy, who subsequently died that same afternoon. Medical evidence showed that the cause of death was a ruptured spleen.

His Honour said that brutality was not the way to enforce discipline; and this kind of thing not only led to loss of life, but also to unfortunate difficulties with fellow miners. "I know," continued His Honour, "the conditions under which you have to work there, alone; wretched food, no society of any kind; troubles with labour very often, I suppose, sickness and malaria. These things get on the mind and affect a man's disposition, and make him do things he could not think of doing under other circumstances, and I am going to take all these facts into consideration in your case."

The accused was sentenced to two years' imprisonment, with hard labour.

Pacific Islands Monthly February 20, 1934

IN THE COURT OF NATIVE
AFFAIRS.

Deki and Torutul, for drinking in-
toxicating liquor, sentenced to be im-
prisoned with hard labour in the
Kokopo Gaol, Deki for three months,
and Toratul for one month.

For being absent from their quarters
after the hour of 9 p.m., the following
natives were sentenced:—Topania 14
days hard labour. Amari, ordered to
pay a fine of 5/- in default seven days
hard labour. Freddi, one month hard
labour.

For creating a noise after the hour
of 9 p.m., Boisa, Tanakula, Kaima,
Batae and Kebae, each ordered to pay
a fine of two shillings in default seven
days hard labour in Rabaul Gaol.

Amona, for assaulting one Kiki,
ordered to pay a fine of five shillings in
default seven days hard labour.

Rabaul Times July 14, 1933

Calaboose, or Kalabus, *is the
Pidgin term for gaol. In the form*
kalabusim *it is a verb meaning
to gaol, or more generally just to
lock up or restrict. A*
kalabusman *is a prisoner, and*
wok kalabus *is the sort of hard
labour that prisoners are given,
but it too has been extended to
cover any sort of difficult,
constant work. It says something
about the experiences of Papua
New Guineans that the word for
gaol has become such a widely
used term and metaphor.*

guilty of murder. Under the Queensland
Criminal Code the death sentence was
mandatory. And in the pre-war New
Guinea the judges and the government
were often willing to exact the full
penalty, but from 1957 no hangings were
carried out. The normal process was for
the judge to announce the sentence then
write, through the Administrator, to
the Governor-General recommending
mercy. As Sir John Minogue explains this
was a complex idea to convey in court:

> you had to go through one or two
> languages to try and explain to both
> the prisoner and the people gathered
> round that you were going to write all
> this in a book; that he was to die, and
> we didn't know when. We were also
> going to write to a big man in
> Australia and see what he said about it,
> and we'd know the answer in a few
> weeks' time.

After successive representations from the
bench the judges were given the power in
1969 to impose sentences other than
death on those found guilty of murder.

In 1940 there were nearly a thousand
Papua New Guineans in gaol. On the eve
of independence over 20 000 were in
gaol. In Pidgin they were the *kalabusman*.
Nearly all of them were serving short sentences with hard labour. They cut grass,
made roads and worked pit saws. To go to
kalabus was one of the common experiences of those Papua New Guineans who
left their home villages. In the eyes of
their own clansmen many prisoners had
done nothing wrong; they had merely
been punished for violating some alien
law. Members of the white community
asserted that gaols were 'country clubs for
kanakas'.

But Papua New Guineans had no
doubt that the *kalabus* was a place of
punishment. Sir John Minogue:

> I noted time and again the look of almost
> despair on the face of some, particularly
> mature men, when they realised
> what was going to happen to them.

Nick O'Neill, too, says that for all of the
hundred or so men that he defended
kalabus was 'the last place they wanted to
go'. The warders, O'Neill believes, were

generally friendly, the food was adequate
and men often emerged healthier than
when they went in, but the restrictions
and the alienation from village society
made prison a place of fear. Yet the
prisoner acquired a knowledge of Pidgin
or Motu, made friends among the police
who were often his warders, and probably
knew more about the outside world than
anyone else in his community. *Kalabus*,
Neil Desailly says, was 'more a compulsory
education' than a form of punishment.

From the start Australians introduced
an adversary system of justice. Where
possible a Papua New Guinean facing a
serious charge was defended by either a
legal or a field officer. In 1962 the Public
Solicitors Office was set up to extend legal
aid to Papua New Guineans. Some people
immediately used the new service to take
land cases to the Supreme Court. This was
taken by some Australians as a demonstration of faith by Papua New Guineans in
the legal system, but others saw the Public
Solicitors Office as bringing massive
amounts of unnecessary work and under-
mining decisions that they had made. Tos
Barnett, one of the first trained defence
counsel to go into many areas, confirmed
the fears of those who saw that the
government's over-zealous concern for
legal proprieties would lead to anarchy.
He earned the name 'Toss-em-out Tos' as
he destroyed the *kiaps'* cases on technicali-
ties. The *kiaps* were naturally irate at what
they took to be an obsession with petty
formalities while justice was ignored. Tos
himself was disturbed when the courts
failed to secure the retribution that the
aggrieved people demanded. In one case at
Kundiawa Tos was one of two counsel
defending a group of men from near
Kainantu who had killed four Chimbus:

> The leading defendant was an old
> gentleman called Takendau. He was an
> old chap, and apparently one of his
> clansmen had been killed in an
> accident while working on a
> plantation on the coast. As it happened
> the accident was nobody's fault, but
> the man was dead. In their custom if
> they suffered a loss either
> compensation was paid or else they

took a life to redress the loss. So they heard that there were some Chimbus in the area who in fact came from a little bit further towards the plantation, but not that much further, certainly nowhere near the coast. These unsuspecting people were travelling through the area collecting bird-of-paradise feathers for a *singsing*. Takendau and his group ambushed them; they lined up on both sides of the path and killed them as they were going through.

The defence was possibly going to be successful. It was based on the fact that under the Queensland Criminal Code you either had to prove that each particular individual had done the killing or had aided the person who did the killing, and knew that he was aiding him at the time. We'd actually made legal history previously in another case which went to the High Court where we exposed a gap in those sections in the Criminal Code. So maybe one of them, or all of them, could have been acquitted. But we never knew because the Chimbus, who were the relatives of the people who had been killed, knowing this possibility, arrived by truck. When the court stopped for the evening adjournment, and we wended our way back from the court house towards the pub where we were all staying, the police took Takendau back towards the gaol, and the Chimbus killed him. The first thing we knew about it, a policeman arrived with two beaming Chimbu gentlemen, each of them still holding an axe with blood pouring down its blade and wanting to tell us that they'd just killed Takendau. Which they had. They were extremely proud and happy that they had managed to accomplish that. You really get the feeling that something is wrong with the system, or certainly that it's not being understood by people having it imposed on them. There were other equally bloody incidents which were undeniable demonstrations of the people's lack of confidence in

the capacity of the courts to deliver what they thought was justice.

A fundamental failing of the Australian legal system was that it was never comprehensive. Although they were nominally under Australian control many villagers continued to run their own systems of settling disputes and punishing those who broke locally accepted laws. The official courts were either too far away, or seen as irrelevant, or the communities were just reluctant to let the fate of their members be decided by outsiders. Sir John Gunther:

I was never confident about justice. I was hearing two groups of people who in their different ways were experts. One said that justice should start at the grass roots and the village should be the first court of justice; the village should manage its own affairs provided the traditional behaviour didn't conflict with the Criminal Code or the Native Regulations. But there were the judges who said no, under no circumstances. You've got to have skilled officials giving out justice to the people. The villagers don't really know what justice means. As far as the public servant was concerned, as far as I was concerned, I think the argument of the judges had to prevail. However once again I thought it would be up to the people to decide what kinds of courts they wanted. By the time they got independence we'd have given them a number of lawyers from the university who could advise them one way or another. If they wanted village courts they could have village courts. And they've got village courts.

One of the first decisions of self-governing Papua New Guinea was to establish village courts.

For the Australian government to carry out its aim of introducing courts that were accessible, universal and presided over by qualified staff, it had to do either of two things: it had to spend more money to extend the national system of courts into the villages, or it had to bring the informally operating village courts into the national system. It never quite did either.

Rabaul Times July 14, 1933

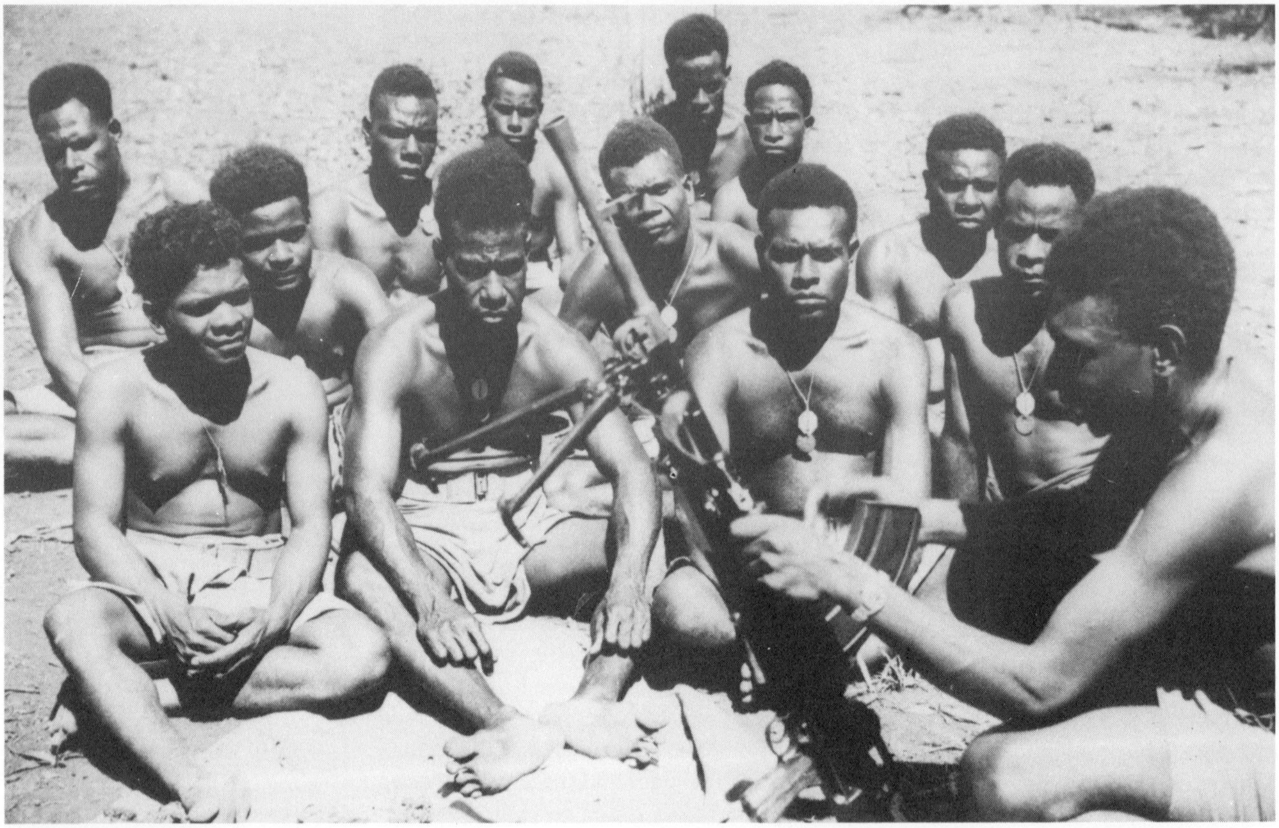

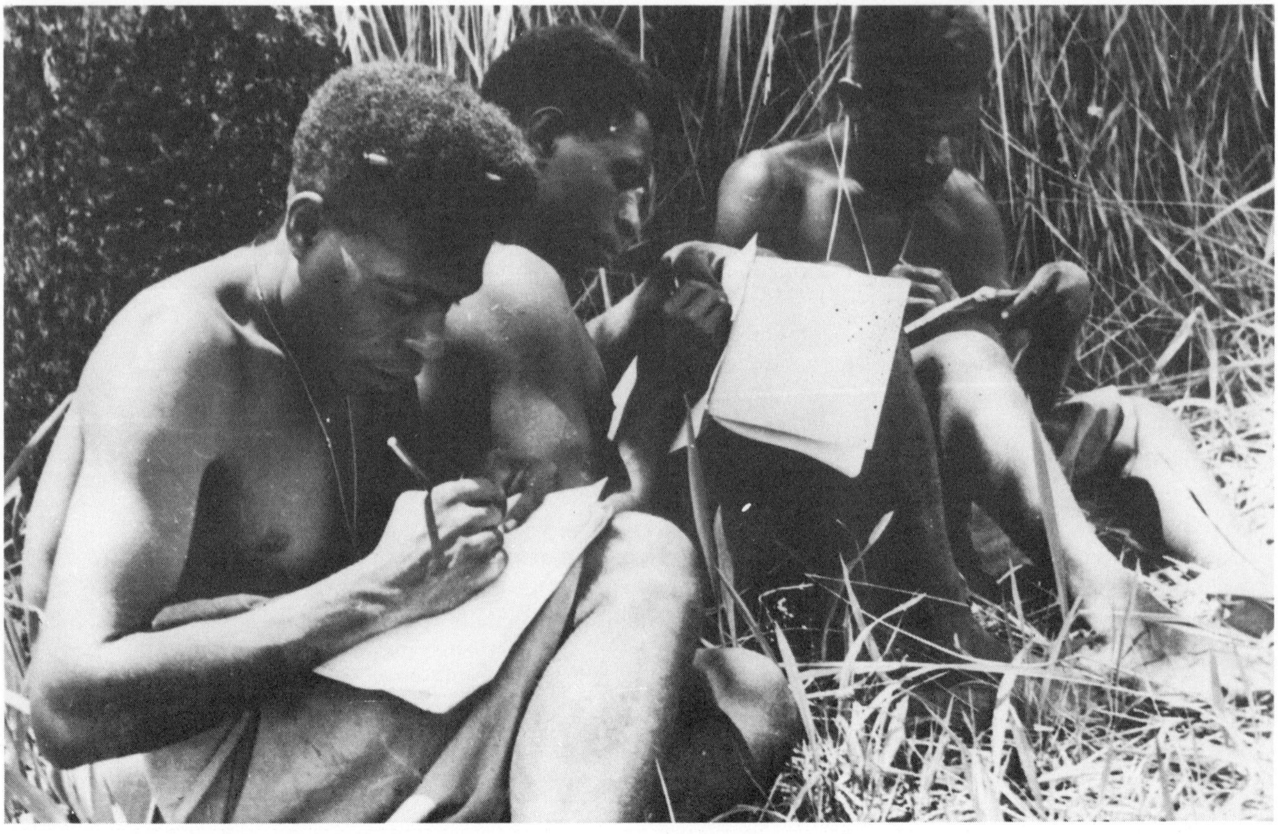

22 War

The Japanese came in and bombed Bulolo, Wau, Lae and Salamaua; and I heard the bombs. That was the end of New Guinea, then. They had evacuated all the women and children. It was a very sad and sorry time. You didn't know what was going to happen. I joined the New Guinea Volunteer Rifles; there were only a few hundred in the whole outfit. It was a Good Time Charlie sort of an army. For the first eight or nine months we were just chasing round the bush, reporting planes as they went over and things like that. There wasn't much defence. You could have taken the whole place with a closet lid. It didn't look as though Moresby or anywhere else would last very long.

Jim Leahy

The war destroyed much of the old Papua New Guinea. By 1945 all of the north coast and the island settlements were a litter of bomb craters, splintered buildings and the wreckage of army camps. The war divided time for Territorians. The *taim bipo* (the time before) became those increasingly hazy days before the war. A 'before' (sometimes 'B4') was a white person who had been in either Territory before 1942.

The war completely changed the scale of foreign intervention. Where in the *taim bipo* there had only been a handful of Asians and Europeans, now there were hundreds of thousands; and they came with the most advanced and horrific engines that their cultures could supply. Papua New Guinea, which had been so marginal to Australian concerns, was in the news every day. The place names— Kokoda, Coral Sea, Milne Bay, Wewak, Lae — became familiar to Australians; they attached history and legend to them.

In 1939 world war seemed remote from the Pacific islands. But suddenly in 1941 Papua New Guinea was midpoint between two armies. The day after Pearl Harbour was bombed Japanese reconnaissance planes flew over Rabaul and Kavieng. And they were there again the next day. At the end of December all

available ships and aircraft were pressed into service to evacuate 1800 white women and children. On one flight from Port Moresby to Cairns fifty passengers crammed into one twenty-one seater DC3. Each departing woman was allowed thirty pounds of luggage for herself and fifteen pounds for each child. Theresa Bloxham:

I knew I was going away in the clothes I stood up in. I picked up—this was psychological really—I picked up a pillow slip, a small towel and a cushion because I was pregnant at the time and I felt it would perhaps be possible for me to lie down when I got extremely tired. We didn't know where we were going, what was going to happen to us, or anything.

Jean McCarthy packed 'a few rags of clothing that I had left after two and a half years in New Guinea without a break', and left her husband standing at the little wharf at Talasea. Given a few hours' notice Mrs Bob Franklin was flown out of Wau and arrived over Moresby at 11 o'clock at night: lights set on forty-four gallon drums guided the plane in. Requests from leaders of the Chinese community were ignored, and no provision was made for the evacuation of Asian or mixed race women and children.

Corporal Ben demonstrates the Bren gun. The war brought the Papua New Guineans praise, opportunity, power, hard work, disaster and death (top left).

The war gave Australians a glimpse of Papua New Guineans as ordinary people (bottom left).

TOK LONG OLEGEDA BOI BILONG OL PLES CLOSTU SALAMAUA

Long MUBO soldia bilong mipala rausim ol Iapan nau kilim plenti.   Yupala lukim plenti balus bilong mipala work wontaem.   Ol i trowei plenti bam nau sutim ol Iapan long gun masin Mipala sitrong tumas. Iapan i laik bakarap nau.   Lik lik taem mipala kum up pinis long ol ples kanaka.

Mipala savi bifor ol Iapan i pulim sumpala man long wok long im.   Supos man olsem i kirap nau kam long mipala i no got tok mor.   Man istop clostu Iapan i kisim bam nau gun masin bilong mipala.   Man i got meri nau pikinini hait gut long bus nau waitim mipala.

Guvman isalim dispala tok.   Salim nabaut long ol kanaka.

Leaflets dropped over isolated people assured them they had not been deserted.

Pacific Islands Monthly

AUSTRALIAN GOVERNMENT'S CRUEL TREATMENT OF EVACUEES
Refusal of Any Promise of Economic Rehabilitation

ALTHOUGH nearly a year has passed since civilians were removed from the Australian Territories of Papua and New Guinea, and their commercial interests disrupted or destroyed by conditions beyond their control, these people still are without any promise, undertaking or reassurance from the Australian Government concerning their eventual economic rehabilitation.

They cannot get even a reassurance or a promise of sympathetic consideration of the position in relation to the two matters which most vitally concern them—namely, compensation for losses, and permission to return, when it is safe, to the occupation of their own properties.

THE indifference of the Commonwealth Government to the distress of these unfortunate people—who are in danger of losing everything, while the people of Australia remain complacently unharmed—is damnable and sickening. Appeal after appeal, by Territories people, individually, and by the Pacific Territories Association, in relation to these two matters, have been fobbed off with official formular and smooth-tongued Ministerial promises to "inquire into the situation." Nothing has been done, nor seems likely to be done.

So the time has come for plain speaking. Ministers are callous and indifferent—wherefore an appeal for assistance will be made elsewhere. A copy of this article will go to the editor of every influential newspaper, and to every member of the Commonwealth Parliament.

It is a disconcerting fact that, under our system of government, the only way in which inarticulate or unimportant sections of the people run get attention by and past consideration of, their grievances is to identify their themselves upon the attention of the Government by various means or has long since been explained to the with an outcry through the newspapers. The idea that an obvious injustice automatically redresses the attention of a statesman or has long since been exploded. Ministers will dodge and duck and temporise as long as they run avoid giving a difficult decision.

"Indirect" War Damage

THE most bitter grievance of the people evacuated from the Territories relates to the definition for the War Damage Commission of "direct" and "indirect" damage. When, under military orders, they came away to Australia, they were certain that all their "war losses" would be covered by "war damage compensation insurance." It did not matter whether their property was destroyed by a shell, or had deteriorated through absence of a staff or was carried off by thieves from unguarded premises—their loss was the same, and was directly attributable to the fact that war had burst into their Territories. Their loss was not any fault of theirs.

To their amazement, the Commonwealth Government took an entirely different view. They were to be compensated for property lost by direct enemy action, like the bursting of a bomb; but they would not be compensated for the loss of property due to lack of guardianship, such as climatic deterioration, or looting.

This Government decision was passed on to the War Damage Commission in the shape of a set of regulations—those three-quarters of worth and much-abused instruments of wartime administration—and the War Damage Commission, of course,

has approached the problem of compensation for Territories residents with its hands tied. It can award compensation only for direct damage; and, even in that regard, all its activities up to date have been marked by a petty, thin-nosed, niggling interpretation of the regulations —all apparently designed to reduce, to the last penny, the Commission's liability to make compensation payments to the Territories.

TAKE, as an example, looting. In the part of New Guinea occupied by the enemy, it may be assumed that all property that has disappeared has been taken by the enemy, and that compensation will be paid accordingly—there is no great problem there.

But a part of New Guinea, and a very large part of Papua, actually have not been occupied by the enemy. But, just the same, property has disappeared or deteriorated—partly through lack of care, partly through looting. The Commission does not propose to pay compensation for that—only for property proven to have been actually destroyed by enemy shells and bombs.

Could anything be more cruel or unfair? It simply cannot be argued about. What is the difference between the loss of furniture destroyed in a bomb explosion, and the loss of furniture carried off by looters during the absence of the owners under compulsory wartime evacuation?

What is the difference, from the owner's viewpoint, between a plantation destroyed by shell-fire, and a plantation destroyed by bitter agencies which could not be controlled because both owner and staff had been sent away by the military authorities?

It is no use appealing to the Commission—it is bound by the Commonwealth Government's decision. The Commonwealth Government, presumably terrified at the thought of what the Pantrypnoids Union would say to it if it allowed compensation to the "monopolistic interests" operating in the Territories, has been deaf to all appeals for a more liberal interpretation of war damage.

No, sir—the tender feelings of the Pantrypnoids' Union are not going to be outraged by the spectacle of Burns Philp, or Carpenters, or BP", receiving compensation for their blasted plantations or looted stores; so every man and woman in the Territories is going to be denied compensation for what is called "indirect" war damage, but which is just as much war damage as if it had been done by a Jap bomb.

A Political Background?

FOR months, we have been carefully studying this situation—acquainting
(Continued on Page 32)

'I think,' Jean McCarthy says, 'it was a blot on our Australian Government'.

In Port Moresby the women were divided, with first priority given to those with large families. They were taken out immediately by boat, although they soon found that they were not privileged. The largest ship, a returning troop transport, had few facilities: no sheets, no milk for the children, and it was 'filthy'. Those who went by plane faced 'four days from Cairns down to Sydney in a dreadful old train'. In spite of acts of generosity by some Australians who met planes and trains with cups of tea and dry nappies, many of the displaced women experienced great hardships. Theresa Bloxham arrived in Sydney knowing no one and with only five pounds in cash. Her baby, born prematurely, died, and she was effectively destitute:

> I went to the Department of External Territories and explained to them what my position was. I needed clothes and I had to pay for my keep as I had no relatives, and could they make some arrangement to give me an allowance from my husband's salary. Word came back to say that they were sorry, they couldn't give me an allowance because they'd have to have my husband's signature. I said, 'I don't even know where my husband is'.

She did not say what she then feared, that her husband was dead. Although many of the officials were personally sympathetic they could do nothing. Eventually she used the last of her money on a bus fare back to the Department where

> I was told that I could be given a small amount of money. I was asked to sign for it on three different slips of paper, and told that it was to be returned in three weeks. Now that was my first type of help. I thought, three weeks is three weeks. I can't return it in three weeks, but I've got to have it.

The evacuation of the women and children had been carried out with skill, daring and pettiness. Pilots risked their lives; women tolerated appalling conditions as they waited on outstations, stood on the rain-washed Port Moresby airstrip and spent days crowded on ships and trains. Yet they constantly encountered many Australians who scarcely knew there was a war on. And by then some of the homes that the women had left had already been bombed. Papua New Guineans, watching the sudden departure of the *misis* and her children, were alerted to approaching disaster with a clarity that no amount of words could have conveyed.

> *The Japanese caught the Anglican sisters and the men there. In 1942 over the radio I had implored them to leave.*
> **Claude Champion**

Isolated groups of Europeans were cut off by the swift southward advance of the Japanese. In the Sepik District eight Europeans and eighty-two New Guineans led by Jack Thurston spent five months crossing from the headwaters of the Sepik to Daru. They had, in effect, made in reverse the famous patrol of Ivan Champion and Charles Karius. In another remarkable journey Danny Leahy guided a group of nuns from the north coast through the highlands to the Mount Hagen airstrip:

> They would have all been over forty, some of them over sixteen stone. Over 10 000 feet we went just near Wabag. Then over the Daulo Pass; that was just a track. When we set off I said to the head nun—she was the biggest one—I said, 'Look, Sister, with these habits and everything, I'll get none of you to Mount Hagen if you don't pull your skirts up'. I said they'd get sopping wet and cold in the mountains and all die of fever. She said, 'Oh, we couldn't'. 'Well,' I said, 'it's up to you. I can't wait for you because I haven't got enough carriers'. I took ninety carriers, and I had to feed them off the country. She said, 'All right, I'll do it. Then the other nuns will see me and they'll do it'. And this big fat nun put a pair of shorts on that I gave her. She had these shorts up to her knees, and sandshoes and socks. They were absolutely wonderful women really. Anyway some of them made rompers

out of their habits and tucked them into their socks. You couldn't carry them. Well, we did try to carry this big sister, the big young one. The only way I could do it was to cut a long pole and make a sort of basket arrangement. But that bloody near killed her anyway. We had to cut her out of the basket in the end, and I said, 'There's only one way'. I had two boys on their arms pulling them up the big mountains, and a couple behind shoving them up. That was a wonderful trip with those women. It was their faith that brought them through. They were truly Christian.

It is not to detract from the nuns' faith to pass a share of the credit to Australian and Melanesian bushmanship and muscle.

The Japanese made their first heavy air raid on Rabaul on January 4, 1942. Many of the New Guinea ports were undefended, but in Rabaul 1400 Australians waited to meet the main Japanese advance. Most were men from the 2/22nd Battalion. Peter Figgis, the Area Intelligence Officer, remembers that 'things were fairly chaotic'. Poorly equipped, their few heavy guns destroyed and their pathetically obsolete aircraft shot out of the sky or shattered on the ground, they were 'in pretty poor shape'. But their orders were to fight:

You've got to remember that this was the time when Mr Churchill was telling everybody that we were going to fight them on the beaches and so on. This permeated as far as New Britain. That was really the basic tactic that we were going to employ: we were going to fight them on the beaches. There had been no preparation for withdrawal because that was regarded as bad for morale and an admission of defeat. In fact what we should have been doing was to build up base stocks back in the mountains and establish a good communications centre to which we could have retreated and then harassed the Japanese. Above all we could have kept the people further south informed as to what was going on.

The troops, Figgis says, 'were pretty wry': discipline 'was quite good' in the face of expected disaster.

Nurses and women missionaries had been exempted from the compulsory evacuation of white women and nearly all had chosen to stay at their various posts. Tootie McPherson was an army nurse on duty at an emergency hospital at Vunapope Catholic mission west of Rabaul:

During the night of January 22 some of the troops came to the hospital with gunshot wounds and we knew the Japanese had arrived. In the morning when it got daylight, from where we were right on the water in this native hospital, we counted forty-nine Japanese ships. Then they stormed us in their little barges. They rushed the hospital. And first of all they wanted food. It appeared that the Japanese when they took troops anywhere didn't feed them. Perhaps it was to make them a little crankier. They were very cruel to a lot of the lads. They took some of them away and we never saw them again. We know they were killed. Some had to dig their own graves before they were shot. They were cruel to us. I, unfortunately, or fortunately, was the first. I didn't bow deep enough to them. Well, I got the most dreadful whack. I was knocked down and given a few kicks. I did bow my head, very begrudgingly; but from then on I did bow deep enough.

They were very suggestive and dreadful in many ways. Many's the time they've chased us, trying to urinate on us while the rest of them just stayed back and screamed with laughter. It was nothing for them to take their trousers off and things like that. Fortunately for us when the advance guard came, they brought all their geisha girls, a terrific number, and they took over the Bishop's house. The Bishop was put out and the geisha girls were put in. They also brought a lot of horses which they put in the beautiful cathedral. Only for the geisha girls, well, we wouldn't be here today.

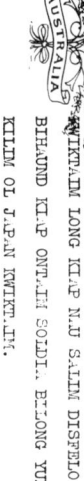

OL BOI H.RIM TOK.

SUPOS YUPELO LUKIM SUMPELO JAP.N I LAIK HAID KLOSTU
LONG ROD BILONG YU. SUMPELO BOI I KAM
WIKIVAIM LONG KLAP N.U S.VIM DISPELO TOK.
BIHAIND KLAP ONL.IH SOLDI. BELONG YUMI S.VI KISIM N.U
KILIM OL J.P.N KWIKT.IM.

195

Survivors from Rabaul on Port Moresby wharf, April 1942

The *Laurabada* crowded with survivors from New Britain, April 1942

The six of us for many nights and days had a phial of morphia in our pockets, and we intended to take that; but thank God we didn't have to. The geisha girls were the only thing that saved us.

There's one thing I must mention. With the first party that arrived every one of them spoke perfect English, and there wasn't one of us that knew one word of Japanese. They told us that they had been taught English for quite some time because they were coming to Australia.

In mid 1942 the nurses were taken in a crowded ship's hold to Japan. All survived the deprivations of prison camp, but one died soon after liberation. The mass grave of the soldiers taken from the hospital was discovered after the war.

Within a few hours of the 5000 strong Japanese South Seas Force coming ashore all effective resistance had ceased. Australian troops, believing that the last order was 'every man for himself', began searching for tracks south. They had been defeated in battle, most found the country alien, and they had little hope of getting off the island. Some surrendered, others struggled on. Peter Figgis:

On the south coast it was bad because they were not getting adequate food, they were all suffering from malaria, some of them were eating things that were giving them dysentery, and by and large they were in poor physical shape. In that situation morale is not good. You see one of your friends dying, then you have to bury him and you're not feeling much better yourself, and there are no signs of any possible evacuation, nor any signs of your own ability to hit back. Rarely did we see any Australian or American aircraft; they were always Japanese aeroplanes overhead. We didn't even really know whether the Japanese might have landed in Australia.

The men, Figgis recalls, 'were a cross-section of the community'. While some selfishly scoffed food before any one else could get a share, others responded heroically. One medical orderly constantly drove himself to save his skeletal companions. Of the 1400 Australians that had faced the Japanese in Rabaul, only 400 finally escaped. They were taken off by crews operating small boats in seas dominated by the Japanese. Figgis was among the 150 soldiers and civilians taken on board the *Laurabada* captained by Ivan Champion. Nearly all of those who surrendered were killed—they were executed by the Japanese or they were on Japanese boats sunk by the Allies.

By February 1942 it seemed that Port Moresby would be the next post to fall. Port Moresby was low on morale and high on disorder as Australian troops pillaged the town. Percy Chatterton suggests that 'the local people followed our example and got away with a bit', but generally Australian soldiers were more destructive of the old town than Japanese bombs. The troops believed that it was better for them to grab what they could rather than leave it for the enemy.

> We had been subjected to quite severe air raids by the Japanese over the preceding days. Obviously they had aircraft carriers somewhere over the horizon. They put the six-inch guns on Praed Point out of action by dive bombing, they had sunk the last remaining ship in Rabaul Harbour, they'd destroyed a fair bit of the town, they'd shot up the two aerodromes, and in particular they'd shot down all the Wirraways. We were in pretty poor shape.
> **Peter Figgis, Intelligence Officer, Rabaul 1942**

The Japanese continued moving south through the Solomon Islands and on to the north coast of New Guinea. In mid 1942 the Allies held the Japanese in battles on the Coral Sea, on the Kokoda Trail, at Milne Bay and at Guadalcanal. About half of Papua New Guinea was under Japanese control. Some Australians, cut off by the Japanese, stayed on as coastwatchers. Other experienced Territorians went back into Japanese-controlled areas by foot and submarine to set up other watching posts. Early in the war the coastwatchers, a section of naval intelligence under Commander Eric Feldt, followed the philosophy of Ferdinand, Walt Disney's bull, who preferred to sit under a tree rather than fight. The coastwatchers were to watch, report and avoid trouble if they could. Malcolm Wright, a pre-war *kiap*, led a party including Peter Figgis, back into New Britain. Golpack, 'a fine old man' and the paramount *luluai* in the area, told Wright that

'I've got the Japanese captain in my pocket and there's no need to worry

about them.' So we lived there for seven months of boredom. Personally I found that the darkness in the bush was worrying me a bit and I got one of the people from the area to make a bit of a clearing so I could go out and take my shirt off and get a bit of sun. We had about four months in the bush without seeing any real sunshine. We got our supplies every full moon. The drops were always very exciting, and there was always a parcel from the Catalina boys tied on the side with particular cigarettes and things like that. We got mail. And I remember sending a request for reading matter, and the person who got this must have thought that we were right among the Japanese because he sent us all pre-war women's magazines. We got *Women's Mirrors*, *Women's Weeklies*, *Woman's Days* for about three years, dated from about 1936. After a while we became experts on diapers and breast feeding and things like that.

Survival depended on keeping good relations with the villagers. To reinforce the position of the coastwatchers, Feldt arranged for well-known Territorians to broadcast to the people. The coastwatchers would tell the villagers to come to the camp to hear, say, Keith McCarthy talk. At the appointed time the coastwatchers would turn up their loudspeakers and the people would hear, '*Apinun yupela*. Makarti.' (Good afternoon to you from McCarthy.) Peter Figgis:

And McCarthy would then hold forth about how they must stand fast, how they must help the Australians, and how the build-up was taking place. With American help the Australians were coming back, and the villagers mustn't help the Japanese. This was tremendous for morale, and it gave them a lot of confidence in us because we said that *Masta* Makarti would talk at such and such a time and he did.

Although the coastwatchers recall boredom, they were under constant tension and some parties suffered sustained harassment. Fifty-three European coastwatchers died during the war.

New Guinea Badly Hit

MELBOURNE, JANUARY 22.

Large scale air attacks were launched against Rabaul throughout Tuesday afternoon and extended on Wednesday to cover practically the whole of the Bismarck Archipelago and coastal areas on the mainland of New Guinea.

Between 100 and 200 Japanese aircraft appeared to participate and hundreds of bombs were dropped in a sustained series of attacks.

Raids also were made on Kavieng, in New Ireland, Madang, Salamaua, Lae, Bulolo and Lorengau on the mainland.

In the raids on Lae, Salamaua and Bulolo, the enemy both bombed and machine-gunned the settlements and aerodromes. A number of commercial aircraft on the ground were damaged. From reports so far received casualties in these raids were few.

In Tuesday's attacks on Rabaul eleven persons were killed and a merchant ship in the harbour was set on fire. Apart from this the effect of the raids was small. Anti-aircraft guns shot down three Japanese machines and damaged several others. Five of our aircraft were lost.

Rabaul Silent

Another large scale raid on Rabaul was reported this morning, following which a message was received stating a large number of enemy ships had been sighted near Rabaul.

Since this time no further messages have been received and it is thought possible that we have destroyed the radio station and possibly evacuated the settlement.

The Papuan Courier January 23, 1942

In the First World War the New Guineans had seen the Germans replaced by the Australians. Now twenty-five years later the Australians had been forced out by the Japanese. Papua New Guineans could not tell how long these new *mastas* would stay. The villagers had no knowledge of what was going on in the rest of the world, or even in the rest of the country. They learnt quickly that they could not believe all that the soldiers told them. They had to make decisions on what they could see. And they knew only too well that if they made the wrong decision they could be destroyed. Few had the privilege of being able to retreat into the bush and become 'neutral bystanders'. Ian Downs:

> In Japanese-occupied areas their loyalty of course was extremely limited. You can't blame them. Anybody with any experience in Europe would realise that this happened not just in Papua New Guinea but all over the world. If you were confronted with someone about to stick a bayonet up your backside it's extraordinary how co-operative you become. Speaking from my own experience, I came in contact with people who were loyal and helped me, and people who were I suppose disloyal and betrayed me, but I never felt any ill feeling because I knew they were under Japanese pressure. Their loyalty was tremendous, especially to the coastwatchers. People like Paul Mason and Jack Read couldn't have existed without the loyalty that they had from the people, particularly on Bougainville. I think that this really shows that the Australian regime couldn't have been all that bad for people to risk their lives and suffer hardships for them. I can remember being up a banyan tree once, somewhere behind Bukawa, with a lot of Japanese looking for me. Two fellows from the village of Hopoi were underneath with the Japanese. They carried on a conversation in Pidgin English, and they normally would have spoken in the Bukawa

language. I'm quite sure that they deliberately carried on that conversation in Pidgin so that I could hear it. They more or less told me by their discussion between themselves where the Japanese were.

Ian Skinner adds that often local politics determined the villagers' response. If their neighbours with whom they 'had a long standing cross' were helping the Allies, then they were likely to side with the Japanese. Where the villagers initially welcomed the invaders as new and generous *mastas*, the Japanese dissipated the goodwill, Ron Garland says, by raiding food gardens, forcing the people to work without pay, or committing atrocities.

As the war flowed across Papua New Guinea many mission men and women were trapped. By the end of the war over 200 foreign missionaries had died. The death of four Anglican women teachers and nurses aroused particular sympathy: they were young, they were not far from safety and their fate was known quickly. Papuans, under threat from the Japanese, had handed them to the Japanese who had executed them. David Marsh found the graves of two of the women and arrested Emboge, the leader of one of the groups that had given early aid to the Japanese. Marsh recorded Emboge's words:

> You people ran away and we were left here. We had to live here. We tried you out and you were hard on us, and we thought we'd try the Japanese. When they failed us we armed ourselves with all the left over rifles and settled our own differences.

The villagers carried on their own war in the midst of world war.

The day after Marsh arrested Emboge he asked Emboge to help build an aerodrome. He responded immediately, bringing nearly 500 people down from Higaturu to Popondetta to cut the runway in a day. The first plane landed that evening bringing twenty-five pound guns that went into action at Soputa that night. Marsh thought, 'whatever he did during the war, he's made up for it today and more; he's saved hundreds of lives'.

But Emboge was hanged. Claude Champion:

> I, with the assistance of the native clerk, Nansen Kaisa, built the twin gallows for the execution. I was so upset with what they were going to do, execute these sixteen natives, I just couldn't bear to stay and watch it. Because several of them were my friends.

The Australian Army hanged sixteen men on the one day, and a total of at least thirty-four Papua New Guineans were executed. Ten of the Papuans were hanged for treason. The charge assumed that they had a loyalty to a government and a nation. At the time they probably had neither, and in practical terms the Japanese were their rulers.

Missionaries who were born in the Axis powers faced equally confusing tests of loyalty and nationality. Adolf Wagner was a Lutheran missionary working on the Huon Peninsula. He was a German citizen, an anti-Nazi, and he had come to think of New Guinea as his home. Adolf Wagner evaded the Australians sent to intern him. His brother, Emil, who had taken Australian citizenship, walked overland to Australian-held territory. Emil recalls his last conversation with his brother:

> He said to me, 'What's the use of me being interned? I have so many people that look upon me as a disloyal German. I am not respected as a Nazi. If I am interned amongst all those people who are praying and yelling for Germany's victory, I have no good future in the internment camp. I will stay with the natives.' Then he said, 'And woe me if Germany wins. I'll be hung.' My brother stayed and presented himself to the Japanese and said he is German, he is neutral and that he is there for the natives and that's all. He said, 'I am not going to help you, or anybody else. I've got no wireless, no machines, nothing. I am just here with the natives to help keep them calm and happy.'

Because Adolf Wagner had evaded the order to leave, some Australians were

The 2nd New Guinea Infantry Battalion buries its dead.

only too ready to believe that he was assisting the enemy. They decided that he should be shot. At that very time he was in fact risking his life to save Allied airmen forced down behind the Japanese lines. After enduring great hardships, Wagner was executed by the Japanese. Wagner had been trapped between two armies and reviled by both.

From the middle of 1944 the Japanese, cut off from their homeland and short of basic supplies, were constantly harassed by Allied bombing, Australian ground troops, and Papua New Guinean regular and irregular forces. On Karkar Island Tim Bowden met a sprightly, slightly-built old man called January who claimed to have personally killed a hundred Japanese. John Middleton translated his rapid Pidgin:

> They would hide their army uniforms and dress up as the local people in torn calico laplaps or whatever bits and pieces were available. Taking bananas, paw paws and taro they would go down to the Japanese camp and trade with them. At the same time they would mark out where the guns and installations were, and count the numbers of troops. At times they would creep back to make sure. They would, as he said, travel like snakes without making any noise. When they had really marked out the camp

properly they would report back to their officers. After putting on their uniforms and picking up their weapons they would go back as a fighting unit.

Ron Garland who served with the 2nd New Guinea Infantry Battalion says that quite a number of Papua New Guineans who could move about freely and fight from planned ambush positions inflicted enormous casualties on the Japanese.

The war in Papua New Guinea was fought at appalling cost. About 150 000 Japanese died. On the mainland alone, from Milne Bay to Aitape, lay the remains of 100 000 men of Adachi's 18th Army. Nearly 12 000 Allied soldiers were killed. How many Papua New Guineans had died is uncertain, but in areas of intense fighting the population had dropped by a quarter. Papua New Guineans would never understand why the foreigners had fought a war across their homeland.

Many of the old government and planter community had been killed. The Japanese had executed thirty of them in Kavieng and another 200 died when the Japanese boat, the *Montevideo Maru*, was sunk by an American submarine. The fate of many was not known until well after the war was over.

In 1941 Jean McCarthy had left her husband, Keith, on New Britain, and at last she got a message from Eric Feldt. It was an official letter that Keith was safe, but that he was on a very dangerous mission,* and that if I valued his life I was not to tell anybody that I knew he was alive because the Japanese were after him. But I was one of the very lucky ones because he did come back to me. I have had people say to me over the years in discussions on the evacuation, 'But then of course you lost all your lovely things like everybody else'. And I have said, 'Yes, but they're only the material things. My most precious possession came back to me'.

It was a terrible thing when the war ended to see the elation on the faces of the women who had been waiting all those years, and then suddenly news came through that they'd all gone on the *Montevideo Maru*. It was a terrible scene. Years and years of waiting, and then—nothing.

The war had given Papua New Guineans a vision of a world in which the foreigners were vastly more numerous and dangerous than they could possibly have imagined. The war was to accelerate their entry into that world.

*Keith McCarthy was awarded the MBE for his work in directing the north coast evacuation of the survivors after the fall of Rabaul.

23 A Reason for Being There

At Baiyer River we had to learn very quickly some of their own language so that we could diagnose what was wrong with them. They would say in their own language, 'One spirit—the agent—the kiliakai is shooting its spears into me'. And we knew that was probably a chest infection. Another was, 'The yamma is eating me'. That meant there was some abdominal problem.

Betty Crouch, Missionary nurse

In that complex mixture of ideas and materials that Australians brought to Papua New Guinea, improved health seemed one of the few that was unambiguously good. Field officers pushing into new country were keen to demonstrate their power and utility by curing a sick person or stitching a wound. It added to their prestige, showed the superiority of one aspect of their culture and strengthened their belief that they were the bearers of benefits. Planter, labour inspector, missionary and humanist could agree that it was desirable for the village to be healthy.

In 1945 a few Papua New Guineans serving with the Allied Forces or living close to military bases had better health services than ever before, but many villagers had no access to any outside skills or drugs. In some areas a child had only a fifty per cent chance of reaching the age of five. Suffering was greatest where fighting had been intense and where the Japanese had remained in control for long periods. During the four years of war the population on Bougainville, the Gazelle Peninsula and in parts of the Sepik had declined dramatically. Most of the deaths were from disease and malnutrition, rather than from violence. In a time of post-war shortages, the problem faced by

the returning civil administration was not how to get funds, but how to get trained men and essential material. Officials were most anxious to carry health services to those communities that had become dependent on Western medicines only to have the supply disrupted by war, and then to extend medical aid to those thousands of peoples yet to see a pill or a hypodermic. The newly appointed Director of Public Health, Dr John Gunther, made adventurous decisions to secure resources, and then apply them to obtain maximum benefit. Gunther recalls that he started the post-war service with 'five doctors, about four Australian trained nurses and twenty-three European Medical Assistants so it was a fairly desperate situation'. The villages, Dr Paul Enders says, 'were full of sickness—yaws, malaria, tuberculosis, dysentery'. People lay in the shade during the day, too ill to work. Without the energy to re-establish their gardens, they were adding malnutrition to their miseries. On Gunther's instruction the small staff concentrated on 'curative medicine'; and he searched for more staff.

One of the greatest boons that we had followed a discussion that I had with Nugget (Dr H C) Coombs who was then head of Post-War Reconstruction. He suggested that

The Papuan Times February 28, 1912

CAUTION.

Prevention of Dysentery and Malaria.

PUBLIC are requested to co-operate with the Government in their endeavours to eradicate dysentery and malaria in populous centres in Papua.

DYSENTERY is caused by a germ, swallowed either in contaminated water or in food or drinks contaminated by flies.

All water should, unless absolutely above suspicion, be boiled before drinking, and all food and drink should be kept in places inaccessible to flies, such as a fly-proof safe.

As flies breed in filth and dirt, and especially in stable manure, no collections of such should be allowed to accumulate. If scrupulous cleanliness of premises is observed by everybody the number of flies would be greatly diminished and the liability to disease consequently lessened. All horses, cattle and stock not in actual use should be kept away from the vicinity of towns.

MALARIA is transmitted by mosquito, and in places where mosquitos are exterminated malaria practically ceases. As mosquitos breed only in standing water it is obvious that, if they are shut off from all such, no more can be hatched, and as the adults die off the plague will disappear.

LOYAL CO-OPERATION on the part of everyone is required to secure success, as a single stable neglected, or a single dirty yard, will supply a whole town with flies, while a single tank unprotected or stagnant pool of water is sufficient to keep up the supply of mosquitos.

(Sgd.) F. GOLDSMITH,
Chief Medical Officer.

CAUTION.

Health Ordinance, 1912.

THE PUBLIC are advised that they should immediately take steps for the prevention of disease as follows :—

All water tanks should be made fly and mosquito proof.

All empty cisterns should be covered, and

All compounds should be weeded and cleared from empty tins, bottles, etc.

The Public are particularly cautioned with regard to their sanitary arrangements.

Prosecution will be undertaken without any further notice, for any breach of the Ordinance.

I. McWM. BOURKE,

Chief Health Officer.

(Acting C.M.O.)

Leprosy detection and treatment

CRTS funds, Commonwealth Reconstruction Training Scheme funds, could be used for Papua New Guineans. It was really stretching the provisions of the scheme to the ultimate, but we grabbed this and started what I called a Native Medical Assistant Training Scheme, afterwards known as the Aid Post Orderly Scheme. I say quite proudly that we were just twenty years in front of the Chinese barefoot doctors. They adopted almost exactly the same principles as we did. We trained people, completely illiterates, to recognise major killing diseases, to use the specific drugs, and we sent them back to their villages. We taught them to their capacity in a matter of twelve months to two years. Now this was the quickest way we could get help to the villages. We had six or seven of these training schools spread through Papua New Guinea.

Supplied with such drugs as penicillin, sulpha and quinine, the Medical Assistants, Dr Tony Radford says, 'could cure some sixty or seventy per cent of the common causes of illness and death'.

Allowing people who were otherwise uneducated to take decisions that could kill or cure their fellow villagers meant that the Department of Public Health was accepting a responsibility that many administrators would have avoided. Sir John Gunther concedes that the Medical Assistants made mistakes:

They killed people; but they saved thousands. One incident was a tragedy. The milk of the coconut is sterile and it can be used injected intravenously. There was an old Medical Assistant in the New Guinea service who had been taught by a doctor in the Salamaua area that if you ran out of sterile water you could use coconut milk to mix up your arsenic for the treatment of yaws. And we had him as an assistant instructor at one of the Aid Post Orderly Training Schools. Unknown to the instructor, he was giving a little bit of extra instruction on the side on how you can use a coconut. One of our orderlies out on patrol in the Upper Ramu ran out of water, got a coconut, opened it, used it that night, and then carried it on with him to the next village. By the next morning, of course, it was highly infected, and I think that seventeen to twenty people died almost instantaneously from an overdose of toxic bacillus. But apart from saving people who were suffering from malaria, pneumonia or dysentery, they got rid of the sores, ulcers and ringworm. We couldn't have done it in any other way.

In fact Gunther could claim that having seen the chance to introduce an unorthodox scheme that could save thousands of lives, he would have been grossly negligent not to have implemented it.

In another radical attempt to obtain staff Gunther recruited European refugee doctors then working as unskilled labourers in Australia. Some could speak little English, their qualifications were hard to verify and they were debarred from practice in Australia. In spite of being 'abused by the Commonwealth Director of Health' who told him that he 'was letting Australia down', Gunther employed thirty-five refugee doctors in the first group. They varied, Maddocks suggests, from 'highly competent surgeons to rascals'. But only two were found to be impostors. One, Paul Enders says, reported smallpox, and when Gunther flew in he found only chicken pox. The other was easily trapped by his colleagues. They would mention that they had recently seen a woman with an enlarged prostate, and he would respond with, 'Oh, I saw three of those myself this morning!' There was 'a degree of friction', too, between some of the immigrant doctors and European Medical Assistants on the outstations before divisions of expertise and authority were defined. But in general the refugee doctors brought the range of skills that would have been expected from a group of Australian graduates; and they came when such skills could not be obtained elsewhere.

The European Medical Assistants, some of whom were ex-army paramedical staff, were responsible for the transfer of primary health service to vast areas of the Territory. At remote stations they built and serviced their own hospitals, often out of necessity developing a range of surgical and medical skills. The demand for precise diagnostic and curative attention came suddenly to Medical Assistant Albert Speer one day in 1948 when he received a deputation of warlike Anga, or Kukukukus, at his remote Gulf District hospital:

They pulled this young fellow out of their midst, stood him up, turned him round, pulled his cloak off, and there was this steel axe head embedded in the back of his skull. It had been there for months as far as I could work out: the Kukukukus said, 'Oh, many, many, many moons.' It was suppurating and the area around was badly infected. I asked if he had walked in. Oh yes, he could walk. Obviously he was in pain, but in full possession of his faculties. I thought, if I dislodge the axe I don't know what's going to happen. I tried to talk on the radio to the medical authorities in Moresby, but I couldn't get on to them. It was bad radio communication. We only had one sked (radio schedule) a day, and we only had a boat every six weeks. The boat had just been and gone, and sometimes that six weeks could be up to two or three months. I weighed all this up and thought, oh well, I'll have a go at seeing what I can do. The Kukukukus said, 'Just pull it out'. But if he died they'd probably attack me or burn the hospital down. I asked the District Officer at Kerema what he would do, and he said, 'If you think you can do it have a try. If he dies, well, anybody seeing that would say he would have died anyway.' I radioed Kerema and they managed to get through on morse key to request penicillin. I got a young patrol officer to administer the anaesthetic and I took the axe out. I had to cut down onto the bone, break an edge of the bone, and ease the axe out. It had penetrated the brain, and there was some infection. I used the old army technique of sulphanilamide and vaseline gauze packs, cleaned up all the mess and hoped for the best. Then the plane came over and dropped some

penicillin, and that was a great source of wonder that this plane would come all the way out just to drop a package.

Anyway, he got much better, and actually the bone seemed to be healing over. One morning we got out of bed, and the head orderly came up and said to me, 'Sir, you shouldn't have done that to him. You know what's happened? They've all gone in the middle of the night and taken every axe and steel knife that the cook had, and there's nothing left in the kitchen.' Even the scissors were gone from the wards. This was their method. If they wanted something they just took it. Bert Speer believes that the Kukukuku were probably grateful. But they had a need for steel, they had few chances of earning money to buy it, the hospital seemed to have so much and they were accustomed to raiding those who were not their kin.

> *Before I first went to Papua New Guinea I had afternoon tea with Mr Chinnery who had been Government Anthropologist in Rabaul for years and years. He said, 'I've got two sets of advice for you, young man, when you go on patrol. The first thing is to put sprigs in the instep of your boots because you will often find you are treading on roots and you will slip. You've got to put sprigs not just in the sole and heel of your boot but also in the instep. The second thing you must do is to carry with you a small bottle of Friar's Balsam. If at any time out on patrol you get any cut or scratch, stop the patrol.' He held his hand up. 'Stop the patrol.' I saw myself pulling my great line to a halt. 'Stop and cover the injury immediately with a little Friar's Balsam and cotton wool.' Now that was quite good advice.*
> **Dr Ian Maddocks**

Doctors and Australian and Papua New Guinean Medical Assistants joined general administration patrols or mounted special medical patrols, and the field staff themselves were frequently involved in direct health work. Although the first Australians to enter the highlands were surprised at the health and vigour of some of the villagers, in other areas they were confronted by the most obvious signs of distress. Malcolm Mackellar recalls the hideous disfigurement that could follow chronic suffering from leprosy and yaws. On one occasion he met a woman who had sat immobilised by ulcers for so long that her calf was apparently grafted to her thigh. When he was patrolling in the scattered hamlets north of Kiunga on the Fly River Jack Baker saw almost 'every skin ailment known to man'. The whole experience, he says, 'was very destructive of the concept of the noble savage'. When he entered one side of a hamlet a third of the people would be

> crawling out the other side because they were unable to walk with either leprosy lesions or yaws ulcers on their legs. It was a fairly horrifying experience, and it brought the whole game back to scratch. You were no longer concerned about whether you had anything to offer these people; you felt damned sure that there was a reason for being there. Probably the most satisfying thing that I've ever been involved in was a small kid so covered with yaws lesions that you couldn't find a piece of good skin to push a needle in. And watching him recover almost miraculously as those filthy lesions closed over. Antibiotics hitting these untouched populations was just sheer magic.

In that area, Baker says, medical work took up most of the *kiaps'* time.

Although the Department of Public Health in the 1950s received more funds than any other department, in 1951 the entire health services of the Territory cost just $2 500 000, a little over a dollar per person. Money spent on buildings could not be used for drugs or dressings. Away from urban centres the hospital was likely to be a basic rectangle, perhaps on stilts, with the top halves of the walls just open space to let the breeze flow freely below wide eaves. 'Men and women' Judy Porter says, 'were to a large extent mixed up.' In a ward designed for twelve or sixteen patients there might be twenty or even forty people. At the end of the ward would be a 'small treatment room-cum-office' and beyond that might be another room used for women in labour. Much equipment and furniture was scrounged: Betty Crouch used jam and fish tins for bowls and kidney dishes when she first worked in outstation wards. New Australian nurses were surprised at the profusion of people in apparent disorder with patients on sleeping mats beside their beds or in the walkway. Joan Durdin:

> Of course when one member of the family was sick it was customary for other members of the family to be there with them. If the wife was sick the husband and several children might be there. The beds in the wards were a cyclone gate style of thing with folding legs. They had no mattresses; the patients used their own mats or mattresses. But as I discovered, it was not at all unusual to find that the sick wife was on her mat on the floor, and her husband had asserted his status by occupying the bed.

It was really a matter of height above ground rather than comfort; and the wife may have preferred the security of floor-level.

Papua New Guinea escaped the 'fatal impact'. Although particular communities suffered a sharp decline, introduced disease did not decimate the general population as it did on some Pacific islands. But the disease pattern altered radically as new illnesses entered the villages, and old diseases were spread more widely. In the post-war the chief causes of death were malaria, pneumonia, tuberculosis, dysentery and gastroenteritis. Life expectancy was only about thirty years. Malaria, the greatest single problem, was responsible for half the infant deaths and left the adults, in Gunther's term, the eighty-percent people. But immediately after the war was over half the patients entering hospital had disfiguring skin diseases of yaws or tropical ulcers. 'What's significant

about yaws,' Ian Maddocks explains, 'is that it is eradicated with a single dose of penicillin'. People would walk for days to have an injection, a *sut* (shoot) as it was called in Pidgin. The very effectiveness of the injection against yaws could skew people's expectations of the health services. Although the elimination of yaws was, Ian Maddocks says,

> almost nothing compared with, say, getting rid of tuberculosis, it was a symbol of our good intentions, of our power, and of curative medicine basically. And to some extent it was counter productive as far as preventive medicine goes because it focused the recipient population heavily upon the injection as the way to health. It's different if you say, look, we want to get rid of hookworm, and we want you all to build latrines and use them. That is much more complex, and it's much less easy to get your message across.

Papua New Guineans were as fallible as the rest of the world in looking for good health in the one quick dose or jab.

Given the few trained health workers available, senior officials could not hope to carry out a comprehensive curative program. 'Even nowadays' Dr Roy Scragg points out, 'I don't think there'd be one doctor for 10 000 persons as opposed to one per 500 in Australia.' To effect a permanent improvement in the people's health there had to be an emphasis on community and preventive medicine. The orderly trained to spray houses against malaria can, Scragg argues, save more lives in Papua New Guinea than the surgeon or any other specialist practising in a major urban hospital. By the end of the 1960s the malaria control program was costing over one million dollars annually. Although thousands of people benefited from the reduced incidence of malaria, the program was never able to attract the funds to completely eliminate the debilitating effects of malaria from broad sections of the population.

Obstructed by local customs, Australian health workers sometimes felt that they had to force change. Betty Crouch:

Papuan Courier January 9, 1931

On only one thing I really had to put my foot down. When a new-born baby had a hard time coming into the world and was very lethargic, they would chop off a joint of the baby's finger. They thought it stimulated the baby to get to the breast. Also, when a baby was born with blood on it, and that was often, it was believed to be unclean; and that was another reason why they chopped a joint off the finger. Now I felt, really, I had to do something about that.

Adults in the Baiyer River area cut their fingers off to demonstrate their sorrow at a death or some other significant loss. Some women, Betty Crouch found, had the tops of many fingers missing. But she accepted that they were adults, they were taking actions only against themselves and she ought not to interfere.

Dr David Bowler adopted a similarly pragmatic approach:

> If mother wishes to bury the afterbirth under the front doorstep that's fine. If mother wishes to have somebody to breathe incantations over the baby, don't comment. If mother wants to cut the umbilical cord with a rusty razor blade, then you try and show her a method of getting a clean razor blade.

When there was a question of expertise at stake not all Australians could be so tolerant. Dr Ian Maddocks:

> Occasionally I would come into a house and there would be *babalau* man, a diviner, who had been brought in at great expense, perhaps from Popondetta or Samarai, and he would be sitting in the household helping the family uncover the why and who, and we might exchange greetings. We never actually became a sort of blood brotherhood of working together, although I wouldn't put that out of court as a possibility. But it didn't seem to be threatening to either side. What was uncomfortable was when in the hospital people who were intolerant of these other views of the world would be aggressive towards families that were trying to uncover the who

or the why, and would throw the diviner out of a ward, or get very impatient with them. This would mean that the family would have to withdraw their patient from hospital and take him home to uncover these answers. So conflicts would occur, and these were unfortunate, and sometimes unnecessary.

Clashes were unnecessary because the diviner and the doctor were usually performing different functions. The Papua New Guineans looked to the diviner to isolate and counteract the malign source of the disease; they expected the doctor to cure the patient who had already been struck by the evil.

> *I was taken on my first patrol by the Assistant District Officer, and I just collapsed. He pumped me full of quinine. In those days the treatment was five grains of quinine in a capsule each day. I recovered the following day. But as long as I was in Gasmata I used to get this form of malaria regularly, every third Saturday morning at 11 o'clock. I had to arrange my movements around that.*
> **Bill Bloxham**

Papua New Guinea has consistently attracted some of the world's best scientists. From Robert Koch, the great German bacteriologist who worked on the north coast in 1900, to Carleton Gajdusek, winner of the 1976 Nobel prize in medicine, Papua New Guinea has been a rich field laboratory. Some of the research has been of immediate benefit to the peoples of Papua New Guinea. Frank Schofield did 'some good work' on immunising women to protect their children against neonatal tetanus; Dr Tim Murrell explained the mysterious highlands disease of *pig bel*, enteritis necroticans; and novel ways were developed to combat endemic goitre. But there has also been much 'scientific imperialism'. Even where scientists have worked on specific problems, the results were published overseas, and the findings were likely to be applied in affluent countries. A study of Papua New Guinean nutrition adds to the stock of Western knowledge, it may well be applied to urban dwellers suffering various forms of excess, and the villagers who provided the data continue to eat as before. They were the victims of an 'intrusive foray'. They were 'bled and biopsied', heard a quick thank you, and that was all.

The early post-war practices segregating the races had, inevitably, influenced the provision of health services. In Rabaul, for example, there were three hospitals: one for whites, one for Chinese and mixed race, and one for Papua New Guineans. A leading citizen of the white community once threatened to horse-whip the Director of Public Health if he shifted one black or yellow man into the European hospital. Maintaining the divisions, Roy Scragg recalls, forced doctors to make potentially embarrassing decisions when they admitted people whose skin colour varied from the norm of their racial affiliation. Europeans objected to change, Judy Porter says, with the expected arguments that 'natives will make our hospitals dirty' and lower the standard of care. Some Papua New Guineans also objected because they feared being 'swamped by the needs of the Europeans'. The first early change came when the Director asserted that a patient requiring specific treatment available in only one section of the hospital would be treated in that section irrespective of race. Full integration was long delayed by the capacity of most white patients to pay for superior conditions.

The breaking of the racial barriers in the hospitals put Papua New Guinean staff under stress, as Jelilah Unia explains:

I found treating white patients the most difficult thing in my life as a student nurse. It was all right if they were unconscious; but I just couldn't face nursing a European while he was conscious because I was afraid of doing something wrong and being shouted at. Once I went to give a man an injection through the intravenous drip. Apparently this sort of injection can really sting as you are injecting through the vein. I don't think he really knew what he was doing, he was quite ill, but I must have hurt him, and I remember him swinging his hand and knocking my cap off. I was really shaken.

For their part white patients were often puzzled by the caution of their Papua New Guinean nurses.

Papua New Guineans began training as doctors immediately after the war when the first group of students went to the Central Medical School in Fiji, but from 1959 students began training at the Papuan Medical College, later to be a faculty of the University of Papua New Guinea. Staff recruited from Australia brought with them a 'pale copy of the sort of medical course that seemed to be operating all over the world'. With the encouragement of Dr Eric Wright they attempted to adapt their teaching to the particular needs of the community that the students would serve. That immediately brought objections from the students; they suspected that something different was something less. The students wanted qualifications with international acceptance and that would be hard to obtain for an obviously local ticket. Other problems arose as the first graduates went into the field. In 1963 Dr Kilawari was appointed District Medical Officer at Manus responsible for the health of all races. In spite of shrill protests from sections of the white community the Director, Roy Scragg, was able to retain him at his new post. Another round of objections took place when the administration decided that Papua New Guinean graduates would be addressed as 'Doctor'. Again the conservative and aggressive white protestors were found to be out of step with changing attitudes and events.

The Department of Public Health had set precedents in placing Papua New Guineans in positions of responsibility, but it too was forced to quicken the rate of change on the eve of independence. Recently qualified Papua New Guineans were 'just rushed into positions'. Eileen Seneve completed her training as a nurs-

Papua New Guineans in the
operating theatre, 1949

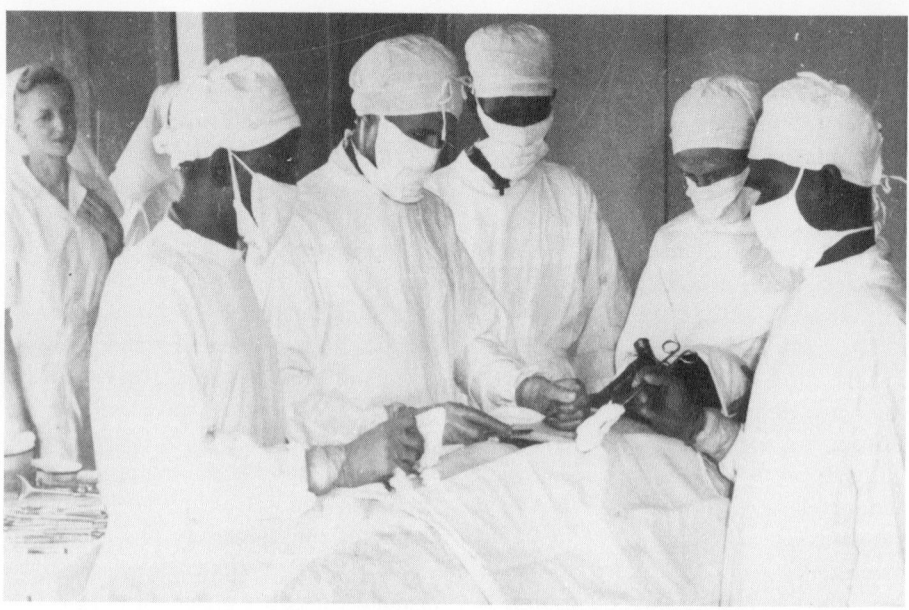

ing tutor in September 1974 and took over as principal of the nursing school in January of 1975: 'it was a really tough job. Apart from just trying to organise the school program, I had to learn to reply to letters, write reports for headquarters and so on.'

As Papua New Guineans settle behind the desks of authority they will begin to assess the Australian-made health service. Dr Ian Maddocks:

Papua New Guinea will eventually decide what system is appropriate for itself. I think we left behind a bureaucratic system which was largely an image of the sort of system that we knew ourselves, and I don't think we could have done much else. The Melanesian style of government in the villages is very different, but then you can't really govern a country the way you govern a village. I don't know what style Papua New Guinea will establish for itself. Decentralisation into provinces appears to me to just increase the bureaucracy and the opportunities for a failure of political will rather than necessarily getting closer to a Melanesian style of government. The health system that we left was not so much a pale copy of Australia's as an incarnation of what Australians believed was an appropriate health service within the

Papua New Guinea context, with our emphasis on prevention and on funding things like malaria control. I don't think it was by any means a great system we left behind. I think it depended too much upon central control, and that was shown to be a problem after the keen, intense sort of administrative authority of the white directors had passed on. But I don't know that we could have done otherwise. I have been continually impressed by the dedication and good intentions and thinking hard work of those people who were there. They were really doing their best to make it work well. What they left behind was not by any means perfect, but I don't know that out of that historical setting it could have been much different.

The work that Australian doctors did in Papua New Guinea was of some significance to Papua New Guinea, but it was also of great significance to their own personal development and growth. They achieved status and confidence and technical abilities that probably they could not have attained so easily had they stayed in Australia. The health workers were in the enviable position of being able to mix altruism and self-advancement and of always being able to do some good for the people of Papua New Guinea.

24 Going Finish

It may seem rather ridiculous that New Guinea natives should ever be independent—yet we contemplate the independence of the Philippines, and in a hundred years the New Guinea natives might easily be the equal of the Filipinos of today.

Sir Hubert Murray, 1939

Kiap: Orait Governor-General em i kam long Maprik tude long bringim tok, bringim save, long Her Royal Highness, the Queen, em i kam long yu.
Lord de l'Isle: I come here to greet you in the name of Her Majesty the Queen, and on her behalf, of the people of Australia. I thank you for all coming here today for this great gathering. My daughter and I are greatly looking forward to the dancing which we hope to see shortly. I bring you the best wishes of the people of Australia who care very much for the peace and prosperity of New Guinea and Papua, and particularly of the Sepik District. You are beginning a long road towards self-government which will demand a great deal from you all so you must send your children to school and remember that in the last result everything depends on you, on your hard work and on your sense of purpose.

When Lord de l'Isle, the Governor-General of Australia, addressed that gathering at Maprik in 1963 neither he nor anyone present would have predicted that self-government was only ten years away. It was an occasion for paternal encouragement about the 'long road

ahead'; and there was no suggestion that the journey would be short and swift.

In 1963 there were few preparations for the speed of change. No Papua New Guineans occupied senior positions in the public service. No Papua New Guinean had graduated from university, and only twenty-five were at the top of secondary school. The Legislative Council, the embryonic parliament, was dominated by whites in numbers, power and voice. There was yet to be a general election in which all Papua New Guineans would vote, and two thirds of the people did not even have a local council in which they might practise the rituals of electing a representative. For most Papua New Guineans 'government' was still a young Australian *kiap* and half a dozen police who came on patrol.

When Australians returned to re-build the civil administration after 1945 little thought was given to radical constitutional change. 'None of us' Jim Sinclair says, 'dreamed of self-government and independence. Indeed the view of the Minister for Territories and the Australian Government was that the country wouldn't be ready for self-government until after this century.' Some officials, Dame Rachel Cleland found, believed independence

Pacific Islands Monthly August, 1951

NG LEGISLATIVE COUNCIL
Strong Feeling in Rabaul
From a Special Correspondent

RABAUL, July 28.
BOTH the Planters Association and the Chamber of Commerce here are planning to make a very strong protest to the Minister for Territories about the proposed Legislative Council, when he arrives here shortly.

We think it is an outrageous thing that our elected representatives should be outnumbered by the officials and their nominees by about 23 to 3.

It is recognised, of course, that these proportions were fixed years ago, when the Act or Ordinance was adopted by the Chifley Government on the recommendation of Mr. Ward. But that does not lessen its iniquity, and we shall do all we can to get an amendment.

C E Barnes—Milne Bay

First Legislative Council,
November 1951

Pacific Islands Monthly January,
1964

More Support For 'New Guinea'

Papuans representing nine Local Government councils in the Central District of Papua recommended in December that the Territory of Papua-New Guinea should be called "New Guinea". This can be regarded as an important move towards finding one suitable name for P-NG.

The Central District includes the Port Moresby area, Papua's stronghold, and one of the objections in the past to P-NG being called simply New Guinea has been the fact that, allegedly, Papuans wouldn't like it. On the New Guinea side of the border there doesn't appear to be any great opposition to the simple term New Guinea. If this name were adopted, presumably P-NG natives would call themselves New Guineans whichever side of the border they came from.

The recommendation of the Papuan Local Government councils will be discussed later this year at a territory-wide conference of councils.

belonged to a future so distant that 'they didn't think that we were getting any closer to it'. Andrée Millar:

> Most Australians didn't believe it was ever going to happen. They said so at Independence. I remember one District Commissioner saying, 'If you'd ever told me that these monkeys would make doctors and ambassadors, I wouldn't have believed you'. They did not see it coming; but then that's because they were administering people from a you-do-this-because-I-tell-you level. A lot of Australians felt that Papua New Guineans couldn't do it and wouldn't do it. And that didn't help the people to do it.

Reform for some Australians meant becoming more efficient at what they had been doing since the 1930s, but not handing power to someone else.

Through the post-war, Australian ministers and senior officials had said that Australia would bring Papua New Guineans 'to the stage where they will be able to manage their own affairs and decide their political future as a people'. To the very eve of Papua New Guinea's nationhood many Australians seemed reluctant to state a constitutional goal and take definite steps to achieve it. But suddenly the Australian government changed its public statements: Australians would make the basic decisions about the time and the form of the Australian departure. Ian Downs:

> Gorton had personally decided that Papua New Guinea should get its independence as soon as possible. His main interest in this was connected with Australian policy and attitudes towards Indonesia. The thing that triggered things off of course was the Whitlam visit in 1970 when he told the people that when Labor came to power, as he anticipated in 1972, Papua New Guinea would become self-governing and then get its independence. This was something new because it was the first time a political leader had put forward the view that this was not a decision which was to await Papua New Guineans.

Six months later the Australian Prime Minister, John Gorton, announced the transfer of significant powers from Canberra to Port Moresby, and in April 1971 Charles Barnes announced that the

Australian Government would 'draw up a flexible program of movement towards full internal self-government'. As Jack Baker says, 'Our last act of colonial arrogance was to say, "You will be independent".' Papua New Guinea escaped the destruction, the unifying effect, and the myth-building power of a fight. 'Independence' Sir Maori Kiki concedes, 'was given on a plate. There was no real struggle.'

Older Papua New Guineans constantly argued for a slowing of the rate of constitutional change. Conservative Australians could always quote the graphic pleas of old village leaders who wanted the Australian mother to stay at the side of its Papua New Guinean child. The trepidation of the older generation was in contrast to the minority of young, educated Papua New Guineans who were pushing for change. Bernard Narakobi:

> The situation was summarised for me by an old man in my village. We'd been sitting all day and it was going on towards evening. The sun was over the treetops, about to sink under the sea. And he said to me, 'Well, young man, look at the sun. We belong', referring to his generation, 'to the generation of the sinking sun. We don't know what independence is, in spite of all your explanations. But if you think independence is a good thing, well, let us have it; but you must remember that the new sun, the next day, is your day. We belong to the sinking day.' He was simply placing his trust in those people who were going to make decisions about independence. This is something that rings strongly in my mind every time I make a decision: the parliamentarians, the judges, the decision-makers must accept that at independence the people had no conception of what was going on. Some knew clearly that they wanted to be their own masters, they didn't want other people to rule them, but beyond that few people knew what it was all about.

Most of the apparent conservatism of older villagers was a reluctance to step into the unknown. In any case Australians, of all people, should have been well aware that a colonial dependence once established was hard to break.

Up to the 1960s Papua New Guineans had made few effective political demands on Australia. Expressions of discontent were usually local and many Australian officials believed that if a group of villagers were hostile then they must be misinformed. If they could be made to understand, their anger would subside and they might even be grateful for what Australia was doing for them. One of the rare consistent complaints that Papua New Guineans made was that they weren't allowed to drink alcohol. But that right was granted to them in 1962. Then in 1964 urban Papua New Guineans suddenly had a new basis for protest and they expressed their anger in new ways. For a long time the Australian government had said to Papua New Guineans that if they obtained the same qualifications as Australians they would receive the same pay. Now, as the first Papua New Guineans were about to benefit from that policy, it was announced that Papua New Guineans would be paid at a lower rate. The decision united the most articulate Papua New Guineans. Sir Maori Kiki:

> We marched from town to Konedobu. There wasn't any violence, but there were plenty of security men around. Sir Donald Cleland was then the Administrator. He received us, talked to us, and said, 'All right, we will put your claim to Canberra, but you may not get it'. Canberra repeated the policy and said, look, it would be very difficult for an independent Papua New Guinea to pay you at the Australian salary level. But the interesting thing is that before the march I had spoken to Lady Cleland and Sir Donald. Now the attitude of Sir Donald and Lady Cleland was quite different from that of Canberra. Lady Cleland was very influential. She did everything. That old woman, I have time for her. I think she had time for Papua New Guineans. She went down to the people's level and she knew

Sir Maori Kiki

Pangu Pati symbol

211

THE NEW GUINEA PARTY

A Policy for the Territory's Security

The Party will contest the House of Assembly elections for Papua-New Guinea with the following main objectives: Representation for the Territory in the Federal Parliament ● A free and independent plebiscite for West New Guinea ● Improvement in the Territory's defence ● A trebled amount for education ● Equal opportunity for all races ● The maintenance of stable government.

People of all races are invited to nominate for pre-selection before January 6 with Charles Kilduff, Barrister and Solicitor, Port Moresby.

Pacific Islands Monthly January, 1964

exactly what the people wanted. She used to come to our house, take our women, and teach them how to cook food and sew dresses and so on. She walked to different villages. Even when we had bitter feelings, I knew that from the top level we had the backing of Sir Donald and Lady Cleland.

The wages decision, Noel Levi believes, quickened the movement of Papua New Guineans into national politics, and gave them a glimpse of the realities they faced in going alone.

> *It is hoped that New Guinea will develop first towards greater participation in the local management of purely local affairs, and eventually beyond that to some form of self-government ... That is a long way ahead. It may be, as I have said, more than a century ahead ...*
> **Hon Paul Hasluck, Minister for Territories, 1951**

When the new salary scales were announced they gave Papua New Guineans well under half the Australian rate. It was that degree of difference as well as the apparent breaking of faith that angered Papua New Guineans. Dame Rachel Cleland recalls her own response:

I was so sympathetic that for the very first time, and the only time that I was here, I became political myself, and I got involved in fighting publicly. I felt so angry about it. You see, we went backwards rather than forwards. And because we went backward we pushed the people forward. We provoked them. I remember having an argument with Warwick Smith (Secretary, Department of Territories) one night when he was staying with us, and saying, 'If you go on as you are going there's one good thing you'll do. Everybody's grizzled that there was so little political awareness amongst the people, but now you'll make them politically aware!' And it came very quickly once this decision was made.

Incidentally, the Administrator heard it over the air, not officially from the government.

Anger over the two salary scales declined, but Papua New Guineans sustained their political activity.

In 1964 the Administrative College, then occupying temporary buildings at Six Mile in Port Moresby, had just begun residential courses. The College became a centre where informal political education was as important as the training of public servants. Michael Somare:

We had this Bully Beef Club. In any college, whether in Australia or here, the food is always lousy. So we would all contribute money and substitute our own food by having navy biscuits, hard biscuits, and corned beef because that was real food as far as we were concerned in those days. We said, well, we'll form a Bully Beef Club. And that Bully Beef Club eventually developed into a political club. We met people who came like Bob Hawke, who spoke to us, and lectures were given on how governments were formed, on introducing political parties and so on. We thought we'd convert the club into something real.

Some of the informal discussions leading to the transformation of the Bully Beef Club into a political party took place at Maori Kiki's house. A few senior Australian officials made it clear that they thought political parties premature, even subversive, and any meeting of Papua New Guinean activists was likely to attract the attention of the security service. One particular meeting of twenty Papua New Guineans and Australians decided on the name Pangu Pati. Maori Kiki:

We said, OK, let's make sure that we don't leak this information to anybody. Before we go we'll swear on the bible. I said, I've got a bible inside but the Catholic group said, we Catholics cannot hold your bible. So we sent Barry Holloway around in the middle of the night looking for a Catholic bible. When he came back we drafted the oath: 'I promise on behalf of my people of Papua New

Prince Charles opens Parliament.

Guinea not to mention the existence of this group or the names of the people who are in it. So help me God.' There we were putting our hands up saying that it would all be secret. But early in the morning after the meeting, at seven o'clock, I received a phone call from the security fellows. They said, 'We heard that there was a meeting in your house'. You see how trustworthy people are! So I said, 'No, there was no meeting'. He said, 'Come off it. We know that there was a meeting in your house last night, and plenty of things were discussed. Do you want to know who was present?' So they read out the names exactly of who was at the meeting. Shit! This was after holding the bible. I don't know if they bugged us or what. I think somebody who was present, some bastard who held the bible and promised to God, leaked the information the next morning.

I am not blaming the authorities of those days because the Mau Mau was very active and a lot of things were happening in Africa and other places. People were then focusing their eyes on emerging leaders in Papua New Guinea. I don't know how many files I was on. Canberra was then becoming scared. But it was just false fear. We

didn't have any idea of having a riot or interrupting anything; we only talked about forming a political party. What worried me was that the United Nations was putting pressure on Australia to give independence to Papua New Guinea. But how can you give independence to just a loosely organised people in Papua New Guinea without political parties?

In spite of tension and harassment, relations between Papua New Guineans and Australian security were touched with the same sense of humour that Maori Kiki now invests in his memories.

Other pressure for early independence came from sections of the Tolai people. Well before the Mataungan Association became prominent in the late 1960s Gus Smales recalls how Epineri Titimur,

stood up at a meeting of the combined councils in Rabaul one day and told a visiting Australian delegation that the time had come for the Australians to get out. That was something akin to blasphemy at the time.

Australians who dismissed Titimur as not being in step with the thinking of Papua New Guineans were surprised to find him elected to Parliament in 1968. After he entered Parliament, Titimur, Smales says, 'changed his name to Frank because all politicians should be frank and open'.

Demand for change among the Tolai was so strong that, Don Penias says,

We got independence just in time. The Tolais for instance, and I'm a Tolai, had been in contact with the outside world for a bit longer than the other areas of Papua New Guinea. At the same time we have suffered more under white rule. But generally the Tolais are a very peaceful people. Now there was a lot of talk about self-government and then independence. Many people said, 'No, we don't want self-government, it's too early, we're not really prepared'. And they really meant it. Some of them from areas like the highlands had been in contact with the outside world for a little less than forty years. But the Tolais, or the islands people, were actually jumping up and down: we've got to have it now.

As Trevor Shearston points out, many highlanders feared that independence meant that all the whites would abandon the area. But part of the highlanders' resistance to constitutional change was based on a shrewd appraisal of the political situation. If independence came quickly most positions of power would be taken by the better educated coastal people; the longer the delay the more highlanders would be trained to replace the departing Australians.

Members of the white community were apprehensive for other reasons. Kevin Goodwin:

My prediction is that they will turn on the Europeans and the Chinese. They're going to get nasty. After that I think the Europeans will have to leave. I personally think I'll have to, and then they will turn on each other.

Goodwin claims that 'definite threats' were made against the lives of the white people in one district.

The Australians in Papua New Guinea were constantly dividing. It was not a case of people with sympathy for the aspirations of Papua New Guineans against those who were in the Territory for their own interests. Some Australians who felt a commitment to Papua New Guineans argued that the people needed more time. Others, equally concerned, wanted to push Papua New Guineans into positions of responsibility. They knew that this might create a privileged group, but they thought that there was neither time nor resources to advance all peoples uniformly. The role of senior Australian officials was further complicated by the fact that in the Territory they were often public defenders of government policies; they did the work of both departmental head and minister. Every three years the United Nations visiting mission made its circuit of New Guinea and called Australia's stewardship to account. Normally the United Nations delegates made gentle criticisms but in 1962 they were more provocative. Sir Hugh Foot (Lord Caradon) spent considerable time 'quizzing' G T Roscoe, the Director of Education:

One of the questions he put to me was this, 'How long is it going to be before you can have sufficient native university graduates to head all the government departments?' I said, 'I don't know'. 'Oh,' he said, 'You must know. If there's anybody in the Territory that knows it would be you'. I said, 'I know this: it's going to be a long, long time'. 'How long?' 'Well,' I said, 'If you want a time, I'll say fifty years'. 'Nonsense,' he said, 'You won't have fifty years, you'll only have five'. I said, 'Very likely, but if we only have five years we won't have any university graduates'. 'Why not?' he persisted. 'Well,' I said, 'It takes a long, long time to make a university graduate out of an Australian boy. He's got to go to primary school for seven years, he's got to have seven years at a secondary school, and then he goes three, four, five or six years to the university; and even then we only regard him as a beginner. Do you think that I can take a black kanaka out of the bush, give him a few years and turn him out as a university graduate? It's not reasonable.' He asked, 'Can't you pressure-cook them?'

But two years later the Commission on Higher Education chaired by Sir George

Currie recommended the founding of a University of Papua New Guinea. When politicians and public servants in Canberra finally decided to accept the Commission's findings the University was quickly established in Port Moresby. It had teachers and students at work before it had buildings—or almost any physical signs of a centre of learning. From the time the University accepted its first undergraduates, there were seven years to self-government.

> *Self-government is coming and we want it as soon as it is practicable. The time has come when our educated and capable men are ready to accept responsibility, and once they get it and are seen to be doing their job the remaining people who have doubts will take confidence and support their leaders.*
> **Michael Somare, Chief Minister, 1972**

When Michael Somare as leader of the Pangu Pati managed to build a coalition government after the 1972 elections, the Australian government's timetable for the hand-over of power was thrown into disarray. Tos Barnett, an Australian lawyer, was seconded to head a small group working directly to the Administrator to speed up the transfer. The blueprint for change was enshrined in an enormous file of documents and graphs, but the situation, Tos says, demanded immediate action. It was a case of, 'Hell, if we're to be taking over foreign affairs, we need a foreign affairs department'. The grand and orderly plan was locked in its specially built chart case where it was to be secure from journalists and never consulted. Tos suspects that it remains unopened.

In the accelerated localisation program the most able Papua New Guineans in the middle level of the public service became departmental heads within months. Former Administrator, Les Johnson:

> The first appointments to head up departments weren't entirely new to senior administrative tasks, but they

Michael Somare

were 'plonked', I suppose that is a fair word to use, they were 'plonked' into foreign environments as departmental heads. They were of course strongly supported by subordinate Australian staff. They appreciated that they were nominal blacks, so to speak, although quite clearly the country was soon going to be managed entirely by Papua New Guineans. But they were conscious that they had been promoted a little earlier than their experience and talents warranted. There was usually a reasonable marriage between the Papua New Guinean head of the department and his immediate subordinate officers, and there was a degree of mutual support. Of course there was always the suspicion, or the feeling perhaps, that you were doing yourself out of a job, and so you would keep in your own hands as many of the strings as possible just to make sure that your senior didn't bolt away with the department and leave you high and dry looking for a job in Australia. I think it was natural for there to be a fairly conservative approach to passing over responsibility to Papua New Guineans, and I don't think Australian officers in Papua New Guinea were any different to people anywhere else in the world.

Papua New Guinea Post Courier
September 16, 1975

The results, Johnson says, were 'patchy': while some Australians 'nurtured and developed' Papua New Guinean leaders, others 'lay back in the traces'.

Noel Levi, who was to become one of the first Papua New Guinean departmental heads, was conscious of the way national public servants could threaten the positions of Australians:

> so Australians would prefer to give assistance in small doses as long as they could calculate the risk to themselves and then calculate their next move. If they were able to get a job in Australia, then they would accelerate the localisation of their position. Of course when the decision was made to give Australians a golden handshake I think that was when most of them opted to give their jobs to nationals. Most Papua New Guineans were then thrown into deep water because not enough training had been given to them to take on the responsibility.

They may have been untrained and in deep water, but most of them swam.

At the same time as they hastened (or delayed) their own replacement, Australian senior officials had to come to terms with new political masters. Tos Barnett remembers an image of physical contrasts: 'the new Ministers were at that stage slender, often young, and wearing comfortable shirts and trousers'. They were formally introduced to their Australian departmental heads: 'much more portly, more elderly, bigger in every way, and rather florid in the face either because of their habits or because they were not used to being kept waiting'. When the two groups adjourned to a side table for drinks the Papua New Guinean ministers disappeared under the towering mass of the 'large white gentlemen with their white socks, shorts and shirts'. It was as though only the Australian officials remained in the room.

While golden handshakes eased the departing of Australian civil servants, the Chinese community faced a difficult choice. Most elected to take or retain Australian citizenship. It gave them 'great security'. They were confident, James

Woo says, that in Australia 'no legislation would be changed to suit the circumstances of your colour'. Those members of the mixed race community who thought of Papua New Guinea as 'home', but felt that they were not 'Papua New Guineans' had to resolve more subtle problems. Sir John Guise:

> They were bought off by the gimmick of giving them expatriate wages with the right to drink, and all of the privileges. By that action Paul Hasluck will always be remembered as the Minister who created a division in the country. There were two groups. One that was led by me and I was saying to the mixed race people, 'Every one of us are natives of this country'. The other group said, 'No, we are Australian citizens'. So there was a clear division. I maintained, and say even to this day, that if the mixed race person went to the Supreme Court for a ruling he would still be considered a native of this country. Now before independence the group that was saying 'We are not natives, we are Australian citizens' they said 'Oh, this self-government is coming', so they started going to Darwin, Brisbane, Townsville, Cairns and Cooktown. Come independence and these ones who were in Darwin suddenly realised how wrong they were. But they couldn't come back. Several of them tried. They wrote letters to me and I wrote back, 'If you want to come back, you come as a foreigner. You've got to have a visa to come back here, and if you want to stay you've got to get a permit to extend the visit.'

When they framed their constitution Papua New Guineans were determined that no one was to have dual citizenship: you were in or out.

Australians who were in business or owned plantations also had to decide on their allegiance. To take Papua New Guinean citizenship they had to have lived in the country for eight years, they had to renounce Australian citizenship, and citizenship by naturalisation did not give the same property rights as citizenship by birth. John Middleton thought that 'a person in my position that has a long association with the country and large holdings here, he as an act of faith would have to take up citizenship, and it would have been rather an insult to have refused'. Five years after independence he says, 'I don't for one second regret the decision'. Edith Watts explains that the local people asked her and her husband to stay, and the Provincial Commissioner told them: 'Look, you and John have been here so many years, and we don't mind as long as you sit out here and don't worry us. We don't mind if you stay here for ever'. But John Watts now sees Papua New Guinea 'moving towards an allegiance and a life style which is not related to Australia, but to Melanesia or Asia'. In those circumstances, he says, 'I don't think it will be for me'. Sir John Guise expresses a more cynical view of some who left:

> There have been many instances of Australians who were very good friends of mine who said, 'We love this country. We are going to die here; we are going to be buried here'. But the moment they fell out of authority, they all left.

They had confused pleasure in position with affection for people and place.

Whether they left with relief or regret, Australians now assess their own, and their country's, role in the building of a new nation. Jim Sinclair:

> I don't believe that we have to make apologies to anybody. In years to come when the final accounts are in and when the final evaluation of Australia's role in Papua New Guinea is made, particularly when it's compared against the achievement of other colonial powers in the post Second World War era, I truly believe we'll come out of it pretty well. That's not to say we didn't make mistakes. We made an awful lot of mistakes, both of omission and commission. But when you consider the size of Australia, when you consider our population, our resources, when you add up the sums of aid that we gave,

Raising the flag

> when you accept that Papua New Guinea achieved independence without any armed insurrection of any kind—in fact we virtually had to force them to accept independence—then our overall record is good.

Ian Downs adds that 'at least we made them into a nation. When I went there in 1936 there were just 11 000 villages'.

Both during Australia's rule and since, commentators and participants have debated whether Australians were too inclined to impose their own institutions rather than adapt them to Papua New Guinean conditions. Sir John Gunther favoured a transplant:

> I never had any reservations about it; I was sure it was the right thing to do. Now I could use two arguments. One is that we introduced what we knew about. I think in these kinds of situations where you're moving rapidly towards independence, experimentation might be dangerous. So you implant what you know rather than try and find something different. Number two is that we never proposed that anything we did should

John Waiko

be everlasting. We always said, 'Look, the day after they get independence they can repeal, amend, do anything they like. But we're giving them something we know about; it mightn't work for them, but it does work for us, and we think it can work for them. So we'll use it.' I remember fulminating at one stage about their stupid land tenure system, saying you can't have economic development until you have individual title and so on; but towards the finish I realised that the worst thing we could possibly do was to try and do what the British and others have done and alter the system. They can do it themselves.

It was not a case of those who favoured adaptation being more sympathetic to Papua New Guinean needs. Where Papua New Guineans were not in a position to say what they wanted, then Australians were presumptuous whether they installed Australian institutions or they told Papua New Guineans what was good for them.

Whatever the merits of its many parts, Ron Galloway believes that the administration bequeathed by the Australians had one general defect: 'we had in ever so many fields a heavily overloaded civil service, and the result was that this new-born country found itself saddled with many complex and difficult procedures'. John Waiko takes his criticism further:

It's not Papua New Guinea's independence. It's what I call 'briefcase independence'. Australia more or less carved out what Australia wanted Papua New Guinea to be in the area, put this in a briefcase, left it in a house, walked out the front door. Papua New Guinea came in the back door, got the briefcase, and when they opened it, inside was an Australian institution.

Waiko sees Papua New Guineans maintaining an Australian creation, and not yet moulding something of their own.

Foreign governments had asserted control over points on the Papua New Guinea coast at the same time as they were slicing the last of the colonial melon in Africa, Asia and the Pacific. Australia

relinquished control at the end of the era of Western empires. In broad terms neither the Australian experience of being rulers nor the Papua New Guinean years of being ruled were unique. But in detail there were important differences. Australian rule was brief. For over half the peoples of Papua New Guinea the Australians came and went within one lifetime. The Australians were neighbours. Papua New Guinea was at the same time Australia's frontier, its Territory, and its colony. If Australians had suffered the tyranny of distance, then Papua New Guineans had known the tyranny of proximity. Papua New Guineans had at times endured too many Australians, too much direction from Canberra, and too much cash—but most of that went back to Australians. When Australia ceased to be the administering authority it continued to have interests in a neighbouring nation.

Australians as colonial officials had not been good at wearing plumed hats, holding ceremonies or building monuments. They left styles, structures and ways to act. Papua New Guinea had been intensely important to a few Australians, but only in war had it been of crucial importance to most Australians.

The way Australians 'went finish' was as good as most things that they did. They were confused about how and when, and seemed to have stumbled; they consulted Papua New Guineans at length then suddenly ignored them on a major decision; they made small mistakes, but got the big issues right; they used no guns or gaols against political opponents; they shook a lot of hands and laughed a lot; they were generous on the final points; and they went quickly.

Just after five o'clock in the evening of September 15 the Australian flag was lowered at the Sir Hubert Murray Stadium in Port Moresby. To the strains of 'Auld Lang Syne' four sergeants of the Defence Force paraded the flag before the crowd, then Warrant Officer George Ibor of the Pacific Islands Regiment presented it to Sir John Guise, Governor-General designate of Papua New Guinea. Ivan Champion remembers:

The ceremony was very moving to me when they lowered the Australian flag. Guise called on everybody to see: 'We are lowering it, not tearing it down'. That was rather nice, wasn't it. At one minute past midnight on September 16 the announcer on Papua New Guinea's National Broadcasting Commission radio introduced His Excellency Sir John Guise:

Distinguished guests, visitors from overseas, people of Papua New Guinea: Papua New Guinea is now independent. The Constitution of the Independent State of Papua New Guinea under which all power rests with the people is now in effect. We have at this point in time broken with our colonial past and we now stand as an independent nation in our right. Let us unite with the Almighty God's guidance and help in working together for the future as a strong and free country.

Australia had been associated with British New Guinea from 1884; it had ruled Papua as a Territory from 1906; and it had administered New Guinea from 1914. That formal control had ended.

'Going Finish' was personal as well as ceremonial. Keith Jackson:

Like a lot of Australians I have a respect verging on love for that country. I will always regard it as having a very important place in my life, perhaps the most important, because I was there from when I was eighteen until I was thirty-one. They were very important years, the years in which I developed my career, married and started a family—the formative years of anybody's life. When they happen in a particular environment like that you just can't walk away from it without feeling a great deal of emotion, and the way I felt was well reflected in my son. We took off in the jet, and Simon who was sitting beside me in the aeroplane started to cry. I said to him, 'What's wrong? Are you frightened?' He said, 'No, I'm leaving home.' And that's exactly how I felt.

Australia holds few visible signs of its relationship with Papua New Guinea. Australian genes, language, clothing, food, recreation and gardens show few of the traces that have been a part of the back migrations of other colonial powers. Papua New Guinea's influence is strongest in the force that it exerts over thousands of Australian memories.

Acknowledgments

The first acknowledgment must be to those who made the radio series: Tim Bowden, production and presentation; Daniel Connell, associate producer; Susan Crivelli, research; and Wayne Chapman, technical production. Interviews were collected by:

Daniel Connell, Sean Dorney, Tim Bowden, Stephen Riley, Adrienne Swanton, Tony Morphett, Ros Bowden, Geoff Heriot, Pauline Hanley, Chris Ashton, Huw Evans, Ray Sheridan, Stephen Rapley and James Peter.

The following were interviewed:

Sue Aboitis
Waiau Ahnon
Simon Akai
Jean Ashton
Peg Ashton

Jack Baker
Lilian Barclay-Miller
Tos Barnett
Cliff Batt
Dibul Belong
Ela Birrell
John Black
Vince Bloink
Bill Bloxham
Theresa Bloxham
Ian Boden
Jack Boland
Yorki Bott
Billie Bourke
Joe Bourke
David Bowler
Eileen Bulmer
Bob Bunting
Rev Ben Butcher

James Canty
Claude Champion
Elsie Champion
Ivan Champion
Pin Champion
Phil Charley
Rev Percy Chatterton
Stan Christian
Jane Clarke
Dame Rachel Cleland
Des Clifton-Bassett
Bob Cole
Tom Cole

Rod Collins
Steve Collins
Betty Crouch
Allan Currey

Lord de l'Isle
Neil Desailly
Olive Dixon
Ken Douglas
Ian Downs
Joan Durdin

Geoff Elworthy
Paul Enders

Denys Faithful
Peter Figgis
Bill Forgan-Smith
John Fox
Tom Flower
Mrs Bob Franklin
Bob Franklin

Ron Galloway
Bill Gammage
Ron Garland
Bobby Gibbes
Jean Gibbes
Sgt Gonene
Kevin Goodwin
Sir John Guise
Sir John Gunther
Archbishop David Hand
Leo Hannett
Lyle Hansen
Sally Hansen
Bertie Heath
Win Herry
Brett Hilder

Tom Hilliard
Prof Ian Hogbin
Elma Holmes
Penelope Hope
Jim Hopkinson
Jane Hopper
Pat Hopper
Audrey Howard
William Morris Hughes
Harry Hugo
Lloyd Hurrell
Jean Huxley
Tom Huxley

Amirah Inglis

Rudolph Janke
Keith Jackson
January
Les Johnson
Peter Jonah

Fred Kaad
Kamuger
John Kaputin
Jack Karukuru
Marva Keckwick
Sister Mary Martha Kettle
Sir Maori Kiki
John Kolia
Helmut Kroenig

Prof Peter Lawrence
Harry Lawson
Dan Leahy
Jim Leahy
Mick Leahy
Jim Leigh
Barbara Lepani

Noel Levi
Gordon Linsley
Phyl Linsley
Geoff Littler

Dudley McCarthy
Jean McCarthy
Malcolm MacGregor
Malcolm MacKellar
Tootie McPherson
Ian Maddocks
David Marsh
Paul Mason
Clive Meares
John Middleton
Andrée Millar
Sir John Minogue
Sevese Morea
Ted Morrison
John Murphy

Bernard Narakobi
Sir Horace Niall

Ebia Olewale
Nick O'Neill
Father Tim O'Neill

Samson Patiliu
Don Penias
Jerry Pentland
Rosa Petch
Peter Pinney
Betty Porter
Ben Probert

Anthony Radford
Robin Radford
GT Roscoe

Father Ross	Jim Sinclair	Jack Thurston	Lynn Watt
Charles Rowley	Ian Skinner	Tabitha Tscharke	Edith Watts
	Marie Skinner		John Watts
Norman Sandford	Gus Smales	Jelilah Unia	Bert Weston
Roy Scragg	Michael Somare	Gwen Ure	Anne Whitehead
Bill Seale	Albert Speer	Rev Eric Ure	Ted Whitehead
Francis Seeto	Gladys Stevens		Darcy Williams
James Seeto	John Sutherland	Chris Vass	Ginnie Williams
Eileen Seneve		Tony Voutas	James Woo
Noelene Shaw	Stephen Takaku		Malcolm Wright
Trevor Shearston	Graham Taylor	Emil Wagner	
Ray Sheridan	Jim Taylor	John Waiko	Otto Zander
Ancie Shindler	Joe Taylor	Merl Wall	Rudi Zander
Andy Siegers	Shirley Taylor	Hetty Warner	
Jan Sinclair	Rev Neville Threllfall	Amy Washington	

Field music recordings were supplied by:

The Institute of Papua New Guinea Studies, ABC Radio Archives, Les McPherson, Colin Simpson, Ray Sheridan, Dr Bob MacLennan and Richard Giddings.

Among many employees of the ABC who provided advice and support a particular debt is owed to Nora Bonney, who transcribed the programs with speed and skill. Helen Findlay and Nina Riemer edited the manuscript of the book without complaining about its untidiness, and were always gentle when pointing out the most gauche of constructions. Leigh Nankervis, the designer of the book, has worked imaginatively to make the written word evoke some of the atmosphere of the spoken. Glenn Hamilton of Merchandising, ABC, has given generous support through various stages of production. Photographs and other illustrations have been located and supplied by the Australian War Memorial, the National Library, *Pacific Islands Monthly,* Claude Champion, David Marsh, Theresa Bloxham, Mitchell Library, Australian Museum and the Bureau of Mineral Resources.

Index

Administrative College, *Port Moresby* 212
agriculture 39–40
Ah Tam 30, 85
Ahnon, Waiau 86, 220
Aid Post Orderly Scheme 202
air transport 15, 53–4, 60–3, 126, 146
Aitape 62, 85, 103, 150, 200
Aiyura 108
alcohol 44, 47, 59, 68
  liquor laws 79, 170, 179, 211
Alexishafen 160
Alois Akun 30
Ambunti 118
Anderson, George 121
Angoram 95
Anio 183
Anis, *Lance-Corporal* 48
Armit, William 54
Arnold, George 93
Asaro Valley 123, 124
Ashton, Des 102
Ashton, Jean 102, 103, **111**, 220
Ashton, *Mrs* Peg 178, 220
Assistant Administrator
  see: under names of individuals *eg*
  Cleland, *Sir* Donald

Assistant District Officers 33
  see also under names of individuals *eg*
  Faithful, Denys; Linsley, Gordon; Mantle, Frederick
Assistant Resident Magistrates 18, 33
  see also: under names of individuals *eg*
  Faithorn, W B
Atkinson, *Mr* O J 100
Australian Broadcasting Commission 179, 221
Australian Expropriation Board 28
Australian New Guinea Administrative Unit 175
Australian Prime Ministers
  see also: under names of individuals *eg*
  Gorton, *Sir* John; Hughes, William Morris; Whitlam, Edward Gough
Australian School of Pacific Affairs 41, 43, 186
Australian Territory of Papua 12, 16

'B4s' 21, 31, 193
Baiyer River 201, 206

Baker, Jack **34**, 48, 56, **183**, **204**, 211, 220
Ballantine, David 17
Ballarat, *Victoria* 13
Bannigan, Fred 95
Barnes, Charles 210–11
Barnett, Tos **188–9**, 190, 215, 216, 220
Barton, *Captain* Francis 17, 46
Bates, Charlie 176
Batt, Cliff **23**, 69, **73**, **78**, 220
Baum, Helmuth 123
Behrmann, *Dr* Walter 116
Bena Valley 123, 124, 125, 126
Benabena 124, 126
Billy the Cook 91
Binandere people 139
Bird, Jack 63
bird of paradise hunters 23
Birrell, Ela 94, 144–5, 220
Bismarck Archipelago 12, 77
Bitapaka 25
Black, John 130, 135, 165, **167**, **176**, 220
Blackwood, Beatrice 102
Bloink, Vince **13**, 220
Bloxham, Bill **206**, 220
Bloxam, *Mrs* Theresa **46–7, 52**,

83, **103–4**, **193**, **194**, 220, 221
Boden, Ian **169**, 220
Bol River 116
Boland, Jack **172–3**, 220
Bolivip 116, 117
Bonagai 107
boredom 44
Boroko 179
Bott, Yorky **169**, 220
Bougainville 69, 71, 76, 77, 80, 85, 110, 133, 198, 201
Bourke, *Mrs* Billie **24**, **30**, **144**, **166–7**, 220
Bourke, Joe 101, 220
Bowden, Ros 9
Bowden, Tim 7, 8, 9, 199, 220
Bowler, *Dr* David **206**, 220
Boy's Own Annual, book 14
Boy's Own Paper, magazine 13
British Government 11, 12
British navy 11
British New Guinea 12, 219
  see also Barton, *Capt.* Francis; MacGregor, *Sir* William; Symons, Alexander Henry
Brown, Arthur 176
Brown, Shanghai 91
Bukawa 198

Bulldog Trail 158
Bully Beef Club 212
Bulmer, Eileen **83–4**, 220
Bulolo 147, 193
Bulolo, ship 14
Bulolo Gold Dredging Company 146, 147
Bulolo River 124, 142, 146
Buna 18, 19
Bundi 158
Burns Philp 14, 58, 141, 146, 163
Burui 61
Butcher, *Rev* Ben 8, 149, **150**, **152**, **154–5**, 220

Cadet Patrol Officers 33, 34, 43
Cairns, *Queensland* 14, 193, 216
cannibals 117, 149
Cape Nelson 19
Captain Blood, film 93
Caradon, *Lord* 214
Carpenters (WR) 58, 141
Carpenters airline 15
carriers 51–2, 53, 115–6, 121, 126, 130, 142, 194
Cecil Hotel, *Lae* 94
Central Court 185, 187
Chalmers, *Rev* James 149, 151
Champion, Alan 120
Champion, Claude **18**, 46, **56**, 120–1, **133**, **194**, **199**, 220, 221
Champion, *Mrs* Claude 99
Champion, Herbert William 18, 19
Champion, Ivan **18**, 53, **89**, **115–19**, 120, **137–8**, 194, 196, **218–9**, 220
Champion, *Mrs* Ivan (Elsie) 19, 99, 220
Chan, *Sir* Julius 161
Charters Towers, *Queensland* 112
Chatterton, *Rev* Percy 20, 21, 149, 154, 197, 220
Cheesman, Evelyn 102
Chester, Henry 11
Chief Judicial Officer 17
  see also: Murray, *Sir* Herbert
Chimbu 63, 129, 130, 158, 189
Chimbu people 79, 191
'Chinatowns' 29
Chinese people 29–30, 87, 170–1, 193, 216
Chinnery, *Mr* E W P 204
Christian, Stan 57, 220
Christianity
  see missionaries
Clark, George 139
Clarke, Jane 112, **113**, 220
Cleland, *Sir* Donald 15, 211
Cleland, *Dame* Rachel **11**, 15–16, **33**, **60**, **106**, **153**, 169, **180**, 209–10, 211, **212**, 220
Clifton-Bassett, Des 83, 89, 133, 220
clubs 70–1
  see also: under names of individual clubs *eg* Lae Club; Papua Club
coastwatchers 197
cocoa 23, 73
'Coconut Lancers' 26, 34
coconut palms
  see copra
coffee 23, 131
Cole, Bob **13–14**, **34–5**, 43, 49, 71, 134, 186, 220
Cole, Tom **75**, 229
Collins, Rod 79, 220
Collins, Steve 160, 220

colonialism 12–13, 14, 23, 206
Commonwealth Reconstruction Training Scheme 202
Connell, Daniel 7, 8, 220
Cooktown, *Queensland* 14, 107, 216
Coolgardie safes 69
Coombs, *Dr* Herbert Cole (*Nugget*) 201–2
copra 23, 59, 69, 75
Coral Sea 11, 193, 197
Cosmopolitan Hotel, *Rabaul* 85, 86
cotton growing 23
Crivelli, Susan 8, 220
crops 39–40
  see also: under names of plantation crops *eg* copra; cotton; rubber
Crouch, Betty 201, 205, **206**, 220
Cruikshank, Captain 58
Currie, *Sir* George 215

Damita, Lili 93
Daru 57, 107, 109, 115, 149, 151, 194
  gaol 37
Daughters of Our Lady of the Sacred Heart 150
Daulo Pass 63, 194
de l'Isle, *Lord* 209, 220
Deckert, Fred 146
Degen, Jumbo 91
D'Entrecasteaux Islands 40, 117
Department of District Services and Native Affairs 34
Department of External Territories 194
Department of Public Health 204, 207
Depression, economic 13, 14, 29, 61
Desailly, Neil **21**, 43, 44, 46, 49, **50**, **83**, **135–6**, **186**, 190, 220
Dickson, *Dr* Ian 146
District Commissioners
  see: under names of individuals *eg* Downs, Ian; Niall, *Sir* Horace; Seale, Bill
District Courts 185, 187
District Officers 33, 92
District Standing Instructions *1925* 51, 52, 53, 54, 56
Dixon, Olive **153**, 220
Dogura 151
Douglas, Ken **58**, **86**, 220
Downs, Ian **13**, 35, **64**, **185**, 186, **198**, **210**, 216, 220
Duke of York Islands 57
Dunantina River 123
Durdin, Joan 205, 220
Durour, ship 58, 85
Dutch East Indies 11
Dwyer, Michael 123

Edie Creek 60, 76, 124, 141, 142, 144–5, 146
education 15, 111–13, 152–3, 177
Eekhoff, Henry 124
Ela Beach 178
Elevala, boat 115, 118
Eliptamin people 137
Elworthy, Geoff **15**, **34**, **68**, **70**, **81**, 220
Emboge **198**
empire building 12, 14
Enders, *Dr* Paul 201, 203, 220
Entrance Island 107
Erave River 120
expeditions 115, 119, 126

Faithful, Denys 15, 49, 96, 220
Faithorn, W B 120
Feldt, Eric 197, 200
Fenbury, David 43
Feramin people 118
field officers
  see Assistant District Officers; Assistant Resident Magistrates; Cadet Patrol Officers; District Commissioners; District Officers; Patrol Officers; Resident Magistrates
Figgis, Peter **195**, **196**, **197**, 220
First World War
  see World War I
Flierl, Leonhard 123
Flierl, Wilhelm 123
Flower, Tom **166**, 220
Fly River 109, 115, 204
Flynn, Errol 93
Foot, *Sir* Hugh 214
Forgan-Smith, Bill 60, **61**, **62–3**, 220
Fox, Jack 108, 130
Fox, John 25, **26**, 143, 220
Fox, Tom 108, 130
Frank, *Brother* Eugene 158
Franklin, Bob 141, **142**, 143, **147**, 220
Franklin, *Mrs* Bob 193, 220
French in the Pacific 11
Fuzzy Wuzzy Angels 172, 175

Gajdusek, Carleton 206
Galloway, Ron **13**, 218, 220
Gammage, Bill 177, **179**, 220
Gapenuo **157**
Garaina 61
Garland, Ron 198, 200, 220
Gasmata 206
Gazelle Peninsula 23, 83, 201
German New Guinea 12, 23–25, 28, 55, 69
Germans in the Pacific 11
Gibbes, Bobby **61–2**, **95**, 220
Gibbes, Jean 109, 220
Gibbes, Julie 109
Gibbes Sepik Airways 54
Giddings, Richard 221
Gira River 141
Goaribari Island 149
gold mining 59, 60, 94, 123, 141–8
  see also: Misima goldfield; Morobe goldfields; Wau
Gona 172
Gonene, *Sergeant* **50**, 220
Goodenough Island 77
Goodwin, Kevin **214**, 220
Gore, *Mr Justice* R T 108
Goroka 63, 64, 123
Gorton, *Sir* John 210
Government House, Port Moresby 19
Government House, Rabaul 26
Government Secretary
  see Champion, H W
Grabowsky, Ian 127
Green, John 139
Grimshaw, Beatrice 102
Guadalcanal 197
Guest of Honour, radio program 27
Guinea Airways 146, 158
Guise, *Sir* John 8, **20**, **21**, **165**, **166**, 167, **168**, **172**, **173**, **177**, **216**, **217**, 218, **219**, 220
Gulf of Papua 115
Gunther, *Sir* John 80, 154, **159**, 162, 177, **179**, **191**, **201–3**, **217–8**, 220

gurias 83–4
Gurney, Bob **124**, 125
guttaim bipo 23

Hagen 130, 158
Hagen people 79
Hamilton, Glenn 221
Hand, *Archbishop* David 155, 159, **160**, 162, 220
Hannett, Leo 25, 37, **161**, **163**, 186, 220
Hansen, Lyle 38, **47–8**, 220
Hansen, Sally **170–1**, 220
Hanson, Jane 107–1, 110
Hanuabada 20
Harris, Geoff 137
Harrison, *Major* G A 126
Hasluck, *Sir* Paul 212, 216
haus kiap 37, 48
Hawke, Bob 212
Heath, Bertie **146**, 220
Hendry, Clem 143
Herry, Win 153, 220
Hides, Jack 13, 119, 120, 121
Higatura 83, 89, 198
Highlands Highway 63
Hilder, Brett **57**, **59**, **78**, **86–7**, 220
Hogbin, *Professor* Ian 15, 38, 80, 105, 166, 220
Holloway, Barry 212
Holmes, *Mrs* Elma 103, 220
Holmes, *Col* William 25, 26
Hope, *Mrs* Penelope **13**, **17**, **67**, 68, **70**, **100–1**, 220
Hopkinson, Jim 79, 169, 220
Hopoi 198
Hopper family 110–11, 220
Hughes, William Morris 26, **27**, 220
Hugo, Harry **29**, 77, **78**, **79**, 85, **86**, **91–2**, 169, 220
Hula people 57
Humphries, Dick 18–19
Huon Gulf 141
Huon Peninsula 44, 199
Hurrell, Lloyd 36, 37, **175**, **178**, 186, 220
Huxley, *Mrs* Jean **84**, **103**, 220
Huxley, Tom **176–7**, 220

Ibor, George 218
indenture system 75
Independence 7, 9, 209–19
Inglis, Amirah 15, 105, **168**, **181**, 220
Inus plantation 110
International Training Institute 41
Ioma 99
Iriwaki 155
Iwunga 128

Jackson, Keith 219, 220
Janke, Rudolph 25, **28**, 220
January **199–200**, 220
Japanese in New Guinea 29, 48, 147, 171, 193–200
Jimmi Valley 60, 128
Johnson, Les 153, **215–6**, 220
judicial authority 185–91
  see also Chief Judicial Officer; Patrol Officers; Resident Magistrates

Kaad, Fred 48, **49**, 171, **172**, **176**, 220
Kaiapit 123, 145
Kainantu 61, 108, 123, 124, 126, 157, 190

Kaisenik 143
Kanaka, Jack 176
Kanga Force 147
Kaputin, John **177**, 220
Karius, Charles 115–19, 194
Karkar Island 85, 199
Kassam Pass 63
Katoomba, ship 15
Kavieng 24, 111, 193, 200
Kavieng Club 71
Keckwick, *Miss* Marva 19, **151–2**, 220
Kennedy, Robert 45
Kerema 203
Kettle, *Sister* Mary Martha **150**, 220
kiaps
    definition of 33
    their courts 185
    went finish' 49–50
    see also references under *field officers*
Kieta Club 71
Kiki, *Sir* Maori 21, 154, 178, **183**, 211, **212–3**, 220
Kikori 56, 99, 115
Kilawari, *Dr* 207
Kipling, Rudyard 13
Kiunga 204
Koch, Robert 24, 206
Kokoda 19, 141, 193
Kokoda Trail 172, 197
Kokopo 25, 87
Konedobu 211
Koroba 56, 134, 135
Kroenig, Helmut **76**, 220
Kudjiru 61
kukboi 45, 47
Kukukukus 203
Kundiawa 50, 189, 190
Kuta 158

Lae 60, 61, 94, 108, 124, 146, 147, 193
Lae Club 180
Liaigam 35, 96
Lake Kutubu 121
Lakekamu River 141
languages
    see Pidgin
Lapumpa 124, 125
Laurabada, boat 18, 19, 20, 67, 100, 196
Lawes, *Rev* William and family 99, 149
Lawrence, *Professor* Peter 24, **41**, **160**, 220
Lawson, Harry **14**, 220
Leahy, Dan 123, 124, 125, **127**, **131**, 138, 157, **158**, **159**, **194–5**, 220
Leahy, Jim 93, **130**, **144**, **145**, **193**, 220
Leahy, Michael 8, 93, 123, **124**, 125, 126, **127**, 130, **138–9**, **141**, 142, 145, 157, 220
Leahy, Paddy 93, 145
leave 13, 45
Legislative Council 209
Leigh, Jim 31, 220
Lepani, Barbara **182**, 220
leprosy 40, 204
Letlet 88
Levi, Noel 161, **177–8**, 212, **216**, 220
Lieutenant-Governor
    see also MacGregor, *Sir* William; Murray, *Sir* Hubert

Linsley, Gordon 43, **47**, 53, 55, 105, 220
Linsley, *Mrs* Phyl **104–5**, 220
Logan, Jack 142
London Missionary Society 149
Lumi 62

McAuley, *Professor* James 41
McCarthy, Dudley 35, **45**, **134**, 220
McCarthy, *Mrs* Jean **85**, **86**, 193, **200**, 220
McCarthy, Keith 48, 85, 176, 197, 200
Macdhui, ship 14
McDonald, Gregor 143
McEnroe, *Father* 158
MacGregor, Malcolm **71–3**, **80**, 220
MacGregor, *Sir* William 16, 45
McIlwraith, Thomas 11
McInerney, *Dr* John 94–5
Mack, Ian 35
Mackellar, Malcolm 39, 44–5, **64–5**, **92–3**, 204, 220
MacLennan, *Dr* Bob 221
McPherson, Les 221
McPherson, Tootie **195–6**, 220
Madang 23, 24, 102, 160, 176
Maddocks, *Dr* Ian 204, **205**, **206**, **208**, 220
Mahony, *Mrs* 91
Mailu people 57
Mailu-Domara 81
Malaita 70
Malaria 45, 51, 69, 79, 100, 205
    see also quinine
Malaya 81
Mambare River 99
Mandated Territory of New Guinea 27–9, 40, 167
mankimasta 47
Manning, Guy 91
Mantle, Frederick 91
Manum 85
Manus 35, 207
Maprik 209
Marienberg 187
Markham Valley 61, 63, 84, 115, 123, 143
Marsh, David **20**, **44**, 134, 135, **137**, **175**, **198**, 220, 221
Marshall, Charles 124, 125
Marshall, Dan 124
Marsina, ship 14
Martyrs School 81
Mason, Michael 8
Mason, *Mrs* Paul (Noelle) 80
Mason, Paul 80, 110, **113**, 133, 198, 220
Massim people 57
masta-boi relationship 7, 71, 128, 165, 171, 176
Mataungan Association 213
Matunga, ship 14
May River 130, 189
Mead, Margaret 102
Meares, Clive 29, 85, **86**, 220
medical work 40, 57, 108, 137, 154, 195, 201–8
    see also: under names of individuals *eg* Gunther, *Sir* John; McInerney, *Dr* John; Speer, Albert; Strong, *Dr* Walter
Mekeo 150
Melanesian art 24, 154
Mendham, George 61
Mendi 64, 162
Mianmin people 130

Middleton, John 199–200, 217, 220
Millar, *Mrs* Andrée **14–15**, **94**, 105, 106, **175**, **210**, 220
Miller, *Mrs* Cassie 70
Milne Bay 193, 197
miners 137
    see also: under names of individuals *eg* Fox, John; Franklin, Bob; Leahy, Dan and Michael; Weston, Bert
Mingende 158
mining
    see gold mining; miners
Minogue, *Sir* John 189, **190**, 220
Misima Island 21
    goldfield 91, 141
missionaries 62, 88, 92, 123, 130, 136–7, 149–55, 157–63, 195, 198, 199
    see also: under names of individuals *eg* Chatterton, *Rev* Percy; Keckwick, *Miss* Marva; Lawes, *Rev* William; Ross, *Father* William; Threlfall, *Rev* Neville; Ure, *Mrs* Eric
Montoro, ship 14, 86, 93
Montevideo Maru, ship 200
Moresby, *Captain* John 139
Morobe goldfields 29, 141, 144, 146
Morschheuser, *Father* Carl 158
mortuary rites 20, 38, 167
Motu people 57
Motuan burial 20
Mount Blucher 116, 117
Mount Elimbari 124, 125
Mount Hagen 49, 53, 62, 63, 64, 108, 126, 128, 157, 158, 194
Mount Kaindi 141, 146
Mount Kubor 123
Mount Lamington 18, 83, 88
Mount Wilhelm 123
Murphy, John 33, **34**, **38**, 51, **52–3**, 187, 220
Murray, *Sir* Hubert 17–20, 21, 34, 46, 55, 67, 117, 121, 123, 149, 187, 209
Murray, *Col* J K 175–6
Murray, Leonard 19, 21, 100
Murray, Terence 19
Murray Range 120
Murrell, *Dr* Tim 206
Musa 81
My Wicked, Wicked Ways, book 93

Namanula 85, 86
Namu 124, 125
Nankervis, Leigh 221
Narakobi, Bernard 37, **186–7**, **189**, **211**, 220
National Broadcasting Commission of Papua New Guinea 7
Native Labour Ordinance 76
Native Medical Assistant Training Scheme 202
Native Women's Protection Ordinance 20, 168
Nauru 25
Neal, Normie 142
New Britain 23, 77, 133, 197, 200
    see also Gazelle Peninsula; Palmalmal
New Caledonia 11
New Guinea Club 71
New Guinea Goldfields Limited 124, 125
New Guinea Volunteer Rifles 193

New Ireland 23, 77, 150
newspapers 57
Niall, *Sir* Horace 34, 38, 43, 51, 220
Nick the Greek 91
Nordup 86
Not a White Woman Safe, book 168
Nuts to You, book 78

Ogamobu 67, 100
Olewale, Ebia 37, 220
O'Malley, Jim 119
O'Neill, Nick **189**, 190, 220
O'Neill, *Father* Tim **163**, 220
Orokolo people 154
Otomata plantation 70
Owen Stanley Range 112

Pacific Islands Monthly, magazine 176, 221
Palmalmal 73
Pangu Pati 215
Paparatava area 24
Papua Club 70–1
Papuan Wonderland, book 120
Patiliu, Samson 85, 220
Patrol into Yesterday, book 48
Patrol Officers 18, 33, 36, 38, 40, 41, 43, 46–7, 51–6, 115, 121, 131, 133
    see also Cadet Patrol Officers
Penias, Don **179–80**, 220
Pentland, Jerry 60–93, 159, 220
Petch, Rosa **170**, 220
Peter, James 150
Phillips, *Judge* Beaumont 86, 176
Phillips, Rusty 95
Pidgin 9, 30, 31, 111, 124, 157, 189
Pidgin English 26, 30, 31, 198
Pilhofer, George 123
Pindiu 44
Pinney, Peter **19**, 220
pit latrines 44
Plain Tales from the Raj, BBC radio feature 8
plantation crops
    see: cocoa; coffee; copra; cotton; rubber; tobacco
planters 28, 59, 67–73, 75–6, 200
    see also: under names of individuals *eg* Batt, Cliff; Douglas, Ken; Elworthy, Geoff; Hope, *Mrs* Penelope; Hugo, Harry; Janke, Rudolph; MacGregor, Malcolm; Sandford, Norman; Thurston, Jack
police 48, 87, 89, 115, 118, 120, 121, 130, 133, 162, 187
Popondetta 198, 206
Porgera 35–6, 136, 159
Port Moresby 15, 24, 68, 94, 99, 106, 117, 120, 149, 178, 180, 193, 194, 196–7, 212, 218
    see also Papua Club
Porter, Judy 205, 207
Powdermaker, Hortense 102
Probert, Ben 157, 160, 220
Proctor, Tom 85
Purari River 119, 120, 123, 124

Queen Emma 91
Queensland 11, 183
    see also Charters Towers; Toowoomba; Townsville
quinine 56, 206

Rabaul 24, 25, 29, 34, 85–8, 111,

126, 141, 147, 161, 171, 176, 179, 187, 193, 207
air raids 195
Rabaul Club 71
Radford, *Dr* Anthony 202, 220
Radford, Robin 157, 220
Radio Australia 72
Ramu River 23, 115, 123, 158
Rapindik Tip 169
Rapolla 88
rats 45, 68
Read, Jack 198
reading matter 44, 197
recruiters 76–8, 143, 145
refugee doctors 203
reprisal raids 24, 55, 139
Resident Magistrates 18, 33
  see also Assistant Resident
  Magistrates
  and see also: under names of
  individuals *eg* Humphries, Dick;
  Kennedy, Robert
Rigo 105
Rigo people 81
Riley, *Rev* Baxter 100
roads 63–5
Robinson, Percival 67
Roscoe, G T **214**, 220
Ross, *Father* William 8, 157, **158**, 159, 220
Rowlands, Ned 123
Rowley, Charles 41, 220
Royal, Bill 60, 141
Royal Commission *1906* 17, 46, 67
Royal Geographical Society 130
Royal Papua and New Guinea
  Constabulary 48
rubber trees 67
Ryan River 119

Salamaua 35, 59, 60, 94, 141–2, 143, 144, 147, 158, 193, 202
Samarai 57, 94, 99, 107, 206
Samberigi Valley 120
Sanders of the River, film 34
Sandford, Norman **15**, 69, 70, 75–6, **77**, **79**, 141, 221
Schofield, Frank 206
School of Civil Affairs 41
schools 111–13
  boarding in Australia 15, 112–13, 177
  mission 152–3
schooners 14, 60
Scobie, Jim 144
Scragg, *Dr* Roy 205, 207, 221
Seale, Bill 28–9, 171, 221
Second World War
  see World War II
Seeto, James 70, **170**, 221
seismic activities 83–9
Seneve, Eileen 207–8, 221

Sepik district 37, 45, 57, 77, 84, 95, 162, 189, 194, 201, 209
Sepik River 115, 116, 117, 118, 130
Shaw, Noeline **180–1**, 221
Shearston, Trevor 47, **162**, 214, 221
Sheridan, Ray 221
Shindler, Ancie 108, 221
shipping 21, 57–60
  see also: Burns Philp; schooners;
  steamers
  and under names of individual
  ships *eg Katoomba; Laurabada;*
  Macdhui; Montoro
Siaguru, Tony 179
Simoi 20
Simpson, Colin 221
Simpson Harbour 25, 26, 88
Sinclair, Jan 112, 221
Sinclair, Jim 34, 39, **43**, 48, **54**, 56, 134, 135, 185, 186, 209, **216**, 221
Sirupu 124
Skinner, Ian **14**, 102, 108, **134**, 198, 214
Skinner, *Mrs* Marie 101, 102, 105, 108, **112**, 221
Smales, Gus **213**, 221
Smith, Staniforth 53
Sogeri plateau 67
Smith, Warwick 212
Solomon Islands 25, 70, 197
Somare, Michael **149**, 154, **212**, **215**, 221
Sopura 198
sorcery 189
Speer, Albert **89**, **203–4**, 221
statehood 12
  see also Independence
steamers 14, 57
Steamships Company 58
Stevens, *Mrs* Gladys 105, **167**, **171**, 221
Stewart, *Mrs* Flora (Ma) 91, 93–4, 144
Strickland River 115, 119, 130
Strong, *Dr* Walter 100
Stuart, Ian 178
Stuart, Robert 78
Sudest Island 141
Sumbago 85
Sunset Creek 61
Supreme Court 185, 187, 188
Surprise Creek 61
Symons, Alexander Henry 107
Symons, Theresa 107
Szarka, Gerald 137

Tabibuga airstrip 60
Taim Bilong Masta, radio series 7–9
Takaku, Stephen 154, 221

Takendau 190
Talasea 38, 193
Tambu signs 133
Tamsimara 117, 118
Tari 83, 121, 159
Tavaua 88
Taylor, Graham 95–6, 221
Taylor, Jim 53, 125, 126, 127, **128**, **129**, 130, 131, 157, 176, 221
Taylor, Joe **29–30**, 221
Taylor, Shirley 105, 178, 221
Taylor, Tony 89
Telefomin 61, 130, 133, 137
Tenekau plantation 69
Territory of New Guinea 21, 51, 52, 53, 219
Territory status 12
Threlfall, *Rev* Neville **161**, **162–3**, 221
Thurnwald, Richard 24
Thursday Island 14, 109, 150
Thurston, Jack 77, 194, 221
Tiger Lil 35, 91
Titimur, Epineri 213
tobacco growing 23
tok masta
  see Pidgin English
Tolai People 83, 111, 213, 214
Tomkins, *Rev* Oliver 149
Toowoomba, *Queensland* 112
The Top End, It's Different Up There,
  radio feature 7
Torres Strait 11, 95
Torricelli Mountains 84
Towakira 24
Townsend, Kassa 28, 187
Townsville, *Queensland* 112, 216
transport
  see air transport; carriers; roads;
  shipping
Trobriand Islands 182
tropical ulcers 40
Tumleo Island 150
Tureture village 37

Umboi Island 23, 149
Unia, Jelilah 207, 221
University of Papua New Guinea 207, 215
Ure, *Rev* Eric 21, 151, 221
Ure, *Mrs* Gwen **17**, **151**, 221

Valaur 88
Vanimo 95
Varoe, boat 67
Varzin plantation 24
Vass, Chris 35–6, 47, **96–7**, **136**, **159**, **186**, 221
village book 37
Village Constables 37, 40
Vitiaz Strait 57
volcanic eruptions 84–9

Voutâs, Tony 44, 80, 221
Vulcan Island 85

WR Carpenters 58, 141
Wabag 131, 138, 194
Wage Valley 121
Wagner, Adolf 199
Wagner, Emil **199**, 221
Wahgi Valley 62, 123, 124, 125, 126
Waiko, John 80, 139, **153**, 181, **218**, 221
Walkie Talkie 94
Wall, *Mrs* Merle **69–70**, **71**, **73**, 221
Walsh, C B 130
Wampit 61
Wampur people 157
Waria people 130, 139
Warner, Hetty 154, 221
Washington, *Mrs* Amy 88, 100, **107**, **109**, 221
Washington, Bill 176
Watts, John 81, 217
Watts, Edith 217, 221
Wau 94, 101, 110, 123, 144, 147, 158, 193
  airstrip 60–1
Weber brothers 23
Wela River 121
The West Coasters, radio feature 7
West Irian 189
Weston, Bert **142**, **143**, **144**, 145, **146**, 221
Wewak 61, 189, 193
White Women's Protection
  Ordinance 20, 168
Whitehead, Anne 110, **112**, 221
Whitehead, Ted 91, 221
Whitlam, Edward Gough 210
Wien, Eric 93
Williams, Darcy 94, 221
Williams, Ginnie 105, 221
Wilmot, Morton 86
Wilson, *President* Woodrow 27
wives 46–7, 99–106, 169, 180
Wolff, Rudolph 24
Woo, James **29**, **170**, **171**, 216, 221
Woodlark Island 107, 141, 149
World War I 13, 25–6
World War II 19, 69, 147, 171–3, 193–200
Wright, *Dr* Eric 207
Wright, Malcolm 197, 221

Yap 25
yaws 40, 204, 205
Yodda River 141
Yule Island 149, 150

Zander, Otto 23, 221
Zander, Rudi **169–70**, 221